Defense Studies Series

Pentagon 9/11

Defense Studies Series

Pentagon 9/11

Alfred Goldberg
Sarandis Papadopoulos
Diane Putney
Nancy Berlage
Rebecca Welch

Historical Office
Office of the Secretary of Defense
Washington, D.C. • 2007

This is the Official U.S. Government edition of this publication and is herein identified to certify its authenticity. Use of the 0-16 ISBN prefix is for U.S. Government Printing Office Official Editions only. The Superintendent of Documents of the U.S. Government Printing Office requests that any reprinted edition clearly be labeled as a copy of the authentic work with a new ISBN.

It is prohibited to use the Department of Defense seal, as appears on the title page, on any republication of this material without the express, written permission of the Historical Office, Office of the Secretary of Defense. Any person using official seals and logos in a manner inconsistent with the Federal Regulations Act is subject to penalty.

Library of Congress Cataloging-in-Publication Data

Pentagon 9/11 / Alfred Goldberg . . . [et al.].
p. cm. -- (Defense studies series)
Includes bibliographical references and index.
ISBN-13: 978-0-16-078328-9
1. September 11 Terrorist Attacks, 2001. 2. Pentagon (Va.). 3. Terrorism—Virginia—Arlington. 4. Rescue work—Virginia—Arlington. I. Goldberg, Alfred, 1918- II. United States. Dept. of Defense. Historical Office.
HV6432.7.P43 2007
975.5'295044—dc22

2007016098

For sale by the Superintendent of Documents, U.S. Government Printing Office
Internet: bookstore.gpo.gov Phone: toll free (866) 512-1800; DC area (202) 512-1800
Fax: (202) 512-2104 Mail: Stop IDCC, Washington, DC 20402-0001

ISBN 978-0-16-089316-2

Foreword

It is fitting that this admirable, firsthand study of the human tragedy that occurred on September 11, 2001 be reissued on the tenth anniversary of that terrible event.

Pentagon 9/11 is, first and foremost, an indelible portrait of the unstable and perilous world in which we live. The tragedies, heroic deeds, and lessons from that infamous day must never be forgotten. The deadly attacks on the Twin Towers in New York and the Pentagon in Washington instantly brought home to the nation a deep-felt consciousness of its vulnerability. But the American people are always at their best in times of crisis. They recall first principles and fight back to protect what is dear to them, life and liberty. That inherent spirit was immediately in evidence ten years ago, too, among the passengers aboard United Airlines Flight 93, when they defeated the terrorists' plan to use that airplane as a fourth weapon of destruction.

Remembering the past does not enable us to predict the future, but it can help is to shape it. Ten years after, we remain acutely aware that our security can be assured only by continuing resolution, vigilance and fortitude. We have no inviolable shield against external or internal attack, but for the past decade our security measures both at home and abroad have kept us safe from further harm. We are fortunate that we have been successful thus far in discharging this responsibility without diminishing either what Alexander Hamilton called our "ardent love of liberty" or our fundamental rights.

To confront our enemies, to defeat those who would destroy our way of life, we must hold true to the spirit of the guiding principles that have shaped our nation and served us so well throughout our history. *Pentagon 9/11* serves as an important reminder of the stakes, and the risk we incur if we lose focus.

LEON PANETTA
Secretary of Defense

Preface

As no other event in U.S. history, not even Pearl Harbor, the deadly assaults on New York and Washington that took the lives of almost 3,000 people on 11 September 2001 shattered the nation's sense of security. The utter destruction of the Twin Towers in New York and the severe damage done to the Pentagon by Middle East terrorists signaled a changed world in the making, one that poses a constant threat of attack that the United States must guard against and defeat if its people are to live in freedom and safety. The nation responded first with stunned surprise and overwhelming grief, then with outrage and stern refusal to be intimidated.

What happened at the Pentagon that day and for days afterwards is a compelling story of trauma and tragedy as well as courage and caring and an instructive case study in coping with such appalling contingencies. Any history of this event must relate the resolve and fortitude exhibited by the military and civilians most immediately affected as well as the indispensable help that came from thousands of responders in the aftermath. In the first terrifying minutes after the plane crashed into the building the swift actions of survivors and rescuers helped save the lives of many who would otherwise have perished. The prompt response and subsequent performance of federal, state, and especially local agencies, in particular their coordination and cooperation with each other and with Pentagon authorities, provided invaluable lessons for dealing with other large-scale emergencies in the future.

The Department of Defense undertook preparation of a history of the 11 September 2001 attack on the Pentagon at the suggestion of Brig. Gen. John S. Brown, director of the U. S. Army Center of Military History. The OSD Historical Office initiated the project as a Defense Historical Study—a joint endeavor on behalf of the Department of Defense. At the request of the director of the Naval Historical Center, the OSD Historian assigned responsibility for preparation of the study to the Naval Historical Center.

Reconstructing and clarifying this complex event required a collaborative effort. A first draft of the history was prepared by Sarandis Papadopoulos of the Naval Historical Center. He performed extensive research, conducted and directed a large number of oral history interviews, and provided an overall framework for further review and revision. Edward Marolda of the Naval Historical Center edited the manuscript and provided a second draft. A third and final version was prepared by members of the staff of the OSD Historical Office—Alfred Goldberg, Diane Putney, Nancy Berlage, and Rebecca Welch. They performed much additional research including oral history interviews, reorganized and rewrote the manuscript, thoroughly edited it, and checked it rigorously to insure accuracy of fact and of use and citation of all sources. Stuart Rochester gave the manuscript a final review and prepared the book for publication. The final product reflects the efforts of all of these participants and the researchers, compilers, editors, and fact checkers who assisted them.

Above all, this book would not have been possible without the cooperation of the more than 1,300 people who participated in oral history interviews conducted by the historical offices of the Army (almost 900 interviews), Navy, Air Force, Marine Corps, and OSD. The interviews were conducted by staff members of these offices and by Army and Navy reservists who entered on active duty for the purpose. Most of the firsthand evidence needed to provide the foundation for an evocative, broad-based historical narrative comes from these far-ranging interviews. Until a fuller and more definitive in-depth history can be written, this account represents the most comprehensive effort to date to capture what occurred at the Pentagon on 9/11. Although there are intricate treatments of the crash scene and the physical impact of the collision, the work is not as much concerned with elaborate technical analysis, which can be found in after-action reports and other literature, as with conveying in accurate and sufficient detail both the essential chronology and the kaleidoscopic nature of the unfolding developments that day, including evoking both the shock and destructiveness surrounding the catastrophe. The focus is on what happened to people and to the building on 11 September 2001 as seen chiefly through the eyes of participants and observers. The huge cast of thousands includes the dead and injured, survivors, rescuers, firefighters, medical attendants, FBI agents, police, Defense military and civilian volunteers, forensic specialists, morticians, representatives of scores of federal, state, local, and volunteer organizations, family assistance staff of the Department of Defense, and the families of the survivors. The many recollections of individual experiences are as fragmented as was the collapsed E Ring section of the building. As with rebuilding of the collapsed area, this account had to reconstruct the sequence and progression of events piece by piece.

The necessary reliance on oral history interviews varying greatly in scope, recollection, and quality presented a challenge in establishing a dependably accurate and consistent record. A number of survivors, rescuers, and responders still suffered from the physical and emotional effects of their traumatic experiences when interviewed days, months, and even years later. Given the circumstances in which those in the impact area found themselves—shocked, injured, dazed, fearful, disoriented, gasping for breath—it is understandable that they could not retain clearly all that had happened to them or that they had observed. Even where witnesses had vivid recollections of their experiences they often acknowledged lack of precision in recalling all that had happened—time, place, people, and circumstances. Physical factors—smoke, darkness, fire, debris, and other hazards—all contributed to disorientation and confusion. It is not surprising, therefore, that versions of the same event by participants or observers viewing the scene from individual perspectives often differed and therefore had to be weighed carefully. Still, it was necessary to make prudent judgments where discrepancies existed. Material used in this study was distilled from the enormous amount of information available from the more than 1,300 interviews, of which we found it possible to use only a representative portion, relying on the corroborative testimony of two or more witnesses wherever possible.

Of the many problems encountered in seeking to render an accurate and authoritative account, the most difficult was to establish an exact timeline for 11 September. Few participants or observers could pinpoint precise times for what happened—the building collapse, arrivals and departures, rescues, treatment and evacuation of injured, the progress of fires, warnings and evacuations, building searches, and escapes from the wreckage. For many of the day's developments the best that can be done to identify time of occurrence is to use such locutions as "about 10:00 a.m.," at "approximately 11:15," "between 1:00 and 2:00 p.m." This is especially necessary where there are conflicting recollections or gaps in the available evidence, and other sources such as physical documentation did not permit the authors to resolve the discrepancies or achieve absolute certainty. In general, there may be confidence in the accuracy of the sequence of events if not the exact time of each.

Space does not allow giving here the credit due many individuals who contributed importantly to this volume. We acknowledge them by name in a list appended after the text and regret any inadvertent omissions. The hundreds of oral history interviews cited in the study appear in a list included in the bibliography.

Finally, although this volume was prepared in the Department of Defense, the views expressed are those of the authors and do not necessarily represent those of the department.

Alfred Goldberg
OSD Historian

Contents

Illustrations

Photographs follow pages 82 and 162.

Defense Studies Series

Pentagon 9/11

Chapter I

Target: The Pentagon

Since World War II the Pentagon has stood as a symbol of American power and influence to the nation and the world. By 11 September 2001 it had been the command center of the nation's military establishment for more than a half century. In retrospect it seems obvious that in some regions of the world, particularly in the Middle East, a U.S. military presence and perceived ascendancy should have made the Pentagon an object of fear and hatred and a likely target of attack by terrorist enemies.

The Building

Knowledge of the purpose, design, and construction of the Pentagon is requisite to understanding the deadly effect of the 11 September attack. The original conception of the huge structure in the summer of 1941 derived from the urgent need for space to house the rapidly expanding War Department headquarters in Washington. The shadow of the war in Europe and a growing threat in the Pacific from Japan had caused the United States to mount a partial mobilization of industry and manpower that greatly multiplied the activities and numbers of the Army in 1940-41. By July 1941 Chief of Staff General George C. Marshall had obtained permission from his superiors to plan for a single building to accommodate the burgeoning War Department staff scattered among 17 buildings in the Washington area.[1]

Where to place the building occasioned much controversy during the summer of 1941 until President Franklin D. Roosevelt decided in August on a site along the Potomac River in Arlington County, Virginia, directly across from Washington. Groundbreaking occurred on 11 September, exactly 60 years before the 2001 attack. The building was declared completed 16 months later, on 15 January 1943.

Originally the Pentagon Reservation had 583 acres; by 2001 it had shrunk to 280 because of transfers to other purposes. The building covers 29 acres; parking lots take up 67 acres. North and South Parking and other smaller parking areas accommodate about 10,000 vehicles. A Center Court of more than five acres provides appealing landscaping and more light for the inside A Ring. Of the 6.6 million square feet in the building, about 3.8 million were originally devoted to office space.

From the beginning, the building architects and engineers had decided on a pentagonal shape and a horizontal rather than vertical projection, limiting the height to four stories. The afterthought addition of a fifth story in 1942 raised the building's height to 71 feet. A low-rise structure of such massive dimensions—almost a mile around the exterior—gives the Pentagon a fortress-like appearance—not inappropriate for a military headquarters. The appeal of the pentagonal shape, second only to a circular shape in efficient design, lay in making it possible to reach anywhere in the huge building by foot in seven or eight minutes. Stairways, escalators, freight elevators,* and wide ramps provide ready access to all parts of the building. At the outset of construction, given wartime austerity and fiscal constraints, all parties involved agreed that it would be a no-nonsense building—no marble, no decoration, no ornamentation. Truly a pentagon, the structure has five concentric rings (labeled A to E from the innermost ring out), five sides, and five floors. Four light wells between the rings, mainly at the upper three floors, provide daylight for most offices. The dimensions are impressive—the five exterior walls are each 921 feet long, and the five innermost walls facing the Center Court each 362 feet long. From the outer face of E Ring to

* Since 2001 renovated sections of the building include passenger elevators and new two-way escalators.

the outer face of A Ring the building has an overall depth of 396 feet. The roofs are concrete and flat, except for those over the more visible A and E Rings and the 10 radial corridors, which are sloped and covered with slate tiles. Outermost walls are faced with limestone and backed with unreinforced 9-inch brick; inner ring walls are of 10-inch architectural concrete. The building rests on more than 41,000 concrete piles, ranging from 27 feet to 45 feet in height, that support an equal number of columns reaching to the roof. The building's structural framework (floors and columns) is made of reinforced concrete.

Ten numbered corridors radiate like spokes from the A Ring apexes on the inside of the building to the E Ring on the outside. These wide corridors and narrower ones running through the middle of the rings provide 17.5 miles of hallways. The five rings are each 50 feet deep separated by 30-foot gaps known as light wells, except for a 40-foot-wide roadway, the A-E Drive, running through the light well between the B and C Rings, that provides access for vehicles to the Center Court from the outside of the building through tunnels at either end. In much of the building on the 1st and 2nd Floors there are no light courts between the C, D, and E Rings, so that office space is contiguous from the E Ring through the C Ring. The five exterior apexes are at the centers of the five "wedges." The five rings are segmented by expansion joints at four locations evenly spaced around the structure. Where load-bearing partitions are not present, non-bearing partitions separate offices. The five interior apexes at the A Ring have exits to the Center Court at the 1st and 2nd Floor levels. The building's five-digit numbering system indicates the floor, the ring (a letter), the corridor, and the specific room. Thus, 2E460 (in the direct path of the crash) is on the 2nd Floor, E Ring, near Corridor 4.

The Pentagon Department of Defense (DoD) work force, numbering more than 30,000 military and civilians during World War II and the Korean War, had diminished to fewer than 22,000 people, more than half civilian, in 1998. After renovation work on Wedge 1 began in 1998, the building's DoD population declined still further to about 18,000, where it stood on 11 September 2001.*

* The authorized personnel strength in the Pentagon for the years 1945-1998 is listed in Department of Defense Selected Manpower Statistics, Fiscal Year 1999, Table 1-7, prepared by Washington Headquarters Services, Directorate for Information Operations and Reports. In addition to DoD employees, the building's population usually included about 2,000 non-DoD employees, chiefly contractors.

Built originally for the War Department, the Pentagon eventually came to include the major headquarters components of DoD after its establishment in 1947: the Office of the Secretary of Defense (OSD) and the three military departments—Army, Navy, and Air Force. The Marine Corps headquarters did not join the other three services in the building until 1996. Accordingly, all of the most senior officials of the Defense Department have their offices in the Pentagon—the secretary of defense, the secretaries of the three military departments, the Joint Chiefs of Staff,* and the numerous high-ranking civilian and military officials who support them.

In 1989, approaching the half-century mark, the Pentagon's historical importance and architectural merit received recognition by placement on the National Register of Historic Places. By that time it had also become apparent that the aging building urgently needed to be thoroughly renovated and made more secure. Concern about the vulnerability of the structure had for some time engaged the attention of responsible officials. There had been security incidents as long ago as the 1960s; on two occasions bombs planted in the building by unknown persons had exploded but caused little damage and no casualties. The growing terrorist threat in the 1980s and 1990s had led to a number of security improvements both inside and outside the building.

The structure's major deficiencies, as reported to Congress, centered on materials and engineering systems failures, fire protection and safety shortcomings, lack of technological modernization, and inadequate security. During its 50 years of existence, the original building systems had never been replaced or significantly improved. Consequently, all systems—heating, ventilation and air conditioning, plumbing, electricity, and telecommunications—required replacement and modernization to bring the building up to code. The 17.5 miles of corridors and the 100,000 miles of telephone cables indicated the scale of the renovation task. Some parts of the ground-supported basement floors between the piles had settled as much as 12 inches. Major structural modifications to the pile-supported foundation were required to create more usable space by enlarging the mezzanine floor to cover most of the basement. Windows, both casement and double-hung, were generally in disrepair and badly in need of replacement. Archi-

*The Defense Department has three military departments and four military services. The chiefs of the military services and a chairman and vice chairman constitute the Joint Chiefs of Staff.

tectural elements—windows, doors, stairways—and the building facade (concrete and limestone), which showed cracks and spalling, required comprehensive overhaul. Removal of hazardous materials, especially asbestos, was another imperative. Moreover, the building did not incorporate modern fire and safety features. Finally, the machinery housed in the Heating and Refrigeration Plant, a separate building nearby, had become obsolete. This long bill of particulars underscored the need for a total renovation of the Pentagon.[2]

In 1990 Congress authorized a complete overhaul of the Pentagon, capping the cost at $1.218 billion in 1994. To plan and eventually oversee this huge undertaking DoD established under Washington Headquarters Services an office that evolved into the Pentagon Renovation Program Office (PENREN) in 1997. PENREN managed all aspects of planning and execution of the renovation and construction work, employing contractors for almost every phase of the project.[3] It soon became evident that the original plan to complete the work within 10 years was optimistic; by 2001 planners projected a completion date of 2014. The first construction phase, a necessary preliminary to all renovation, was the new Heating and Refrigeration Plant and associated exterior utility projects beginning in 1993 and completed in September 1997. There followed the renovation of the basement and the extension of the basement mezzanine floor, a project of high priority and longer duration. Upgrading security stood high on the list for the next stage of reconstruction and renovation of the building proper, which began in 1998 with clearance of Wedge 1, most of whose approximately 5,000 occupants were moved to leased facilities in Northern Virginia by the end of the year. By September 2001, Wedge 1 had been largely reoccupied and work was under way on adjacent Wedge 2, which had been cleared of all but about 700 occupants.

Extending from midway between Corridors 2 and 3 to midway between Corridors 4 and 5, with more than one million internal gross square feet of space, Wedge 1 was only five days from official completion and housed about 3,800 people on 11 September. Corridor 4 provided access to Wedge 1 on all floors, but a temporary construction barrier wall midway between Corridors 4 and 5 limited access to Corridor 5 by Wedge 1 occupants in all rings on most floors.[4]

Under the renovation plan all of the walls, utilities, and asbestos in Wedge 1 were removed. The outer wall was reinforced with structural steel tub-

PLAN OF THE BUILDING - FIRST FLOOR

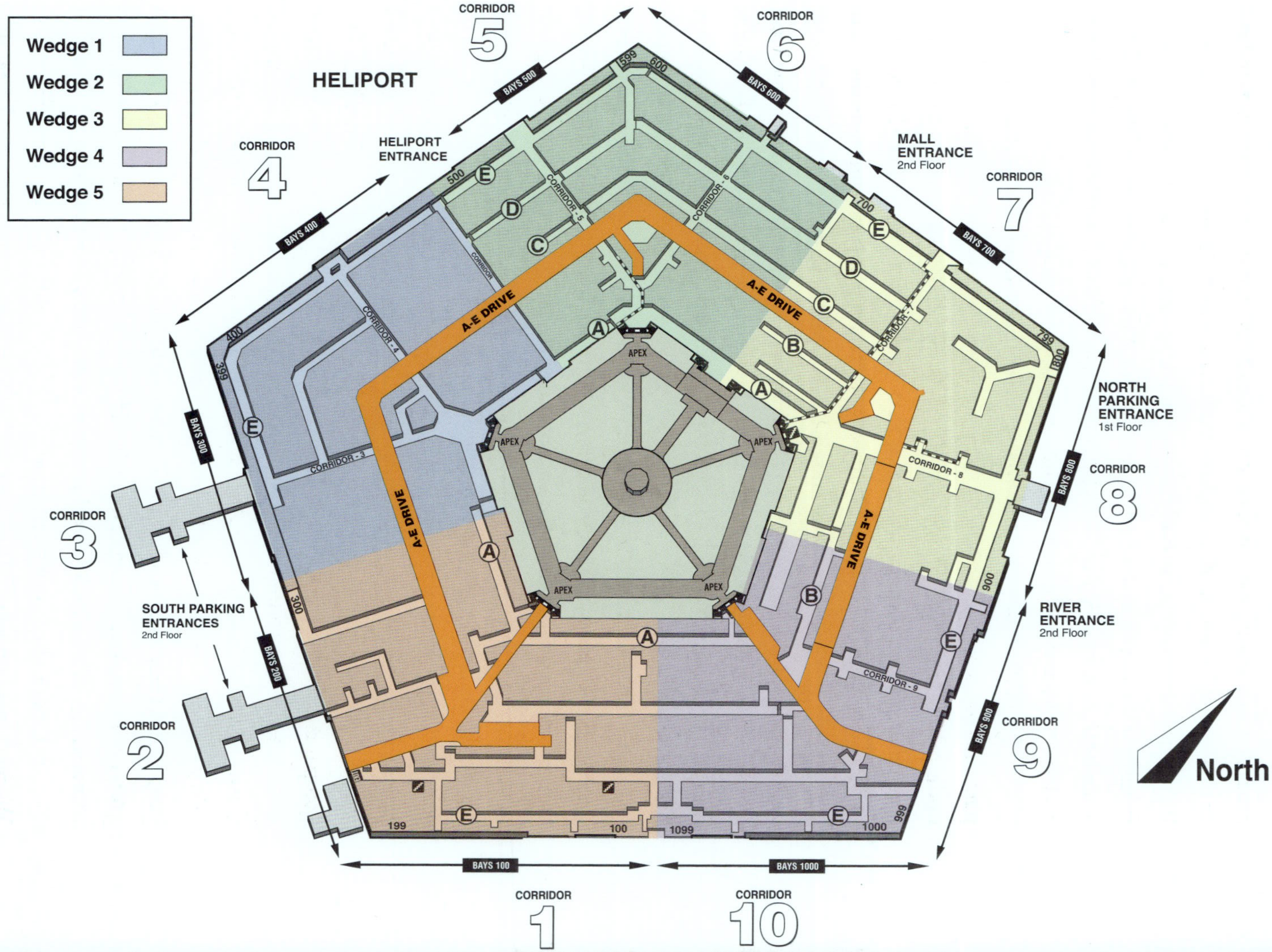

ing to increase its lateral stability and provide support to new blast-resistant windows. The building's windows indeed required special attention. Analysis of attacks on large structures elsewhere bore out that flying glass from blast-shattered windows caused many casualties, including deaths. The Pentagon's original 7,748 mostly casement-type windows, varying in size from 5'x6' to 6'x7', offered no resistance to blast-generated fragmentation. Reinforcing the windows on the outside of the E Ring and the A Ring would diminish the blast and fragmentation effects of exterior explosions. New windows for the E Ring,* the same size as their predecessors but with glass 1 1/2 inches thick and weighing more than a ton apiece, were welded into special tubular steel frameworks. On 11 September many survived the blast.[5]

Long regarded as a physical security risk, the extensive south side loading dock for truck deliveries was replaced in August 2000 by a new 250,000 sq. ft. Remote Delivery Facility (RDF) adjacent to North Parking, some hundreds of yards from the Pentagon. Named for David Cooke, a longtime DoD administrator popularly known as the "Mayor of the Pentagon" and familiar to all as "Doc," the RDF was linked to the Pentagon by tunnel in February 2002, permitting unloading of large vehicles at a safe distance from the building. After deliveries were x-rayed, goods came into the Pentagon by electric-powered carts via the tunnel. Built largely for security reasons, two new pedestrian bridges at the south side of the Pentagon, entryways into Corridors 2 and 3 at the 2nd Floor level, provided massive barriers separating vehicular and pedestrian traffic.[6]

While security concerns received increasing attention as renovation progressed, the measures planned, under way, or instituted could neither anticipate nor fully defend against the powerful attack that came on 11 September 2001. Indeed, it is difficult to see how any realistic physical changes to the Pentagon could have deflected or greatly diminished the effects of the attack.

The Attack

For their assault on the U.S. homeland on 11 September 2001 the terrorists, identified as belonging to the al Qaeda network headed by Osama bin Laden, chose four targets known to the world as prominent symbols of American

* New A Ring window glass was not as thick as the E Ring window glass.

prestige and power. The first two, the Twin Towers of the World Trade Center in New York, were icons representing American economic strength. The third, the Pentagon, represented U.S. military might. A fourth and highest-value target selected—presumably the White House or the Capitol—escaped attack when the hijacked plane destined for it crashed in Pennsylvania.

Previous attacks against U.S. official facilities by radical Muslim terrorists had occurred overseas: most notably the suicide truck bombing that killed 241 American military at the Marine barracks in Beirut, Lebanon, in October 1983; a similar strike against the Air Force Khobar Towers housing complex in Saudi Arabia in June 1996; the massive attacks on the U.S. embassies in Nairobi, Kenya, and Dar es Salaam, Tanzania, in August 1998; and the small-boat bombing of the destroyer USS *Cole* in Yemen's port of Aden in October 2000. The only strike within the United States by Middle Eastern terrorists occurred in February 1993 when they exploded a truck bomb in a parking garage under the World Trade Center in New York City, killing six people. Before 2001 the al Qaeda terrorists had decided to aim at more high-value and high-visibility targets in the United States.[7]

Over a period of two years before September 2001, in accordance with plans conceived by a network of al Qaeda plotters, the chosen agents entered the United States and made preparations for their stunning assault. They selected the most practical, lethal, and obtainable means of achieving their purpose—large aircraft carrying huge loads of explosive fuel. Beginning as early as July 2000, 14 months before the hijackings, several of the terrorists took flight-training courses. They acquired flight deck videos for Boeing 747, 757, 767, and 777 aircraft. By September 2001 the hijackers were ready.[8]

On the morning of 11 September, the terrorists hijacked four airliners, two from Boston's Logan International Airport, one from Newark Liberty International Airport, and one from Washington Dulles International Airport, in Northern Virginia. The two aircraft departing from Boston—American Airlines Flight 11 (11 crew, 76 passengers, 5 hijackers) at 7:59 a.m. and United Airlines Flight 175 (9 crew, 51 passengers, 5 hijackers) at 8:14 a.m.—were Boeing 767s bound for Los Angeles. Their flight crews each stopped transmitting within half an hour of departing, when they were over central New York State. Air controllers first registered concern at 8:21 a.m. when American Flight 11 turned off its transponder; the

Federal Aviation Administration (FAA) sent its first warning of the hijacking of American Flight 11 to the Northeast Air Defense Sector (NEADS) of the North American Aerospace Defense Command (NORAD) at 8:38 a.m.[9]

The call from the FAA did not come in time. The military had less than 9 minutes' warning before the first airliner hit the World Trade Center and 25 minutes before the second. The Air National Guard launched two F-15 fighter planes from Otis Air Force Base, on Cape Cod, Massachusetts, at 8:53, too late to intercept the hijacked aircraft. Flights 11 and 175 hit the North and South Towers of the World Trade Center at 8:46 a.m. and 9:03 a.m. respectively, with the fighters still 70 miles distant at the time of the second crash. Otis and Langley Air Force Base in Virginia, each with a pair of fighters at the ready, were the only two alert sites available to NEADS for air defense of New York and Washington. Just 14 fighter planes on alert guarded the whole of American airspace that morning. The New York City attacks caused the South Tower to collapse at 9:59 a.m. and the North Tower at 10:28 a.m., killing more than 2,700 people.[10]

United Flight 93 (7 crew, 33 passengers, 4 hijackers), a Boeing 757 bound for San Francisco, left Newark at 8:42 in the morning. At approximately 9:24 a.m., NEADS ordered Langley Air Force Base, near Norfolk, Virginia, which had been put on alert at 9:09, to prepare to scramble fighters presumably to intercept not Flight 93, but Flight 11, mistakenly thought to be moving south, this almost 40 minutes after Flight 11 had struck the North Tower. Another 40 minutes later, after a struggle between the hijackers and passengers, Flight 93 crashed into the ground near Shanksville, Pennsylvania, killing all on board.[11]

The conspirators no doubt chose and methodically planned the takeover of these particular flights to maximize explosive damage. Because all four aircraft were headed nonstop for the West Coast, they carried large loads of highly volatile fuel. The full force of their destructive power became apparent when Flight 175 hit the South Tower in New York; the resulting jet fuel fireball exploded downward into lower floors.[12]

Near-simultaneous departure and subsequent hijacking of the four planes, all of which took off within a period of 43 minutes, maximized the element of surprise, allowing the FAA little time to warn pilots in U.S. airspace. The huge number of aircraft—more than 4,600—aloft over the continental United States

BOEING 757 SCHEMATICS

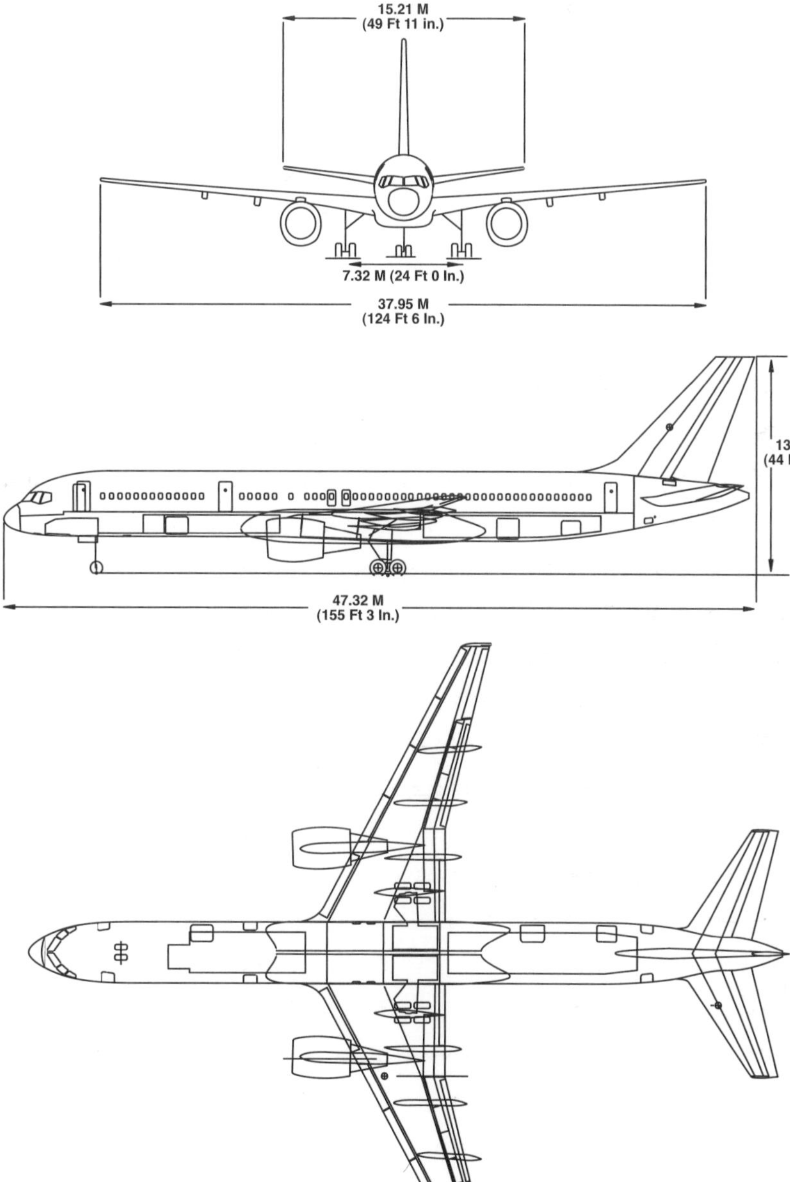

Source: Boeing Company

made it difficult for NORAD to identify the four rogue aircraft. Finally, the element of surprise reduced the time available to launch interceptors to divert or shoot down the hijacked aircraft, assuming that a decision to do so could have been made in time.[13]

At Dulles International Airport five hijackers boarded American Airlines Flight 77 bound for Los Angeles: Khalid al Midhar, Majed Moqed, Nawaf al Hazmi, Salem al Hazmi, and Hani Hanjour, of whom the first four were subsequently listed as "possible Saudi" nationals. Although some of the men set off metal detector alarms, they were passed through the security checkpoints. When the plane lifted off at 8:20 a.m. it had 64 people on board—a crew of 6 plus 58 passengers, including the 5 hijackers with their weapons, probably small knives and box cutters.

In a speculative reconstruction of what took place in the plane, it seems likely that over eastern Kentucky the hijackers made their move, probably between 8:51 and 8:54, and took over Flight 77. They either waited for a cabin attendant to knock on the flight deck door and then rushed the cockpit or took an individual cabin crew member or passenger hostage and used threats against the victim to gain access. Once on the flight deck the attackers either incapacitated or murdered the two pilots and then took over the aircraft. With one hijacker as pilot, the other four herded the passengers to the rear of the aircraft and forestalled any attempts to retake control of the aircraft before it reached its target. Under the control of the five terrorists, at about 8:55 a.m. Flight 77 turned south and then five minutes later turned eastward from a point near the junction of West Virginia, Ohio, and Kentucky. Hani Hanjour, who had received FAA pilot certification, no doubt piloted the aircraft.[14]

Tracking Flight 77 would not have been easy, even if controllers had been able to identify the plane to follow. Its transponder, a transmitter that broadcast the course, speed, and altitude of the airplane, was turned off at 8:56. The hijacker pilot refused to answer any radio messages, adding to the uncertainty of making a decision to dispatch military aircraft to intercept the airliner. For air traffic controllers the lack of a transponder signal meant they could not find the Boeing 757 until it crossed the path of a ground-based radar. In any event, there was not enough warning time for NORAD to take effective action. The only relevant action taken came in response to the erroneous FAA notice that Flight

11 was flying south toward Washington. At 9:30 a.m. Langley Air Force Base launched three* F-16s that were still about 150 miles away from Washington when Flight 77 crashed into the Pentagon seven minutes later. The fighters had flown over the ocean in accordance with standing instructions and did not turn toward Washington until ordered to do so at almost the same time that the Pentagon was struck.[15]

The crashes into the Twin Towers, quickly perceived as terrorist attacks, were a call to action at the Pentagon. The acting deputy director for operations in the National Military Command Center, Navy Captain Charles Leidig, initiated a call for a "significant event" telephone conference of senior military leaders at 9:29. Leidig rejected the erroneous FAA warning that Flight 11 was heading for Washington. At 9:33 the Ronald Reagan Washington National Airport tower passed to the Secret Service Operations Center in Washington the alarming word that "an aircraft [is] coming at you and not talking with us." A minute later the plane, Flight 77, turned south below Alexandria, Virginia, then circled back to the northeast and flew toward Washington again. Its destination was the Pentagon, not the White House or the Capitol.†[16]

The final minute of the airliner's flight took it along an east-northeast course above an Arlington County, Virginia, roadway, Columbia Pike. County Police Department Corporal Barry Foust, stopped at a traffic light at the intersection of Walter Reed Drive and Columbia Pike less than two miles from the Pentagon, spotted the aircraft flying low, saw a plume of smoke, then radioed, "We just had an airplane crash . . . must be in the District area." Three blocks further along, at the intersection of Columbia Pike with South Wayne Street, Police Motorcycle Officer Richard Cox observed the airliner flying so close to the ground that the polished underside of its fuselage reflected the images of the buildings it passed on its flight; then he heard an explosion.[17]

* The two fighters on alert were joined by a third, a spare aircraft that had not been placed on alert. NEADS had ordered Langley to send up three fighters.

† "At 9:34 AM the aircraft was positioned about 3.5 miles west-southwest of the Pentagon, and started a right 330-degree descending turn to the right. At the end of the turn the aircraft was at about 2000 feet altitude and 4 miles southwest of the Pentagon. Over the next 30 seconds, power was increased to near maximum. . . . The airplane accelerated to approximately 460 knots (530 miles per hour) at impact with the Pentagon. The time of impact was 9:37:45 AM." (National Transportation Safety Board, "Flight Path Study — American Airlines Flight 77," 19 Feb 02. See Appendix B.)

FLIGHT PATH OF AMERICAN AIRLINES FLIGHT 77

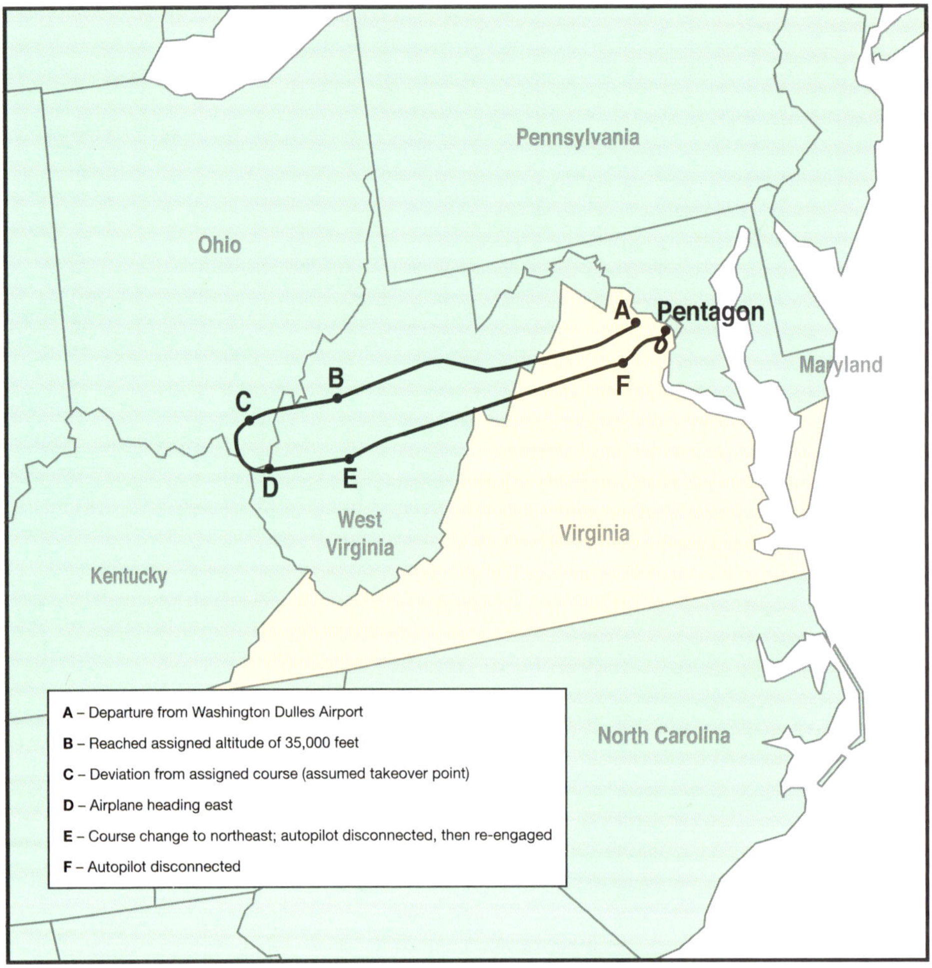

Sources: NTSB Flight Path Study, 19 February 2002, and 9/11 Commission Report

Flying just above the Navy Annex Building and a Virginia State Police radio mast, both uphill from the Pentagon and adjacent to Arlington National Cemetery, the hijacker pilot guided the Boeing 757 downhill and turned it in a northeasterly direction. Less than two seconds before the plane hit the Pentagon, R. E. Rabogliatti, a building management specialist at the Navy Annex, peered out of his office window and saw the airliner looming over the building. Later, recalling its screaming engines he judged that the pilot must have pushed the jet's throttle to the limit; he estimated its altitude at less than 150 feet. In the Army Operations Center in the Pentagon Basement, Brigadier General Peter Chiarelli

AIRCRAFT'S FINAL MANEUVER BEFORE IMPACT WITH PENTAGON

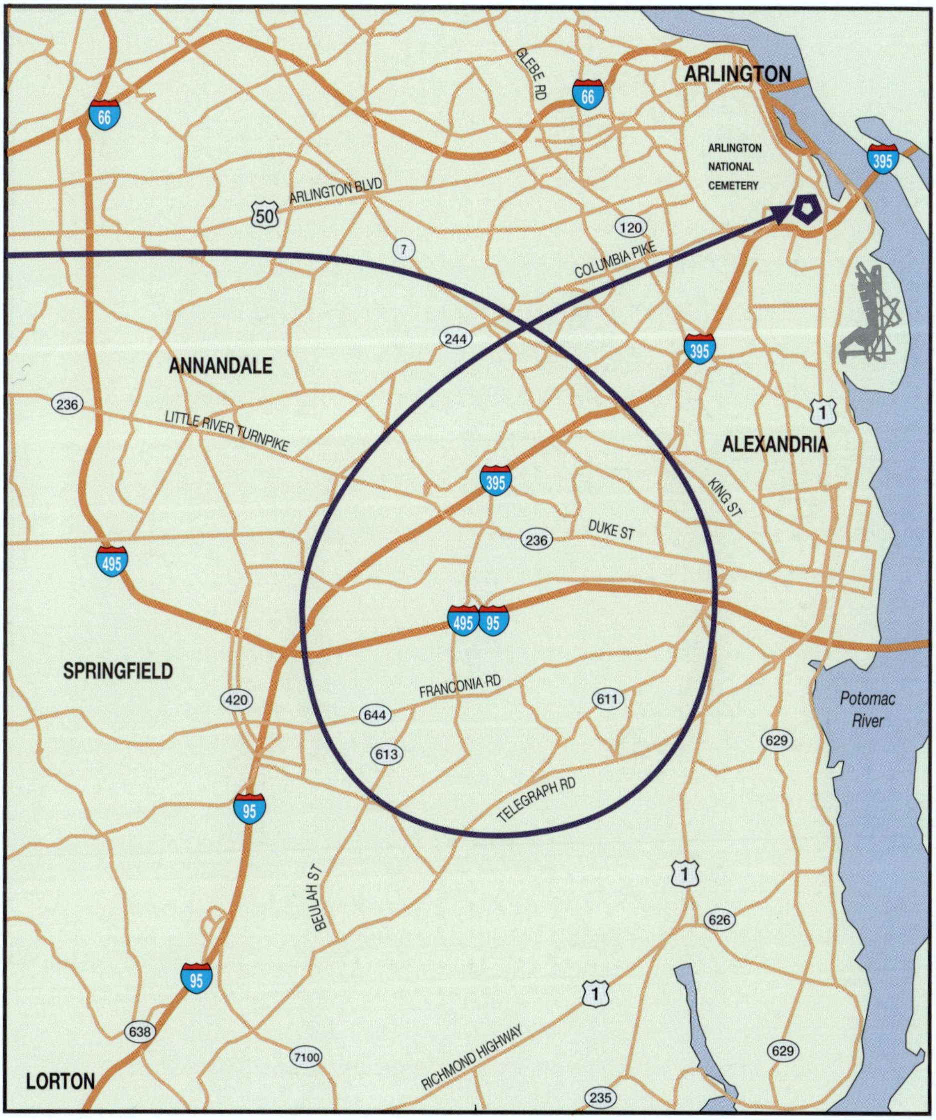

Source: Adapted from NTSB Flight Path Study, 19 February 2002

was told by "the INTEL folks" that an "aircraft was headed for D.C. and it was right about then that we heard the noise and the building had been hit."[18]

Others in the immediate vicinity who witnessed the impact recalled that the airliner struck several obstacles, including light poles on Route 27, on the way to its target. The right wing hit a portable generator and the right engine crushed a chain link fence. The left engine smashed an external steam vault. Observers saw debris falling from the plane and the building. Five images from a Pentagon security camera, approximately a second apart, recorded the approach, the crash, and the immediate effect—a huge fireball.[19]

Witnessing the fiery crash from above was the crew of a C-130 transport plane that had taken off from Andrews Air Force Base, Maryland, minutes before. As Flight 77 descended toward the Pentagon it crossed the C-130's flight path. An air traffic controller asked the C-130 pilot, Lieutenant Colonel Steve O'Brien, to reverse course and follow the airliner. O'Brien turned and followed, watching in disbelief as Flight 77 smashed into the Pentagon. Ordered to leave the area immediately because fighter aircraft were approaching, the C-130 flew on to its destination—Minneapolis-St. Paul.[20]

Flight 77 hit the Pentagon at 9:37 a.m.* A description of the moment of impact on the building is contained in a report by the American Society of Civil Engineers—*The Pentagon Building Performance Report*:

> The Boeing 757 approached the west wall of the Pentagon from the southwest at approximately 780 ft/s. As it approached the Pentagon site it was so low to the ground that it reportedly clipped an antenna on a vehicle on an adjacent road and severed light posts. When it was approximately 320 ft from the west wall of the building (0.42 second before impact), it was flying nearly level, only a few feet above the ground. . . . The aircraft flew over the grassy area next to the Pentagon until its right wing struck a piece of construction equipment that was approximately 100 to 110 ft from the face of the building (0.10 second before impact) . . . . At that time the aircraft had rolled slightly to the left, its right wing elevated. After the plane had traveled approximately another 75 ft, the left engine struck the ground at nearly the same instant that the nose of the aircraft struck the west wall of the Pentagon . . . . Impact of the fuselage was . . . at or slightly below the second-floor slab. The left wing passed below the second-floor slab, and the right wing crossed at a shallow angle from below the second-floor slab to above the second-floor slab.[21]

The impact proved devastating. The aircraft had taken off with a total weight of over 90 tons, roughly 25 percent of it in fuel. Allowing for the hour-and-a-quarter flight from Dulles Airport to Kentucky and back, Flight 77 still had most of its original 7,256 gallons of fuel on board, the greater part of it in the

* *9/11 Commission Report*, 9, 25-27, 461 (n 154), puts the time at 9:37:46.

wings, when it hit the Pentagon. Traveling at 530 m.p.h., the aircraft, and the subsequent fuel explosion, delivered enormous destructive power. The catastrophe might well have been even greater had the Pentagon been struck by either of the two Boeing 767s that crashed into the World Trade Center. These larger aircraft, carrying thousands of gallons more fuel than the Boeing 757s that departed from Newark and Dulles, would have done far more damage.*[22]

Flight 77 struck the west side of the Pentagon at the 1st Floor level just inside Wedge 1 near the 4th Corridor and proceeded diagonally at an approximate 42° angle toward the 5th Corridor in the mostly vacant and unrenovated Wedge 2. After the nose of the plane hit the Pentagon a huge fireball burst upward and rose 200 feet above the roof. Multiple explosions occurred as the plane smashed through the building. The front part of the relatively weak fuselage disintegrated, but the mid-section and tail-end continued moving for another fraction of a second, progressively destroying segments of the building further inward. The chain of destruction resulted in parts of the plane ending up inside the Pentagon in reverse of the order they had entered it, with the tail-end of the airliner penetrating the greatest distance into the building. Remarkably, these circumstances meant that the bodies of the passengers in the rear of the aircraft traveled deeper into the ground floor of the building than did those in the front. The largest concentration of body parts was found at the deepest area of penetration—the C Ring.[23]

While the immediate building interior area hit by the nose of the aircraft was small, the section subsequently wrecked by the large plane debris and multiple explosions of jet fuel from the ruptured tanks seconds after impact spanned a larger irregular area of more than an acre on each of the 1st and 2nd Floors. Office spaces and corridors on these floors accounted for the locations of all but two of the DoD victims. On the ground floor, the impact damage extended as

* The Boeing two-engine 757-200 aircraft had a wingspan of 124 ft. 6 in., overall length of 155 ft. 3 in., and tail height of 44 ft. 6 in. According to American Airlines, Flight 77 carried "approximately 7,256 gallons of 'Jet A' fuel" on board when it departed Dulles (ltr D. Douglas Cotton, Legal Department, American Airlines, Inc. to Dalton West, OSD Historical Office, 24 Mar 06). According to the National Transportation Safety Board, Flight 77 carried 48,983 lbs. of fuel while on the ramp prior to departure and still had 36,200 lbs. of fuel on board when it hit the Pentagon. A standard conversion factor of 6.7+ lbs. per gallon of fuel yields the 7,256 gallons figure that American Airlines provided as above. See NTSB Office of Research and Engineering, "Study of Autopilot, Navigation Equipment, and Fuel Consumption Activity Based on United Airlines Flight 93 and American Airlines Flight 77 Digital Flight Data Recorder Information," John O'Callaghan and Daniel Bower, 13 Feb 02, 8.

PATH OF PLANE INTO BUILDING

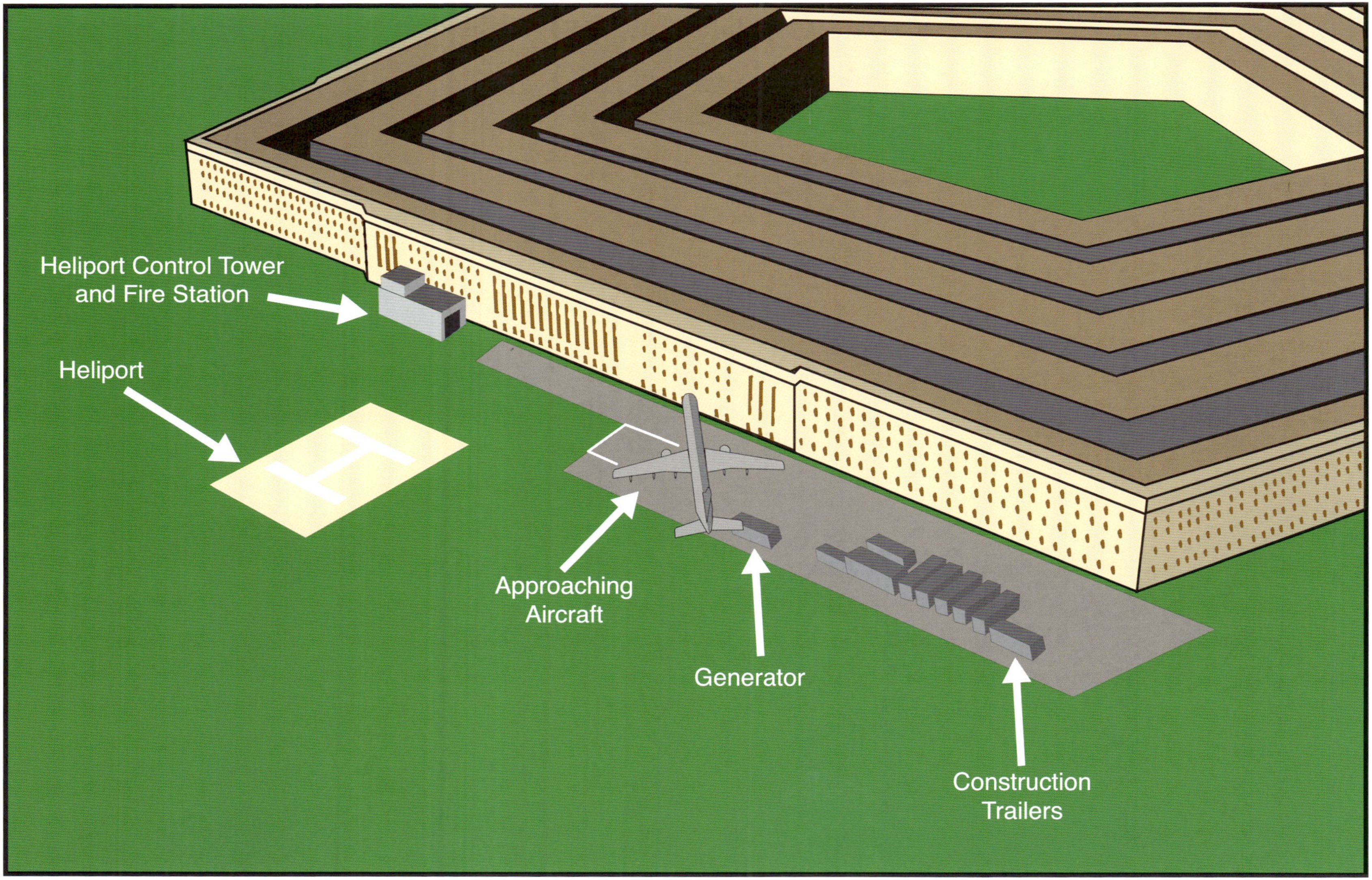

far as the inner wall of the Pentagon's C Ring adjoining A-E Drive, a depth of 210 feet, although the plane traveled about 270 feet along an angled path into the building. A-E Drive in Wedges 1 and 2 marked the C Ring back end of the 1st and 2nd Floor areas that suffered almost all of the fatalities. Impact damage on the 2nd Floor proved much more limited than on the 1st Floor, with no supporting columns destroyed at a distance more than 50 feet from the outside wall. Above the 2nd Floor most of the damage in the D and C Rings resulted from fire and smoke and collapsed ceilings and light fixtures.[24]

The velocity of the plane's fuselage expended itself by the time it reached A-E Drive, which dissipated the remaining explosive energy of the crash. But the blast had enough force left to blow holes in the C Ring wall and force open the doors of an electrical vault opening into the drive; the openings proved the salvation of many survivors. Parts of the aircraft—including a tire part—hurtled through the outer three rings of Pentagon offices, emerged from a so-called "punch out" hole in the C Ring wall, and came to rest in A-E Drive. The plane's voice recorder and flight data recorder were not recovered until several days later, 14 September.[25]

The report of the American Society of Civil Engineers concluded that "the direct impact of the aircraft destroyed the load capacity of about 30 first-floor columns and significantly impaired that of 20 others." Moreover, "this impact may have also destroyed the load capacity of about six second-floor columns adjacent to the exterior wall." Shattering the many columns essentially doubled the span between columns, thereby imposing severe stress on the stability of the affected building section and causing collapse of the four floors in the E Ring above the impact point at 10:15 a.m. The collapse started with the 2nd Floor just north of Corridor 4 along an expansion joint in the E Ring, and opened a hole to the outside about 95 feet wide at the 1st Floor level. The collapsed zone extended approximately 50 feet from the outside to the still-standing inside E Ring wall.*

* Establishing an exact time for the collapse of the Pentagon's floors above the impacted E Ring area required extensive research. The "Arlington County After-Action Report" cited an incorrect time (9:57 a.m.) in its Appendix 1, page 1-1, seeming to confuse the warning of a collapse with the collapse itself: see A-29-30, A-66. Time-stamped video images provide the best evidence for 10:15 a.m. as the time of the collapse. See WUSA 9 News video, David Statter reporting from the Pentagon, 11 September 2001, 4100 Wisconsin Ave., Washington, D.C., and ABC News video, "World Trade Center and Pentagon Bombings," 11 September 2001, 705204, Television News Archive, Vanderbilt University, Nashville, Tenn. (local Nashville time), http://tvnews.vanderbilt.edu/tvn-month-search.pl. See also Rossow, *Uncommon Strength*, 83, n 1.

The D and C Rings did not collapse. The low hit reduced the damage visible from outside.[26]

No building could have absorbed the energy of such a crash without suffering structural damage and, if occupied, casualties. Nevertheless, the Pentagon fared better than less sturdy buildings would have. The greatest power of the interior explosions was confined to a limited area bounded by concrete floors and sturdy walls. Major structural damage ended with the collapse of the impact zone. Additional damage incurred over the next 36 hours extended deep into the Pentagon, with a considerably larger area beyond the impact site damaged by fire and smoke as well as the water from sprinklers, burst pipes, and fire hoses. The worst damage came from the volume and flammability of the fuel rather than the structural strength of the plane.

Although never designed to offer the protection of a bunker, the building's steel-reinforced concrete and brick construction protected most employees in Wedges 1 and 2 from fires and explosions and saved their lives. Moreover, the rigidity of the Pentagon's facade caused some of the fuel in the wings to detonate on impact, diminishing the inside destruction and probably reducing the number of dead—all 64 on board the plane and 125 from the building. The lighter structure and largely glass facade of the World Trade Center buildings presented much less impact resistance.[27]

In other respects, the structural strength of the building proved a mixed blessing. Concrete and brick, not yielding easily to the energy of the impact, channeled the ensuing explosion and flames along paths of less resistance. The new windows, frames, and walls in Wedge 1 held up under extraordinary pressures, but they diminished venting of the fires, heat, and smoke. Consequently the explosion's constrained energy coursed through offices, corridors, elevator shafts, and stairwells, where doors offered less resistance than concrete. The furious energy of the explosion made the bottom two floors in the immediate vicinity of the crash site death traps, compromised stairwells as escape routes, and made firefighting more difficult.

The delay in the collapse of the E Ring in Wedge 1, almost 40 minutes, proved critical to the survival of occupants of the upper three floors, where the immediate impact of the plane claimed only two lives, both on the 3rd Floor. The

PATH OF AIRCRAFT THROUGH THE FIRST FLOOR

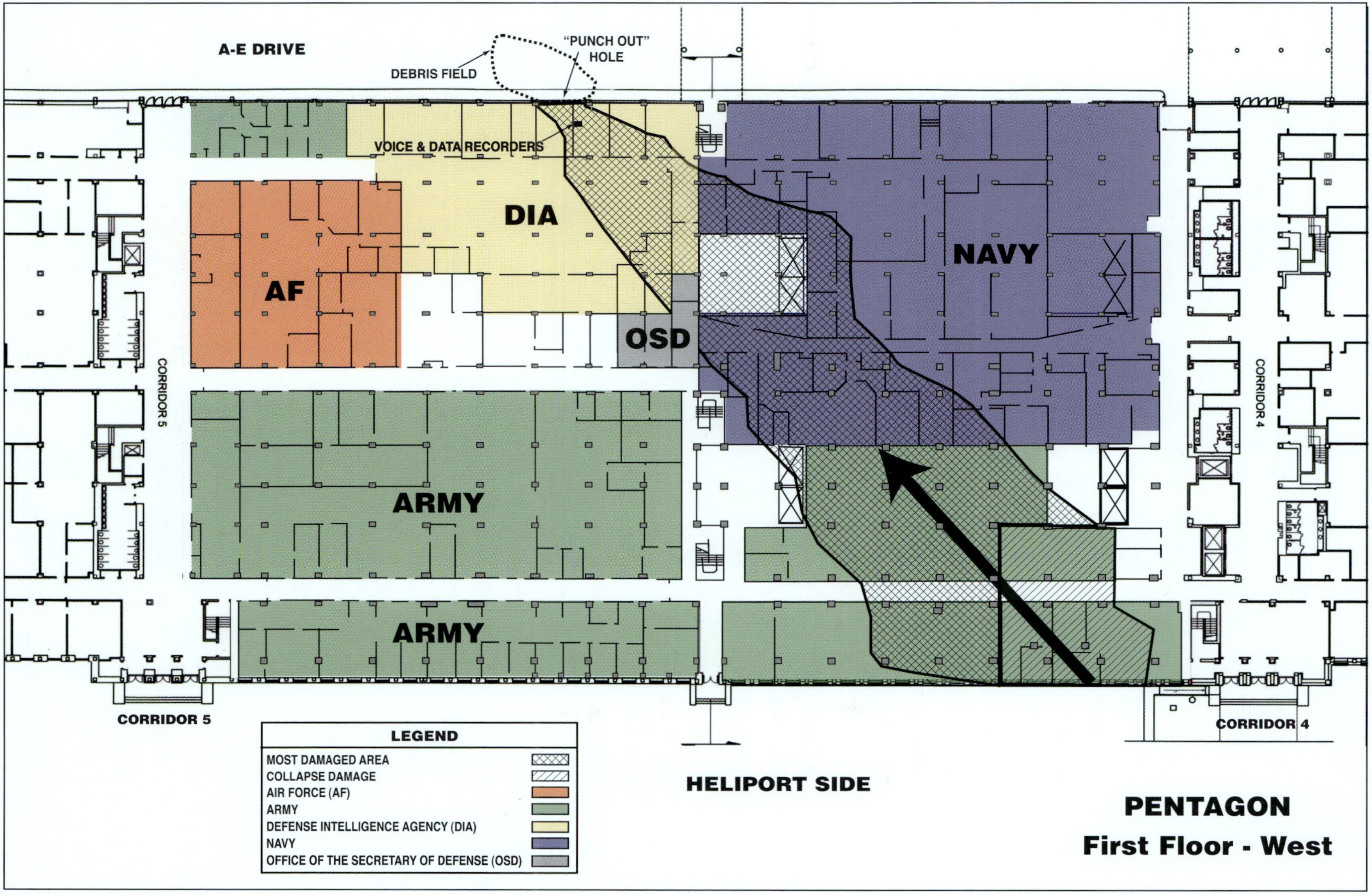

Pentagon's sturdy construction served to delay the collapse, affording time for hundreds of people on the upper floors to escape.

The destruction and, more importantly, the loss of life, would have been worse without the reinforcement of the exterior wall of Wedge 1 and installation of the blast-resistant windows and fire suppression systems. Hitting just inside Corridor 4 in Wedge 1, the plane penetrated into the unrenovated Wedge 2. On 11 September the offices in or near the impact point were not completely occupied, either awaiting new tenants in Wedge 1 or mostly vacated in preparation for renovation in Wedge 2. Had the aircraft hit fully-occupied unrenovated Wedge 5, several hundred yards to the right, the toll of dead and injured, as well as structural damage, would have been much greater. If the plane had missed Wedge 1 entirely and plowed through only unrenovated and nearly-vacated portions of Wedge 2, the structural and fire damage would have been far greater, but the death toll might have been less. No matter where it might have struck the Pentagon, Flight 77 would have wreaked havoc.

Chapter II

The Deadly Strike

At 9:37 a.m. on 11 September the 20,000 people present in the Pentagon had no hint of the stunning explosion and firestorm about to engulf those in the path of the doomed airliner only seconds away from striking its target. A few of those witnessing the televised horror of the crashes into the World Trade Center's Twin Towers in New York did, indeed, wonder aloud if the Pentagon might be next. Their worst fears became reality when 34 minutes after United Flight 175 struck the South Tower of the World Trade Center at 9:03 a.m. American Flight 77 smashed into the west side of the Pentagon, bringing great damage to the building and death and injury to many of its inhabitants.

Despite the fortuitous circumstance that only 3,800 of the 4,500-5,000 intended occupants had moved into newly renovated Wedge 1 with its strengthened walls and windows and that Wedge 2 had been largely emptied of personnel (about 700 remained) as renovation began there, the exploding airliner exacted a heavy toll of dead and injured.[1] Of the 125 Department of Defense fatalities in the Pentagon, 92 occurred on the 1st Floor, 31 on the 2nd Floor, and 2 on the 3rd Floor, all between Corridors 4 and 5. The dead included 70 civilians (10 of them contractor employees) and 55 military.* The Army incurred the greatest loss—

* There is evidence that one OSD contract employee, Allen Boyle, may have been outside the building just before the plane hit.

75 men and women.* Another 106 injured were taken to area hospitals.[2] On the periphery of the damaged area many persons suffered from inhaling the dense and noxious smoke that engulfed a large part of the building on all five floors, reaching beyond the 2nd and 7th Corridors on either side and as far as the A Ring and even the Center Court on the lower floors.

On the airliner, all 64 people died, including the 5 hijackers, most of them instantly. Among the six crew members were a husband and wife pair of flight attendants. A party of eight from the Washington area—three teachers, three 11-year-old students, and two escorts from the National Geographic Society—had looked forward to a field trip to the Channel Island Marine Sanctuary in California. One of the children was the son of a Navy chief petty officer on duty in the Pentagon. A family of four, including two small children, and a honeymoon couple bound for Hawaii were among the victims. What befell two passengers—William Caswell and Bryan Jack—was especially ironic. Both were Department of Defense employees on official business trips and had offices in the Pentagon.† [3]

The attack killed 189 people, all of whom, with a few exceptions, died within minutes. Antoinette Sherman, an Army employee, died six days later in the hospital. Caswell and Jack on Flight 77 brought the total of DoD-affiliated fatalities in the Pentagon to 127.‡

A life-and-death drama for many hundreds of Pentagon occupants played out on the large stage between Corridors 4 and 5 and mostly on the 1st and 2nd Floors in Rings E, D, and C—an area of some two acres on each floor. Those floors contained numerous offices and hundreds of individual cubicles creating mazes awkward to negotiate even under normal conditions. The layout of the building and the drastically altered state of their surroundings caused by the crash dictated the escape routes taken by survivors. The main escape routes from the impact area to the outside of the building from the E Ring were Corridor 5 and the Heliport entrance midway between Corridors 4 and 5. In the opposite direction, Corridors 4 and 5 provided the chief exits through the A Ring to the Center Court. Some survivors from Wedge 2 managed to escape through blown

* For a complete list of fatalities see Appendix A.

† Still another DoD employee, Herbert Homer, was killed when the plane on which he was a passenger, American Airlines Flight 11, smashed into the World Trade Center.

‡ See Appendix A.

windows in the E Ring outer wall. On all floors and most rings a wooden construction barrier midway between Corridors 4 and 5, a temporary product of the renovation, often prevented people in Wedge 1 from reaching Corridor 5 and those in Wedge 2 from reaching Corridor 4.* In large measure, this particular obstacle determined routes taken by many of the survivors. Other main escape exits from the impact area were through Corridors 4 and 5 into A-E Drive from the C Ring. Three openings in the C Ring wall between Corridors 4 and 5, one of them the blown doors of the C-4 electrical vault, and a forced window at the 2nd Floor level proved the salvation of many survivors from the 1st and 2nd Floors. The holes into A-E Drive also made it possible for rescuers to enter the building and bring to safety lost and injured occupants who would otherwise have perished.

For people in the immediate vicinity of impact and along the path of destruction the first minutes brought surprise, disorientation, fear, panic, danger, and death. For those spared annihilation, the first minutes began a grim, desperate struggle for survival. In the menacing darkness and smoke, fear for their lives caused some to panic and cry out or scream; many prayed silently or aloud. Others, although frightened and expecting to die, did not panic and strove single-mindedly to find escape for themselves and their coworkers. Close to the crash, bewildered and shaken men and women, their thought and senses clouded by shock, had to function at whatever levels of instinct and willpower they retained. They faced a host of instant hazards: utter darkness, toxic smoke, fire, immense heat, piles of hot debris, collapsed ceilings and walls, live electric wires, blocked exits and stairways, and the beginning of a structural collapse within the critical zone. Hardly any knew or guessed what had precipitated the appalling chaos that had descended on them, even though most were aware of the crashes into the Twin Towers little more than half an hour earlier.

In sections of the building as much as two or three corridors removed from the Corridor 4 crash site, people could not help but notice the effect of the impact—variously described as a loud noise, a sudden shudder of the structure, an explosion, a concussion, the firing of large guns. Most of the occupants

* The wooden construction barrier wall on all floors midway between Corridors 4 and 5 separated Wedge 1 from Wedge 2. Doors in most of the barrier walls permitted access to corridors on either side of a barrier, but they were often obscured by the smoke and most of the escapees from Wedge 2 turned toward Corridor 5.

in these areas departed in orderly fashion, some after encountering smoke and obstacles. A number stayed behind to help rescue others. Army Major Craig Collier recalled that he and his colleagues remained in their office, 2C638, after the plane hit:

> Moments later the building jolted and we heard a muffled boom, then a rumble. Some loose plaster and dust fell from the ceiling, but otherwise there was no other indication of what had just taken place about 200 feet away. All of my peers in the area are experienced combat arms officers, and we quickly agreed that it sounded and felt like a bomb. Most of us stayed in place watching the news and waiting for more information as one or two officers walked out into the hallway to see what was going on. Remarkably, my boss walked in and asked us what was happening. He had been in the latrine next door and hadn't felt or heard a thing. Within about 2 minutes the TV banner below the video of the burning towers changed from "World Trade Center" to "Pentagon," but before I could hear any of the details the word came to evacuate the building. Two of our female civilian secretaries bolted out of the office but the rest of us took the time to calmly turn off computers, call our wives, grab our bags, and exit.[4]

Away from the impact area, 1,000 and more feet removed, many occupants had no inkling that an attack had occurred and felt little or no immediate effect. They heard the fire alarms, smelled smoke, and heeded instructions from the Defense Protective Service (DPS) to leave the building. Unlike the skyscraping World Trade Center, the low-lying Pentagon's numerous exits to the outside and to the Center Court facilitated rapid evacuation; for most of the 20,000 inhabitants the evacuation proved orderly. Once outside the Pentagon no one could miss the immense column of smoke rising from the crash site.

During the renovation sophisticated fire alarm and sprinkler systems had been installed in Wedge 1. These operated initially after the attack, but many were soon damaged or destroyed and ceased to work. Surviving sprinklers helped limit the spread of the fire and toxic smoke and provided survivors much needed relief from the great heat. The older alarm systems in the rest of the building had false alarm and other functional failures. These systems included an automated recorded message giving instructions to evacuate. A backup public address system, called "Big Voice," complemented the automatic announcements by indicating the best escape route. Unfortunately the systems performed poorly. In some sections of the building workers heard no alarm at all or received a garbled announcement. In Wedge 2 there were no sprinklers.[5]

Many occupants in the newly renovated Wedge 1 on the 1st and 2nd Floors were not yet fully familiar with their new quarters. In windowless, blacked out, and smoke-filled areas, disoriented, they had difficulty knowing where to turn to find exits leading to safety. Even occupants of Wedge 2, more familiar with their surroundings, found themselves at a loss in the smoke and darkness.

Knowledge of what happened to the hundreds of people in Wedges 1 and 2 and nearby areas most immediately affected by the explosion and fire comes from an abundance of eyewitness testimony and forensic evidence. The accounts of death and survival that follow are representative of the range of experiences endured by most of those unfortunate enough to find themselves in or near the path of the exploding airliner.

Among those who actually saw Flight 77 hit the building, perhaps closest to the crash site were Air Traffic Controllers Sean Boger and Army Specialist Jacqueline Kidd, in the air traffic control tower between the building and the Pentagon Heliport, from where they directed helicopter landings and departures. On hearing the news of the crashes in New York, Boger wondered aloud, as he had on other occasions, why no airliner had ever accidentally hit the Pentagon, given its close proximity (approximately a mile) to Reagan National Airport. Moments later, after Kidd had gone downstairs to the restroom, Boger, looking out the window, saw "the nose and the wing of an aircraft just like coming right at us, and he didn't veer. . . . I am watching the plane go all the way into the building." He stared as the Boeing 757 "smacked into the building" less than 100 feet away.

When the plane exploded into the Pentagon, Boger "hit the floor and just covered up" his head because he was "surrounded by glass." As the tower's alarms sounded and emergency lights flashed, he rose, yanked open the control room door, and plunged down the stairs, jumping steps to avoid a clutter of ceiling tiles, light fixtures, and broken stair railings. On the ground floor he met Specialist Kidd, and the two ran from the scene. About 25 yards distant they fell to the ground and turned to look at the conflagration that had set on fire their cars, parked next to the tower.[6] Inside the building, others in the path of the plane did not have the opportunity to run.

First Floor

On the 1st Floor of the E Ring and part of the D Ring, directly in the path of the oncoming airliner, the U.S. Army's Resource Services—Washington (RSW) office, part of the Office of the Administrative Assistant to the Secretary of the Army, employing 65 to 70 people, managed money and personnel for the headquarters staff. By 11 September two RSW divisions had moved from their older, unrenovated offices to their new 1E400 area workplace. However, the RSW director, longtime government employee Robert Jaworski, and many of his people from the personnel, financial management, and accounting staffs, had not yet moved into their new spaces and were still working in the D Ring, Corridors 6 and 7 area, 500 feet or more removed from their colleagues.

In his 3D735 office Jaworski heard radio broadcasts of the World Trade Center attacks. After the second airliner hit, Jaworski and his staff realized the crashes were terrorist attacks; he remarked to one staff member visiting from the new E Ring office that the Pentagon would be a likely target. Seconds later Jaworski heard the building shake and the sound of shattering glass—instant, staggering confirmation of his speculation. He and his nearby colleagues got up from their desks, moved quickly down Corridor 7 to the A Ring, then to Corridor 9, down the ramp into the Concourse, and out an exit leading to South Parking.

For the RSW staff in the E Ring, location determined their fate. Jaworski later observed sorrowfully that "they didn't have a chance." Just two occupants of one office along the inner side of that part of the E Ring survived, only because they had stepped out to the restroom moments before the airliner slammed into the building. None of their immediate office mates escaped. RSW's Program and Budget Division, hit especially hard, lost 25 of its 28 members. Across the E Ring hallway, along the outside wall of the building, the jet's impact proved almost as lethal. Of the Managerial Accounting Division's 12 members present, only 3 survived. For these three the fireball and partial collapse of a wall almost proved their undoing; not one escaped without injury. All told, 34 of the 40 members of the Program and Budget and Managerial Accounting Divisions present that morning perished.[7]

Among the six who survived, Sheila Moody was one of the luckiest. Seated at her desk in 1E472, she heard a "whistling sound. . . . And then there was a rumble, and a large gush of air and a fireball that came into the office and just blew everything all over the place and knocked us over." Trapped in "a lot of smoke and just darkness," she could not see that the hole blown in the outer E Ring wall was only a few feet away. Then, in the silence that had descended, she heard the working of a fire extinguisher and a voice calling out. She called back but "then the smoke and the fumes started taking my breath away, and I couldn't really call out to him. So I started clapping my hands." Her rescuer, Staff Sergeant Chris Brahman, extinguished the flames between them and led her to the outside. Moody was hospitalized for burns to her hands that proved worse than she initially realized.[8]

Two other survivors from the RSW offices, Juan Cruz Santiago and Louise Kurtz, were less fortunate than Sheila Moody. When the plane hit, Cruz was thrown to his knees and engulfed by fire. Most of his body was scorched with second-, third-, and fourth-degree burns. Reduced to a state of semiconsciousness, he became aware of water being poured over him and he vaguely perceived someone carrying him out of the building. As the initial shock wore off he experienced excruciating pain. Hospitalized for three months, Cruz underwent nearly 30 surgical procedures, including skin grafts to his face, right arm, hands, and legs. He was left with cruel damage to his face, eyes, and hands.[9]

Louise Kurtz was standing at a fax machine in her RSW office when, she later recalled, she was "baked, totally. . . . I was like meat when you take it off the grill." In spite of her pain and shock she managed to crawl on top of a table and through a window to the outside of the E Ring. She lapsed into unconsciousness in an ambulance and woke up in the hospital; doctors gave her a 50 percent chance of survival. After more than three months she left the hospital without her fingers and her ears, with multiple skin grafts, and with other severe disabilities.[10]

Another Army office under the administrative assistant to the secretary of the Army, the Information Management Support Center (IMCEN) on the 1st Floor, suffered six fatalities. Room 1E460 lay in the direct path of the airliner; its three occupants—Michael Selves, Lieutenant Colonel Dean Mattson, and John Chada—perished. Three other IMCEN employees—Teddington Moy, Robert Maxwell, and Scott Powell, a contractor—died at other locations occupied by IMCEN in the E Ring.[11]

More fortunate than her six fellow IMCEN employees was Specialist April Gallop, in Room 1E517 in Wedge 2. On 11 September she brought her two-month-old son Elisha to work with her because her babysitter had been hospitalized. With Elisha in a stroller alongside her desk, Gallop sat in front of a computer. "And as soon as I was about to turn the computer on, boom ... the computer blew." The walls and ceiling crumbled, and she found herself covered in debris up to her waist. Frantically looking for her son in the smoke-darkened room, with flames providing the only light, she saw that the stroller was on fire but empty. Freeing herself from the debris, Gallop searched desperately for her baby and found him covered up in the litter. "He's in a ball, like that .... So I was thinking, oh, my God, his bones are broken."

Two of Gallop's office mates, Corporal Eduardo Bruno and Sergeant Roxanne Cruz-Cortez, soon came to her aid after freeing themselves from the rubble that had trapped them for a few minutes. They helped her climb over the half-demolished office wall and passed the baby from hand to hand as they moved toward an outside window in the E Ring that led to safety. Followed by perhaps as many as 10 civilian workers, Bruno and Cruz-Cortez reached the window. Cruz-Cortez pushed and pulled two hysterical women to the window. The baby was passed outside and the others followed, dropping one by one. Bruno, although injured and later hospitalized, helped catch people dropping from the window. Once on the outside Gallop lost consciousness. When she awoke in George Washington University Hospital she called for her baby. Fortunately he had survived without serious injury.[12]

Beyond the Army offices in Wedge 1, the newly opened Navy Command Center (NCC) occupied a much larger space than the RSW offices between Corridor 4 and the wooden barrier midway between Corridors 4 and 5. Including much of the D Ring and all of the C Ring, bridging the light well between the D and C Rings, the center's area exceeded a third of an acre.

The Command Center tracked movements of U.S. Navy vessels and aircraft and monitored significant international events, keeping the chief of naval operations and other senior Navy leaders informed of important developments. The Watch Floor, focal point of the NCC, was staffed 24 hours a day. Seven other offices shared the center's spaces with the Watch Floor. Five-foot-high movable partitions separated most of the office cubicles. For meetings, including daily briefings during the workweek, a theater and conference room provided larger spaces. Between 50 and 70 people were normally on duty during a workday. Although its near end was some 80 feet from the outer wall of the Pentagon, the NCC had no real protection from the exploding airplane. In a matter of seconds it became an inferno of explosion, fires, and tangled wreckage that killed or injured most of the occupants.[13]

At work in the Meteorology and Oceanography section of the center on 11 September were the officer in charge and two petty officers. Early that morning, Lieutenant Nancy McKeown, a former chief petty officer, gave a briefing on global weather patterns. After completing the morning briefing, McKeown returned to her office, where she and her two aerographers, Petty Officers Edward Earhart and Matthew Flocco, watched as United Airlines Flight 175 struck the South Tower in New York City. Soon after, McKeown returned to her own cubicle nearby and sat down. Almost immediately she heard a roaring crescendo of sound as ceiling tiles came down and she fell from her chair. It felt like an earthquake (she had experienced quakes in Japan) and the roar became louder. McKeown yelled "Bomb!" and dived under her desk; the office plunged into darkness and began to fill with smoke. Within moments the thunderous din subsided, the smoke thickened, and she emerged from her now "deathly quiet" office calling out for her two petty officers; there was no response. Only flickering lights overhead illuminated the "pitch black" space.

Disoriented, McKeown walked the wrong way, toward the path the jet had taken through the building. Feeling the wall growing hotter, seeing visibility dropping further, and finding breathing more difficult, McKeown turned around and headed back toward her office, stopping momentarily under the spray of a broken sprinkler line to ward off the intense heat. On spying a small bright spot in the distance she moved toward it, eventually recognizing the glass doors at the 4th Corridor entrance to the Command Center. Although the dense smoke choked her, she somehow succeeded in gaining the attention of two rescuers who took her into Corridor 4 and sat her down. Sputtering, McKeown told them that "we had to go back in and get my two guys." She thought that one of the nearby rescuers headed back into the center. As she awaited further assistance McKeown "could hear people yelling, 'Don't jump! Don't jump!'" Looking up, she could "see ... silhouettes falling from the second floor down. I don't know if they were jumping or falling. . . . All I could actually see was the silhouettes coming down and ... people kind of reaching up trying to grab people as they were coming down." After reaching a triage center in North Parking, McKeown was transported by ambulance to the nearby Arlington Urgent Care Center where she was treated for smoke inhalation. Unfortunately, Petty Officers Earhart and Flocco did not survive.[14]

Another junior officer in the Command Center, Lieutenant Kevin Shaeffer, a 1994 graduate of the U.S. Naval Academy who worked in the Strategy and Concepts office, also watched the attacks on the Twin Towers on the center's large-screen television sets. Shaken, Shaeffer returned to his cubicle, where he stood and continued to watch over the tops of the partitions. Suddenly the walls "exploded," and "the next moment was just a gigantic fireball with obviously a ton of force coming through the space." A "huge flash of fire" erupted with such force it blew him to the floor.

Despite suffering grievous injuries Shaeffer never lost consciousness and his actions remained purposeful. Realizing that his hair and skin were on fire, he rolled around on the floor to put out the flames. In those same few seconds he wiped his hands through his hair, and found it charred. When he managed to stand up, smoke-filled air increasingly irritated his mouth and throat and limited what he could see. As far as he could tell, no one around him remained alive. Aware that he was badly hurt, and neither hearing nor seeing anyone, he began looking for a way out. Judging that the explosion had come from the E Ring, he crawled in the opposite direction.

Piles of blown-down light fixtures, ceiling tiles, duct work, wiring, and cubicle furniture made the going difficult, and Shaeffer resorted to crawling under and over these heaps, cutting his badly burned hands. Following a zigzag path he worked his way towards the back of the Command Center, where he saw a dim light ahead. Gasping from the choking smoke, he crawled through rubble, scaled more piles of wreckage, and finally staggered out into A-E Drive through a hole blown in the C Ring wall. Later, he reckoned it had taken about five minutes to crawl the roughly 70 feet to A-E Drive.

After receiving on-the-spot first aid, Shaeffer was transported to the DiLorenzo Clinic in the 8th Corridor, from where he was carried outside on an electric cart and taken by ambulance to Walter Reed Army Medical Center. His burns were so severe (over 42 percent of his body) that he was transferred to the Washington Hospital Center where he underwent many weeks of painful treatment in the intensive care unit. After an ordeal of more than three months he was able to leave the hospital. Having suffered permanent damage to his lungs and to the right side of his body, Lieutenant Shaeffer was retired on medical disability.[15]

In the Intelligence Plot section, tucked into a corner of the Command Center in the C Ring, 13 people were present on the morning of 11 September. This area was a SCIF (Sensitive Compartmented Information Facility), a highly secured space containing especially sensitive classified materials. It lay almost 200 feet from the outer E Ring wall of the Pentagon and along the course taken by Flight 77. The officer in charge, Commander Dan Shanower, and six coworkers had completed briefing Deputy Director of Naval Intelligence Susan Long and members of her staff about 20 or 30 minutes before the impact. Also in the Intelligence Plot that morning were six others: Lieutenant Commander Charles Capets, using a computer on the Watch Floor alongside Lieutenant Megan Humbert and Petty Officer of the Watch Jason Lhuillier, while Petty Officers Steven Gully and Jesse Polasek and Seaman Sarah Cole worked in the adjoining Graphics space.[16]

Lhuillier interrupted a meeting in Shanower's office to report the second World Trade Center strike. A few minutes later, after returning to his desk, Lhuillier heard a "Kaboom," and was thrown to the floor and under an adjacent desk. Within seconds of the impact, as the fire intensified and the smoke thickened, Lhuillier began to have difficulty breathing. Capets, visiting the Intelligence Plot from his office on the 5th Floor, was present when the Watch Officer received information that a hijacked aircraft was headed toward Washington. Thinking that his boss should know, he picked up the phone to call when "this thing hit." Like Lhuillier he was flung to the floor of the wrecked office and experienced the fire, heat, smoke, and darkness. After initial confusion and failed efforts to find an exit, Capets saw the beckoning light from a hole blown open in the C Ring office wall to A-E Drive and crawled toward it. Finding the office door jammed shut by the explosion, Lhuillier followed Capets, scrambled over a barricade of office equipment, and escaped with him through the same large hole. The two turned back to pull Humbert to safety through a pile of debris. Capets and Lhuillier assisted in frantic rescue efforts that helped survivors get out of the building into

A-E Drive.[17] For Shanower and his briefing team there was no escape. The rapid spread of the fire and the deadly smoke quickly killed all of them.

Other survivors from the Intelligence Plot also had a close brush with death. The force of the blast slammed Steven Gully into a huge copy machine, knocking the wind out of him, "kind of like taking a head-on in football." Gully recalled that "my smoothie [drink] went flying. I actually saw my smoothie fly away from me, which you know … was kind of surreal." On extricating himself, he scrambled through a hole in the C Ring wall to safety in A-E Drive. Polasek remembered "a huge force throwing me from behind," expelling him through a hole into A-E Drive as he was still seated in his chair. Blown off her chair, Cole landed in A-E Drive as well, dazed but only slightly injured. These 3, plus Capets, Lhuillier, and Humbert, were the 6 survivors of the 13 Intelligence Plot occupants.[18] All of the Navy's losses occurred in the Command Center—42 military and civilian dead, including 3 contractor employees.[19]

The deadly force that ravaged the NCC penetrated the wooden barrier separating Wedge 2 from Wedge 1 and slammed into Defense Intelligence Agency (DIA) offices where about 70 employees occupied a large space in 1C535. The remnants of Flight 77 ended the plane's path of death and destruction at the inner wall of the C Ring, adjacent to A-E Drive, claiming seven victims in 1C535, members of the DIA Program and Budget Office, who must have died immediately.* Among the 11 survivors, Paul Gonzales, a former Navy officer and chief of the office, later related that he could not "even describe the sound.… And then I got hit from behind by a blast of air and heat.… I remember looking and just watching things go flying past me .… Just flying and I started flying with them." Although injured and burned, Gonzales remained alert and sought to find survivors during what he remembered as a chaotic 20 or 25 minutes of frantically seeking an escape route through the thick choking smoke, which forced the survivors low to the floor.[20]

Kathy Cordero, in the same office, felt "a real big gush of wind," saw a "big ball of … red, orange fire," and felt herself on fire. Gonzales came to her rescue. With others they crawled under, over, and through the debris until they emerged through a hole into A-E Drive from where they were led to the Center Court.

* Rosa Maria Chapa, Sandra Foster, Robert Hymel, Shelley Marshall, Patricia Mickley, Charles Sabin, and Karl Teepe.

Severely burned, Cordero was taken on a stretcher to North Parking and from there to the Virginia Hospital Center in Arlington where she woke up six days later in the intensive care unit. The ensuing surgery, including skin grafts, kept her in the hospital for more than three weeks. Gonzales, badly hurt and suffering from severe lung damage, was taken to Walter Reed Hospital. He believed that doctors used heroic measures to save him. After two weeks he was able to go home to recuperate. Four of Gonzales's colleagues, including Cordero and Christine Morrison, later testified that they owed their lives to his courageous leadership.[21]

Christine Morrison gave a singularly striking description of her first fleeting awareness of what happened:

> From the back of the room there was a heat wave like haze extending from the back of the room up to the ceiling.... You could see through it. It was moving. Before I could register or complete that thought, this force hit the room, instantly turning the office into an inferno hell. Everything was falling, flying, and on fire, and there was no escaping it. The swiftness and force has no comparison, my body mass didn't exist and my body was useless. I was slam-dunked backward into another co-worker's cubicle and a piece of a hot heating and ventilation duct trapped the top half of me. I was stunned, desperately trying to do something; I did not understand what was happening.
>
> I felt the heat and I heard the sizzling of me. My eyes had a front seat to the horror.... I couldn't move any part of my body.... Everyone in our office area was struggling for breath and life.
>
> The majority of the lights went out in an instant. Oxygen disappeared; my lungs felt like they were burning and collapsing. The room filled with overpowering thick gaseous smoke with heavy particles before you could get a chance to take the next breath.... Somehow I was bartering for just one breath of air. I finally managed to stand up.
>
> My mind was like sludge and thoughts took forever to form and longer to reach the brain and even longer to make use of them. I was barely able to think through what was a button and how to do a simple function like unbuttoning each section of my blouse to get some relief from the heat. We would later discover that the blast had shifted the cubicles and blocked two of our exits. By then, everyone lost his or her sense of direction.[22]

Morrison finally managed to stand. The heat and the smoke drove her back down to the floor where she lay for many minutes before she could manage to summon whatever willpower and strength she had left and begin crawling. She saw an area ahead that appeared to be lighter; hearing someone say "over here," she went toward the sound. By now barefoot, somehow she managed to "navigate the wreckage," finally emerging upright into A-E Drive after more than 20 minutes of horror. Suffering from head lacerations and smoke inhalation, Morrison was sent to the Virginia Hospital Center where she received treatment in the intensive care unit.[23]

Second Floor

On the newly renovated 2nd Floor, the Office of the U.S. Army Deputy Chief of Staff for Personnel (DCSPER) had just moved 275 people into a section of the C, D, and E Rings between Corridor 4 and the barrier halfway to Corridor 5. The senior officer, Lieutenant General Timothy Maude, and his immediate staff occupied a large expanse in the E Ring with windows facing west toward Arlington Cemetery.

Most of the DCSPER space, across the hall from General Maude's office, held a "bay" of cubicles that extended through the C Ring, adjacent to A-E Drive. From the E Ring to the windows overlooking A-E Drive, the DCSPER occupied an area of about an acre. The common area held 138 cubicles with five-foot-high partitions for military and civilian personnel serving in two directorates—Military Personnel Management and Plans, Resources and Operations. The bay also included a conference room, enclosed offices, spaces for contractors, and four copier areas. Occupants entered the office spaces through three doors—two leading from the 4th Corridor on the south, and one from the E Ring hallway; they could leave the area through three staircases, one in each of the E, D, and C Rings at the Corridor 4 end of the office. Restrooms lay outside the space, along Corridor 4.

General Maude was meeting with eight members of his staff (including three contractors)* in his conference room along the windowed outer wall of the Pentagon when Flight 77 smashed into the building almost immediately below that exact point. The impact penetrated the 2nd Floor slab, scattering lethal

* Major Ronald Milam, Sergeants Major Larry Strickland and Lacey Ivory, civilians Gary Smith and Max Beilke, and contractors Gerald Fisher, Terence Lynch, and Ernest Willcher. (Historical Project Notes, Individuals in DCSPER Conference Room, 11 September 2001, OSD Hist.)

debris throughout the area; Maude and his colleagues probably died instantly or within a short time after impact.[24]

A huge conflagration* spread quickly in the DCSPER area. The Jet A fuel atomized and quickly combusted, causing explosive bursts as the plane hurtled into the building. A detonation 150 feet inside the building resulted from a "fuel-air" explosion after the Jet A tanks disintegrated on impact. Here, as elsewhere, there was no uniform pattern of death and destruction. The vagaries of the fuel-air explosions and freakish blast effects meant deaths occurred randomly inside the Pentagon, with the occupants of seemingly more secure interior offices sometimes suffering worse fates than those nearer the outside wall.[25]

Although the Army and Navy offices on the 1st Floor bore the brunt of the kinetic energy created by the aircraft striking the building, the DCSPER 2nd Floor offices also felt its effects as an immense upward force penetrated the reinforced concrete floors of the bays. These offices suffered chiefly from the fuel explosion and fire. Some notion of the intense heat in the 2nd Floor offices may be gained from the experience of Librarian of the Army Ann Parham, who had resumed work in the bay after watching television coverage of the second airliner striking the World Trade Center. Fortunately, she had stepped away from her desk in 2D470 to send a fax to the library at Fort Benning, Georgia, and was returning to her office when the plane hit. A colleague in a nearby space, Marian Serva, was killed while seated at her desk. Recalling her own predicament, Parham described the heat as suffocating and the smoke-filled air as so dense that it "felt like I was in London and I actually had thought that I was in London and this was a very foggy ... night." Through the gloom, office furnishings appeared shapeless. Worse, she was coated by a mist of foul-smelling, dangerous Jet A fuel. The fireball caused flash burns on her face and hands, her eyes were burning, and a flaming ceiling tile burned off a two-inch swath of hair. With help she made her way out of the bay and to the River Entrance and out of the building. When she arrived at the Alexandria Hospital in a Defense Protective Service car, still wearing her plastic Pentagon identification badge, she realized it had curled in the heat from the fire. Doctors attended to her burns and a lacerated foot and broken toe.[26]

* This might more properly be termed a deflagration—a chemical process burning extremely rapidly and producing intense heat, flames, and sparks.

AFFECTED AREAS ON SECOND FLOOR

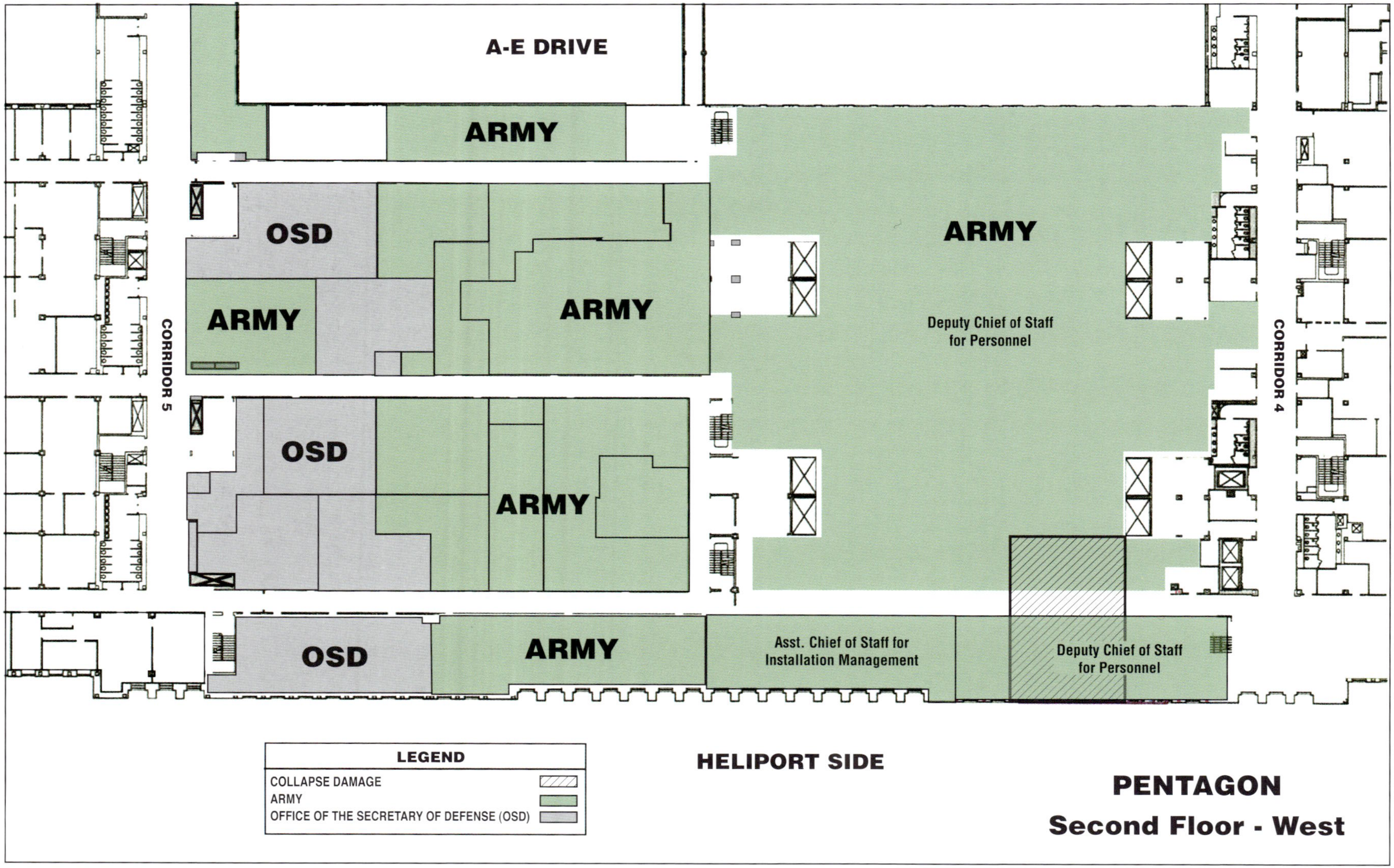

As with many other people in the Pentagon, for Lieutenant Colonel Stephen Zappalla the morning's main event was the attack in New York City. Still watching television in the 2nd Floor C Ring office of his absent civilian supervisor, Raymond Robinson, he felt the impact shake the building. Seated in Robinson's chair, Zappalla suffered a blow on the head from falling ceiling tiles and was thrown against a wall. Dazed but otherwise unhurt, he arose and got out of the office, swearing he would never again sit in his boss's chair. On emerging from the office Zappalla saw fire coming toward him from the E Ring. Abruptly the flames changed direction, veering to the right in the direction of Corridor 5. Disoriented, he blundered about until he heard voices through the smoke that directed him to Corridor 4; from there rescuers assisted him to the A Ring, where he went first to the Center Court and then to South Parking.[27]

For two civilians and two noncommissioned officers the erratic path of the fire proved their salvation. Tracy Webb, Dalisay Olaes, Specialist Michael Petrovich, and Sergeant First Class Michael Weaver all worked in 2E477. Seated across from one another in a quartet of cubicles, they heard radio reports of the attacks in New York. Shortly thereafter, as the floor beneath them shuddered and fractured, they heard a bang followed by an explosion. Olaes felt her hair burn as the fire passed through the office. Screams of surprise and pain from other office occupants filled the air; furniture blew about and a blizzard of papers surged around them. Petrovich looked for Webb and Olaes, but could find only Olaes in the smoke. The pair crawled below the smoke outward toward the E Ring exit, but when Petrovich felt the door hot to the touch and saw an orange glow radiating from under it, they turned around and headed inward towards the C Ring. Weaver, after seeing the fireball pass, initially headed towards the E Ring door as well, found it impassable, and escaped by going toward the inside of the building.[28]

As the fireball roared through her area, Tracy Webb turned to escape the flames, which had set her hair afire. Batting out the fire in her hair, she saw Petrovich and Olaes heading towards the nearby E Ring exit and tried to follow, only to become lost among the cubicles and unable to find her way. Without realizing it, she was moving northward toward the D Ring exit. Confused, and with little to guide her in the increasing gloom of the office, Webb panicked and stood up only to feel the heat and smoke sear her lungs as she tried to breathe. Sinking to the floor, she was convinced she was about to die. Fortunately her desperate attempt to stand had brought her to the attention of Major Regina Grant, who had fled from 2E487 where she had been attending a meeting. Convinced, too, that her end was near, Grant had given up moving and had started praying when she spotted Webb trying to stand. Grant crawled over, grabbed at Webb's clothing, and pulled her down to the floor. Grant's anguished cry for help was heard by Sergeant Major Tony Rose, who had been helping people out of the large DCSPER bay area. Rose had been knocked down by the blast and had gotten out of his C Ring cubicle to join others in leading survivors out of the bay to safety. When Rose answered Grant's cry, Grant and Webb followed the sound of his voice, staggered over to Corridor 4, and met up with him. They escaped down the corridor into the Center Court.

At the moment of impact, Dr. Betty Maxfield, an Army demographer who had come from her office at 2B659, stood at Tracy Webb's desk talking about personnel matters. Maxfield remembered "a fireball went passing through the area in which I [was] standing. . . . And everything went black. . . . The smoke was very, very dense. And the burning ceiling tiles began to drop on us like hot cinder balls. . . . The only damage to me personally was that the hair on my arms ... [was] burned." After turning back from the direction of the E Ring, she dropped to the floor and joined a chain of crawling people, some of whom were crying and screaming. In two separate groups, one led by Petrovich, the crawlers reached the C Ring windows at A-E Drive several minutes apart.[29]

For Olaes, Webb, Petrovich, Weaver, and Maxfield, their good fortune came about because the Jet A fuel had largely passed over their heads without exploding. Army people further inside the building were not so lucky. Explosions on the 1st Floor directed energy upward with such force that they ripped and "buckled and penetrated" the concrete deck of the 2nd Floor.[30] Four soldiers from the Officer Accession and Sustainment Branch* were killed in their cubicles by one of these detonations and the thick toxic smoke and immense heat that accompanied it.

Elsewhere in DCSPER, 12 officers and civilians assembled for a regular biweekly meeting at 9:00 a.m. in Conference Room 2E487, along the inside of

* Lieutenant Colonels David Scales and Karen Wagner, Chief Warrant Officer William Ruth, and Sergeant First Class Jose Orlando Calderon-Olmedo.

the E Ring. Seated around a table or along the walls were Colonels Philip McNair and Larry Thomas; Lieutenant Colonels Robert Grunewald, Dennis Johnson, Marion Ward, Curtis Nutbrown, and Marilyn Wills; Majors Regina Grant and Stephen Long; and civilians Max Beilke, Martha Carden, and Lois Stevens. Beilke* left early to attend General Maude's meeting and was killed. Because the previous meeting had been postponed, this one in 2E487 ran long, so that at 9:37 a.m. none of the participants knew of the World Trade Center attacks.[31]

As Marilyn Wills was making her report to the group, Flight 77 struck. One attendee later remembered seeing a fireball behind Carden at the north end of the table; then the lights went out and parts of the ceiling came down at Carden's end as well. Several conferees in the room, including McNair, shouted to get down on the floor below the smoke that filled the room. Grunewald called out to Carden, and when she "yelled, help . . . [he] said, Martha, I'm going to come get you . . . and dove over the table." Most of those in the room turned to the exit that opened into the E Ring hallway, near where Johnson and Carden had been seated. Wills found the door to the flame-engulfed hallway, but it was locked, so the participants reversed direction and headed out into the DCSPER office bay.[32]

The bay was dark and eerily quiet. In the smoke and great heat, they quickly split into smaller groups, each seeking to find the best way out by crawling below the smoke. Holding on to Grunewald's belt, Carden followed him into the bay towards Corridor 4. Grunewald, the most familiar with the area, cleared debris from their path through the office. With others following, Grunewald and Carden continued crawling, the officer encouraging his companion to keep moving. Competing with his words was the recurring sound of the Pentagon alarm system, repeating, "Attention, a fire emergency has been declared in the building. Please evacuate." As Grunewald and his followers traversed the full length of the bay the overhead sprinklers began spraying. Shortly thereafter Grunewald realized he was no longer on carpeting but on the tile floor of Corridor 4 at the C Ring exit. The pair stood up and headed inward toward the A Ring. Subsequently, Grunewald went back into the stricken area at the C Ring to look for other survivors, but the roiling black smoke that discouraged even crawling along the floor forced him to turn back. Carden was escorted to safety in the Cen-

* As an Army master sergeant in 1973, Beilke had had the distinction of being the last U.S. serviceman to depart Vietnam, other than Marine guards and military attaches at the American Embassy in Saigon, following the Paris peace agreement that concluded the Vietnam War.

ter Court, followed shortly after by Grunewald. They made their way out of the building to North Parking. Both later received hospital treatment. Carden later said: "I absolutely could not have done it. Rob literally saved my life."[33]

Fortunately, most of the others in the conference room also managed to escape. Carden especially was lucky, as her office (2D460) was opposite the E Ring hallway, where she would have been instantly killed at her desk, as were most of her colleagues. McNair and the other escapees got out into Corridor 4 and headed for the inside of the building. As previously noted, Major Grant met up with Tracy Webb, and the two followed Sergeant Major Tony Rose to safety. Sadly, one pair did not reach safety. Johnson and Long got out of the conference room only to perish in the E Ring near the bay's exit door after becoming trapped in the inferno there. They may have taken the wrong turn, as several staircases around the DCSPER spaces were blocked and inaccessible because the fuel-fed fire had already spread over two floors.[34]

Another group from the meeting had an equally harrowing experience. Wills and Lois Stevens began crawling toward the back of the bay. They feared they would collapse from the smoke until a sprinkler doused them with water, soaking their clothes and allowing them to use some of the clothes as filters. At one point Wills carried another woman on her back as she crawled. Wills, Stevens, and later Maxfield followed McNair and crawled through the darkness and smoke to the back of the office bay next to A-E Drive where they found Specialist Petrovich and Dalisay Olaes at the windows.[35]

Petrovich and Olaes had reached the 2nd Floor windows overlooking A-E Drive several minutes before McNair, Wills, Stevens, and Maxfield arrived. Finding no way to open one of the renovated windows, Petrovich had picked up a nearby laser printer and begun hammering away at the already bowed window and its twisted steel frame. Joined in the effort by McNair, who got on the sill and used his feet to push out the frame, the two finally managed to create a human-size opening. McNair and Petrovich then lifted Stevens to the window ledge and lowered her out of the opening, not letting go of her wrists until she had only a short distance to fall into the arms of catchers below. Stevens did not realize she had a broken foot until she was let down on the ground. The military and civilian rescuers in A-E Drive cushioned her fall, then did the same with Maxfield and Olaes; the latter sustained a broken leg. Petrovich, who had begun to experience trouble breathing, slipped down next with McNair's help. Wills and McNair repeatedly called out for additional survivors. Finding none, the colonel lowered Wills to the driveway and then dropped down the wall to safety. Suffering from burns and smoke inhalation, Petrovich eventually reached Walter Reed Army Medical Center where he spent several days in treatment. Also at Walter Reed, Wills received extended treatment for similar injuries and a frozen shoulder. Olaes underwent an operation on her leg at Virginia Hospital Center. Stevens, too, spent the night being treated in the hospital.[36]

The last man out of the large DCSPER bay was probably the luckiest. Lieutenant Colonel Michael Beans had been watching the television set next to Marian Serva's desk. Turning away from the view of the World Trade Center, he recalled he had moved about 20 feet toward his cubicle in 2D470 when he heard and felt a "loud concussion" and was thrown on the floor. The lights went out and in the dark room Beans could see small fires burning around him. He tried to escape through the nearby E Ring door, only to see fireballs rolling down the corridor. He hurriedly shut the door and turned back into the bay, crawling below the dense smoke. Part way through the bay the sprinklers began spraying water on him and he heard the automated system announcing the fire. He crawled slowly and painfully to the C Ring wall where he wielded a chair in a vain attempt to smash one of the windows overlooking A-E Drive. Beans then decided to try to reach Corridor 4 and crawled through C Ring as fast as he could. When he felt the tile floor of Corridor 4, he paused to catch his breath, and then got up and ran for the safety of the A Ring. As the smoke cleared, he spotted a DPS officer motioning him toward an exit into the Center Court. From there he was taken to the Pentagon's DiLorenzo Clinic and then to the Virginia Hospital Center for treatment of wounds and burns.[37]

Overcoming pervasive confusion from the suddenness of the attack, the cataclysmic and unpredictable nature of the fire, and the lack of visibility brought on by the choking smoke, most of DCSPER's office workers evacuated speedily and helped each other as best they could. Individually or in small groups they managed to improvise escape routes. Although many of its people escaped, DCSPER suffered 29 military and civilian (including 4 contractor employees) dead and 27 injured.[38]

Another Army work area, adjacent to DCSPER on the 2nd Floor, the Office of the Assistant Chief of Staff for Installation Management (2E486), also sustained casualties. Lieutenant Colonel Brian Birdwell,* a field artilleryman, had left his desk to use the Corridor 4 restroom. As he was returning to his office he heard a "very loud explosion." He was still in Corridor 4 when a fireball enveloped him and flung him onto his back. Birdwell tasted jet fuel vapor and suffered severe burns over much of his body. Soon he felt cool water on his face as the ceiling sprinklers came on, providing him a measure of relief and hope. Dazed, he struggled to stand up and managed to stagger down the corridor toward the B Ring until he collapsed again. This time he was seen by Colonel Roy Wallace, Colonel Karl Knoblauch, and others who, after securing emergency treatment for Birdwell, carried him to a nearby triage point from where he was evacuated to Georgetown University Hospital in Washington and later to the Washington Hospital Center. Although he could not have imagined it during his agonizing ordeal, Birdwell was lucky. Had he been in his office he would not have survived. Two people who were in his office, Cheryle Sincock and Sandra Taylor, were killed.[39]

Third Floor

Before 11 September the Directorate of Strategy, Plans, and Policy, an element of the Army's Office of Deputy Chief of Staff for Operations and Plans, had moved into a large area of Wedge 1 in the vicinity of the E Ring and Corridor 4 on the 3rd Floor. The director, Major General John Wood, and his immediate staff had offices in the E Ring, 3E450, looking out on the Heliport. When Flight 77 struck the building the concussion blew Wood out of his chair and onto the floor. Outside his bulging windows, he could see flames; smoke began filling the office. Unable to open his jammed office door he frantically pounded on it. Fortunately his deputy, Brigadier General Karl Eikenberry, who had been thrown against the wall of his own office, was alerted to his boss's plight by the screams of Linda Moore, Wood's secretary. Unable to open the door manually, Eikenberry lay down on the floor and kicked it in, freeing Wood from what would have been certain death.[40]

* See also Chapter III.

Wood, Eikenberry, and others emerged into the blackness of E Ring, where the floor had already buckled. Uncertain about escape routes, after some false starts they turned into Corridor 4, collecting people from offices as they went, urging them on toward the A Ring through the thickening smoke. Eikenberry and several other officers remained behind for a time in the C Ring to assist others. The group made their way to the Center Court, where they encountered what Wood described as "pandemonium." Instructed shortly after to leave the building because of warning of an anticipated second attack, they made their way to South Parking and beyond.[41]

Unfortunately, in an office next to Wood's, there were two fatalities—Major Wallace Hogan, executive officer to Major General Philip Kensinger, assistant deputy chief of staff for operations and plans, and the general's secretary, Diane Hale-McKinzy. The freakish shock wave spared Wood but not Hogan and Hale-McKinzy. Their bodies were found on the 1st Floor. Both died of multiple blunt force injuries and smoke inhalation.[42]

Fourth Floor

On the 4th Floor, above the direct impact area in Wedge 1, occupants of the Marine Corps Office of the General Counsel counted themselves fortunate that they did not suffer the fate of Army and Navy offices on the floors below. General Counsel Peter Murphy, in Room 4E468, remembered hearing a "huge noise, louder than any noise I've ever heard before." He was standing with his back to the window that looked out on the Heliport when he felt himself lifted and "tossed" perhaps 15 feet to the other side of his office. He saw a huge fireball at the window and the ceiling started to fall in. He observed the wall move, "actually . . . moved in several inches. But the windows just stood absolutely tall and never splintered, never cracked, nothing." Murphy's deputy, Robert Hogue, and Major Joe Baker were also thrown to the floor. Unlike most other survivors, Murphy and his companions "were pretty certain it was a plane and it was a terrorist," even though they had not seen the plane coming in. They had been watching the attack on the Twin Towers and had speculated about such an attack on the Pentagon.

The office began filling with smoke. The office administrative clerk, Corporal Timothy Garofola, succeeded after a few minutes in forcing open the heavy office door, which had jammed, and the four men emerged into the hall. After making certain that their other offices were clear of people, they made their way to Corridor 4, noticing flames coming up through the floor seams. Through the black smoke they heard "Follow my voice. Follow my voice." Crouched low, they made their way to the A Ring and from there to the 2nd Floor. After rejecting going to the Center Court and failing to get through to North Parking, they emerged into South Parking. Murphy recollected that "once we got down to the second deck there were now hundreds and hundreds of people all going in different directions. Most, very disciplined and moving quick and not running, but moving quickly."[43]

Elsewhere on the 4th Floor the damage was immediately evident. Commander Joan Zitterkopf, a Navy helicopter pilot assigned to a training aircraft redesign group, was standing at her desk in 4C453 at the moment of impact. Actually standing astride one of the Pentagon's expansion joints, Zitterkopf felt the shift of the seam between her feet and later remembered "one foot going up and it felt like one foot going down." She toppled and fell. The bright orange fireball she saw through a window left no doubt in her mind that the Pentagon was under attack.

Recovering her balance, Zitterkopf joined colleagues in filing out of the office. Black smoke from the fuel fire spewed down Corridor 4 toward them. One of the Pentagon's new automatic smoke and fire suppression doors began to close across the corridor, adding to her anxiety. These doors had not been demonstrated to Pentagon occupants, nor had their override switches been made known to them; the corridor barriers deployed automatically to limit the spread of smoke and fire. This one threatened to block Zitterkopf's exit. She instinctively ran to the door and somehow tripped the override switch, locking it open to permit escape from the smoke-filled side of the door. Keeping up their pace along the corridor, the evacuees walked down the escalators in the A Ring and eventually reached the safety of North Parking.[44]

Fifth Floor

There were no fatalities on the 5th Floor, but only because the occupants of the E Ring offices managed to fight their way out before the floor, directly above the impact zone, collapsed. Fortunately, because the 5th Floor was furthest removed from the lower floors' inferno, they had more time to get away. The largest and best organized group that escaped, 30 Navy civilian employees of the Surface Warfare Group from Crane, Indiana, had come to Washington as part of an industrial management course. Shortly after 9:00 a.m. they were attending a briefing by Under Secretary of the Navy Susan Livingstone in 5E490. As she began answering questions after the conclusion of her remarks, the attendees felt the building lurch and saw a light fixture and ceiling tiles fall as smoke began spilling from air vents. Captain Dennis Kern, Livingstone's executive assistant, had a vivid recollection of a "very loud explosion" that "rocked the room." He likened it to the sudden jolt of an earthquake. Livingstone instinctively exclaimed "there has been a terrorist event . . . . And we need to evacuate and get out of here." She and Kern then led the way out of the room to seek escape from the building. Kern was the only one who knew the 5th Floor layout.[45]

Because none of the offices on the floor had windows facing the outside of the building, neither the meeting participants nor the occupants of other offices in the E Ring had a clear notion of what had happened. While these offices were not seriously damaged, light fixtures had dropped from the ceiling and hung loosely from their cables, and broken acoustic ceiling tiles lay across the floor in the corridor, adding to the uncertainty of movement. As moments passed the air filled with the black smoke spewing from the ventilators, making it hard to see and breathe.[46]

When Livingstone and Kern tried to descend the same staircase that they had used to get to the meeting, they found the way blocked. Later inspection revealed that the explosion had made the stairwell into a chimney full of smoke and flames. Unable to get through to Corridor 5 because of the wooden construction barrier wall across the E Ring near the conference room, Livingstone and Kern turned back toward Corridor 4, encountering some 15 people who had emerged into the hallway from another Navy office. One of this group, Gail Wirick, customarily used a motorized wheelchair to move about the Pentagon. This time, with the help of two colleagues, she used a walker to evacuate her office.* The group, grown to almost 50 people, pushed on in its search for a way out.[47]

* Some disabled workers needed help to escape. On the 4th Floor, departing Navy workers encountered a disabled custodian with limited language comprehension. Clearly disoriented by the alarm and smoke, she had to be escorted out of the building.

When another effort to use a staircase in the direction of Corridor 5 proved futile, Livingstone and Kern concluded that the route toward Corridor 4 offered the only escape and reversed direction in the E Ring once again, encountering a drop of about eight inches in the floor at the major building expansion joint next to the area that later collapsed. Livingstone warned those behind her of the downward "step"; the warning was passed down the line. At this point, the evacuees were walking directly over the impact area hit by the airliner minutes earlier. The drop traced the line of an expansion joint of the building where the upper four floors were nearing collapse because of the loss of supporting columns below. Almost 40 minutes after the initial impact, that section of the E Ring collapsed. Pressing forward, many holding hands by this time, the group turned into Corridor 4. Sam Cardenas and Laurie Burrow helped Gail Wirick negotiate the full distance. Without their support Wirick would have been unable to manage on her own with her walker, which she eventually abandoned.[48]

As the group emerged into Corridor 4 the smoke became so black and dense it forced them to crawl, still hanging on to one another. Low to the floor along Corridor 4 and scarcely able to see their way, they could feel the heat from the burning floor below. Unexpectedly, they heard a voice calling through the black smoke, "Is anybody back there?" Kern, still in the lead, returned the hail and asked the caller to keep yelling so that the group could move in his direction. The caller, Commander Dan Braswell, had gotten out of his office, 5D453, into Corridor 4, immediately after impact. He and some fellow officers "looked to the left and realized hey, there's nobody coming from the E Ring yet. So we started yelling back there." Braswell urged the Livingstone group to continue moving and drew their attention to an emergency strobe light flashing from a place of relative safety. As the smoke thinned to a gray haze, the evacuees stood up. When Kern saw a fire and smoke suppression door closing across the 4th Corridor, threatening to block their path out of the building, he quickly leapt forward, smashed it back against the wall, and held it open. After the group passed that point, the smoke in the air thinned, and they emerged into the A Ring. Livingstone and Kern, separated from the rest of the group, descended to the 1st Floor, where, instead of exiting into the Center Court, they made their way to the Concourse and out to South Parking. The Crane group, still pretty much together, also left the building and reached South Parking. Using verifiable time references, members concluded that their harrowing journey had taken about 15 minutes.[49]

Along with thousands of other evacuees the Crane group had to move further away from the building when warning of a second aircraft attack on the Pentagon before the collapse at 10:15 a.m. led to orders to evacuate the crash site and the vicinity. In North and South Parking, evacuees were pushed further and further back until they were hundreds of yards away.[50]

Concern for others, particularly in the area most affected by the impact, was almost universally reflected in the anxiously repeated efforts by office leaders and staff members to account for all of their colleagues. They checked and rechecked to ensure that all known to them had gotten out safely. Once outside, they searched among the milling crowds until they accounted for all of their people. Some went back into the building in an effort to get a complete tally. Sadly, they had to accept that not all had reached safety.

Within minutes of the crash, the toll of Pentagon occupants dead and injured stood distressingly high. In addition to the 124 killed, not counting the Army employee who died of injuries days later, the Arlington County Fire Department reported that of the 106 victims transported to hospitals, 49 were admitted.* For those in the impact area lucky enough to escape, finding a route out of the building afforded the key to survival. This was especially so for those in the newly refurbished Army and Navy offices on the 1st and 2nd Floors as well as those on the upper floors. Both military and civilians, in spite of their fear and confusion in the chaos that engulfed them, displayed uncommon courage and comradeship in assisting one another to escape the stricken building.

* The others were treated and released. About a hundred more received treatment for minor injuries on site. For injured disposition see Chapter V; for causes of death see Chapter VIII.

Chapter III

The Rescuers

There could not have been as many survivors of the attack on the Pentagon without the persistent and selfless acts of others—military and civilian—who were themselves caught in the maelstrom or came unhesitatingly from elsewhere in the building to respond to the desperate circumstances facing the many victims trapped in the wreckage. The suddenness and split-second penetration of the attack, followed by the instantaneous havoc wrought in the stricken area, allowed no time for organized rescue efforts. Necessarily, much of the assistance rendered by rescuers came from the improvised action of individuals or small groups. Men and women from within the devastated area—themselves directly threatened by fire, smoke, and explosive force—provided the leadership, encouragement, and physical assistance that enabled hundreds of shaken and injured people to escape death. From elsewhere in the building outside the immediately affected area, daring rescuers, with a minimum of equipment and relying only on their knowledge of the building and sheer will, plunged into the smoke and debris of corridors and offices to seek out bloodied and burned survivors and deliver them from the inferno. Others entered the burning E Ring from outside the building and helped victims they described as "charred" to reach safety. Using flashlights and voice direction they showed lost and disoriented wanderers the way of escape. Some, perhaps many of the rescuers, risked their own lives or, at the very least, injury.

Almost all of the successful rescues of survivors occurred within the first half hour after the attack. For all the daring acts, in some instances, especially subsequent to the initial response, the large numbers of impatient military and civilian volunteers seeking to engage in independent actions compounded confusion and impeded the work of the firefighters. When the first fire companies arrived only minutes after the impact to assist in the rescue efforts, they found volunteers searching for survivors in parts of the building near the impact site. The firefighters ordered them to leave the building because they were not trained or equipped to deal with the dangerous conditions they encountered.

As the volunteers were forced to abandon the search, they congregated outside at the Heliport, in the Center Court, and in A-E Drive. They organized into groups to assist medical and firefighting efforts however they might. Some teams served as stretcherbearers; others lined up ready to follow the firefighters into the building and bring out survivors. Their impatience was reined in when the collapse of the ruptured E Ring made it clear that what remained to be done was a job for professionals.

Fully engaged in directing Emergency Medical Service (EMS) efforts, Assistant Fire Chief John White found that his primary challenge was managing the mass of eager helpers during the morning. Anxious to assist, volunteers of all ranks donned gloves, handled IV bags, grabbed backboards, and provided other services. At one point, feeling that the professional emergency responders were not doing everything they should, some volunteers tried to get back into the building; Defense Protective Service officers helped the firefighters block them. In the Center Court, Arlington Fire Battalion Chief Jerome Dale Smith stopped a squad of Marines from marching into the building. Luckily, the officer leading the squad cooperated. Fort Myer firefighter Sergeant Thomas Hodge understood the volunteers' desire to reenter the building but knew they could not help and would only put others in jeopardy. The last thing the firefighters needed was "another victim." When Major General James Jackson, commander of the Military District of Washington (MDW), arrived about noon, he saw the need to "get some kind of cohesive unit in here, specifically the Old Guard" (3rd Infantry Regiment) from Fort Myer and to move the volunteers out of the way.[1]

On receiving reports from his officers that throngs of volunteers were impeding the firefighters and EMS workers, Incident Commander James Schwartz, assistant chief of the Arlington County Fire Department, left the command post to investigate. When he encountered an Army brigadier general and a line of soldiers protected only by thin dust masks preparing to go into the Pentagon he confronted them. Asserting command of the site, he ordered that all nonemergency people be prevented from going inside the building. Schwartz believed the order saved the life of one defiant soldier seeking to enter who got into a scuffle with firefighters shortly before the E Ring collapsed. He later explained that while he respected the "truly heroic" efforts of the civilian and military rescuers, such "freelancing" was inexcusable and could lead to death and injury. "And that's what we were trying to stave off."[2] Still, the early efforts of Pentagon volunteer rescuers, the very first responders, undoubtedly saved the lives of many, probably most, who would otherwise have perished.

Close by the unfortunate Defense Intelligence Agency office in the C Ring of Wedge 2 was a clutch of Army offices including the Quadrennial Defense Review (QDR) Office.* The Army QDR people in 1D536, although closer to the outside of the building than the DIA group, did not suffer the full brunt of the impact because the plane's angle of approach skirted the D Ring in Wedge 2 but penetrated the C Ring. Still, the effect on the D Ring offices was life-threatening. The shock wave blew people over, caused walls and ceilings to collapse, and flung furniture about. The rubble, fires, and dense smoke threatened to thwart the occupants' frantic struggles to escape. Members of the QDR office who managed to get out testified to the generally calm and purposeful behavior of their colleagues in effecting the rescue of most of those in the office. Most of the officers there possessed command experience and were trained to deal with emergencies, albeit not this particular one. Colonels Mark Perrin and Sean Kelly and Captain Darrell Oliver, the last initially rendered unconscious for a time by a blow to the head, led others out of the badly damaged, smoke-filled area. Twice Oliver carried frightened people on his back, scaling debris and climbing over a ruined office wall. The first was the office secretary, who had been blown from one office into another and covered by debris. He described her as "not emotionally able to get over that wall . . . . I didn't have time to debate with Desireé, so I said, hey, just get

* The QDR is a recurring Department of Defense four-year report required by Congress.

on my back. . . . I took her and threw her on my back and scaled the wall and there ... [were] two walls at 45 degree angles—the walls just collapsed." After passing his burden to Lieutenant Colonel William Delaney, Oliver returned and carried a second person, this time a frightened man, on his back over the wall and to an exit. Meanwhile, Perrin assisted others and sought to account for all of his people. Once over the wall, the survivors made their way into the E Ring and down Corridor 5 toward the exit to the outside. Unfortunately, two members of the QDR office—Lieutenant Colonel Jerry Dickerson and Staff Sergeant Maudlyn White—did not escape.[3]

In A-E Drive a group of approximately 20—civilians and Army, Marine, Navy, and Air Force officers and enlisted men—mounted dangerous but successful rescue efforts. Two of the group, Marine Lance Corporals Dustin Schuetz and Michael Vera, had come from their office, 4E487, above the crash site in an unrenovated part of the 4th Floor in Wedge 2. The two young Marines were discussing the attack on the World Trade Center when Flight 77 hit the building. The blast knocked Schuetz to the floor and slammed Vera and his chair into a wall where his books and manuals fell on him. Undeterred, the two collected themselves, helped their panicked and confused colleagues evacuate the offices down Corridor 5, and pointed them the way to leave the building. As Vera described it, "myself and Cpl. Schuetz, we just, I guess, did a telepathic connection or whatever you want to call it . . . and without thinking we went back to the site and started helping people out." After looking into E Ring offices for injured victims they ran to the 1st Floor and A-E Drive, where they joined a group that included a party of five sailors from the Navy staff's security detachment, several Marine officers, three or four Army soldiers, and perhaps five to eight civilians. Responding to screams and pleas for help from trapped victims, the rescuers entered the dense smoke and fumes and the flames of the C Ring through the holes in the wall with only rudimentary equipment—handheld fire extinguishers, a single flashlight, and shirts dampened in the ankle-deep water in A-E Drive for use as face masks against the suffocating smoke. The only illumination other than from the flashlight came from the flames.

Because of the choking, toxic smoke, parties of three or four rescuers crawled in relays into the destroyed areas, where they had to dig through and move collapsed furnishings and rubble to create exit routes for trapped victims.

To protect their skin from fire and heat, they rolled in pools of standing water in A-E Drive, despite which some of them suffered burns. When teams could no longer bear the heat and smoke inside, they retreated to A-E Drive and handed over the meager equipment to another group to use in the rescue effort. By the time firefighters relieved them these daring rescuers had made a number of forays into the smoking, ruined space. In a period of perhaps 30 to 40 minutes Schuetz and Vera estimated that the group saved a dozen people suffering from cuts, burns, and smoke inhalation. Fortunately, the two Marines incurred only minor injuries.[4]

Schuetz later explained what drove them. "We're Marines, that's what we're supposed to do. It may sound corny to somebody that ... is not a Marine, but that's something we've always been trained to do. . . . But we were mentally prepared and we just used instinct and went directly into the smoke." Expressing the same compelling sentiment another rescuer, Air Force Master Sergeant Paul Lirette, a medical technician from the Pentagon's Air Force Flight Medicine Clinic, who had also helped evacuate survivors, asserted that "as far as going into the building, I mean I figure that's what we get paid to do. Somebody was hurt, we're military, and that's what we've got to do."[5]

One of the most heroic deliverers, Lieutenant Commander David Tarantino, a Navy flight surgeon, served as a disaster relief specialist in the Office of the Assistant Secretary of Defense for Special Operations and Low Intensity Conflict. His office, 4A531 in Wedge 2, did not experience the direct impact of the collision. Aware of the attacks in New York City, Tarantino suddenly "felt a violent shudder and a loud explosion." He left the office, but instead of departing from the building as did most others from his area, he decided to make use of his medical skills at the crash site. Making his way to smoke-filled Corridor 4, he moistened paper towels in nearby restrooms, passing them out to persons with breathing trouble, while continuing on toward the impact area. When the smoke and noxious fumes became too dense for Tarantino to walk upright, he dropped to the floor and crawled slowly on his belly. He moved down to the lower floors and at each level helped dazed and confused people to reach the Center Court. Moving on to A-E Drive, Tarantino encountered human remains, a large hole in the C Ring wall, a large airplane tire, and smoke billowing along the roadway. Cries for help coming from trapped victims compelled response.[6]

After first helping evacuees in A-E Drive, Tarantino joined Navy Captain David Thomas, who had come from Corridor 6 in the E Ring area, and other volunteers preparing to enter the building. Thomas later explained that he "went to the scene because that was where … [I] thought … [I] should go. It was just an instinctive thing for me. I don't even know why, but it was like being back on the ship. You go to where your shipmates are having a problem." He wanted to search for Captain Robert Dolan, the commanding officer of the Navy Command Center, his Naval Academy classmate and the best man at his wedding. Unbeknownst to Thomas, Dolan was already dead. Other volunteers included Commander Craig Powell, a Navy SEAL new to the building who came from the 5th Floor; Surgeon General of the Air Force Lieutenant General Paul Carlton, Jr.; Lirette; and an unidentified Army sergeant. Of this multi-service party the general, who had organized a medical rescue team, later observed, "I don't know how we could get any more joint than that."[7]

The rescue group went into the building from A-E Drive through one of the holes spewing smoke. Working his way into the impact area, Powell came upon dazed and injured Nancy McKeown* and helped her reach safety. Powell then joined Army rescuers in A-E Drive working to get people out of a 2nd Floor window in the C Ring. Another participant, Army Lieutenant Colonel Kenny Cox, had run to A-E Drive from his office in 1D711. The group positioned a six-foot ladder on top of a dumpster hoping to reach the 2nd Floor window, but finding the ladder not long enough, Cox had the ladder hoisted to his shoulders. This still did not do the job. Finally, group members returned to catching escapees dropping from the 2nd Floor window.[8]

Meanwhile, armed with fire extinguishers and flashlights, some of this group made their way from A-E Drive into the Navy Command Center on the 1st Floor, a scene of utter devastation and chaos. Tarantino described the scene as he and Captain Thomas sought to respond to calls for help:

> At this point in this area there were live electrical wires. I got shocked twice. It's so hot that the debris is melting and dripping off the ceiling onto your skin and it would sear your skin and melt your uniform. We went a little farther, turned a corner and came into this bombed out

* See Chapter II.

> office space that was a roaring inferno of destruction and smoke and flames and intense heat you could feel searing your face.

With only a moistened T-shirt to beat back the fire, he made "a serpentine path" through the debris.[9]

Calls for help heard by Tarantino and Thomas came from Petty Officers Christina Williams and Charles Lewis, trapped beneath collapsed partitions and other debris, as was Darrell "Jerry" Henson, the office chief. Henson's deputy, retired Navy Captain Jack Punches, had died at his desk. The door to their office was jammed shut. The two young sailors trapped in the debris remained conscious but had increasing difficulty breathing. They had talked with each other and Henson for about 15 minutes after the explosion, repeatedly calling for help, but smoke and heat gradually sapped their energy and hope. Encouraged by the rescuers calling out, Lewis squeezed out from under the wreckage and escaped with their assistance. Williams, unable to escape from under a pile of rubble, had to wait until the rescuers could pull her out and take her to safety.[10]

Thomas described the scene as he and Tarantino struggled to reach Henson, trapped in a mountain of wreckage: "There is this face … almost like a caricature of a face. It appeared to be floating in space, just this face at an angle, cut up. It looked like a Halloween thing. . . . It was just sitting there. It looks like it's floating. . . . Then I focused a little further in and it's actually a guy's head squashed between furniture and his desk, actually his computer." Tarantino crawled into the "little tiny space" alongside Thomas and shone his flashlight on Henson, a retired Navy pilot with 72 combat missions in Vietnam to his credit. Sitting upright at his desk, Henson was saying "Help me! Help me!" His "bruised and bloody" head was pinned against his left shoulder by a massive weight; he couldn't move in any direction. The injured and weakened Henson, with flames licking ever closer, had almost given up hope when Thomas and Tarantino found him. Craig Powell had also inched into the room and helped by clearing some of the debris.[11]

Crawling into the cramped space where Henson lay entrapped, Tarantino reassured him: "I'm a doctor, I'm here to help. We're going to get you out of here, but you have to help yourself. You've got to fight your way out." But Henson, pinned down, couldn't move. At first Tarantino alone, then with Thomas, tried but failed to move the partition or clear the wreckage atop Henson. It seemed to

Thomas that the debris entrapping Henson looked like "a couple of tons." Adding to the urgency, the flames and smoke were starting to weaken the rescuers who feared also that the ceiling was about to collapse on them. Finally, "out of desperation," Tarantino lay on his back underneath Henson and leg-pressed against the cubicle wall, while Thomas lifted with his shoulder. After Herculean effort the two officers finally succeeded in raising the confining mass a few inches. Exerting himself mightily, Henson wriggled almost free of the wreckage when a computer cable snagged his shoe; leaving the shoe behind he made good his escape, crawling over Tarantino. Thomas "dragged him the rest of the way out of the hole."[12]

Other members of the rescue party, including General Carlton, who witnessed Tarantino's and Thomas's heroics, helped Henson out of the Command Center, placed him on a stretcher, and carried him out to the Center Court. Tarantino, while still holding up the heavy weight with his legs, called out for other victims but heard nothing. Urged by others to get out, he rolled over and crawled out. When Powell saw that the ceiling might collapse, he held up the ceiling mesh until all had gotten out of the room.

Later, in A-E Drive, Tarantino and Thomas, "coughing and retching," wiped "the crap off our faces and tears from our eyes." Thomas remembered: "I'm thinking . . . I was motivated looking for my friend [Dolan], I don't know what the hell is motivating this guy, but he's just as insane as I am. He might not make it and I don't even know who the hell he is." So that he wouldn't forget the man with whom he had just been through so much, Thomas reached over and ripped Tarantino's name tag off his uniform, exclaiming, "in case one of us doesn't make it, at least if I do, I'll know who you were and I'll tell your parents." "Hell of a guy," Thomas later pronounced him. Tarantino provided medical assistance to Henson and saw to it that he was loaded on an ambulance bound for the hospital. For the rest of the day, Tarantino assisted with triage outside the building.[13]

On the 2nd Floor C Ring, in the Wedge 1 area occupied by the Army's Office of Deputy Chief of Staff for Personnel, Colonel Karl Knoblauch and Lieutenant Colonel William McKinnon felt the crash. Knoblauch described it as a "thunderous strike and rocking of the building"; he thought that there had been a gas explosion. Fire alarms sounded and sprinklers activated, as the two officers made their way through the ravaged area calling out to colleagues in the darkness, urging them to leave the building. Acrid, pungent smoke forced them to crouch close to the floor. Emerging into Corridor 4, where the air was much better, they met Colonels John Davies and Roy Wallace; Lieutenant Colonels Gerald Barrett, Thomas Cleary, and George Richon also joined them.[14]

Soon afterward, on spying someone lying in Corridor 4 in the direction of the E Ring, the rescue party gently picked him up and went back down the corridor toward the A Ring. McKinnon later recalled the "skin was hanging off his fingers in shreds" and that he was bleeding. As the officers carried the injured soldier toward safety, McKinnon looked down at him but failed to recognize his Army Command and Staff College classmate and friend; facial burns and a covering of soot prevented recognition. Only when he glimpsed the injured man's name tag did he realize the identity of the man he was carrying—Lieutenant Colonel Brian Birdwell.[15]

At the intersection of Corridor 5 and the A Ring the group paused to irrigate Birdwell's wounds with bottled drinking water. Here they encountered the commanding officer of the Pentagon's Air Force Flight Medicine Clinic, Colonel John Baxter, who was also Secretary Rumsfeld's flight surgeon and accompanied him on trips. On learning of the emergency situation Baxter and his medical team had snatched up medical trauma packs from their clinic at 4A750 and gone to the DiLorenzo Clinic. Hearing of casualties elsewhere in the building, they proceeded to Corridor 5 on the 2nd Floor, where they found and immediately attended to Birdwell and other injured people. Baxter observed that Birdwell was "very badly burned, had blast injuries and inhalation injuries. He had obvious soot in his mouth." Baxter gave him an injection of morphine to ease his terrible pain. As Baxter and his team worked on Birdwell, the latter kept asking McKinnon to telephone his wife and reminded his rescuers that some of his colleagues might still be trapped in their C and D Ring offices on the 2nd Floor. The medical team placed Birdwell on a motorized cart that took him past the DiLorenzo Clinic and out to North Parking.[16]

At the triage site where Colonel Baxter had treated Birdwell, Navy financial manager Natalie Ogletree, on her way out of the building, observed Birdwell. Her own experience of being burned as a child led her to believe that Birdwell needed a comforting presence. After glancing at his name tag, she took his hand and said, "Brian, we're going to pray." The officer responded, "OK, Ma'am," and the two recited the 23rd Psalm together. Producing a Bible, Ogletree read aloud the 91st Psalm. When the called-for ambulance failed to arrive in North Parking after some 30 minutes, medical personnel hoisted Birdwell into an Army captain's sport utility vehicle for transport to Georgetown University Hospital.[17]

In the meantime, the Knoblauch/Davies group returned to the 2nd Floor by way of Corridor 5 to look for other victims. Despite the threat to their lives and the grim reality of their surroundings, they hesitated self-consciously before entering a women's restroom in search of water to soak their T-shirts for use as face masks. They continued toward the crash area, but their improvised protection could not shield them from the dense smoke and intense heat that prevented them from getting any further along the E Ring. They headed back toward the center of the building.[18]

Soon the officers encountered Army Major John Thurman hobbling along wearing only one shoe. Thurman, whose 2D491 office was uncomfortably close to the impact site, had been flung, still in his chair, across his cubicle by the force of the shock wave. Crawling out from under his desk where he had managed to find refuge, Thurman called for his coworkers, Lieutenant Colonel Karen Wagner and Chief Warrant Officer William Ruth, and sought to lead them to safety. Unfortunately, he became separated from them in the smoke. Thurman found an emergency exit that permitted him to get out into Corridor 5. He propped the door open with his shoe because he saw that the outside handle was missing and the door would otherwise lock automatically. At Thurman's urgent plea, Knoblauch's group then searched for Wagner and Ruth but could not penetrate the smoke that poured out of their office. Neither survived. Thurman eventually wound up at the Walter Reed Army Medical Center from which he was discharged three days later.

As the search party reversed course and headed toward the Center Court, its members ensured no one remained in nearby D, C, and B Ring offices.[19] At one point, Davies and other members of the group descended to the 1st Floor, entered A-E Drive, and then sought to enter the building through one of the holes in the C Ring wall. Rear Admiral Phillip Balisle, the Navy's director of surface warfare, already engaged in helping rescue efforts, dissuaded them from entering the space unless they equipped themselves with fire extinguishers. Finding none, the Army officers returned to the D Ring to continue their rescue efforts. When they heard the warning of another hijacked airliner headed for the Pentagon, they left the building and joined in the assistance effort outside.[20]

Efforts to control movement in the building led to confrontations between police carrying out orders to keep people from entering dangerous areas and rescuers passionately eager to do their utmost. The police seemed not to take sufficiently into account that they were dealing with people, chiefly military and retired military, many of whom by instinct and training responded unhesitatingly to such emergencies.

With other rescuers, Commander Samuel Perez, who had come down from the 5th Floor to A-E Drive, reentered the building in the vicinity of the Navy Command Center on the 1st Floor. Even though voices could be heard calling for help from behind a jammed door, a Defense Protective Service officer and a Navy shore patrolman ordered Perez and the others to vacate the area. When Perez objected, the shore patrolman made an implied threat to use his pistol. Complying for the moment, the would-be rescuers returned when the security guards had moved on. Although they failed to get into the room and heard nothing more from behind the jammed door, they later thought that those trapped in the room eventually made their way to safety.[21]

In other instances, people ignored the order to evacuate and returned again and again to help in any way possible. In A-E Drive, Admiral Balisle and other rescuers would not leave when toward 10:20 a.m. they received word that security authorities had ordered complete evacuation of the building following the report of another presumed hijacked airliner headed for the Pentagon. Later Balisle recalled the order "was tough because there was nobody there yet as a fire party." Earlier, he had seen people jumping from a C Ring second-story window into A-E Drive and had supervised rescuers going into the burning building. In response to his urgent calls for help, relayed by DPS officers' radios and messengers, Balisle learned that the attack had taken place on the E Ring west side and that the firefighters there had their hands full, as did those fighting the fire from the Center Court. In the absence of firefighters, many military personnel did not want to quit their search for survivors, viewing departure as tantamount to abandonment of wounded on the battlefield. Standing fast, the admiral and many others would not leave until it became painfully evident that the overpowering smoke prevented them from reentering the building.[22]

Not long after, Federal Bureau of Investigation (FBI) agents, who had begun arriving at the crash site before 10:00 a.m. (Special Agent Christopher Combs was first), declared the area a crime scene. Still, for a few more hours some military and civilians persisted in their desperate rescue efforts, evading FBI and other guards. Some slipped into the building hoping to account for colleagues for whom they felt responsible or to salvage records and even equipment. Others helped injured Pentagon workers outside the building, serving in less dramatic but still timely and beneficial ways. Navy Captain William Toti, an engineer officer serving as an assistant to the vice chief of naval operations, had made his way from his office at 4D620 out an exit to the Heliport area. He joined a team of stretcherbearers to carry a badly burned man from the impact area in Wedge 1 and then went back inside to help bring out a badly burned woman from the Army's Resource Services Office. As he helped her, Toti saw smoke coming from his mouth as he exhaled. Outside on the lawn, medical personnel started an intravenous drip and gave the injured woman oxygen. Kneeling beside Antoinette Sherman, Toti asked her if she felt better. She responded, "Doctor, am I going to die?" Convinced that she would survive, despite her critically burned body, Toti responded, "No … you're not going to die . . . . We have a helicopter coming for you, I'm going to stay with you until you're on it." Sherman nodded. Six days later she died in the hospital.[23]

One notable Pentagon worker also helped render assistance to victims of the attack. Soon after the airliner hit the building, Secretary Donald Rumsfeld left his office, went out a 1st Floor emergency exit, and hurried to the affected area. There he joined a stretcher party and helped carry injured persons to a medical treatment area. Once satisfied that enough help was on hand, the secretary returned to the building, where during the course of the morning he spoke by telephone with the president and the vice president.[24]

Another rescuer, Army Captain Lincoln Leibner, who was in South Parking about 100 yards from the point of impact, saw Flight 77 come in "full throttled, wheels up, a controlled flight." He ran toward the impact site, "hyper aware" of what had happened. Leibner entered the Pentagon through a door to Corridor 5 that had been blown off its hinges and immediately encountered a badly burned woman whom he helped out of the building. He went inside again and found that the smoke had greatly worsened. Hearing voices calling for help, he called back to give guidance out of the smoke.

Close to the doorway Leibner saw two women trapped in debris. He freed them and walked them out, glad to have a chance to clear his lungs of smoke. Once more he returned through the same door and this time had to leave because of the smoke. Observing a broken window in Wedge 2, he pulled himself up through it and worked his way through and around debris toward a line of people, some of whom were injured. He "was able to grab people and lower them down [from the window] to other people who were taking them out." When he heard a warning to "get away from the building" he climbed from the window and walked over to a triage area. Unable to walk further because of the smoke in his chest, he got down on one knee. Refreshed a bit and in spite of his burns and cuts, he got up and helped carry the injured to ambulances. By this time Leibner had attracted attention to his own condition and he "got put into an ambulance." After receiving treatment at the Virginia Hospital Center, he returned early in the afternoon to the Pentagon and to his job in the communication section that directly served the secretary of defense. As one just returned from the trenches, he was summoned to tell his story to Secretary Rumsfeld, who, according to Leibner, wanted to hear his firsthand account of the explosion. Leibner recounted witnessing Flight 77's plunge into the building. He remained on the job until after 9:30 p.m. when he was ordered to go home.[25]

It is possible that the fire might have been contained sooner and more people spared injury had the firefighters and other rescuers not been forced to pull back from the site on receipt of the warning of another incoming hijacked aircraft. This presumably was the fourth of the hijacked planes—United Airlines Flight 93—that crashed into a field near Shanksville, in Somerset County, Pennsylvania, at 10:03 a.m. Some time after the attack on the Pentagon, before 10:15 a.m., FBI Special Agent Combs received warning of a possible second attack from the FBI field office in Washington, which had been informed by the Federal Aviation Administration. Using a radio provided by a firefighter from the Reagan National Airport, he confirmed the warning directly with the airport's control tower. Combs immediately informed Incident Commander Schwartz, who ordered evacuation of the building and the surrounding area. Thousands withdrew to what were thought to be safe areas. The firefighters and other emergency responders returned only after about 25 minutes (shortly after 10:40 a.m.) when they received the all clear signal.[26]

In the first hour or two after Flight 77 struck, the scene in the Pentagon was one of confusion, fright, panic, escape, injury, and death. But for the presence of the many powerfully motivated rescuers—most of them volunteers and some of them victims themselves—who repeatedly placed themselves in harm's way, the outcome would certainly have been worse. In a long day of suffering and tragedy, their heroics provided moments of emotional uplift as defining as the terrible pain and sorrow.*

* See Chapters IV and VII for rescue work by the Defense Protective Service, firefighters, and other responders.

Chapter IV

Fighting the Fire

The fierce fire, powerful explosions, and chaos caused by Flight 77's plunge into the Pentagon confronted the hundreds of firefighters on the scene with what must have been the worst disaster they had ever encountered. The great size and uncommon configuration of the building permitted full play for the furious kinetic energy generated by the plane's impact to cause death and destruction on a stunning scale. For 36 tense and exhausting hours the firefighters performed their most critical missions—at first to save lives, and then to save property by containing the blaze. Strengthening their grim motivation was awareness of the vital importance of keeping the Pentagon up and running.

The First Responders

At the Pentagon Heliport, 150 feet from the west side of the building, preparations were under way early on 11 September for the expected arrival of President George Bush around noon.* On duty in the Air Traffic Control Tower were Tower Chief Sean Boger and Army Specialist Jacqueline Kidd. Soldiers from a bomb ordnance disposal unit were en route from Fort Belvoir, 15 miles

* The president was scheduled to return from a trip to Florida. On occasion he used the Pentagon Heliport instead of the White House grounds for his helicopter when going to and from Air Force One at Andrews Air Force Base. He had left from the Pentagon on 10 September. The helipad at the White House was not available for use because of preparations for a social function on the grounds.

away, to do a routine sweep of the Heliport before the president landed. To cope with helicopter emergencies, three civilians from the fire department at nearby Fort Myer manned the fire station next to the Heliport.[1]

Inside the fire station, Alan Wallace, Mark Skipper, and Dennis Young watched the TV coverage of the World Trade Center attacks until Fort Myer Fire Chief Charlie Campbell telephoned and warned them to stay alert as "Washington, D.C., could be a target." Skipper and Wallace went outside to check on the new crash truck (Foam 161) equipped with the special chemical foam used in fighting jet fuel fires. Wallace had parked it outside the station with the back end toward the Pentagon.[2]

The two men stood next to the truck discussing the New York attacks when Wallace glanced up and saw an airplane "coming at us." He yelled to Skipper to run for cover. Instantly Wallace thought: "Now it's happening here . . . we are being attacked in Washington," and then, "I [am] going to be on fire very soon." Diving under a nearby vehicle, Wallace felt the blast and the explosion's enormous heat and pressure as Flight 77 smashed into the Pentagon, just 20 feet from the corner of the fire station. Skipper heard a tremendous crash and saw the orange glow of a huge fireball bursting from the blast site and rising above the building. Boger and Kidd ran from the control tower, fleeing its shattered windows and collapsing ceiling.[3]

When the falling debris began to settle, Wallace and Skipper quickly checked that neither was seriously injured; only later would they realize they were flash-burned. As flames engulfed the building, Wallace jumped into the crash truck and started the engine, but it would not budge—the back end was ablaze and belching smoke. At the same time he radioed the fire department headquarters at Fort Myer that an airliner had hit the west side of the Pentagon, probably providing the first report of the exact crash location.[4]

Within moments, people near the impact site began streaming out of the Pentagon, escaping any way possible—from damaged exit doors, blown-out windows, and through holes in the inside C Ring wall. Black smoke clouded the air. On emerging from the building, Navy Captain William Toti was stunned to see the Heliport "all torn apart." When he saw Wallace sitting in the burning fire truck, he ran to help, wondering, "Is he dead? No, he's moving. He's making a radio call . . . what a stupid thing to do." Only later did he realize how important that radio call was.[5]

Wallace and Skipper salvaged medical supplies, fire extinguishers, and breathing apparatus from the crash truck, grabbing what was left of their equipment and gear. Wallace's boots were filled with debris and the suspenders on his fire pants were burned. Although the explosion had caused part of the ceiling to collapse around him, Young emerged from the station house unharmed. When they heard cries for help coming from inside the building, the three firefighters rushed to help workers attempting to escape through a blown-out, first-story window. With others they helped move the injured to an area beyond the Heliport.[6]

Meantime, area first responders learned of the crash and reacted immediately, arriving at the Pentagon within minutes despite initial uncertainty about the location. They came from nearby Arlington County Fire Department (ACFD), the Pentagon's primary emergency service for fire and medical incidents, and the Fort Myer Military Community Fire Department, which operated the Heliport fire station. From Reagan National Airport came emergency crews that had special aircraft fire and rescue training and equipment and automatic authority to respond to any crashes within a five-mile radius of the airport. These units belonged to the Fire and Rescue Department of the Metropolitan Washington Airports Authority.[7]

They were able to respond rapidly in part because the Arlington County Emergency Communications Center (ECC), focal point of all police and fire 911 calls for the county, received early warnings from county emergency workers who saw the low-flying plane. Captain Steve McCoy and firefighter Andrea Kaiser, on ACFD Engine 101 traveling north on Interstate 395 for a training session, caught sight of an airliner descending steeply and disappearing over the horizon, heard an explosion, and then saw a plume of smoke. McCoy radioed ECC and reported, "We got a plane down, it looks like in the Crystal City area by the 14th Street Bridge." Police Corporal Barry Foust radioed that it might have crashed in Washington, D.C., while Officer Richard Cox identified the Pentagon as the possible site. A flood of similar calls coming into ECC overwhelmed phone lines and radio channels, making it difficult for dispatchers to determine the location of the crash, assign an alarm rating, and direct the types and number of units to respond. Finally, ECC confirmed the Pentagon as the crash site and assigned an augmented first alarm rating to the emergency and dispatched Arlington fire and Emergency Medical Services (EMS) units.[8]

When the plane struck, nine ACFD medical and fire units were less than two miles north of the Pentagon in Arlington's Rosslyn area responding to an apartment building fire that had been extinguished by the time the first unit reached the scene. ECC diverted them to the new emergency, and the first unit, Truck 105, roared into the Pentagon's South Parking about five minutes after the crash and pinpointed the Heliport as the incident site. Confronted by a huge tower of black smoke rising from the building and people streaming out, the crew instructed ECC to call for additional resources. Other Arlington units took the step of self-dispatching when they heard the radio reports, barely discernible through the chatter. Incident Commander Schwartz later explained that ECC found it difficult to make assignments because of the confusion and heavy radio traffic: "And quite honestly, all of the units in Arlington County ... knew they were going to the dance. So they all just started responding."[9]

ECC notified the Fort Myer and Reagan National fire departments, both of which had already begun to respond. Dispatchers also asked Alexandria and Fairfax County fire and EMS services to stage units in readiness near the Pentagon. All of these departments were signatories of the Northern Virginia Response Agreement, a "mutual aid" pact that allowed regional fire and EMS organizations to respond automatically to emergencies and share resources across jurisdictional boundaries. As one responder put it, "You get the closest available unit of the type needed for the incident, and it doesn't matter whose name is on the side of the truck." ECC also asked the District of Columbia Fire and Emergency Services to stage units nearby; the District shared a mutual aid agreement with Arlington, but rather than authorizing automatic dispatch it required the party seeking assistance to first request it.[10]

Arlington's first responders converged on congested South Parking, stopping at the corner of the building nearest the impact site. Renovation construction trailers and equipment parked near the corner made it difficult to get to the Heliport. Firefighters abandoned their vehicles, grabbed their equipment, and ran to the building. Senior ACFD officers began arriving in South Parking within six minutes and immediately initiated command and control protocols.

Training Captain Chuck Gibbs was followed by Robert Cornwell, a seasoned battalion chief who knew the Pentagon well. Cornwell assumed overall command of the scene and began to assess the situation. Battalion Chief Dale Smith raced from Virginia Hospital Center, arriving around the same time as EMS Supervisors Captains Ed Blunt and Alan Dorn, who at once set up makeshift triage, treatment, and casualty collection areas. ECC dispatched additional medical services, and Arlington County Police soon arrived to control traffic to enable emergency units to get through.[11]

At the time of the crash, most of the firefighters at Fort Myer, about a mile west of the Pentagon, were attending an aircraft rescue and firefighting class led by Captain Russell Dodge, Jr., assistant chief of the Fort Belvoir Fire Department. Ironically, they were discussing aircraft fuel loads when they heard of the New York attacks over the station's radio. Suddenly, Vance Valenzo heard a "horrendous explosion" and Jeff Afforder felt a "jolt" like "somebody shutting a door." Immediately, there was confused radio chatter about a "plane going down," location unknown. The station simultaneously received Alan Wallace's radio call from the burning Heliport truck identifying the target. Momentarily stunned into disbelief, the firefighters reacted quickly. Captain Dennis Gilroy, acting Fort Myer department commander for the day, recalled that "everybody just got up [and] we're gone. . . . We didn't wait for anybody's dispatch. . . . We just responded." "Self-dispatch," Gilroy called it.[12]

Speeding toward the Pentagon, Fort Myer crew members, aware that two planes had crashed in New York, feared the possibility of another hit and "kept looking around like something [was] going to happen." Rescue Engines 161 and 162 and the command vehicle arrived at about 9:42 a.m., mere moments after the first Arlington unit, followed by a reserve pumper, Engine 163.[13]

The Fort Myer crews encountered what they later described as a surrealistic scene. Brian Ladd of Engine 161 spotted people "just coming out the windows," some badly burned. Expecting to see pieces of the wings or fuselage, he saw instead "millions of tiny pieces" of debris spread "everywhere." Through the heavy black smoke, Sergeant Thomas Hodge and Bruce Surette on Engine 162 caught sight of large crowds of people, some coming out the doors, others "walking through the field ... burned, injured." For Hodge, the "devastation" on their faces "was terrible" to see. Roger Reardon on Engine 161 felt that he had entered "a war zone" or a film set. "It was like Hollywood. . . . People were sitting there screaming or standing [or] running around yelling 'medics' and 'we need firefighters and police officers.'"[14]

Better informed than the first Arlington units thanks to Wallace's radio call, the crew on Fort Myer Engine 161 knew to go to the Heliport. But when an Arlington fire truck inadvertently blocked their access to Heliport Road, Ladd and Reardon impatiently jumped off and ran toward the burning area where, with relief, they saw Wallace, Skipper, and Young, apparently unharmed, helping people out of the building. Sergeant William Harris quickly managed to drive Engine 161 around the Arlington truck. The first to arrive at the Heliport, the crew hooked up to a hydrant in minutes. Reardon and Wallace, helped by civilians and military, pulled five-gallon canisters of foam agent out of the damaged fire station for later use. Meanwhile, the Engine 162 crew stopped in South Parking and considered the best way of entering the building. Along with ACFD firefighters they directed the outpouring of escapees away from the building, assisting those who needed help.[15]

Gilroy arrived about the same time as his units. Stopping his command vehicle on the shoulder of Heliport Road to assess the situation, he viewed the scene with amazement; injured people seemed to be "everywhere" and people were still trying to get out of the blazing building. For a moment he wondered why he saw no aircraft parts, then sped to the Heliport "hot zone," where he assumed command of his units. Dodge, the instructor who had ridden with Gilroy, ran to a blown-out office window behind the burning foam truck and with "an army captain, another civilian, and two deputy sheriffs" helped workers climb out. Although lacking protective gear, he searched in the building until the thick smoke drove him out; then he joined other firefighters setting up at the impact site.[16]

Little more than a mile south of the Pentagon at Reagan National Airport, a stunned Captain Michael Defina watched the TV coverage of the New York attacks. Defina commanded the airport's emergency units that day; some of his firefighters were attending an officer training class or taking part in antiterrorism exercises at the District of Columbia Fire and EMS Training Academy in preparation for possible incidents at upcoming International Monetary Fund and World Bank meetings. When notified of an automobile accident in front of the terminal Defina responded, thinking it suspicious coming so soon after the New York attacks.[17]

Standing on the upper-level roadway of the airport around 9:37 a.m. Defina heard a low rumble and then observed smoke rising to the northwest. Captain John Durrer, also on the scene, saw a "flash" followed by smoke billowing up; with three others he jumped into Rescue Engine 335, a pumper carrying hoses, water, ladders, and rescue equipment, and headed in the direction of the smoke. Confused reports came over the radio: the airport's River Rescue boat reported a crash near the 14th Street Bridge; others identified a Crystal City location. Durrer switched to Arlington's channel and heard voices shouting, "It's into the Pentagon!"; he headed toward South Parking, arriving just after the first Arlington and Fort Myer units. He reported to Arlington officers gathered there, urgently engaged in assessing the situation and determining which resources had arrived and what tactics to employ. Awaiting his assignment from Captain Gibbs, Durrer noted the gaping hole and fire but felt something was missing. Like Fort Myer's Brian Ladd, he had expected to see large parts of the plane and thought, "Well where's the airplane, you know, where's the parts to it? You would think there'd be something."[18] The near total disintegration of the plane had left only a multitude of bits scattered outside the building.

Firefighter Cary Henry left Reagan National about the same time as Durrer. As he drove Foam 331 toward the smoke, he noticed that people stood in the streets pointing north toward the Pentagon. When the radio confirmed the location, he sped the wrong way down a ramp to Route 27 (Washington Boulevard) and quickly reached the Heliport. As he parked close to the great gash in the building, he felt the heat from the fire and recognized the smell of fuel residue. The fire seemed to be advancing rapidly to all the E Ring floors. Gibbs assigned Durrer's specially trained team to help operate the foam truck; the crew immediately attacked the fire with the chemical foam used on jet fuel.[19]

Defina arrived at the Heliport in the command vehicle a few minutes later than the other Reagan National units after mobilizing the rest of his department. Like his colleagues, he had been uncertain of the crash location: the airport's control tower reported several possible locations, but finally Arlington's ECC confirmed the crash into the Pentagon. En route he summoned all off-duty airport fire personnel to duty. Once on the scene he called for the truck (Foam 345) that

PENTAGON AND VICINITY

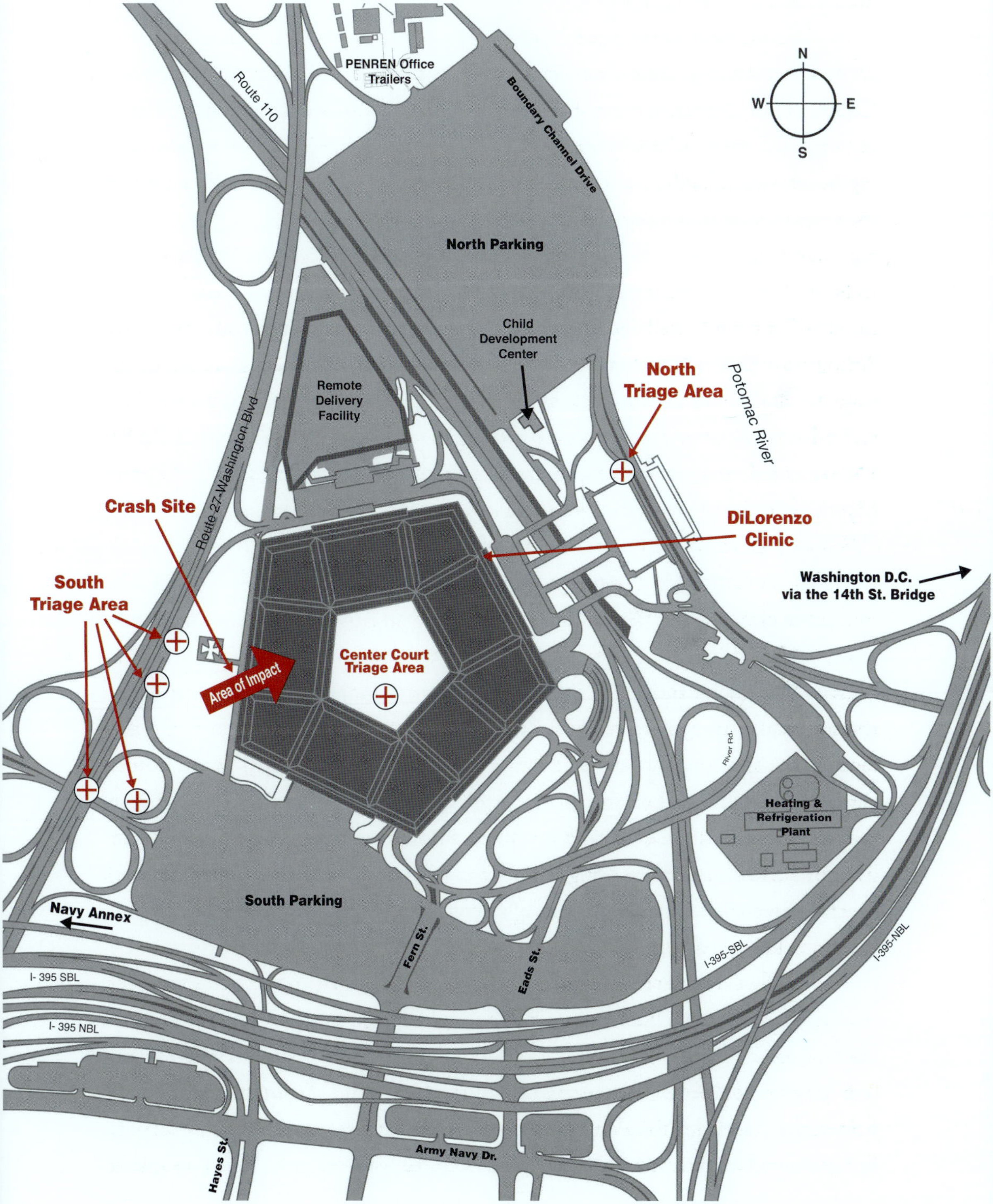

had stayed behind to protect the airport. With all U.S. civilian aircraft supposed to be grounded, the truck would no longer be needed at the closed airport. Later, Defina had Dulles Airport send an additional foam truck to the Pentagon.[20]

Immediately following the New York attacks, but before they received reports of the Pentagon strike, District of Columbia Fire and Emergency Services units kept busy responding to a spate of alarms. Some units mobilized in anticipation of calls, while others checked on the White House after receiving reports of an explosion and an inbound plane. On learning of the crash at the Pentagon, the D.C. services responded to Arlington's request for assistance (received around 9:44 a.m.) and dispatched units across the river. After inching their way through traffic, the first components went directly to the building, while others staged nearby. D.C. Deputy Fire Chief James Martin arrived approximately 15 to 20 minutes after impact to take command of his firefighters. The D.C. firefighters communicated with the Arlington County command post and jumped in with other units "helter skelter" to help with efforts to rescue people still in the building.[21]

Command and Control

The number of departments responding and the confusion at the scene underscored the need for the exercise of effective command and control, which became the responsibility of ACFD Assistant Chief James Schwartz, who arrived at the Pentagon within 10 minutes of impact. Over the radio, he heard the report that a plane was down near the 14th Street Bridge and then that the Pentagon was hit. Making his way down Route 27 in "a wave of emergency response vehicles," he gave ECC specific instructions for requesting additional emergency resources and for recalling off-duty members. As he pulled into South Parking, he saw tremendous smoke and fire, a "sea of people" trying to assist the injured lying "strewn" across the lawn, and military forming small groups to reenter the Pentagon.[22]

Schwartz immediately implemented the incident command system (ICS), used to coordinate response efforts at all incidents but especially important for large-scale events involving multiple agencies and jurisdictions. The ICS was first developed in the 1970s after a series of inadequate responses to disastrous wildfires in Western states demonstrated the need for firm command, planning, and communications procedures that could be used within and across organizations. Over the years increasing numbers of emergency services had come to use some variant of the ICS. After the defective response to the Air Florida jet crash into the Potomac River in 1982, some fire and EMS organizations in the Washington region began to use the ICS.

In March 2001 the Metropolitan Washington Council of Governments, a regional agency addressing problems of mutual concern to its 19 members, advised area fire and EMS departments to implement a standardized ICS. By 11 September, mutual aid partners in Northern Virginia had for the most part done so, but other services in the metropolitan region had not yet fully complied. The goal was to have standard operating procedures so that responders at the scene, no matter their locality, would integrate into this single system, know what was expected of them, and communicate effectively with one another. Chief Schwartz and other commanding officers later attributed the overall success of the emergency response at the Pentagon to the ICS.[23]

The Arlington County Fire Department took initial command of the scene even though the Pentagon was federal property; under the ICS, the agency responsible for the most critical functions at any given stage was to assume authority. While the Pentagon attack created both a fire scene and a crime scene, fire suppression and rescue clearly demanded priority. As the highest-ranking ACFD officer on the scene, Schwartz relieved Cornwell as incident commander, a position ICS protocols vested with top authority in managing the incident. While Schwartz was entitled to operate under a single command structure, giving him sole responsibility for decisionmaking, he exercised tact and diplomacy in dealing with the innumerable participating federal, state, local, and private organizations, particularly the Federal Bureau of Investigation, which was designated the lead agency for investigating domestic terrorist events.* For 10 days, until the fire was officially declared extinguished, the ACFD retained control, relinquishing it on 21 September to the FBI.[24]

Schwartz set up the Incident Command Post in South Parking. Operating initially out of his "command buggy," a Chevrolet Suburban (later in the day switching to the Arlington County Police Department command vehicle and still later to a Fairfax County vehicle), he assigned the tactical missions that

* See Chapter VII.

INITIAL INCIDENT COMMAND STRUCTURE

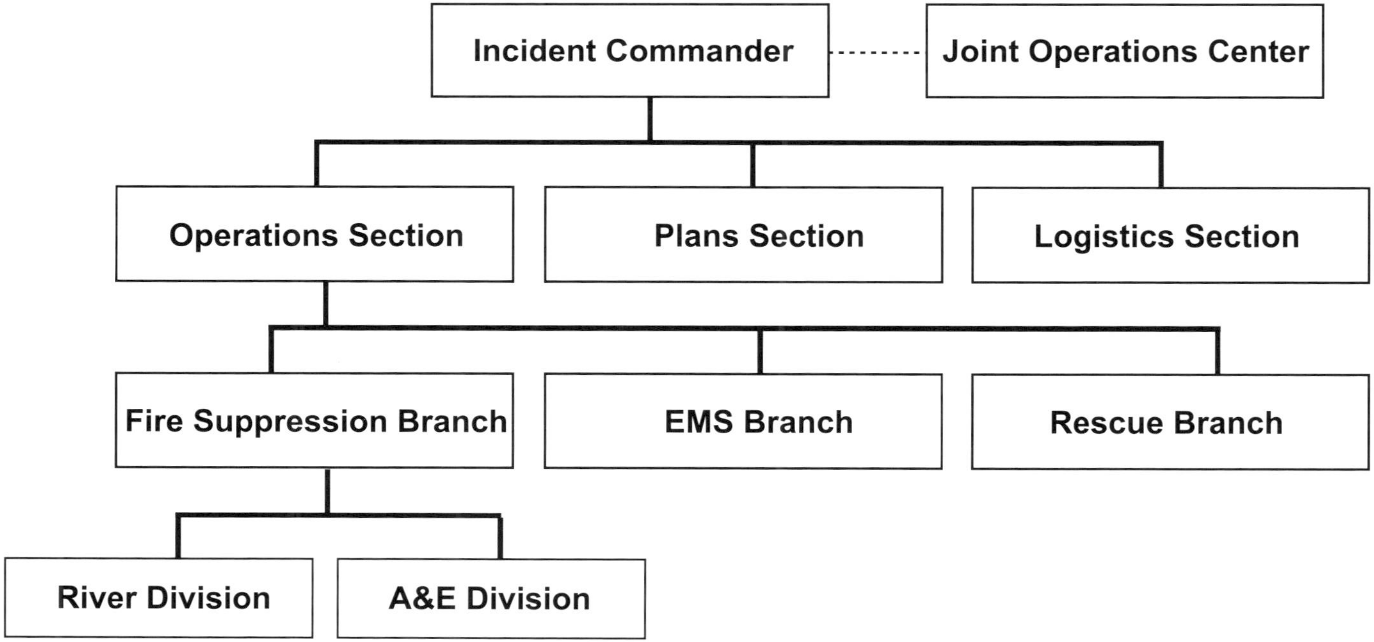

Source: Arlington County After-Action Report

needed the most urgent attention. Since no one yet had a good sense of the damage inside the building he assigned several fire companies under Chief Cornwell to rapidly assess the interior.[25]

The huge scale of the conflagration compelled Schwartz early on to establish the tiered working groups prescribed by the ICS for the most urgent tasks at hand. He appointed Gibbs to command the River Division,* which fought the fire and performed search and rescue missions at the Heliport "hot zone." Operating from the Center Court, Battalion Chief Smith commanded the A&E Division, which took its name from A-E Drive. The EMS Division (initially called the South Parking Division) was commanded first by Assistant Chief John White and then by Battalion Chief James Bonzano. As the morning progressed, Schwartz created the upper supervisory levels. He assigned Battalion Chief Randy Gray command of the Fire Suppression Branch, overseeing firefighting in the A&E and River Divisions; the EMS Branch handled medical activities, by that time centered mostly in South Parking. Around noon, he created the Operations Section to run the Fire Suppression and EMS branches, and around 1:00 p.m. he established the Logistics Section. This organization allowed the commanders to focus on their own sectors and functions and at the same time broadened Schwartz's span of control. He delegated authority at first to his own ACFD officers, later turning to other departments to help sustain the high level of effort.[26]

When radio communications failed, "runners" carried information between the sectors and the command post. In general, the division commanders communicated face-to-face with subordinate officers, who in turn led the firefighting companies on tactical missions. Division commanders had a better grasp of the situation on the ground than the command post, and they had discretion to use what tactics they thought necessary. Because they were so intensely engaged the first day commanders had little chance to interact with Schwartz. In the opinion of some officers it was exactly this flexibility that allowed for success. Indeed, firefighters at all levels often had to exercise their own judgment, especially in the early going.[27]

* Schwartz derived the name from a nearby sign directing motorists to the Pentagon's River Entrance, which was some distance from the impact area.

Schwartz was setting up the Incident Command Post when FBI Special Agent Christopher Combs arrived about 9:50 a.m. Combs served on the FBI's National Capital Response Squad, an antiterrorism rapid response unit. Until additional FBI personnel arrived not long after, Combs served as on-scene FBI commander and stayed with Schwartz at the command post. The two knew each other and had a comfortable working relationship. As the regular FBI liaison to the fire services, Combs routinely cross-trained with regional departments; earlier that morning he had been at the D.C. Fire Academy training firefighters in counterterrorism tactics.[28]

The outpouring of fire departments to the scene, some of them self-dispatched, complicated Schwartz's efforts to establish effective command and control. Those closest to the scene—Arlington, Fort Myer, Reagan National, and Washington, D.C.—raced in first and bore the brunt of the battle. Manpower was short at first, but the number of units arriving from other departments throughout the day became overwhelming. Many had to remain on standby, some at a considerable distance from the Pentagon, and never saw any action. Other units ignored staging protocols, drove to the building, and jumped into action on their own, further aggravating the control problem and causing hard feelings among those who awaited instructions. Different types of units came from Alexandria, Falls Church, Fairfax City, Fort Belvoir, Dulles Airport, and Fairfax, Prince William, and Loudoun Counties in Virginia, and from Montgomery, Prince George's, and Frederick Counties in Maryland.* Dealing with hundreds of trucks and other vehicles and thousands of firefighters, medical people, and other responders sorely taxed the capacity of the command post.[29]

Chief Edward Plaugher of the Arlington County Fire Department gave strong support to Schwartz. After hearing of the attack he raced to the scene, lights flashing and sirens wailing, arriving around 10:00 a.m. As the county's senior firefighter Plaugher could have assumed the role of incident commander, but he recognized that Schwartz, already on the scene for some time, had a better grasp of the situation. Instead, the 30-year veteran of both the Fairfax and Arlington County Fire Departments took control of administrative and support mat-

* In these localities mutual aid agreements allowed firefighters from municipal and volunteer fire departments to "backfill" the many fire stations left empty when units raced to the Pentagon. They provided the resources to meet other fire and medical emergency needs. Some of these volunteers also served at the Pentagon.

ters. Throughout the event, he monitored the overall functioning of the response effort, serving in a "senior advisor-responsible party" capacity.[30]

When he arrived, Plaugher expressed concern that the command structure still lacked the information to calculate medical and firefighting needs. To better judge the scale of the disaster, he commandeered a nearby U.S. Park Police helicopter to fly him over the Pentagon rings, as near to the flames as possible. From that aerial vantage he saw that the fire had not progressed inward beyond the C Ring. When the pilot warned that the helicopter's air intakes would suck smoke into the engines if they got any closer, Plaugher decided he had seen enough. They returned to the ground just as Schwartz ordered a site evacuation because of a report of an inbound plane.[31]

Initial Search, Rescue, and Firefighting Efforts

It took about an hour for the formal ICS structure to become fully operational at all levels. Communication between arriving first responders was difficult; the radio channels were so overwhelmed that some found them almost useless.[32] Nevertheless, during this time the firefighters "knew what needed to be done and went ahead and did it." They followed the systematized approach used at every fire. While the situation was huge and complex, involving multiple emergency organizations, the tasks to be performed were familiar. The firefighters drew on their training and experience. Fort Myer firefighter Vance Valenzo found the situation daunting, but he "just didn't have time to focus on one specific area. You had to make a decision based on your training, based on our job, and you just went ahead and did it. . . . There were so many decisions to be made, and not one decision you made was wrong, because there was so much needed to be done. You just reacted to your job." Several firefighters who described the early situation as one of "organized" or "controlled chaos" noted that initially the command structure was as shocked as everyone else.[33]

Because saving lives is paramount in all catastrophic incidents, some of the first responders entered the building immediately to look for survivors and to reconnoiter the scene so that tactical decisions could be made. Arlington crews entered the building from South Parking through Corridor 3 and began to assess conditions on all floors and to direct workers to leave. As they advanced toward the impact point, they encountered heavy smoke.[34]

Firefighters from Reagan National, Fort Myer, and Arlington did the same from the Heliport side via Corridor 5. Vance Valenzo's group searched through offices on the 2nd Floor, finding debris everywhere. The black smoke was so thick that Valenzo could not even see his hand in front of his face. The firefighters went as near the blast zone as possible before a hole in the floor stopped further progress. They found no one, dead or alive.[35]

Initial search and rescue missions were exceedingly dangerous. The firefighters did not know how far the fire had spread nor to what degree the building's structural integrity was compromised. Furthermore, the plane might have carried chemical agents or secondary explosives. The ruined interior that reminded Roger Reardon of a movie set was all too real as he and his colleagues crawled through dangling lights, loose electric wires, fallen ceiling tiles, and concrete. It was an experience he wanted never to repeat.[36]

Additional responders from Reagan National, Fort Myer, Arlington, the District, and elsewhere continued to arrive during the confused first hour after the attack, although traffic congestion and crowds near the building slowed them. Some had been in classes or training, others had been off-duty. Reagan National's Battalion Chief Walter Hood, Jr., Captain Robert Mott, and firefighters Michael Murphy and Greg Long had been attending the counterterrorism class at the D.C. Fire Academy. The police provided an escort, clearing the way so that they arrived around 10:00 a.m. Hood checked into the command post and was given charge on the Heliport side of several firefighting companies from surrounding jurisdictions. They searched as much of the E Ring as they could, but calls to vacate the building interrupted them.[37]

Captain Charles Howes and Michael Murphy, from Reagan National, joined a rescue group that entered Corridor 5 and the E Ring to search for survivors. The firefighters searched room to room, using axes, crowbar-like tools, sledgehammers, and a hydraulic device to pry doors open. They encountered damaged and destroyed office areas with tables and equipment thrown about and everything on fire or falling down. The firefighters used a thermal energy (infrared) camera to look for bodies (indicated by a heat signature) through the smoke and darkness, but they found no one alive. At least three times during the day they were forced to leave the building because of evacuations triggered by the E Ring collapse and two reports of incoming planes.[38]

Despite their strenuous efforts, emergency personnel made fewer rescues near the blast site than might have been anticipated. Indeed, most rescues occurred immediately after impact, before emergency assistance arrived. Chief Schwartz later acknowledged that military and civilian personnel "saved far more lives in those first few minutes than we saved at any time." When the Fort Myer units first pulled up to the impact site at about 9:42, rescuers were still "grabbing" some people out of the building, but shortly after the rescues from the E Ring seemed to stop. Reagan National units arriving only moments later assisted a few survivors "staggering around," trying to find a way out of the building. Defina noticed that very few survivors came out from near the impact site; Gibbs, also on scene in the first minutes, saw no victims come out near the blast zone. It became clear to the firefighters early on that there would be no more survivors from the impact area. Nevertheless, throughout the day, as fire suppression teams made headway against the blaze, rescue groups would follow, searching against all odds for survivors.[39]

In the first minutes, while some firefighters searched near the impact site, others set up the fire suppression equipment as rapidly as possible, with the immediate imperative to suppress the external fires caused by the spewed jet fuel that saturated whatever lay in its path. The explosion had generated a huge fireball that blasted outward, up and over the building. The spilled fuel, a highly combustible kerosene derivative known as Jet A, burned itself off. Whatever was near the E Ring blast hole burst into flames, including the Heliport crash truck, two cars parked near the air control tower, a construction shed, and a diesel fuel tank and generator on a flatbed trailer. Oxygen bottles stored near the trailers apparently exploded, adding to the pandemonium. Firefighters connected multiple hoses to Reagan National's foam trucks 331 and 345 and Fort Myer's Rescue Engine 161 to fight the exterior fires, drenching everything around the building that was burning.[40]

Defina and his Reagan National firefighters attacked the visible E Ring fire from the outside. They sprayed the foam and water mixture into the hole where the plane had hit. When they ran out of foam they had to switch to water. Reagan National's spare crash truck arrived shortly after 10:00 a.m., bringing a new supply of the chemical agent.[41]

Under Gilroy's supervision the Fort Myer crews set up a "deluge gun," a cannon-like portable device used for applying high volumes of water to large fires, directing it at the building and a doorway where "people were trying to come out." Also known as a "deck gun" or "master stream," it required several firefighters to operate it. Crews began to lay water supply hoses into the building and attacked the fire with hand lines, switching nozzles where necessary to adjust the pressure and reach of the spray.[42]

Smith, commander of the A&E Division, directed fire suppression efforts from the Center Court. When he drove his command vehicle in there and took charge, he saw "hordes" of people everywhere fleeing the building. Although Arlington firefighters and a three-person truck unit from the D.C. Fire Department soon appeared and more help arrived later, Smith, short of firefighters for much of the day, at times deemed the situation out of control because of the limited resources he had on hand to deal with such a large fire and complex building. He did not know that a plane had hit until he later saw aircraft fragments inside the building. To Smith, the Center Court seemed a separate world, a sentiment echoed by others. (Gilroy similarly observed that the Heliport site "became a small world" to those working there.) According to Schwartz, the untelevised and generally unrecognized Center Court operation constituted a significant portion of the overall suppression effort.[43]

E Ring Collapse

As they battled the blaze at the blast site, the firefighters watched the building closely, fearing structural failure. One firefighter explained that they "pretty much knew that the building was going to collapse because it started making weird sounds and creaking." When Battalion Chief Tim Lasher of Reagan National noticed a crack in the structure and Gilroy saw a cornice of the building move, Defina warned of imminent collapse and urged everyone near the impact site to evacuate. Immediately all units on the Heliport side were ordered to leave the area.[44]

Minutes after the warning, around 10:15 a.m., an E Ring area above the hole carved by the plane collapsed, pulling down the 2nd through 5th Floors and the roof. Narrower than the swath of damage created by the plane crash, the collapse zone was about 95 feet at its widest point along the building's outer wall

FIRST FLOOR DAMAGE

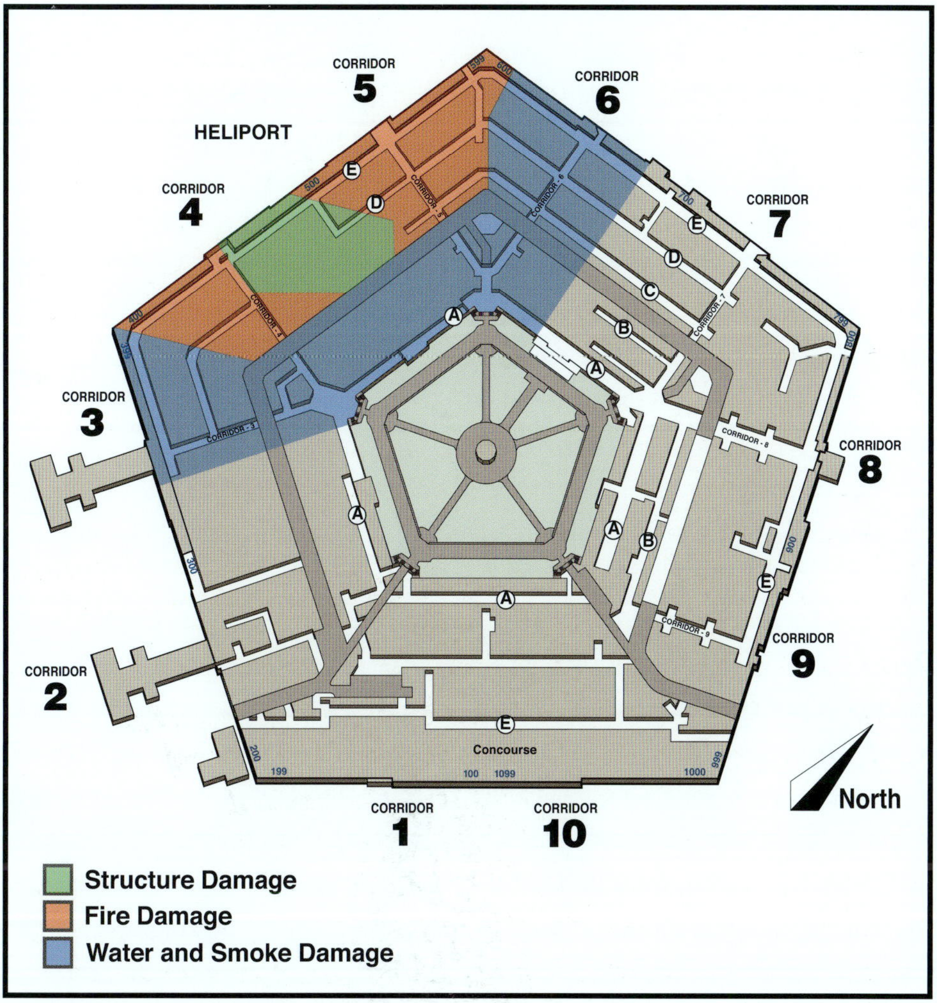

and approximately 50 feet at its deepest point, reaching to the E Ring's inner wall, which remained standing. The force of the plane's impact and the ensuing fire had destroyed or damaged a number of 1st and 2nd Floor columns in the plane's path, increasing the span between the remaining ones. Through a complex redistribution of forces, the weight normally supported by the missing columns temporarily shifted to other structural elements that held long enough for upper-floor occupants to escape. Eventually, when the load became too much, more supporting columns collapsed and a break occurred along an expansion joint between Corridor 4 and the Heliport entrance.[45]

Gibbs and other firefighters searching for survivors left just in time. Onlookers saw buckling floors sag and swing downwards as though hinged. The section of the building seemed to "pancake" down on itself, looking as if someone had "cut it with a knife" and "left it to crumble." As hundreds of tons of concrete and bricks rumbled down, onlookers watched in fear and anguish. PENREN worker Michael DiPaula, "completely numb and in a daze" after his escape from a construction trailer near the impact site, was horrified as he watched the collapse, "just not knowing who got out." For U.S. Park Police helicopter pilot Keith Bohn, the image of "the building collapsing and burning and people fleeing" was imprinted forever on his mind.[46]

Inbound Plane Rumors and Evacuations

Warnings and rumors of more plane attacks caused apprehension and disrupted the firefighting. Schwartz ordered evacuations in the morning and afternoon of the 11th and another evacuation the next morning. The first warning came before the 10:15 a.m. E Ring collapse, when FBI agent Chris Combs received a call through his FBI radio that a hijacked plane thought to be headed toward Washington was only 20 minutes away. Notified by Combs at the command post in South Parking, Schwartz considered the options. If he did not evacuate and another plane hit, the cost in lives could be staggering. If he retreated, the firefighting and rescue efforts would be delayed. With the New York attacks fresh in his mind, Schwartz decided to order a full incident site evacuation, urging emergency workers to seek cover under nearby highway overpasses. He relocated the Incident Command Post from South Parking to beneath an Interstate 395 overpass near Hayes Street, several hundred yards from the building.[47]

The order to evacuate was broadcast repeatedly on fire, police, Defense Protective Service, and other radio channels, and the countdown began. Portable radios, however, were not always fully functional, cell phones did not work, and there were few of the more reliable Nextel radio phones available. Consequently, evacuation orders were passed by word of mouth, shouted out through bullhorns, or sounded by air horns and honking fire trucks to clear the area rapidly. But it took time to disseminate the command and even longer for everyone in and around the building to respond. Every five minutes or so radios announced the time remaining until the aircraft was expected to arrive.[48]

Images from a security camera video as Flight 77 strikes the Pentagon.

Indistinct view of aircraft.

Zoomed image focusing on aircraft.

Impact at 9:37 a.m.

Above: Foam residue visible on the Pentagon facade, before the collapse.
Below: Military and civilian personnel cluster close to the Pentagon, hoping to aid first responders in search and rescue efforts.

Carrying the injured.

Emergency treatment of injured victims in the first triage area.

Above: Secretary Rumsfeld (foreground, second from right) assists with carrying a victim on a stretcher toward an ambulance on Route 27. (Courtesy of WUSA-TV, Washington)
Below: View of the burning Pentagon from the Washington side of the Potomac.

Above: Volunteers and firefighters at the Heliport entrance, planning to search the building for victims.
Below: Firefighters and volunteer rescuers in front of the impact site and burning generator.

Above: Firefighters pull back as part of the E Ring collapses.
Below: Dark smoke rises from the flaming Pentagon shortly after the collapse of the E Ring.

Above: Impact scene with the Capitol in the background.
Below: Fort Myer firefighter Vance Valenzo carries a hose across the debris-covered Helipad.

Incident Commander James Schwartz at a press conference on 14 September 2001.

Evacuation from Corridor 2 to South Parking.

Above: Evacuating injured by helicopter.
Below: Volunteers and emergency responders offer aid in the Center Court.

Above: In A-E Drive, debris and airplane tire remnant.
Below: The "punch out" hole in A-E Drive.

Above: Debris covering the Heliport area.
Below: District of Columbia Fire Department Tower 10 fighting fire in upper stories.

Above: Removing a damaged building column.
Below: Weary workers emerge from Heliport entrance.

Above: Search and rescue workers.
Below: Rescue worker indicates an area has been searched.

Above: Firefighters battle the roof fire on the morning of 12 September 2001.
Below: The burnt roof of the Pentagon on 14 September 2001.

President Bush thanks responders while visiting the Pentagon crash site on 12 September 2001.

Firefighters and military personnel unfurl the flag from the Pentagon roof during President Bush's visit on 12 September 2001.

As the orders passed down the chain of command, the firefighters dropped their hoses, shut off their equipment, and abandoned the search missions. Some moved their fire trucks away from the building, withdrew across Route 27 and Interstate 395, and sought shelter behind barriers or under overpasses. As word of the evacuation spread around the vast Pentagon perimeter, Pentagon police, helped by military volunteers, steered the many clusters of people away from the building and ordered those still inside to leave. Army Lieutenant Colonel Bill McKinnon recalled, "I was standing out there . . . and the police started coming to us and told us that another plane was heading inbound to Washington . . . and that we needed to get away from the area. So you had this migration of thousands of people just moving away from the Pentagon—just a sea of people, civilian and military, just migrating across the fields and the highways, the ramps and everything, to move away from the area."[49]

Most complied readily, some more calmly than others. While a group of Defense Intelligence Agency colleagues waited in North Parking, rumors of additional attacks abounded. The atmosphere seemed "strangely calm yet uncertain," Karl Glasbrenner recalled, until an armed sailor passed by yelling, "Take cover NOW!!! There is another plane inbound that will arrive in less than two minutes!!!" Running to the Potomac River bank from North Parking, some DIA employees brought the children from the Pentagon's Child Development Center. As they waited, "everyone's eyes turned skyward, searching for the alleged inbound aircraft that carried the threat of yet more deaths." Airboats, with armed police clothed in black tactical gear, patrolled the river. "Sirens could be heard almost continuously." Glasbrenner later described the thoughts that had raced through his mind: "Where do you go? Where do you hide? You are outside, with nothing to provide cover. . . . There is virtually nowhere you can run in one minute. . . . Panic filled the air, as people ran screaming through the park, many in circles, as they attempted, in vain, to choose a safe destination."[50]

In the crowded Center Court, by the time Smith received the evacuation order he thought it too late to clear the area. Although he ordered his firefighters from the building, they remained in the Center Court, along with a number of volunteers and Pentagon workers who had not yet made it to the outside.* Smith felt "helpless," because "we were trying to do our job" while "under attack."[51]

* See Chapters III and V for evacuation of medical personnel and patients from the Center Court at this time.

Elsewhere, military volunteers seeking to carry on with rescue work were dismayed by the interruptions. Major Craig Collier, who had evacuated from 2C638, lined up in South Parking with other volunteer stretcherbearers when police "began screaming for us to move to the other side of I-395, as there was another aircraft inbound just minutes away." Commander Randall Lescault, who continued to search the building after he escaped from Corridor 4, D Ring, reluctantly left when a firefighter insisted. In retrospect, he believed that the evacuations "really interrupted the rescue operations," but he also recognized that at the time the danger seemed genuine: "Everybody else is thinking World Trade Center. You know that plane number two is going to kill all the firefighters while they are in place."[52]

Some military and civilians objected to the decision to evacuate. A few still combing the building for missing colleagues ignored the order, insisting that live victims remained trapped inside. Angered, some felt that FBI officials cared more about protocols and collecting evidence than finding survivors. Ensign Will Parks later experienced a feeling of guilt and wondered long after what might have been if he had been allowed back into the building.[53]

Minutes after the countdown reached zero and the threat did not materialize, Combs received a communication that the hijacked aircraft had crashed into Camp David, the presidential compound in Maryland—learning only later that it had crashed in rural Pennsylvania. At about 10:40 a.m. Schwartz announced the all clear, and the firefighters converged on the building again.[54]

Testimony about evacuations of the building on 11 September is confusing and often contradictory; the prevailing turmoil surely blurred perceptions of time and space. While it is clear that there were three major evacuations—two in the first hour and one in the afternoon—some groups may have had to leave the building more than three times during the day. The Reagan National firefighters who tuned in to the airport's control towers rather than the Arlington channel reported pulling back for multiple inbound plane warnings in the morning; TV reporter David Statter and the Fort Myer Fire Department log both described receiving another inbound aircraft warning around 11:30 a.m. Some people pulled back mistaking as threats the military jets and helicopters that flew over the Pentagon in the morning. Rumors of bomb threats and other alarming hearsay also caused some responders to retreat. No doubt localized evacuations of some parts of the building occurred because hazardous conditions endangered firefighters and rescuers.[55]

The disruptive evacuations kept firefighters "on the get go," requiring them to scramble back and forth in full protective gear between the building and safer areas, draining their energy. Captain Durrer from Reagan National remembered that on two or three occasions he had to drop everything, run back across to Washington Boulevard, and stay there for a while. "Then they'd clear us and we'd come back across and, you know, we kept getting them." Search and rescue efforts were also interrupted. Captain Howes found that the periods between evacuations were too short for his Reagan National firefighters, loaded with heavy tools, to complete their assignment. Each time they got into the building, they made it "virtually nowhere" before being evacuated again. Of most serious consequence, the morning evacuations cost firefighters progress already made in suppressing the E Ring fire and allowed it to rekindle with greater intensity. Frustrated as he waited behind a barrier, firefighter Cary Henry saw the outer fire gain strength. The interruptions also delayed firefighters from advancing on the interior fires and suppressing them.[56]

Still, fire officers gained a few precious minutes during the morning inbound plane evacuation to regroup and organize their plans of attack. Arlington's Chief White held an impromptu meeting with EMS officers so they could be "smarter going back in." Howes used the time to plan search missions and update newly-arriving colleagues. Alan Wallace and Mark Skipper, the firefighters who had been at the Heliport during the attack, finally had a spare moment to realize they were burned and needed medical attention.[57]

The arrival of some units was delayed by the second evacuation. Several District of Columbia units had reached the perimeter of the Pentagon area when they were told to stop and take cover under the overpasses because of the inbound plane report. On "pins and needles" as they waited 15 to 20 minutes, the firefighters were relieved when they saw a military jet fly overhead. After the all clear, they moved up to the Pentagon. Battalion Chief John Thumann and Sergeant Richard Zegowitz and their companies joined the Arlington firefighters on the Heliport side. Although Thumann checked in with the command post via radio and worked "in liaison" with Arlington's Suppression Branch, some of the D.C. units operated independently under their own commanders. This generated friction between the departments until Gibbs and Thumann, who knew one another, succeeded in achieving a measure of coordination.[58]

Fighting the Fire "Tooth and Nail"

Interruptions made it difficult for the firefighters to make progress; not until about an hour after impact could they mount a sustained effort against the interior fires. When the firefighters first arrived, the fire burned most intensely on the first two floors near the blast hole and in the E, D, and C Rings. After the collapse and during the evacuations, the interior fires intensified, spreading upward and northward into unrenovated Wedge 2 toward Corridor 5. Although the fire suppression system in the renovated area had helped slow the fire from spreading more widely in Wedge 1, by this time it was blazing on all five floors in the outer three rings of the unrenovated areas. The immediate goal was to prevent the fire from jumping past the C Ring.[59]

After waiting on the Pentagon outskirts until the threat of a second aircraft attack had passed, David Tinsley steered D.C.'s Tower 10 truck carefully across the lawn to avoid the thick debris that might puncture his tires. Observing the still expanding fire, he positioned the truck with its long ladder to the left of the impact site and hooked up to a water supply. Gary McKethan operated the bucket at the top, while Tinsley operated the levers below. For the next few hours, they directed a stream of water into the interior through windows that had been burned out, carefully avoiding hitting the firefighters below going in and out of Corridor 5. McKethan operated in stop-and-go fashion, waiting for crews to assess the interior before he "threw" more water from the bucket. Later, to avoid getting stuck in the wet ground, Tinsley repositioned the heavy truck from the grass onto a cement pad. As specialized tower truck operators the two understood their mission and had little interaction with other departments or the Arlington command structure.[60]

Firefighters at the Heliport found the foam mixture worked well to extinguish the external fires and those in the outer ring, but when they directed it toward the blazing inner reaches of the blast zone, whirlwinds blew the foam back out. It seemed evident to Gibbs, in command of fire suppression there, that the foam was ineffective for fighting the interior fire.[61]

The depth of the building made it difficult to attack the innermost part of the conflagration, in the C Ring. Even Tower 10 had a limited reach. As the interior continued to blaze, it soon became clear that the firefighters had to go deeper inside the Pentagon and fight the fire up close, a far more dangerous and labor-intensive undertaking than directing streams from the outside. They had to "tooth and nail it," as D.C. Deputy Fire Chief Martin put it, resulting in "some pretty hairy moments" for some of the firefighters battling inside.[62]

After about 11:00 a.m., the firefighters concentrated a two-pronged attack on the interior fires. On the Heliport side, multiple teams of firefighters moved inward from the E Ring using Corridor 5 as their primary route. From the Center Court, firefighters went outward toward the E Ring, moving through the rings and floors successively. The fires that raged in the C Ring, deep in the building, proved the most difficult to extinguish. There were too few firefighters to fight the inner ring fires effectively until additional help arrived as the day advanced.[63]

The firefighters carried heavy, large-diameter supply hoses into the building and connected them to thinner, hand-held lines. The size of the Pentagon, its honeycomb structure, and the diverse layout of areas and offices on the different floors and rings, made this an arduous, energy-draining task. To reach the fires on the upper floors the firefighters connected sections of hoses together and stretched them down the long corridors and up the stairwells. Because the building's damaged water system now had very low pressure, the water supply had to come from exterior hydrants, rather than the building standpipes. From the Center Court the firefighters had to extend large-diameter supply hoses to hydrants outside the building, where civilian and military volunteers assisted in connecting and stretching out the fire hoses.[64]

The fire suppression efforts required careful coordination as the firefighters advanced into the inner rings. Working from both directions and on different floors, the teams were out of sight of each other. Under no circumstances did they want to move forward while an inferno raged beneath them. As Martin explained, they made sure there was no floor space between groups of firefighters: "If you were on two, there was somebody on one, because fire below you is a really bad thing." Seeing puddles of water boiling on the concrete floor under

SECOND FLOOR DAMAGE

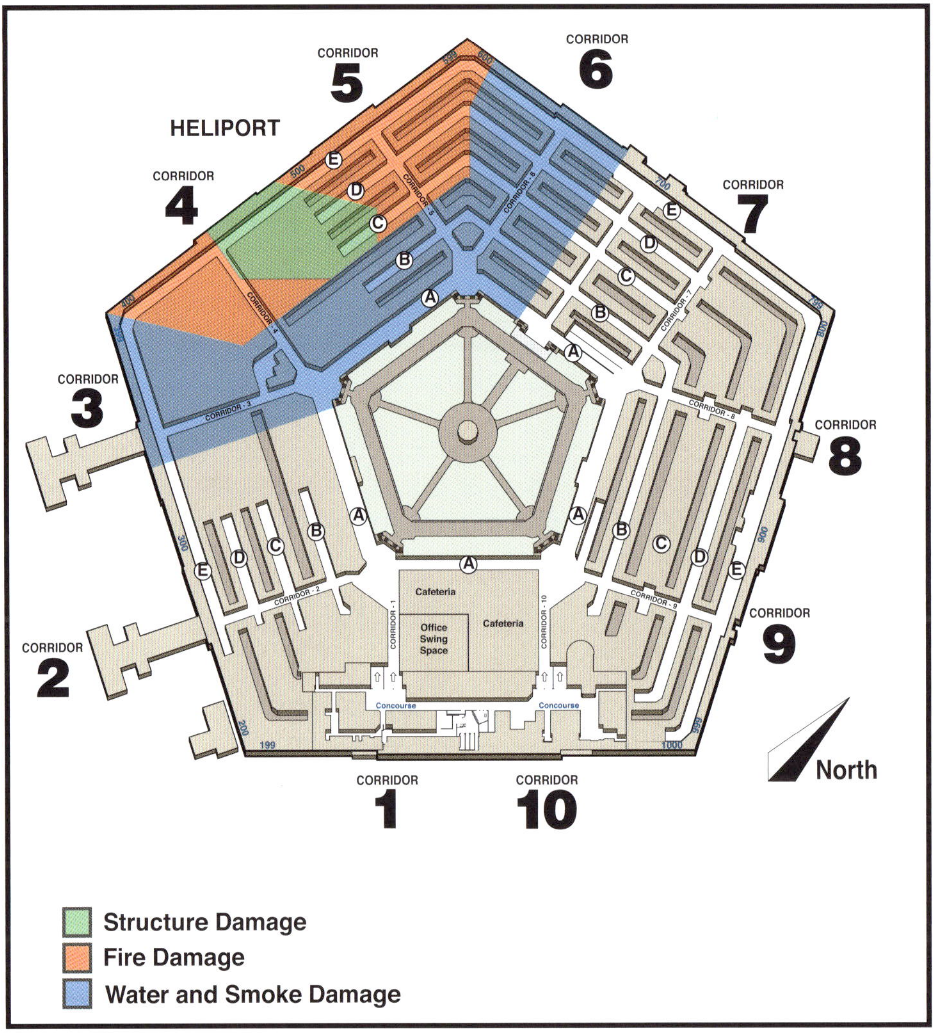

their feet, one group of firefighters backed out because the fire burned too hot on the floor below.[65]

Dense smoke and limited visibility made for dangerous and challenging conditions. Many of the electrical fixtures were damaged or destroyed, and the darkness obscured hazards such as the "hot" electrical wires strewn about. With water pooling on the floors, electrocution remained a threat until building engineers managed to shut off the electrical power to the affected areas. Moreover, the firefighters "encountered some of the highest heat conditions they had ever experienced in any fire." The jet fuel burned fiercely hot, intensified by the radiant heat coming from the center of the crash site. Estimates of maximum interior temperatures ranged up to 2,000° Fahrenheit.[66]

Each firefighter working inside carried a respirator such as the "SCBA" (self-contained breathing apparatus), but the air supply lasted only 45 to 60 minutes, not much time to navigate the large building and fight the blaze. Despite the risks, some delayed using the respirators, breathing in the smoky air as long as they dared, to prevent being "out of air before they got to a place at which they were able to do any kind of significant tactical operations." One unit tried several times to extend to the 3rd Floor a supply hose and attach hand lines to it. Because they had difficulty getting the hoses connected, their air supply ran out before they could finish. In the end, the unit commander refused to let them try again until more of the fire was extinguished. Some units ran short on respirators and air bottles. As a result of this experience, after 11 September departments enlarged their stocks and ensured that air packs were interchangeable between regional departments.[67]

After most of the fire had been put out in the E Ring, units moved into the D Ring through Corridor 5. Battalion Chief Thumann led a group of D.C. firefighters deep into the building, going first, checking the walls and ceilings for spalling (cracking) that might cause hot blocks of concrete to fall on them. They put out pockets of fire as they moved through burnt-out office suites. Their hand-held lines reached far enough for them to avoid having to crawl over charred desks and shifting debris, but the full hoses were heavy. The work was exhausting and no doubt seemed endless.[68]

As the fire suppression units beat back the fires, moving up successive floors and deeper into the rings, other teams continued to search. By late afternoon they could search the upper floors more thoroughly. Reagan National's Defina led Arlington and Fairfax firefighters from the Heliport to the E and D Rings to check for bodies and survivors. Advancing down long corridors and breathing hard from their labor and load of equipment, they rapidly exhausted their air supply, making it difficult to reach some of the inner locations. Another group from Reagan National and Alexandria wielded hydraulic and other tools to force entry through closed doors but found no one. While working on the 5th Floor they used a part of the 3rd Floor, burned so badly it was open and ventilated, as a refuge where they could regroup and breathe freely. Tower 10's long ladder came in handy to reach the upper floors; when one Alexandria firefighter was overcome by heat exhaustion and dehydration, he was hastily lowered to the ground in its bucket.[69]

Additional ladder trucks arriving during the afternoon allowed the firefighters to gain greater access to the interior fires on the upper levels. They set up "ladder-pipe" operations—hoses running up the ladders and attached to a nozzle at the tip—to reach the upper floors, sometimes dropping the heavy hoses over windowsills or down the facade of the building rather than lugging them down corridors and up stairwells to reach the inner rings and upper floors. Still, it was not easy. Reagan National's Michael Murphy recollected that it took his group about 20 minutes just to smash through a 2nd Floor E Ring window from the inside in order to drop a hose down to a pumper truck.[70]

The building's structural complexity compounded the firefighters' problems. While Arlington, Reagan National, and Fort Myer responders had some familiarity with the building, firefighters from other jurisdictions did not. Military personnel gladly provided directions. One firefighter from Greenbelt, Maryland, operating out of the Center Court was confused by the layout. By sheer coincidence he spotted Commander George Navas, a naval officer he knew slightly through his son's Little League, and asked for help. Navas pulled down from the wall a renovation guide map and traced a path through the interior. Navas was not surprised that outsiders had difficulty finding their way around the "puzzle palace." Sailor Kevin Hazelwood, who remained in the Center Court for much of the day, led firefighters into and around the building.[71]

The renovation had made changes in Wedge 1 not yet familiar to most occupants. PENREN and building engineers advised the fire officers of corridor changes and structural peculiarities, providing them with maps and drawings of the building. Richard Fitzharris, a PENREN group leader, speaking in the morning with Schwartz about the building, noticed the chief had an outdated drawing. Fitzharris initiated a search for Stacie Condrell, a senior PENREN planner; somehow a DPS officer found her among the crowds by calling over a bullhorn. Condrell retrieved current drawings, took them to the command post, and explained the overall design and layout. She spent the day with the fire suppression command team at the Heliport and helped orient firefighters, FBI agents, and search and rescue teams. Captain Gibbs found the maps crucial as did D.C. Deputy Chief Martin, who used them to plot assignments and keep track of the firefighters, an absolute requirement for ensuring their safety. The extremely hazardous conditions made it a priority to maintain accountability. Fire Marshal Charles Burroughs from Reagan National and others at the Incident Command Post tracked the location of crews and what they were doing. Officers at the crash site set up their own systems to account for their units.[72]

During the afternoon, another evacuation disrupted the attack on the fire. Around 2:00 p.m. Schwartz received notice of another unidentified aircraft headed for the Pentagon. Once again, the firefighters had to drop their hoses, climb down high ladders or flights of stairs, and take cover several hundred yards away. When Schwartz learned that the plane bore federal officials, he ordered his men and women back to fight the fire.[73]

The Roof Fire

As the firefighters made progress against the interior fires a new challenge emerged. Early in the day Fitzharris warned Schwartz that a hidden layer of highly flammable old wood under the Pentagon's slate roof might pose a threat. If the wood ignited, fire could spread rapidly through the roof and affect much of the building. By late afternoon it was evident that the fire had indeed ignited parts of the Pentagon roof.[74]

The original pitched roofs, capped by slate shingles, covered the E and A Rings and the 10 radial corridors, while the rest of the building had flat concrete roofs covered by a layer of granite chips. The pitched slate roof began from the bottom with a 4 1/2-inch inverted V-shape concrete slab supported by columns. Underneath the slab was a 2-inch layer of insulation, above it a covering of tarpaper on which stood 2"x2" sleepers (timbers) 16 inches apart that had a wooden sheathing of random-width planks nailed to them. At the very top, 1/4-inch to 3/8-inch slate shingles were affixed to the wood below. The open spaces in the sheathing/sleeper structure made conditions ripe for open combustion, allowing the fire to spread rapidly. With few, if any, "stops" (breaks that flames could not jump across) in the pitched roofs, the blaze could run freely along the wood layer. Burning between the hard slate and concrete, the fire was difficult to access.[75]

Several hypotheses suggest how the wooden layer caught fire. The blast may have spewed jet fuel onto the roof, saturating it, although it is difficult to envision how the fuel seeped through the slate layers. Or, when the giant fireball rolled over the top of the building, falling debris may have penetrated the roof line. Another plausible theory is that the collapse exposed wooden roof areas of the E Ring, making them vulnerable as the fire intensified and spread upward.[76]

In the afternoon a team searching the 5th Floor unsuccessfully attempted to reach the fire. Typically with a roof fire, firefighters would "poke holes in the ceiling and rip the ceiling down" then "take a ladder and stick a nozzle up in there and put the fire out." But Captain Howes found that this "bullet proof building," with its concrete decking, rendered these tactics useless. The roof fire burned so long because they "just couldn't get to it."[77]

Crews climbed up truck ladder extensions or from the 5th Floor onto the roof and tried to put out the fire from above. D.C.'s Tower 10 used its bucket to ferry equipment up to the roof. Groups of firefighters attacked different sectors. Some time after 2:00 p.m. D.C. Chief Charles Drumming took command of several Alexandria and Arlington companies that worked on one sector of the obstinate fire for "a long period of time," he remembered. These firefighters thought the roof had been "breached" from below but were not certain where or how. They called on the Fairfax County Urban Search and Rescue team to use a powerful saw known as a "Dig Bird" to cut a hole in the E Ring roof. Even with the special tool this took considerable time. After finding the inner layer of wood and the concrete below, they concluded that the fire was "moving along the various sections of the roof" above the crash site.[78]

As darkness fell on 11 September, Chief Schwartz withdrew the crews from the roof, switching from an offensive to a defensive strategy. He distrusted the pitched roof's safety as a working platform for the fatigued firefighters since he knew neither the scope of the damage done to the roof nor its soundness. Also he was uncertain about the structure and composition of the roofing materials and whether there was insulation that might be acting as an accelerant.* Danger threatened at every turn; in the dim lighting one could easily slip on the sloping roof and fall into the wide gaps between the rings and radial corridors.[79]

* It is unclear to what extent insulation, known by the name of horsehair, proved an accelerant, in that it lay above the 5th Floor ceiling but below the concrete slab, and was not present in the wooden sheathing layer of the pitched roof through which the fire spread.

Until daybreak firefighters fought the roof fire from the outside with large streams of water pumped up through ladder pipes and large monitor nozzles to try to contain the fire. Not everyone was happy with the decision. One participant likened this standoff to "babysitting" the fire. An onlooker, Lieutenant Colonel Harold Campbell, found the battle dramatic. He saw outlined against the night sky a fireman standing on a ladder, shooting water down onto the roof: "The fire goes away and he stays up there because it comes right back. . . . It just doesn't go away."[80]

By daybreak the roof fire was still making significant headway. Determined DoD workers who returned to their offices on the morning of 12 September saw firefighters still pumping water onto the burning roof. The overnight spraying had done little to stop the flames; they stubbornly kept rekindling. Ultimately, the roof fire did not critically affect the building's structural stability, but the televised scenes of the flames that allowed the world to watch the Pentagon burn overnight made things seem worse than they were. According to Schwartz, the night of 11 September Secretary Rumsfeld kept asking when the fire was going to be out so "he could have his building back." A report that the roof fire was approaching crucial communication equipment heightened anxiety; if damaged, Defense command and control capabilities would be seriously compromised. Fortunately, the firefighters prevented the fire from reaching that far.[81]

New crews rotated in. The only way to reach the fire was to open up the roof. In a backbreaking task, the firefighters swung heavy sledgehammers to smash through the slate and wood and put hose streams into the holes to stop the fire's spread. It became a chase: "If you put some water in the middle, then the fire is going to go out to the left. If you put water out to the left, it's going to go back to the right." Once a fire had gotten into the wood in the open spaces, the best thing was "to cut it off" on two ends. The most viable and safest tactic, although time-consuming, was to make trench cuts on either side of the fire to serve as firebreaks and so prevent the flames from traveling all the way around the building. There were hazards; if the firefighters did not make the cuts sufficiently far from the wood burning underneath, they could fall through the weakened structure. Fatigued as they were, their judgment could easily be impaired. To avoid risk, they made the cuts well away from the burning areas and then left the fire to burn

ROOF DAMAGE

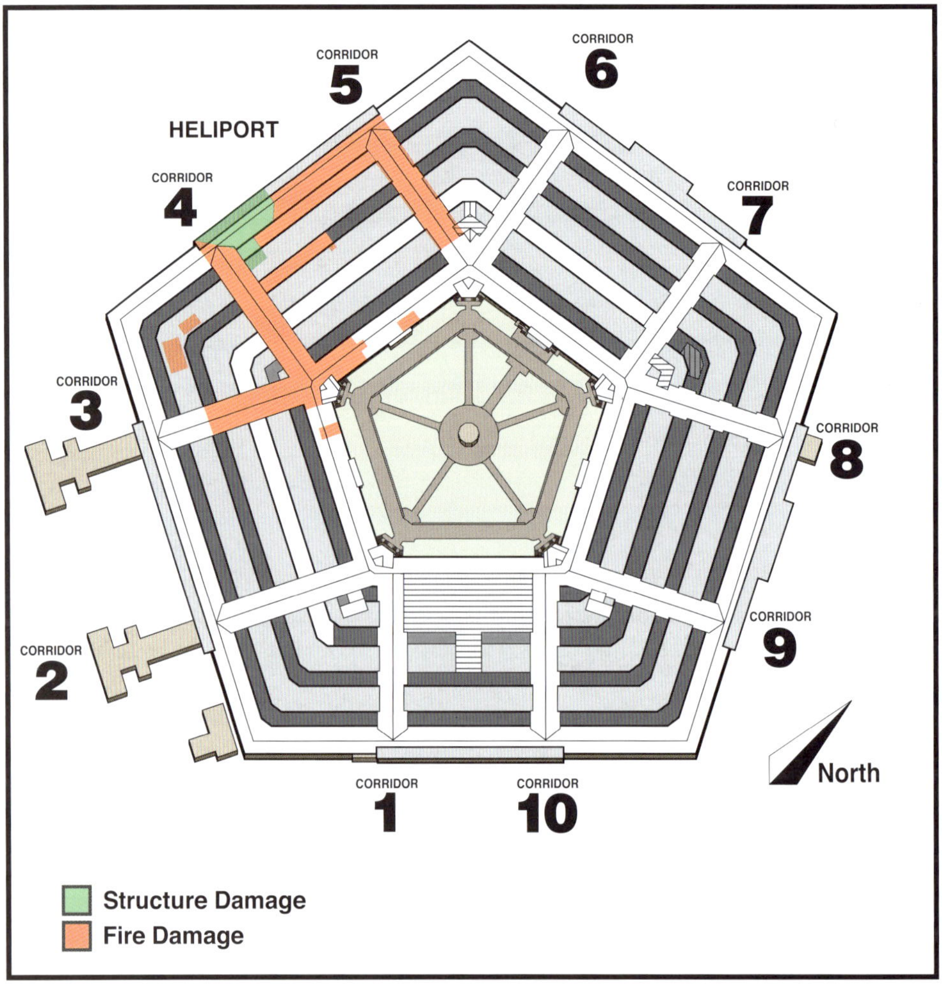

between the cuts. While this may have allowed more of the roof to burn, it kept the firefighters safe.[82]

The firefighters continued battling the roof fire throughout the morning and afternoon of the 12th except when they were interrupted briefly around 10:00 a.m. by another evacuation order in response to a mistaken warning of an inbound plane.[83] By early evening, for the most part both the roof and the interior fires had been contained. At 6:00 p.m. Arlington County issued a cautious press release stating that the Fire Department considered the fire "controlled" but not fully "extinguished"; it might flare up again. Over the course of the next few days, firefighters mopped up some hot spots on the roof, but the need to do so was minimized when a contractor cleared debris all the way down to the concrete roof base. In the end, fire burned the roof of E Ring between Corridors 4 and 5, as well as the roofs of those corridors, part of A Ring near Corridor 4, and part of Corridor 3.[84]

In succeeding days, the firefighters extinguished small fires caused when residual heat ignited pools of jet fuel that remained in the building. On the 13th, TV cameras caught a flare-up of rubble in the collapsed area that Schwartz knew had continued to smolder. It led to a wryly humorous moment when a concerned television viewer in San Francisco called the Arlington County 911 number to report that "the Pentagon was on fire again." As Schwartz remarked, the visual was graphic, but the flare-up posed little threat.[85]

Searching and Shoring

Fighting fire is only one of the tasks confronting fire departments. Integral to the central work of firefighting is searching for survivors and preventing building collapse. A huge and intense fire such as that at the Pentagon demanded search and shoring resources far beyond those possessed by the Arlington and other fire departments that came to its assistance. As the fire raged on during the morning of the 11th, Schwartz recognized that the formidable task facing him would require the services of many more highly skilled, specialized, and well-equipped professional units. Fortunately, such assistance was available from Army engineers and Urban Search and Rescue Teams (US&R) from Fairfax County, Virginia, Montgomery County, Maryland, and elsewhere. Schwartz requested the dispatch of the US&R teams.

Although highly qualified for search, rescue, and shoring operations, these units could not arrive in time—within the first hour after the attack—to rescue any survivors. The initial mission assigned them by Schwartz after they began arriving in the afternoon of the 11th was to search the impact area to the extent possible and report on the conditions they encountered. They noted bodies and body remains but in accordance with instructions left them for the FBI to deal with. Their main contribution thereafter—an indispensable one—was shoring up areas of the building in danger of collapse.[86]

The only one of its kind in the U.S. Army, the engineer company of the Military District of Washington (MDW), stationed at Fort Belvoir, 15 miles south of the Pentagon, had the mission of rescuing survivors of building breakdowns and preventing such collapses in emergencies. Intended chiefly for employment in the National Capital Region, before 11 September its services had never been called on.[87]

The company's 76 soldiers included a heavy platoon equipped with bulldozers, bucket loaders, dump trucks, and other equipment; a light platoon of four squads, each with a leader and two three-soldier teams to carry out confined-space rescue operations and render medical assistance; and a command and logistical platoon. Equipment included high-speed saws, steel-cutting torches, jackhammers, breathing equipment, and lumber and other materials for use in shoring up structures.[88]

Shortly after the attack, MDW alerted the company and Captain Aaron Barta prepared his troops for deployment; within 40 minutes, they were ready to go. At the direction of MDW Commander Major General James Jackson, Barta flew by helicopter with his Initial Reconnaissance Team (IRT), one of the four light rescue squads, to Fort McNair in the nation's capital. There he conferred with Jackson, who told him to delay committing the engineer company because of concerns about another possible attack in the Washington area. Jackson and Barta then proceeded to the Pentagon, which they reached after 12:00 p.m., and reported to Schwartz. Soon after, Jackson gave the order to deploy the full company to the site. The IRT arrived from Fort McNair by 1:00 p.m. With the help of a police escort, the rest of the company from Fort Belvoir reached the Pentagon sometime between 2:00 p.m. and 3:00 p.m.[89]

About a half hour after his troops from Fort Belvoir arrived Captain Barta ordered one three-soldier rescue team into the impact area to assess damage and rescue any survivors on the 1st and 2nd Floors. Although equipped with breathing equipment, the team could not progress very far into the building because of the intense heat and thick smoke. In the short time spent in the building the soldiers found no survivors but reported seeing "lots of bodies [but] ... no signs of life."[90]

Less than an hour later another rescue team headed by Sergeant Eric Godbehere entered the Pentagon from the south side between Corridors 3 and

4 and approached the impact area, making their way through hallways littered with rubble. When they opened doors "to some of the rooms . . . the temperature would jump up 50 to 100 degrees." As the team members advanced, the more they encountered "rooms that ... [weren't] even recognizable as rooms anymore." They found no one alive. Godbehere estimated that his team encountered about 20 bodies or remains during the days that they searched.[91]

Like the firefighters who had preceded them, the search teams had to endure an environment of high heat, toxic smoke, poor lighting, and mounds of rubble in a still smoldering building. During the early searches the possibility existed that more of the partially collapsed building might fall on them, a calamity they later helped to avoid by laboring desperately to shore up weakened areas.

To keep track of rescuers inside the building, each soldier had a Velcro name tag attached to his helmet. As the soldiers entered the Pentagon, each removed his name tag and handed it to a checker, who placed it on a display board indicating each team's working area. Team members retrieved their tags and returned them to their helmets as they left the building. Each team had a hand-held radio for communication with the command post. Team members also wore an alarm that sounded if they failed to move after a short period of time. By 5:30 p.m. the Army engineers had determined that no one remained alive in the searched areas.[92]

In an additional dangerous task some of the engineers assisted the firefighters in battling the persistent roof fire that continued to imperil the building through the second day. Working on the sloping roof they cut and punctured holes in the slate to permit ventilation of the fire in the wooden sheathing below. They spent many hours on the roof, not descending until about 9:00 p.m. on 11 September.[93]

In response to Schwartz's morning request, highly-trained Federal Emergency Management Agency (FEMA) units joined in the search phase during the afternoon and in subsequent work in the building for the next 10 days. Trucks and buses brought in the US&R teams from Fairfax and Montgomery Counties. Schwartz and the Army engineer company had worked with both of them previously. The Fairfax team pulled into the Pentagon staging area about 2:00 p.m.; the Montgomery team arrived later in the afternoon.[94]

Established in 1989 by FEMA, the national Urban Search and Rescue Team program received half of its normal operating and training expenses from the federal government while local jurisdictions covered the other half. In September 2001, 28 US&R groups around the country, each with about 62 members, were subject to recall on six hours' notice, drawing federal pay only when activated. The well-trained men and women of these groups, working at civilian jobs until called to duty, possessed emergency firefighting, engineering, construction, medical, search-dog handler, and other specialized skills. Normally, each team deployed search, rescue, technical, and medical sections.[95]

The US&R teams, equipped with "sensitive listening equipment . . . medical supplies as well as enough food, water and shelter . . . for up to 72 hours," provided emergency response to natural and man-made disasters. Their availability to provide direct support in local emergencies largely relieved state and local jurisdictions subject to fires, earthquakes, floods, hurricanes, and tornadoes from having to buy and maintain specialized equipment and train personnel.[96]

Late on 11 September Schwartz asked FEMA to deploy two more teams to the Pentagon site to assist the Fairfax and Montgomery units. A team of 77 people from Virginia Beach, Virginia, arrived in Washington that evening, spent the night awaiting orders, and did not reach the Pentagon until early the next afternoon. Meanwhile, after driving all night, a team from Memphis, Tennessee, arrived at the site at noon, shortly before the Virginia Beach team. Thereafter, the two Virginia teams worked the 6:00 p.m. to 6:00 a.m. shift; the Maryland and Tennessee teams handled daytime duties. During the second week of the operation, a US&R team from New Mexico arrived to relieve the Fairfax and Montgomery units.[97]

Over a two-week period teams performed with dedication and perseverance under the direction of a FEMA Incident Support Team (IST)* responsible to Schwartz. The US&R teams joined the Army engineers in searching for survivors and body remains and reporting conditions in the building. With more people and resources than the Army engineer company could muster they did most of the shoring on the 1st and 2nd Floors and helped fight the roof fires.[98]

* ISTs are composed of highly experienced specialists drawn from all parts of the country who are rapid responders to crises and coordinate and supervise the US&R teams. They are responsible to the Incident Commander.

Preventing the collapse of ceilings, floors, and walls, and especially the supporting columns greatly weakened by the impact of Flight 77 and the resulting fire, became the major task of the US&R teams and the Army engineer company. Once the teams had determined that no one remained alive in the affected area, it became critical to protect the lives of other responders, who could not be permitted to enter damaged segments of the building until they were judged safe.

The shoring units faced a formidable task. The building had sustained massive damage. "Exterior blast, interior blast, kinetic impact, and fire all impacted the structure with enormous force." Most of the columns in the collapsed zone had been destroyed and some of the remaining ones were "stripped and bowed, retaining little structural strength," causing the E Ring section collapse almost 40 minutes after the attack.[99]

The first shoring operation did not begin until 11:45 p.m. on 11 September. To safeguard entry into Army and Navy offices on the 1st Floor E Ring, Army engineers and Fairfax and Montgomery US&R team members reinforced an exterior Pentagon wall just north of the impact point toward Corridor 5. Around a damaged column, the teams typically placed a "crib," chiefly 6"x6" wooden timbers 4 to 6 feet long in a box as high as 15.5 feet, even using cribs to replace columns completely eliminated by the crash. The box-like reinforcement rose as alternating pairs of timbers emplaced from floor to ceiling like "Lincoln Log" toy structures. The teams also employed a "nine-point crib" three-by-three layout that had a load capacity of 68 tons; one solid crib of eight-by-eight layout had an estimated capacity of 576 tons.[100]

The fast pace of work by the engineers and US&R units soon consumed the lumber brought with them to the site. To assure the speediest delivery of the huge supply of timbers still required, PENREN officials and FEMA authorized purchases of materials on the local retail market. Commercial firms responded quickly in supplying the additional structural reinforcing materials, estimated to have cost hundreds of thousands of dollars.[101]

Overall, US&R teams and the Army engineers shored 42 damaged or destroyed columns on the 1st Floor and 6 columns on the 2nd Floor. Some of this shoring created supports where none had existed before, further guaranteeing the stability of the building. Another 40 columns on the two floors received some shoring. No shoring was needed on the upper floors. For more than a week the US&R and Army engineer units worked in shifts 24 hours a day on structural operations, laboring long hours under appalling conditions that afflicted the senses. Their labors prevented further deterioration of areas adjacent to the collapsed space.[102]

To oversee the emergency shoring work PENREN called on Allyn Kilsheimer, head of several Washington, D.C., structural engineering companies and widely experienced in dealing with building disasters. Kilsheimer arrived on the scene about 5:00 p.m. on 11 September and soon after entered the building to assess its condition, especially how far inside it was safe to go, providing guidance to emergency teams and occupants seeking to reenter. He directed shoring teams on what had to be done and where, seeing the work through to a successful conclusion during the next weeks. Subsequently, he accepted responsibility for demolition and rebuilding of the destroyed area of the Pentagon. His contribution to the recovery effort—saving endangered areas—would be widely acknowledged.[103]

Logistics

A number of agencies, of which the Arlington Emergency Operations Center (EOC) was chief, provided crucial communications and logistics support to the firefighting. Activated only in times of disaster, EOC was staffed by county officials and workers who supported all emergency field operations. Around the clock for 14 days EOC oversaw to good effect the flow of replacement personnel, equipment, shelter, food, and water to the Pentagon; yet the center was not without deficiencies in performing these difficult tasks, especially in the early days.[104]

Within 15 minutes of the crash, the EOC was in full operation at municipal headquarters two miles north of the Pentagon. Captain Mark Penn, on only his second day as deputy coordinator of emergency services, assumed management of staff operations with the assistance of Battalion Chief Ray Blankenship; both were from the Arlington Fire Department. The county manager led the decisionmaking, and senior county officials, including the fire chief, served as policy advisers.[105]

Penn ran the center for some 20 hours straight. The first few hours at EOC were "chaotic." Fire and police officers at the Pentagon could not be reached, forcing the center to rely on media reports until direct communication with the command post was finally established. DoD officials communicated directly with the incident commander rather than coordinating through EOC.[106]

Expecting large numbers of casualties, Penn immediately secured additional EMS assistance. With the help of the Virginia Department of Emergency Management, Penn arranged for ambulances and medical units to come from as far away as Fredericksburg and the Shenandoah Valley, 50 to 100 miles to the south and west. Around 11:30 a.m. Arlington County Manager Ron Carlee declared a local state of disaster after consulting with Schwartz. Working with the Virginia state government, Carlee cut through the cumbersome process for obtaining state and federal assistance, facilitating rapid deployment of FEMA's Urban Search and Rescue Teams that Schwartz urgently needed.[107]

From start to finish, EOC had the primary responsibility for ensuring that the emergency workers received whatever they needed, even as requirements changed. By early afternoon, Schwartz had assigned Chief White to set up a logistics section at the site to coordinate equipment requests and pass them to EOC. Working with White and commanders who succeeded him, EOC requisitioned materials and specialized equipment. Supplied with catalogs, computers, and telephones and given carte blanche, purchasing agents culled from county offices secured a wide range of supplies—fencing, boots, bottles, hoses, airpacks, cranes, gloves, thermal imagers, fuel, dump trucks, school buses, and public works vehicles.[108]

Logistics also involved providing for daily needs—clothing, shelter, health, food, and sanitation—a gargantuan task, given that crews numbering many hundreds worked 24 hours a day. On scene, White found EOC staff indispensable, especially when portable toilets became an urgent necessity the first afternoon. For the first several days, EOC coordinated the supply of food and beverages. Penn relied on the food services contractor for the Arlington County Jail to feed emergency workers before the Red Cross, Salvation Army, volunteer agencies, and restaurant chains set up a variety of food services at an area designated Camp Unity on the Pentagon grounds.[109]

Help came from other quarters also. On the first day, when fire suppression was still crucial, private companies donated truckloads of bottled water, flashlights, batteries, and other critical equipment. On 12 September, a Wisconsin factory delivered specialty boots that workers desperately needed to replace their rubble-damaged ones. Early on, after Plaugher made a chance remark that the site would become a quagmire if it rained, the Army Corps of Engineers rapidly built an all-weather road that became the primary access route to the site for all vehicles; the engineers also installed telephone and electric cables. PENREN, too, supplied equipment, supplementing the EOC system. On the first day it procured backhoes, dump trucks, dumpsters, cranes, generators, and light towers—all indispensable for the heavy work under way. At White's request the Fairfax County Fire Department sent an experienced logistics team to assist. In Schwartz's opinion logistical needs were met handsomely, but from time to time there were anxious moments.[110]

The EOC also helped coordinate activities of the many supporting organizations, including the Department of Health and Human Services, Environmental Protection Agency, Occupational Safety and Health Administration, U.S. Forest Service, Red Cross, and Salvation Army. "You name it . . . everybody that we possibly could need was brought to bear on the problem," Penn later observed. A spirit of generosity and fellowship pervaded these support efforts, from the Arlington County Sheriff who brought 40 pizzas to the workers in the middle of the night to the local businessman who provided a warehouse.[111]

Operational Coordination

On the afternoon of 11 September Schwartz decided to institute a unified command team* in the belief that he would benefit by incorporating in the decisionmaking process key representatives from the principal responding agencies with jurisdictional responsibilities. Finding that some newly arriving agency representatives were not checking in at the command post or were unfamiliar with the Incident Command System, Schwartz also wanted to ensure that organizations operated within the system. He anticipated that more units from many local, state, and federal agencies and volunteer groups would arrive in the follow-

* The ICS provided also for adoption of a Unified Command (UC), "an important element in multi-jurisdictional or multi-agency domestic incident management. It provides guidelines to enable agencies with different legal, geographic, and functional responsibilities to coordinate, plan, and interact effectively. . . . In a UC structure, the individuals designated by their jurisdictional authorities jointly determine objectives, plans, and priorities and work together." (*National Incident Management System*, Dept of Homeland Security, 1 Mar 04, 14, 16.) Schwartz modified this UC by retaining final authority for the Incident Commander.

ing days, some of them unsolicited, making a centralized command team all the more essential to prevent utter chaos.

At a meeting in the Pentagon on the evening of 11 September, agency representatives—more than a hundred—introduced themselves. After describing the ICS Schwartz announced that he was appointing a unified command team, all the while emphasizing that his fire department had ultimate command and he would remain the final decisionmaker. At the end of the meeting, MDW Commander General Jackson introduced himself as the DoD representative "appointed to make sure" Schwartz got everything he needed. Later in the evening Schwartz met with the unified command team, including FBI agent Combs, Jackson, Arlington Police Chief Edward Flynn, and two FEMA representatives. Over the next days, the team held meetings at regular intervals to keep each other informed about developments.[112]

The evening of the 11th the FBI announced plans to set up a Joint Operations Center (JOC) at the Fort Myer Community Center that all responding federal agencies could use to facilitate their assistance to local entities. The FBI also planned to run its criminal investigation from the JOC. Although uncertain that it could be as effective at Fort Myer, Schwartz agreed to the FBI's request to move his command post to the JOC, which became operational by early morning on the 12th. The inadequacy of the new setup became apparent on the morning of the 12th when the air traffic control tower at Reagan National informed fire officers at the Pentagon that an airplane was approaching the building. This transmission bypassed the Incident Command Post at the JOC, which knew that the plane bore FEMA personnel. Arlington Assistant Chief Shawn Kelley—who replaced Schwartz at the JOC as incident commander for the day shift on the 12th and then regularly took over the night shift beginning the 14th—had difficulty breaking through the radio chatter but finally managed to inform the Pentagon firefighters that the plane was friendly.[113]

Schwartz realized that the incident commander could not function effectively so far from the action, especially when his only view of the incident scene was through fuzzy television monitors. On the 13th he moved the command post back to the Pentagon vicinity. Chief White served as Schwartz's representative at the JOC. FBI agent Combs returned to work on-site with Schwartz. White believed this arrangement worked well for the most part and that the two posts succeeded in making joint decisions as necessary.[114]

Presenting a "public face" was an important element of the unification and coordination process. While functioning as senior adviser to Schwartz, Chief Plaugher took on responsibility for managing public relations for the duration. As evening fell on 11 September he realized that no arrangements had been made to provide the public with reports. DoD's press office, although active, focused on the broad picture rather than details, and to Plaugher's disappointment the FBI had declined to set up a joint information center to fill that role. Americans urgently wanted news, particularly of the human toll, about which the media had only unofficial bits of information. To meet this need, Plaugher conducted a joint press conference with General Jackson at 11:00 p.m. Subsequently Dick Bridges, the Arlington County deputy manager, assumed the spokesman role, although Plaugher continued to make appearances.[115]

Dealing with the press could have misleading outcomes as Plaugher learned the day after the attack when he conscientiously estimated a range of 100 to 800 casualties. The press melodramatically reported the higher number. Among his other tasks, Plaugher greeted the vice president, members of Congress, and other high-ranking officials and dignitaries visiting the scene. He came away from the experience thoroughly convinced that the ICS should add a senior adviser akin to an "executive incident commander" to serve as "a big picture person."[116]

On the morning of the 12th, the incident commander began releasing firefighting crews from the District of Columbia and other nearby jurisdictions; fresh units replaced them. There were no fatalities among firefighters and other responders. Finally, at 7:00 a.m. on 21 September, the Arlington County Fire Department turned over control of the site to the FBI, which continued its search for evidence and remains at the declared crime site. Thereafter only a firefighting company, a technical rescue team, and paramedics remained on scene until control was turned back to DoD.[117]

After the fire was contained, late in the afternoon on 12 September Captain David Lange (Fairfax County) led a crew of firefighters and soldiers to the roof where they draped a huge American flag over the side of the building, just south of the impact point, near Corridor 4. The flag was unfurled moments before President Bush arrived at the Pentagon to witness the tragic scene and thank emergency workers. The president and Secretary Rumsfeld joined the gathering of fire and rescue workers and soldiers, shaking hands and offering words of encouragement. Secured on top of the roof, the flag waved gently in the breeze. For those present, the unveiling of the flag and the president's arrival helped lift morale after two days of unremitting toil and raw emotion. The picture of the huge flag flanked by firefighters and soldiers would become familiar to many, symbolizing not only the tragedy of 11 September but also the prevailing spirit of endurance and hope.[118]

Chapter V

Treating the Injured, Searching for Remains

In the hours and days after the attack firefighters, medical personnel, trained rescue teams, and other military and civilian responders and volunteers initially searched for survivors and later for human remains. They made their way into smoke-filled corridors to rescue the wounded, set up triage stations outside, and transported victims to local hospitals and clinics. During the terrifying time between the attack at 9:37 a.m. and the building evacuation ordered around 10:15 a.m. under threat of another attack, virtually all the injured who could be recovered were removed from the building.

The dead remained. Some were entombed under tons of rubble, some perished intact in their offices, some lay in stairwells or corridors where they had tried to escape, and some bodies were too battered or fragmented to be identifiable. Remains recovery proceeded in two steps—locating and removing bodies from the building, and sifting through debris gathered and deposited in North Parking. The difficult task of searching the wreckage for victims or parts of them, documenting their whereabouts, and removing them for identification fell principally to Federal Emergency Management Agency search and rescue teams, Army engineers, FBI agents, Marine Corps photographers, cadaver dogs and their handlers, and the young soldiers of the Old Guard (3rd Infantry Regiment) from Fort Myer. Not until 26 September was this sad work declared finished.

Medical Assistance

To nurse Deborah Lutgen, director of the Arlington Urgent Care Center a few blocks from the Pentagon, the concussion "felt like we . . . [were] in a huge warehouse . . . . A lot of the roof is metal and . . . the whole place kind of vibrated for quite some time afterwards."[1] Nearby at the Rader Army Health Clinic at Fort Myer, after announcing a "Code Yellow" for a mass casualty situation, officials ordered an evacuation of the building and once an all clear sounded stood by to receive casualties. Arlington County's Emergency Communications Center alerted several local hospitals to activate their disaster and emergency preparedness plans. Other trauma centers were notified by airport authorities or learned of the attack from news reports. The ECC dispatched Arlington County Emergency Medical Service units and asked nearby Fairfax County, Alexandria, and District of Columbia fire departments to send theirs.[2]

Two medical facilities, the Army's DiLorenzo Tricare Health Clinic (DTHC) and the Air Force Flight Medicine Clinic, provided outpatient care in the Pentagon. With over 200 staff people in newly relocated basement offices just inside the Corridor 8 entrance, the DiLorenzo Clinic offered primary and emergency care to DoD civilian employees and military from all of the services.[3] The smaller Air Force Clinic on the 4th Floor at 4A750, the apex between Corridors 7 and 8, served only Air Force military personnel. The attack did not find this in-house medical community unprepared for a large-scale disaster. Just as local and federal emergency preparedness units had trained to cope with contingencies involving weapons of mass destruction, the two clinics routinely staged mass casualty "tabletop" exercises. The scenario changed for each drill; presciently, training carried out the previous May supposed casualties resulting from an accidental crash of a twin-engine airliner into the west side of the building. This premise was adopted at the suggestion of Colonel John Baxter, commander of the Air Force Clinic, who, like everybody else in the building, was reminded often that the Pentagon was on the Reagan National Airport's flight path. The exercise assumed that the two Pentagon clinics would treat patients inside their facilities.[4] Instead, circumstances on 11 September compelled the medics to perform triage in the Center Court and in the parking lots, grassy areas, and roads surrounding the Pentagon.

Unlike many of their colleagues elsewhere in the building, people in the below-ground DiLorenzo Clinic did not feel or hear the impact of the crash. No lights flickered, no phones went dead. Ironically, the clinic's director, Army Colonel James Geiling, on duty that day at the Walter Reed Army Medical Center in northwest Washington, learned of the crash before his staff did. On phoning his office, he later recalled, he asked his secretary what was going on "and she said, 'What do you mean what's going on?' She hadn't even heard."[5] Moments later an Air Force officer raced into the clinic and shouted that a plane had hit the building and for everybody to get out. At first nobody knew the location of the disaster area; calls to the Defense Protective Service for information went unanswered. But there was an announcement to "evacuate, evacuate, evacuate" and hundreds of people and billowing smoke began filling the hallways. As patients began arriving or were carried in, the clinic activated its mass casualty plan.

Mass casualty situations called for the staff to assemble in the clinic's front lobby or, in the event of evacuation, rally outside the River Entrance by the flagpole. Major Lorie Brown, chief nurse and chairperson for the DiLorenzo Action Response Team, took charge in Geiling's absence. Her job, she later explained, was "to manage, medically, the scene, directing traffic as it were." Fairly quickly the team set up medical aid stations at several locations and, when communication was possible, deployed to areas as requested by the DPS. A 10-person team remained inside the clinic. Brown directed the triage site outside in the North Parking area near the Pentagon Athletic Club (PAC) and constituted new teams as needed.[6]

Pushing their way through the crowds leaving the building, the chief nurse of the Acute Care Section, Army Captain Jennifer Glidewell, and another medic headed inside toward the Center Court. Since she was familiar with mass casualty exercise procedures, Glidewell assisted patients there and directed other medically trained volunteers until the evacuation order about 10:15 a.m. forced most medical personnel and patients to leave the Center Court and retreat to the outside of the building.[7]

Colonel Baxter was attending a patient in the Air Force Clinic when he heard the alarms sounding. On going out into the 4th Floor hallway he realized "that this was not a fire drill. This was a true emergency." Baxter and others in the clinic grabbed prepared portable trauma packs and hurried to the DiLorenzo

Clinic where all Pentagon clinic staffs were to receive instructions. From there they went to Corridor 5 on the 2nd Floor at the A Ring where they treated a badly burned Army officer.*[8]

Despite the evacuation order, Baxter and five members of his medical team then headed upstairs to search for other wounded. As they moved up from floor to floor they encountered noxious smoke and a few people, whom they encouraged to leave the building. Finding no one on the 5th Floor they returned to the 1st Floor, eyes burning and throats choking. On reaching the Center Court the team began to treat patients lying on the ground. When the warning of another airplane threat came around 10:15, Baxter recalled, "we gathered up our equipment, the patients, and ... actually ran through the building" and out Corridor 8, where the team joined in the triage work near the PAC. Subsequently Baxter and his assistants made their way to the crash site on the west side of the building and helped set up triage areas for the critically injured. Concerned that he had left his clinic unlocked, later in the day Baxter and "several others were able to basically talk our way back into the Pentagon." In the clinic they "turned off all of the electrical equipment, secured the pharmacy, secured the safe with controlled substances, and then got . . . back out to the site." Late in the afternoon, when it seemed certain there were no more survivors to assist, Baxter sent his people home.[9]

Air Force Surgeon General Lieutenant General Paul Carlton, Jr., who had approved the Air Force proposal for the May exercise, made his way from his office on the 5th Floor to the DiLorenzo Clinic, volunteering to head one of the teams of medics that deployed to the Center Court, a seemingly safe area where people had begun to gather as they staggered from their offices. There he established a casualty collection point near the apex of Corridors 3 and 4, then led one of the teams back into the building to A-E Drive to rescue survivors from the C Ring. Based on a "lesson learned" from the recent exercise, medical personnel donned newly purchased blue flame-resistant vests with bright reflective stripes so that amid the confusion they could be identified as medics.[10]

Joining other medically trained personnel on duty in the building that morning was a skilled veteran of an earlier tragedy, Army nurse Lieutenant Colonel Patricia Horoho. In March 1994, as chief nurse of the hospital emer-

* Lieutenant Colonel Brian Birdwell. See Chapter III.

gency room at Fort Bragg, North Carolina, she had participated in the urgent response to the "Green Ramp" disaster, a terrible accident in which an Air Force F-16 fighter collided with a C-130 transport, then plummeted to the tarmac and careened into a parked C-141, killing 24 paratroopers and injuring and burning another 43.[11] On 11 September Horoho was assigned to the Army's Personnel and Health Management Policy Office, located on the north side of the Pentagon. Leaving from the Mall Entrance after the crash she came around the building toward the Heliport where she directed people to the safer grassy area near a tree that became known as the "triage tree." A driver who had stopped on Route 27 (Washington Boulevard) gave her a first-aid bag containing basic medical materials, and she borrowed a belt from a senior officer to use as a tourniquet. She instructed volunteers how to employ an intravenous tube and treated survivors with puncture wounds from blast fragments and others who were burned or had inhaled toxic smoke.[12]

In the first hours after Flight 77 struck the Pentagon, many health care providers materialized from off-site to offer their services. Eventually, Horoho recalled, "we had physicians from Walter Reed. We had physicians from Bethesda [Naval Hospital]. We had physicians and nurses from all civilian hospitals in the area, as well as the medical . . . students from the Industrial College of the Armed Forces" at Fort McNair in Washington.[13] From the Rader Clinic at Fort Myer came a team of five physicians and a physician's assistant led by Colonel John Roser, who had been alerted virtually at the time of impact that morning. Roser thought they could reach the Pentagon more quickly on foot than by vehicle so they "high tailed it down there"; partway they were picked up by a man driving a van. Eventually other Rader medics with two patient transport vehicles joined them. At the Pentagon they divided into smaller teams under the direction of Arlington County Fire and EMS officers, treating an estimated half-dozen patients. Remaining at Fort Myer, Colonel Lorraine Jennings, deputy commander for clinical services and nursing, set up three triage areas for possible use in an adjoining parking lot, and oversaw the emergency operations center inside the clinic.[14]

Dr. James Vafier, medical director of Alexandria's Fire and Emergency Medical Services, accompanying a unit of paramedics on a mission that morning, was less than two miles from the Pentagon when the airplane struck. When

Vafier arrived shortly after 10:00 a.m., Arlington County Assistant Fire Chief John White, commanding the EMS Branch under the incident command system, appointed him the command physician. Beside Route 27 Vafier set up the standard color-coded triage arrangement for determining the order of treatment and evacuation of patients: red for people needing immediate care, yellow for those whose treatment could wait, and green for those whose injuries were slight. Vafier did not set up a black site for those with injuries so severe they had little chance of survival and could benefit only from palliative measures.[15]

Vafier and Horoho assumed primary responsibility for coordinating medical operations near the impact site. Assisting them was Air Force Master Sergeant Noel Sepulveda, one of the first people on the scene. A reservist on active duty at an Air Force office in Arlington, Sepulveda had been a combat medic in Vietnam many years earlier. That morning he had gone to the Pentagon to take a promotion test only to learn that it had been cancelled. On returning to South Parking to get his motorbike, Sepulveda watched Flight 77 smash into the building. The explosion knocked him back against a pole, but not realizing that he had sustained a head injury he ran around the building to join rescue efforts and help set up the triage station, using a bullhorn to summon medical personnel in the immediate vicinity.[16]

The main difficulty in treating casualties resulted not from organizational confusion or jurisdictional disputes but from the immense size of the Pentagon and its many exits, which made it difficult at times to determine where available resources were most needed. Firefighters battled the blaze on two fronts—on the west side of the building and from the Center Court. The injured were evacuated via several routes, emerging randomly hundreds of yards apart. Victims who could not be evacuated through the blazing outer rings to the west side were initially taken to the Center Court, where many of the most seriously injured were gathered. Also, in the first half hour many people stopped at the DiLorenzo Clinic for treatment. From both places and from the triage site near the Pentagon Athletic Club area, people moved to the huge North Parking area.

Sometime around 10:15 a.m., medical operations were disrupted when Incident Commander Schwartz, alarmed by reports of another attack, ordered evacuation of the crash site and building vicinity. Chief White remembered telling the medics on the west side, "I don't care what you've got to do, get these people ... out of here, and you all figure out where you're going to take them once you get en route. Just get them out." As a result, he added, "no matter what their criticality was, they immediately became load-and-go patients. And within five minutes, they were gone."[17] Major Brown of the DiLorenzo Clinic found that the evacuation order "really hindered us, the chaos began again."[18] Medical personnel helped patients who were in the clinic out of the building, taking whatever equipment and supplies they could carry. From the Center Court the injured were loaded onto small vehicles used for moving cargo through the wide hallways of the Pentagon, and then taken out to the north side of the building. Treatment of injured at the casualty collection point near the Pentagon Athletic Club close by North Parking was moved across the road to a grassy area along the Potomac River. Those victims already outside near the impact area relocated beneath the overpass at the intersection of Columbia Pike and Route 27. When it was learned that the fourth hijacked airliner had crashed, search and rescue efforts resumed around 10:40. On the north side, although the DiLorenzo Clinic staff never received an official all clear, some medical teams gathered up their equipment and supplies and headed back inside.[19]

On the west side, the treatment area from beneath the overpass was moved onto Route 27 in the lane adjacent to the Heliport.[20] Chief White described the scene:

> And finally it got to a point where I commandeered one of our EMS supervisor's vehicles that had a public address system in it and I got in and identified myself to the crowd . . . [and] said, "Here's the plan. So just stand fast where you are. As the casualties are brought out by the firefighters, they're going to come to this particular point out here on the heliport. When they do, they're going to be transferred to you people and here is where they're going to go and here is who is going to tell you where to take them."[21]

After the evacuation, with all medical people outside and more visible, tighter organization became possible. Vafier confirmed that "once a command structure was set up, it really started to flow much, much better." Some medics were relocated; Major Brown took over the red triage area for acute care near the impact site. That area became known informally as the "triage street," according to Staff Sergeant Keith Pernell, who commented that it "became a famous meet area for the medics, that was our meeting point for all meetings, commander briefs, and all that stuff."

By the time the reorganized triage operation materialized it became clear, as White noted, that there were "no [more] casualties" at the impact site. "All the casualties got taken care of prior to the first evacuation."[22] No victims remained in the Center Court, so medics there treated firefighters and volunteers suffering from smoke inhalation, dehydration, and exhaustion. Brown summarized the status of the medical response by mid- to late-morning: "Getting more organized; getting more equipment on the scene and more drugs. At one point we had the police bring in narcotics and paralytics [relaxants] to the scene in case of more serious patients. That's what we spent the next couple of hours doing, just finessing what we already had and then no one came out. That was it."[23]

Even during the first hour after the attack, in spite of shock and fear and uncertainty, the improvised teams of emergency medical responders worked exceptionally well. Nurse Suzanne Bucci had come to the USAF Flight Medicine Clinic for an interview that morning, and remained at the side of Colonel Baxter throughout much of the day. "Major Brown or Dr. Geiling, or whoever," she recalled, accepted the authority of the civilian "command doctor"—Vafier. "There wasn't any, 'Wait a minute. We're the Army and so we're in charge here.' None of that."[24] Master Sergeant Paul Lirette, also from the Air Force Clinic, had a similar reaction. "To me, it was like a movie. I mean it just worked. . . . A lot of times you train and you simulate a lot, but it worked like clockwork. I was impressed with the way things were handled. The people... [with] high ranking positions, they stood back and let people do what they get paid to do. They helped when they could help."[25] A member of an ambulance crew from the DeWitt Army Hospital at Fort Belvoir expressed the spirit of cooperation: "Everyone had thousands and thousands . . . of dollars worth of equipment that would belong to their hospital, and everyone was just great about unloading it and just giving it to whoever needed it."[26]

The west side of the Pentagon at the impact point remained the focus of the medical response, but as the morning wore on the number of health care personnel around the impact site far outnumbered the Pentagon employees and firefighters needing medical assistance there. Vafier recalled that "by 1 or 2 in the afternoon, it looked like a MASH unit. . . . We had tents with six bays. . . . It was the most incredible thing. We were ready to handle a large, large number of casualties and there were none."[27]

Ready road access brought rescue responders principally to the impact side of the Pentagon along Route 27 and to South Parking. Three wounded patients were airlifted from a makeshift landing pad on Route 27, two of them by a U.S. Park Police helicopter. Most of the ambulances that raced to the Pentagon congregated close to the crash area and there they idled. The greatest number of people, however, had exited the building elsewhere. Once many of the burned and injured reached safety in the North Parking area they sometimes waited up to 30 minutes for transportation. Only two private ambulances stood ready to pick up patients on that side of the building.[28] Meanwhile, frustrated ambulance crews on the southwest side felt a sense of helplessness brought on by inactivity, a reaction undoubtedly intensified after collapse of part of the building at 10:15 a.m. One Rader Clinic driver found the waiting "a little disturbing and disappointing, and I think that was the worst part of it, because we couldn't do our job or at least save some people. It just made us realize that nobody else was coming out, and that all those people were dead in there."[29]

Communication problems greatly hindered efforts to care for the injured on the north side, in particular evacuating them to hospitals. Almost immediately radio traffic gridlocked, land lines were unavailable, and cellular telephone networks became so overloaded that for a time Pentagon officials and employees as well as some emergency responders could not call outside. Neither the DiLorenzo Clinic at the Pentagon nor the Fort Myer Rader Clinic could establish reliable communications; the DiLorenzo staff called repeatedly to DPS to request ambulances.[30] Hospitals and clinics could not be informed about the flow of casualties, and perhaps more damaging, communication between the fire and rescue and the emergency medical elements on-site was severely impaired. Fighting the blaze from the west side and from the Center Court, the firefighters in direct contact with Incident Commander Schwartz had little idea of what transpired elsewhere in or about the building. From the Center Court firefighters saw victims being taken toward the north side of the Pentagon, but they had no idea what happened to them thereafter. They did not realize the need to request ambulances until communications improved, and by then emergency transportation was not needed. ACFD Captain Mark Penn said, "I had ambulances all over the place ready to come but we never got the call so they just stood by."[31]

In the absence of ambulances, people took the initiative to get themselves to hospitals or to send or accompany others. In one of the first ambulances to arrive, Army Sergeant First Class Donald Workman rode with badly burned Navy Lieutenant Kevin Shaeffer on what the lieutenant recalled as a "roller coaster" ride to Walter Reed Army Medical Center in Washington. Shaeffer, seriously hurt but still conscious, later said, "we were off-roading . . . hitting cars, ... kind of nicking some bumpers," and remembered someone commenting, "there's another Volvo bumped."[32] An ambulance transported one person to the Arlington Urgent Care Center while two other injured walked there. Three victims treated at the George Washington University Hospital arrived on their own. One man, his clothes smoldering, hailed a taxicab to take him to the nearest hospital. Captain Holly Pierce, a public affairs officer with the Army's DCSPER, which incurred the largest number of casualties, carried a number of people in her pickup truck to one of the hospitals.[33]

The DiLorenzo staff called on passing SUV and minivan drivers to take victims to area emergency rooms. Volunteers had to maneuver their private vehicles, not equipped with sirens or flashing lights, through heavy traffic and, when heading for Washington hospitals, across the clogged Potomac River bridges. Often they were unaware of the best medical facility for their charges. Very few patients were taken to the regional trauma center, Fairfax Hospital; a large number went instead to the closer Virginia Hospital Center in Arlington or to the Alexandria Hospital. Others arrived at hospitals not equipped to handle them and had to be stabilized before being moved elsewhere.[34] When a van carrying five injured people wearing color-coded tags pulled up to the Virginia Hospital Center emergency room, nurse Jean McGuire assumed that a private vehicle transporting coded casualties meant that there were so many victims that ambulances were overwhelmed. Although this was not so, she later said, "I can even hear my voice now saying, oh my God, we are losing control."[35]

To the contrary, because of the strategic importance of the National Capital Region its hospitals and clinics were unusually well prepared to handle mass casualties. They routinely conducted drills to practice for chemical or biological attacks. On learning of the events that morning, several facilities shut down non-

ROAD SYSTEM AND MEDICAL FACILITIES

essential services, implemented their emergency disaster plans, and geared up for a wave of casualties.[36] Even before the plane hit the Pentagon, in accordance with established procedure the Dulles Air Traffic Control Tower notified Fairfax Hospital, the largest in Northern Virginia, that a hijacked aircraft was missing, alerting Dr. Thomas Mayer, chair of the Department of Emergency Medicine and medical director for Fairfax County Fire and Rescue. Mayer recalled: "We knew that something was headed towards the national capital area. We didn't know where. But we knew we needed to get ready. So we immediately went on disaster planning mode." The hospital moved patients from the emergency rooms to other areas, halted all elective surgery, freed up 37 of the 40 operating rooms, and activated eight trauma teams.[37] As it turned out, these splendid resources were not required.

Thus, both the Pentagon and local medical facilities and personnel were equipped to handle a far greater flood of people than became necessary. Aware that medical care for the Pentagon casualties more than sufficed, the Headquarters Air Force Crisis Action Team relocated from the Pentagon to nearby Bolling Air Force Base, ready to prepare for assistance to New York where the need was thought to be more urgent and far greater than in the well-served Washington area.*[38] As Dr. Mayer observed, "The problem was that there was tremendous capacity to care for patients and not enough patients to care for."[39]

In all, 106 Pentagon patients reached Washington area medical facilities; 49 were admitted and 57 cared for as outpatients. The Virginia Hospital Center and the Alexandria Hospital received almost two-thirds of the injured as well as most of the people hospitalized overnight. The Washington Hospital Center in the District of Columbia, with one of the nation's most highly regarded burn-care units, admitted eight patients, the most grievously injured.[40]

The improvised nature of much of the medical and evacuation activity complicated the task of accountability, of determining the whereabouts of those wounded and hospitalized, as well as the numbers and identity of the dead. The Army's Office of the Deputy Chief of Staff for Personnel, for example, which suffered heavy casualties, set up a phone bank of 20 lines to send and receive calls about its people. The difficulty in producing a casualty list was compounded because many of the injured had been transported to civilian rather than military

* See Chapter VI.

INJURED DISPOSITION

Facility	Patients Received	Treated/ Released	Admitted
Virginia Hospital Center - Arlington	44	26	18* *2 transferred to Washington Hospital Center
Inova Alexandria Hospital	23	4	19
Inova Fairfax Hospital		1* *Transferred to HealthPlex	
Northern Virginia Community Hospital	6	6	
Inova Emergency Care Center (HealthPlex)	3	2* *Transferred to Inova Fairfax Hospital	
George Washington University Hospital	3	3	
Washington Hospital Center	13	5	8* *Includes patient from Georgetown University Hospital
Arlington Urgent Care Center	10	7	3* *Transferred to other hospitals
Andrew Rader U.S. Army Health Clinic	4	3	1* *Transferred to Virginia Hospital Center - Arlington
Totals	**106**	**57**	**49†**

† A few of the 49 patients listed as admitted above wound up at Walter Reed Army Medical Center.

Source: Arlington County After-Action Report, amended

facilities. Teams dispatched to local hospitals sought to find out who had been checked in and then subsequently admitted or released.[41]

As it happened, an unusually large number of Army chaplains—33—were in the vicinity on the morning of the attack, most attending a meeting in the

Office of the Chief of Chaplains in Crystal City, Arlington. When they learned of the strike they hurried to the Pentagon. Army Chief of Chaplains Major General Gaylord T. Gunhus, on leave at his home in Minnesota at the time, knew the chances of catching a plane back to the city were slight. He drove straight through to Washington, staying in touch by cell phone and arriving the next day. Among the chaplains on the scene several congregated in the Center Court to comfort the injured and frightened streaming out of the building. Thereafter, a few joined the extraction teams as stretcherbearers, entering the burned and smoke-filled offices. Another group took up posts at the triage site near the Pentagon Athletic Club. A third contingent remained with people huddled alongside Route 27 and the nearby first aid stations.[42]

As the fires subsided and then flared up again during the afternoon, the focus of the chaplains' attention shifted from first response to recovery. After the collapse of the E Ring area it seemed probable that no more survivors would be found; the seriously wounded had already been removed to trauma centers. In early afternoon the deputy chiefs of chaplains of the Army, Navy, and Air Force developed a coordinated plan for their ministry. They shared a tent with the Red Cross and decided to staff it with six Army chaplains until 9:00 p.m., Air Force chaplains standing by until 3:00 a.m. the next morning, and Navy chaplains taking the shift thereafter until 9:00 a.m. Their pastoral care embraced consoling the soldiers engaged in the gruesome recovery efforts, the injured who had been hospitalized, and the families of those killed or missing. Army Chaplain Art Pace and his team would perform the hospital ministry for another two months.[43]

Removing Remains

Greatly concerned about the need for more help in rescue and recovery operations as the morning progressed, Incident Commander Schwartz requested reinforcement by FEMA Urban Search and Rescue teams from Fairfax and Montgomery Counties.[44] In the afternoon, shortly after arrival, these and other recovery teams entered the building, which was still burning, unstable, and toxic. Army troops from an engineer company stationed at Fort Belvoir were the first such teams to survey the interior, finding no survivors but noting the presence of human remains. By early evening a more intensive reconnaissance confirmed the much earlier presumption that there could be little hope that anybody remained alive.

It fell therefore to FBI agents and photographers to record the location and condition and photograph the human remains, and for members of the 3rd Infantry Regiment—the Old Guard, of Fort Myer—and on the first day a group of Marines, to carry bodies to the morgue set up on the grounds outside.[45] ACFD Captain Penn spoke appreciatively of the soldiers brought in "to handle the bodies." They felt they knew "how to do it" in a way that would "pay the proper respect." To Penn, "that was really the part of the job that everybody dreads . . . . The Old Guard and the other folks they brought in were wonderful at it and very professional at it and did a great job and never blinked doing it."[46]

On their first sweep on the 12th, recovery teams moved into the south side of the Pentagon and proceeded through the E Ring until they reached the Navy Command Center in the D and C Rings, fanning out to scour the primary damaged area on the 1st and 2nd Floors.[47] Because of the collapse, no bodies were found above the 2nd Floor and only 20 were discovered on the 2nd Floor, most close to the site of impact. Allen Boyle died near an exit to the building, and Antoinette Sherman died in the hospital. The other 167 fatalities were strewn along the diagonal slice of the 1st Floor that marked the path of the airliner. Some remains were blasted through holes in the C Ring's inside perimeter into A-E Drive.[48]

In addition to removing remains, the strong, self-described "able bodies" of the 3rd Infantry performed much manual labor during the following weeks. They had already spent the night of the 11th and the day of the 12th securing the corridors leading into the impact area and clearing debris to the left of it on the 1st Floor.[49] So immense was the scale and extent of the destruction that some likened the interior to the set of a disaster movie or "kind of like going into a haunted house because it didn't look real."[50] To another "it was like walking into hell."[51] Yet there were occasional scenes of normalcy; an office adjacent to an area of total devastation might contain intact computers, books, and desks holding food and drinks hurriedly abandoned—bags of pretzels, cans of soda, a copy of the *Washington Post* opened to the sports section. For the occupants who got out of these rooms it was a matter of "meters between life and death," as one observer remarked.[52]

Searchers often had to make their way through several feet of rubble. Water from broken mains and fire hoses had pooled on the floors six inches deep and even knee-high in some areas. Ceiling grids sagged, electrical wiring snaked down walls and across floors, and plastic light fixtures melted by intense fire hung down like ribbons of caramelized sugar. Plumbing, burned batteries, twisted pipes, heating ducts, and air conditioners were heaped among the ruins, along with jagged metal, nails, and broken glass. Wood, plaster, and tiles had fallen from the floors above. Desks and filing cabinets were reduced to scrap metal. Asbestos lay exposed and lead paint peeled off walls. A layer of black soot covered virtually every surface. Without lights it was pitch dark; even with flashlights dust in the air limited visibility to 10 feet in places. The noxious atmosphere and standing water carried the threat of infectious disease. Fires still smoldered, adding to the acrid stench and smell of decay from the jet fuel, burned plastic, metal, and human flesh.[53]

A body recovery team typically consisted of one or more FBI agents, one or two FEMA representatives, a photographer, and four body or litter carriers from the Old Guard. For the recovery work the FBI drafted Navy and Marine photographers already on the scene taking pictures of the impact site and pieces of evidence strewn as far away as Arlington Cemetery. Inside the building, body recovery teams followed the trail of the earlier teams that had spray-painted a door or remaining column or panel with an orange fluorescent X. In the top quadrant of the X appeared the initials of the team that had cleared the room, on the right the number of bodies believed to be there, and in the other quadrants a code to indicate the location of a body.[54] The agents created a numbering system, noted the condition of the dead, and chalked the number on a slate as an identifier code. The photographers recorded the scene, including wide-angle and close-up shots of bodies in the position found, along with the crime scene designation numbers. After debris was lifted away, bodies and body parts were photographed from several angles, including close-ups of faces to aid identification.[55]

Some remains were unrecognizable, so badly charred that in one case, Navy photographer Kevin Rimrodt recounted, only a remnant of clothing that appeared to be a scrap of a blue bra indicated that the body was of a female. Moreover, without ambient lighting in what resembled an endless junkyard, accurate identification was difficult. In the Navy Command Center on the 1st Floor where

42 people died "there were so many bodies," Rimrodt recalled, "I'd almost step on them. So I'd have to really take care to look backwards as I'm backing up in the dark, looking with a flashlight, making sure I'm not stepping on somebody."[56] A soldier added that "it was dark; you couldn't tell what was wreckage and what was a human being."[57] Such circumstances made drawing up the numbering and location grid an exacting task.[58]

All evidence including human remains had to be removed from the building since, according to FBI Special Agent In Charge Arthur Eberhart, otherwise "we would have been there for months and months and months."[59] After having been photographed *in situ*, the dead and any personal or identifying effects were taken outside by the soldiers. On the afternoon of the attack many body bags had been laid out in the Center Court in anticipation of it becoming the field morgue.[60] But by the time Old Guard soldiers began bringing out bodies, a protected and controlled temporary morgue had been set up in North Parking.

Moving bodies through the clogged passageways could be laborious. For one of the first, a heavyset victim, the soldiers created a rolling chain, walking on top of the rubble and passing the body from hand to hand, with the last man in line moving to the front and the others repeating the process until they were clear of obstacles. They quickly learned that putting a body on a stretcher and handing it down the line made the sad task easier. Sometimes in the less-damaged corridors the bodies or body parts could be wrapped at the scene before being carried outside to the refrigerated trucks.[61]

For biohazard protection at the toxic impact site, soldiers handling the human remains wore a thin, disposable plastic coverall, rubber boots, safety helmets, carbon-filter face masks, and up to three layers of gloves. Early in the operation these items were in short supply. Some soldiers initially had only goggles and about 40 had to share a little more than half that number of face masks; later there were complaints of respiratory problems. The gloves, boots, masks, and helmets were cumbersome. Because the suits were taped shut at the wrists and ankles, the temperature became punishingly hot inside the clothing. Goggles fogged up. For those with masks, frequent filter changes became the rule. After finishing a shift soldiers cleaned their hands and faces with hand scrubbers and wipes and then entered a decontamination tent.[62]

Widespread destruction made recovery of remains slow. As more resources became available in succeeding days the pace picked up, becoming a round-the-clock operation with some 60 soldiers working with the FBI in 12-hour shifts. Sergeant Steven Stokes recalled putting in the half-day shifts five days in a row, and some soldiers worked longer hours than their assigned shift. After 17 September each platoon split its shift into thirds, alternating four hours of work inside the building with guard duty, light labor for the Red Cross, and short break periods.[63] The Old Guard soldiers accomplished an enormous amount of back-breaking work. ACFD Captain Penn extolled their "tremendous job," remarking on how gratifying it was to see them marching down from Fort Myer for the shift change.[64]

Members of the Old Guard, participating annually in hundreds of burials at Arlington National Cemetery, learn that their job demands a level of "ceremonial composure" and emotional detachment, but handling remains proved tough duty for these soldiers.[65] Most were in their late teens or early twenties and had never seen a dead person outside a formal setting or funeral parlor. Specialist John Myers acknowledged that "most people have never seen anything like this in their life at all."[66] Even the more seasoned soldiers were unprepared for the ordeal. Sergeant David Davis, not a new recruit, said, "I can just say that I have seen things there that I don't wish anyone else would have to see, because it's just—it's just unbelievable."[67] For Sergeant Robert Farrar, the "thick charred smell," noticeable even from the highway outside, "is something that I'll never forget . . . . You just cannot get rid of that smell."[68] Lieutenant Mark O'Neill agreed: "I don't think I'll ever forget the smell of it."[69] Over and over, soldiers remembered the "smell of it."

Removing the dead in these circumstances, admitted one soldier, "doesn't hit you until you're there." Some victims were found in relatively normal positions, seated at their desks or clustered around a conference table where they had worked up to the moment of death.[70] Some people had suffocated quickly because of the sudden and intense heat. Others had died from smoke inhalation, trapped in a stairwell as they tried to escape. Many bodies were badly burned, disfigured, or dismembered. It could be hard to dissociate from the human tragedy; seeing a recognizable person was often more disturbing than finding disconnected body parts. Farrar remembered looking at a corpse with a wedding ring still on its finger, knowing "there's some woman at home right now that's praying."[71] Marine Sergeant Michael Farrington was moved by "a child's doll floating around in there and that just kind of got to me because I know that there was a child that went along with that doll."[72] Private First Class Glen Litchfield had to sit down for a few minutes to regain his composure when he too spotted a toy.[73] Family and baby pictures stuffed into a day planner—"those faces keep reappearing," reported one soldier.[74] Sometimes they were undone by the ghastly sights they encountered. One soldier was so traumatized by his experience that he had to leave the site.

Usually the FBI bagged the remains. And although the situation was too chaotic to permit clear and consistent assignment of duties, Old Guard senior enlisted men and officers, when they could, assisted with this most painful job, leaving the younger soldiers to carry the remains outside.[75] Rotation of troops assigned to body recovery helped, as Private Joshua Frauman said, because otherwise "you'll go numb. . . . Both mentally and emotionally we just couldn't handle it anymore, couldn't do it."[76] Military chaplains and mental health counselors stood by to help. Either the regimental commander, the deputy commander, or the executive officer was always there for support.[77] Officers were concerned about their men, as Lieutenant Gilbert Munoz explained:

> We tried the best we could to keep a close eye on them . . . while we were actually inside the building, and then again as they were coming out, to make sure—you know, everyone was shaken a little bit, just from the hard work and the sweating and the real long hours. But we did the best we could to look eye-to-eye with the soldier and see if he was . . . a little more disturbed, or if he was a little more shaken up and needed to maybe . . . talk through his emotions a little bit with some of the chaplains that were on hand.[78]

Private Joel Reynolds confirmed that chaplains "were everywhere. You couldn't walk ten feet without a chaplain asking you if everything was all right or how you were doing. They definitely played a big part in helping the people who needed their services."[79] Many of the soldiers claimed that they bore up quite well without any help, but several confessed that Army culture discouraged talking about the feelings aroused by what they saw.

The soldiers came away from the experience with an enhanced respect for all civilian and military responders, especially the firefighters. They spoke appreciatively also of agencies such as the Red Cross and Salvation Army; the businesses and volunteers—even a North Carolina Baptist church—that provided supplies and food; the FBI, the local police, and many other units from far and near. And they were rightfully proud of their own effort. Even though there were "countless guys that didn't want to go in and do body recovery," nonetheless, Sergeant Farrar declared, "they got up, they put their stuff on, they went in, and they didn't do anything halfheartedly."[80] Private First Class Matthew Malmquist's Old Guard company spent most of their time clearing rubble, but inevitably they encountered body parts. He was "very impressed with . . . how respectfully" those were handled. They were put "in a body bag and then carried out on a stretcher." No matter what was found, "everything was treated as a full human body." And on the site, he observed, "it didn't matter who you were, who you worked for, you were all a part of the same team ... all working towards the same goal." It was, "for lack of a better word ... inspirational."[81] Until the last day of their duty at the Pentagon, "our guys," Lieutenant Rob Wolfe recalled with pride, were "on hands and knees looking for anything because those are our brothers and sisters in there. . . . Character, the honor and dignity that [the soldiers] had every day was just amazing."[82]

Many remains could not be retrieved through the normal recovery process: tons of debris were carted from the Pentagon, loaded into trucks, and deposited in North Parking adjacent to the morgue for a final sifting. An FBI agent rode in each vehicle to ensure a continuous chain of custody over all potential evidence. In the recovery area two FBI agents ran round-the-clock shifts to comb through the wreckage for crime scene evidence, personal effects, and remains of the dead.

Volunteers from several federal, local, and nongovernmental agencies as well as Old Guard companies assisted the North Parking operations.[83] In search and rescue and remains recovery in the aftermath of man-made or natural disasters, the FBI frequently employed teams of dogs and their handlers, usually bureau agents or law enforcement officers. The highly trained animals possess a keen sense of smell that allows them to locate body parts or even minute pieces of skin too small for the human eye to detect in the surrounding debris.[84] Dogs and handlers played an important role here as well.

Four days after the attack, on 15 September, Officer James Lugaila and his dog, from the D.C. Metropolitan Police Department's K-9 unit, accompanied an Urban Search and Rescue team into the building to search for remains. Lugaila suggested that other cadaver dogs be brought in to assist with remains recovery. Captain Eileen Roemer, an FBI employee who was also a naval reservist, kept and trained a cadaver dog. Roemer and Lugaila contacted their own cadaver dog networks and essentially became the day and night team leaders, respectively, of the handlers and their canines who came to work at the Pentagon. The dog teams assembled quickly. At 5:00 p.m. on Sunday evening, 16 September, Roemer and the first six dog teams checked in. The 29 teams in the search worked alongside members of the Army's 54th Quartermaster Company (Mortuary Affairs) and other volunteers under the direction of the FBI and FEMA.[85]

Like the soldiers, the dog handlers wore protective suits, gloves, and face masks. But because of the constant distractions and noise and the need to communicate with their dogs, the handlers didn't always cover their mouths with the breathing apparatus. The dogs did not take to their safety "uniforms" much better than their handlers or the soldiers; for them to get traction and scale the piles of debris safely, booties were placed over their paws. A team usually remained on the scene for an eight-hour shift, but often a dog could only work about 20 minutes before its concentration waned and it needed a break. Although dog teams sometimes participated in the search for remains inside, they spent most of their time searching the debris in North Parking. They uncovered numerous pieces of flesh and bone, internal organs, bloody clothing, or anything with traces of human protein. At the end of a shift dogs and humans were decontaminated in a pair of tents. Volunteer veterinarians and technicians washed and checked out the dogs.[86]

The searchers in North Parking carried out the work in stages. First, to dampen the concrete dust, soldiers hosed down the debris heap. The dogs, working on leads held by their handlers, sniffed for human remains. When a dog signaled that it had found something by pawing, sitting up, or otherwise indicating the spot, investigators and mortuary affairs personnel raked through the rubble or placed it on sifting screens. Remains were photographed and tagged with an identifying number, put in an evidence bag, and taken offsite for future identification. For the final search small front-end loaders spread out the debris to as little as a six-inch depth. Then the dogs went over it again.[87]

Roemer recalled that there were times when a dog was "alerting," but people working at the scene were disbelieving; all that could be seen might be a piece of bent, crushed metal. When the handler insisted that it be investigated, "they would then pry it open and find something in there." The dogs had "figured it out," she said. "One of the early things I learned was trust your dog, and I definitely trusted them every time in this, and I was very proud of the work they did."[88] Besides their invaluable contribution to remains recovery, when "off duty" the cadaver dogs were affectionate and agreeable companions to their human partners in the stressful work and were credited by at least one handler with helping to relieve tension.[89]

The large-scale sifting of the debris in North Parking probably accounted for most of the body remains that would be processed at the morgue.[90] The remaining debris was loaded onto trucks for transport to a hazardous material site. Ten days after the attack, on 21 September, control of the crime scene shifted from the Arlington County Fire Department to the FBI; on the 26th the FBI relinquished control to the Defense Department.[91] By this time, all human remains had been flown to the Dover Port Mortuary at Dover Air Force Base, Delaware, where after identification they would be returned to their families.

Chapter VI

Up and Running

The destruction wrought by the attack on the Pentagon threatened the ability of the Defense Department to carry out its most vital function—maintaining effective command of worldwide U.S. military forces. Recognition during the Cold War that government operations might be interrupted by attack from without or by devastating fires and storms and mechanical failures had led the government to prepare for such contingencies. DoD developed "continuity of operations" plans to ensure performance of essential military functions in times of emergency. When disaster at the Pentagon on 11 September confronted DoD officials with a stern test of their "continuity of operations," they realized that preparations had not taken sufficiently into account an attack of the nature and on the scale that occurred. A major immediate effect was that all of the command centers in the Pentagon had to resort to improvisations to continue or reconstitute their operations.

Despite the explosion, fire, and smoke hazard, Secretary Rumsfeld remained in the Pentagon continuing to direct departmental operations and exercise control of the U.S. armed forces. The attack did not prevent him from communicating with President Bush, a critical need because the president and the secretary comprise the National Command Authority from which overall direction of military operations emanates. When the secretary chose not to follow emergency plans that called on him to move to an alternate command site outside Washington, most other Defense leaders also stayed in the Pentagon—or close to it. The Joint Chiefs of Staff and the Army, Navy, and Air Force each maintained a command and operations center in the building that provided up-to-date information for decisionmaking. So extensive was the damage inflicted that it seemed for a while that all of these centers might have to be abandoned. The building maintenance staff of the Washington Headquarters Services, responsible for DoD facilities in the Washington area, worked with great intensity to keep the National Military Command Center, operated by the Joint Staff, and the other centers up and running. They could do nothing, however, for the Navy Command Center, utterly destroyed in the first minutes of the attack.

National Command Authority

Word of the attacks on the World Trade Center reached President Bush in Sarasota, Florida, where he was visiting an elementary school. At approximately 9:30 a.m. in the school's crowded media center, he spoke briefly to educators, parents, and reporters about the New York attacks, asked for a moment of silence for the victims, then immediately departed for Air Force One to return to Washington. En route to the airport he learned that an airplane had struck the Pentagon. The presidential aircraft was airborne at 9:55 a.m.; the pilot, after conferring with the lead Secret Service agent on board, flew the plane as high and fast as possible for better security. By telephone Vice President Richard Cheney advised the president to delay his return to Washington, repeating advice already given by the Secret Service. At approximately 10:10 a.m., Air Force One changed direction and headed west, eventually landing at Barksdale Air Force Base, near Shreveport, Louisiana. While the aircraft refueled, the president recorded a short broadcast message pledging that "the United States will hunt down and punish those responsible for these cowardly acts." Stating that he was in contact with the vice president, the secretary of defense, other members of the cabinet, and national security advisers, he assured the nation that "we have taken the necessary security precautions to continue the functions of your Government."[1]

The vice president and the Secret Service again advised the president against returning to the nation's capital because of the confused and uncertain conditions there. By this time Cheney and other officials in Washington believed that a threat existed against Air Force One, known by its codename "Angel," a concern later proven to be unfounded. Continuing to heed their advice the president flew from Barksdale to Offutt Air Force Base near Omaha, Nebraska, the highly secure headquarters of the U.S. Strategic Command. There, with his safety assured, the president could use elaborate command and control communication systems and facilities. At about 3:15 p.m. during the president's video teleconference with key administration officials, Director of Central Intelligence George Tenet reported that evidence pointed to the al Qaeda organization as the mastermind behind the attacks.[2]

In the Pentagon Rumsfeld was hosting a breakfast meeting with members of Congress when word came that a plane had crashed into the World Trade Center; following the meeting he was told of the strike into the second tower in New York. In his office listening to an intelligence briefing at the moment Flight 77 struck the Pentagon, Rumsfeld recalled, "The plane hit the building, and the building shook and the tables jumped."[3]

Thinking bomb, the secretary opened his office door and asked Vice Admiral Edmund Giambastiani, his military aide, "What the hell's happening?" On peering out the window and seeing nothing unusual he went into the hallway and asked his plainclothes security guards, Officers Aubrey Davis and Gilbert Oldach, what was going on. Listening to Pentagon police communication traffic via his radio earpiece, Davis stated that there was a report of an explosion at the Mall side of the building. Rumsfeld immediately hastened down the E Ring in that direction, accompanied by his two guards, his communications officer, and the deputy director of security for the secretary's office. At the undamaged 2nd Floor Mall Entrance, after Davis relayed new reports of a plane crash at the Heliport, Rumsfeld pressed on through the smoke and down the stairs to the 1st Floor, where he exited the building just north of the Heliport.[4]

"Oh, my Lord, the whole place was burning," he later remembered. He smelled jet fuel and saw hundreds of pieces of metal on the lawn. He picked up a piece and examined it. Hearing someone shout "We need help!" he ran over to assist in carrying a badly burned victim on a stretcher to the sidewalk by Route 27. From there he had a direct view of the inferno and destruction before the floors collapsed. His questions about what had happened elicited the answer that an airliner had flown into the building.[5]

After a few minutes, observing that the injured were being attended to, Rumsfeld reentered the building on the Mall side, went directly to his office, and tried without success to telephone the president. Then proceeding to the Executive Support Center on the 3rd Floor he joined a White House video teleconference in progress. From Air Force One the president telephoned the secretary after 10:00 a.m. Rumsfeld told him that despite the severe damage the Pentagon still functioned. Because the Executive Support Center had too few phones, desks, and computers and its teleconference screens were small, shortly before 10:30 a.m. the secretary and his staff moved one floor down to the National Military Command Center. The spacious, compartmented center, although smoky and without air conditioning, had electrical power, and its communication and computer systems were operating adequately. General Richard Myers, vice chairman of the Joint Chiefs of Staff, had come to the command center about 10:00 a.m., standing in for Chairman General Hugh Shelton, who was on his way back from Europe.[6]

Soon after arriving at the command center the secretary participated in an air threat conference call with officials from the North American Air Defense Command, a representative from the Federal Aviation Administration, and Vice President Cheney and others in the White House shelter conference room. At 10:39 a.m. Cheney gave Rumsfeld a situation update. At 10:53 Rumsfeld raised the military Defense Condition from level 5, the lowest level, to 3, an intermediate level, requiring a heightened alert status for U.S. armed forces worldwide. During the morning, while in the support and command centers, the secretary focused on immediate questions relating to control of U.S. airspace: the status of the fourth hijacked aircraft, grounding of all civilian flights, tracking of unidentified aircraft, the possibility of more hijackings and attacks, possible orders for launching intercept aircraft, maintaining combat air patrols, and providing rules of engagement for fighter pilots. He sought information on the security of the nation's borders, the identity of the terrorists, and forces available in the Persian Gulf area. He also telephoned Defense Minister Sergei Ivanov in Moscow requesting that the Russians terminate a military exercise—which they did—and he ordered the U.S. Strategic Command to end its Global Guardian exercise testing nuclear command and control procedures. Reports on the number of people killed and injured at the Pentagon and the World Trade Center helped him provide guidance for public information statements.[7]

Despite acrid smoke seeping into the NMCC, the possibility of a second air attack against the Pentagon, and a White House request to begin implementation of continuity of operations measures, Rumsfeld ignored repeated suggestions that he leave the building. Instead he directed Deputy Secretary of Defense Paul Wolfowitz to relocate to the alternate headquarters outside Washington, established at the height of the Cold War. Within minutes a helicopter landed on the parade ground on the River side of the Pentagon and carried off a reluctant Wolfowitz and a few others.[8]

Chief Edward Plaugher of the Arlington County Fire Department suggested that the NMCC be evacuated but chose not to press the issue with Rumsfeld who was determined to stay, largely because the communications network enabled him to keep in touch with key government officials and military commanders. Plaugher worried that carbon monoxide, odorless and colorless, would possibly reach the NMCC and render its occupants "irrational" before it killed them. At the same time he appreciated the magnitude of the crisis and the determination to continue operations in the Pentagon. The firefighters provided the NMCC occupants with a carbon monoxide detector and respirators along with instructions for their use, but by 12:19 p.m. their eyes and throats had become so irritated by smoke that the secretary and others returned to the Executive Support Center where the air was better. During the afternoon the secretary again spoke with the president by telephone; later he participated in the president's video teleconference from Offutt Air Force Base.[9]

Besides tracking aircraft—at noon there were still dozens of planes in U.S. airspace and some airliners inbound from other countries (one later sent a false signal indicating a hijacking)—Defense officials remained vigilant against coordinated "cyberspace" attacks on the nation's computer and communication systems. Information flowed to the secretary from Defense Department components, the FBI, the FAA, and other sources. Calling from the alternate command post, Wolfowitz reported that the computer and communication systems there functioned poorly or not at all. He could, however, participate in video teleconference calls.[10]

Military Command and Operations Centers

The Army, Navy, and Air Force command and operations centers in the Pentagon, operating 24 hours a day seven days a week, normally provided leaders with timely intelligence and information about operations around the world. Explosions and fire quickly destroyed the Navy Command Center on the 1st Floor and killed many of its people, confronting the Navy with the urgent need to improvise a functioning operations center.[11]

Deprived of his command center, Chief of Naval Operations Admiral Vernon Clark, outside the building near North Parking shortly after 10:15 a.m., told his vice chief, Admiral William Fallon, and Vice Admiral Patricia Tracey, director of the Navy staff, that he would not relocate to the Pentagon's alternate command post. Instead he would move to the Washington Navy Yard, a few miles away in the District of Columbia; some staff members had already left to prepare accommodations there in the headquarters building of the Naval Criminal Investigative Service (NCIS). Secretary of the Navy Gordon England joined Clark at the temporary site. NCIS agents kept them informed of efforts to account for missing personnel, a top priority.[12]

Earlier, at Clark's direction Fallon had traversed the short distance to the Navy Annex building on Columbia Pike to establish a command center that would allow Navy leaders to operate in close proximity to the Pentagon. By the time Fallon arrived the Annex had been evacuated. He heard alarms still blaring there. The building had electrical power but had lost its air conditioning, a breakdown that could cause computerized communication systems to overheat and shut down.[13] Still, the Marine Corps Command Center in the building was functioning. After its director, Major General Gordon Nash, offered space to the Navy, Fallon made arrangements for the Navy's leadership and support personnel to move there and to other space in the building. Maintenance crews began to set up portable air conditioners and exhaust fans for the center. Because of fear of another attack, however, only mission-essential personnel might enter the Annex.[14]

Navy officers accepted an offer from the Virginia Department of Transportation to use a conference room in its building on Columbia Pike across from the Annex where, with a laptop computer and a large white pad on an easel, they began to track casualties and those who had gotten out safely. Captain Thomas

McAtee and a few others who drove to local hospitals reported by phone the names of the injured arriving for medical care. They also exchanged names with Army personnel trying to account for people at the hospitals.[15]

Throughout the night Captain Mary Jo Sweeney and staff officers summoned technical support teams to prepare offices in the Annex for the Navy's leadership. The casualty tracking and muster undertaking moved to the Annex, where Admiral Tracey spent the night directing the effort. The next day, with the building's utilities functioning normally, the Navy leadership worked from the Annex.[16]

Commandant of the Marine Corps General James Jones was leaving the building to attend a funeral in the District of Columbia when the plane hit. While he attended the funeral his driver tried to maintain communication with the general's staff at the Pentagon. On returning after 11:00 a.m. Jones went directly to a second office he maintained in the Navy Annex, meeting with his staff continually and receiving updates on casualties and extent of damage. Later in the day Admiral Clark and his staff moved from the Navy Yard to the Annex and joined Jones for meetings in the commandant's conference room.[17]

The Army Operations Center (AOC) in the Pentagon basement functioned throughout the day. Half a world away in Singapore, Army Chief of Staff General Eric Shinseki learned of the attack on the World Trade Center and immediately telephoned the Operations Center, speaking with Brigadier General Peter Chiarelli, in charge of current operations there. Chiarelli gave Shinseki as much up-to-date information about the New York attacks as he could glean from CNN.[18]

As executive agent for DoD the Army coordinated with the Navy and Air Force on proposed action to support civilian authorities during emergencies involving mass casualties. Chiarelli told Shinseki that in his additional capacity as director of military support he had activated the Crisis Action Team to respond to the contingency in New York if requested by state and local officials. He anticipated that the World Trade Center disaster would require enormous rescue, firefighting, and recovery efforts.[19]

During the conversation with Shinseki an intelligence analyst interrupted to inform Chiarelli that other aircraft had been hijacked. One was thought to be headed toward Washington. Sensing the urgency of the situation, Shinseki ended the phone call, saying that he would call back later. Shortly thereafter Flight 77 hit the Pentagon; Chiarelli later described the impact as a "muffled noise."[20]

Soon senior Army leaders including Vice Chief of Staff General John Keane and Secretary of the Army Thomas White streamed into the Operations Center. Word came that the Pentagon's continuity of operations plan required White to leave the building for the alternate command site. He wanted to stay but his staff advised that he go; like Wolfowitz, he departed by helicopter.*[21]

All day smoke threatened to close down the crowded Army Operations Center. Colonel Bruce Bachus, head of the Command and Control Support Agency responsible for keeping the center functioning, depended on engineer Alvin Nieder to operate fans and open regular and emergency doors to create strong drafts that pulled out much of the smoke. Water from fire hoses and burst pipes flowed down corridors, hallways, and stairwells, and seeped through floor and wall cracks toward the AOC's computer and telephone lines and electrical systems. Nieder monitored the water flow all evening. At 1:00 a.m. on 12 September he and NMCC engineer Michael Bartos waded through water over a foot deep in A-E Drive to clear debris from drains, especially the heavy muck from water-saturated ceiling tiles. Their efforts prevented short-circuiting of systems, allowing their respective centers to function continuously during the crisis.[22]

The center's immediate task was to account for Army personnel, an effort spearheaded by the Personnel Contingency Cell, with members of the Crisis Action Team assisting. Initially working with a social roster sent to her by e-mail a week earlier, Major Corrina Boggess and her colleagues located other rosters and compiled personnel lists. Colonel Mark Lewis, director of plans, resources, and operations in the Army's devastated personnel office, called the cell with valuable information about the impact site and escapees from the building. He had departed his office in the B Ring, could not reenter the building, and now led a team of four as they operated from an empty trailer of the Pentagon Renovation Program Office near North Parking. His team spent the entire day and night making phone calls, coordinating information about the injured, missing, and safe.[23]

* The secretary of the Army was second in the line of succession, after the deputy secretary of defense, to assume responsibility as the acting secretary of defense.

In the Air Force Council conference room on the mezzanine level of the Pentagon basement, General John Jumper was chairing his first staff meeting as Air Force chief of staff when he learned of the attack on the World Trade Center. At approximately 9:00 a.m. a large screen displayed coverage of the burning North Tower after the first hijacked airliner had slammed into it. The group then saw United Airlines Flight 175 crash into the South Tower. After viewing televised news for about eight minutes, Jumper resumed the meeting, concluded it quickly, and departed for his office.[24]

When Flight 77 struck the Pentagon, Jumper and Secretary of the Air Force James Roche rushed to their Operations Center on the mezzanine. Members of the Air Force Crisis Action Team had already begun to assemble there for a 10:00 a.m. briefing; one of their responsibilities was to work with the Army to provide assistance to civil authorities in New York. They soon activated a team to focus on continuity of operations.[25]

Over the next few hours efforts to ventilate the smoke penetrating the Operations Center failed. At 12:20 p.m., about the time conditions forced Rumsfeld to move from the National Military Command Center, Air Force leaders and assistants left their center for Bolling Air Force Base, just across the Potomac River. Like their Navy counterparts, the secretary and the chief of staff chose to stay near the Pentagon and not travel to the emergency headquarters well outside Washington. They went to Bolling by helicopter; by 1:00 p.m. the new operations center was functioning. Surgeon General Paul Carlton, who had come from rescue operations at the Pentagon, briefed Roche and Jumper on medical assistance—equipment, people, and air evacuation—that the Air Force could provide to both New York City and the National Capital Region. The leaders approved Carlton's plan to send medical personnel and equipment to McGuire Air Force Base, New Jersey, to stand by to assist civilian efforts in New York as needed. At 3:00 a.m., after conditions on the mezzanine had improved, operational command was moved back to the Pentagon; the Operations Center became fully operational in the Pentagon at 5:30 a.m. on 12 September.[26]

Keeping the Building Operating

To keep the building going required a prodigious effort by the managers, engineers, and mechanics of the Building Management Office and the Heating and Refrigeration Plant. Their leap into action immediately after the plane hit the Pentagon helped save lives and limit damage. At the Building Operations Command Center (BOCC) on the 1st Floor in Wedge 1, usually two or three people kept watch around the clock, receiving maintenance calls from building occupants and monitoring the functioning of utility systems. On 11 September Kathryn Greenwell, answering calls and preparing work orders, sat at the control desk viewing multiple computer monitors that displayed data about heating, air conditioning, ventilation, steam, electricity, elevators, escalators, and fire alarms. The information appeared also on huge high-definition color screens above and behind the desk on one wall of the center. To the right of the large screens two television sets displayed the Weather Channel and CNN.[27]

When CNN reported that an aircraft had crashed into the World Trade Center, Greenwell notified her supervisor, Assistant Building Manager Steven Carter, in his office opposite the control panel. As they watched the second aircraft hit the other tower Carter realized the crashes were deliberate; he immediately ordered the lockdown of all mechanical and electrical rooms in the building to secure utilities against attack. Carter had issued this order previously, but only during security exercises. He notified key staff of the lockdown: Michael Bryant, the building manager, and John Irby, director of the Federal Facilities Division of the Washington Headquarters Services. He also telephoned the Pentagon's Defense Protective Service and learned that the Threat Condition for the building remained at "Normal." Should it change, DPS would notify the center. WHS maintenance managers came immediately to the BOCC; anticipating a raised Threat Condition they discussed additional procedures for securing the building's utility systems, after which they returned to their offices.[28]

When the plane smashed into the Pentagon minutes later it destroyed part of Wedge 1 where the BOCC was located. Carter and Greenwell felt the impact and heard what the latter described as a "thwoom." The two tried to comprehend the information rapidly displaying itself on screens as alarms beeped and data flashed. Greenwell saw the fire alarm system go "berserk" as the number of alarms climbed incredibly fast, 1-2-3-4-5-6-7-8-9-10- and on to 20 … 30 … 40 … 50 … 60 … relentlessly to 100 … 200 … 300 and higher. She knew that for each fire alarm, two smoke detectors had activated. From the hallway just outside the center she clearly heard the public address system instructing everyone to evacuate the building. Judging that no danger immediately threatened the BOCC, Carter instructed Greenwell to continue answering phones while he went to investigate and to keep in contact with him by radio. Because he served as the Building Management Office's representative to incident commanders, usually ranking officers from the Arlington County Fire Department, Carter asked her to let him know when the incident commander arrived and the location of his command post.[29]

In the Center Court Carter received radio calls from Greenwell telling him of people trapped in Wedge 1. He ran to A-E Drive and entered Corridor 4, where he encountered dark, dense smoke, heat, and water from burst pipes pouring into the drive. Nevertheless, he joined in helping others flee the building. Returning to the drive he entered Corridor 5, again assisting occupants to leave the building. In A-E Drive he could see dense smoke issuing from holes in the C Ring wall. People were dipping their shirts in rapidly accumulating water in the drive to sustain them in the search for survivors. Walls had collapsed, debris lay everywhere, and fires still burned. Going back to the Center Court in search of the incident commander, he saw DiLorenzo Clinic medical personnel conducting triage for the injured lying on the grass. Incident Commander James Schwartz was already on the scene but on the west side of the building near the crash site. Building management established direct liaison with him when Charles McCormick, a building repair and alterations supervisor standing outside when the plane hit, linked up with the commander when he moved his command post to beneath the I-395 overpass near South Parking.[30]

The BOCC received a steady stream of calls from civilian and military officials inquiring about conditions in the building. For people who intended to remain in their offices, smoke, not fire, now posed the main threat. During his quick examination of the Pentagon between Corridors 4 and 5 Carter had gained a good idea of the extent of damage and the locations of heavy smoke concentrations. Back in the BOCC he had Greenwell bring up "Metasys," a computer software program for monitoring and controlling utility systems. Contractors had not yet completed its installation as part of the Wedge 1 renovation, but it operated sufficiently to permit manipulation of components of the ventilation system.[31]

Greenwell and a contractor, Chad Hensen, could not connect to Metasys from the computers in the BOCC, but they were in radio contact with workers in the Control Group, a section of the Building Management Office elsewhere with access to Metasys through their computers. Carter asked them to shut down air handlers—air conditioning and heating system components that blew air through the ductwork—in Corridors 3, 4, 5, and 6 and set up air barriers in Corridors 1, 2, 7, and 8.[32]

When Arlington Fire Department Battalion Chief Dale Smith arrived in the Center Court some time before 10:15 a.m. and established an auxiliary command post, he thought the entire building had been evacuated. He relayed an order from the incident commander to close down all air handlers, not knowing that Rumsfeld and many others in command centers intended to remain in the building. Carter informed Smith of the critical work by building maintenance personnel to keep essential elements functioning; an officer from the NMCC also impressed on fire officials the importance of continuing operation of that center. The incident commander and subordinates later directed the manipulation of the air handlers to reduce the amount of smoke in certain undamaged sections of the Pentagon.[33]

As the morning wore on dense smoke that wrapped around the building thwarted efforts to bring fresh air into the structure until wind shifts temporarily blew away the fumes. Control Group crews and contractors operated the ventilation system all day and into the night to ease the task of the firefighters. Despite their persistent efforts smoke and soot permeated the building.[34]

Around 10:00 a.m., within minutes of returning from his inspection of the impact site and while focusing on the ventilation system, Carter received an urgent call from Donald Kuney, the manager of the Heating and Refrigeration Plant, located a few hundred yards from the Pentagon, asking him to send mechanics immediately to basement tunnels near the destroyed areas to turn off valves to keep chilled water from gushing from large burst pipes. Water normally flowed through pipes and coils around the building to cool air and then returned to the plant. Closing the valves would prevent the water from reaching broken pipes and hemorrhaging. Failure of air conditioning would cause large, sophisticated computer and communications systems to close down, leaving the nation's military headquarters without a means of command and control. Backup generators and portable air conditioners could be substituted in certain areas, but those alternate sources were not adequate under the existing extraordinary circumstances. To conserve water for firefighting and to increase pressure for the chilled system Kuney also wanted valves closed on broken pipes carrying water from city lines.[35]

At the Heating and Refrigeration Plant Kuney and operations manager Brian Maguire noted with alarm that the pressure in the chilled water system had fallen rapidly from 80 to 38 pounds per square inch. If the pressure reached 30, it could create cavities that would seriously damage pumps. As the pressure continued to drop, Kuney ordered engineers to shut down the chillers, pumps, condensers, and other sub-systems, effectively closing down the cooling plant, not to be restarted until the maintenance crews at the Pentagon stopped the massive loss of water from the broken pipes there.[36]

While Carter was turning off valves he learned of the warning of another hijacked airliner flying toward Washington and heard the Pentagon police in the Center Court ordering an evacuation. Some of the mechanical and electrical crews communicated by radio and split into two teams; one went to South Parking and the other to North Parking. If the plane crashed into the building or near it at least one of the crews would survive and return to help minimize damage. Carter and a few workers, including electrician Daniel Murphy and maintenance inspector Dennis Smith, stayed behind and waded through water in dark, smoky tunnels to turn off valves on broken water and steam pipes, taking care not to touch red fire valves that controlled water flow to ceiling sprinklers.[37]

Some workers returned to the Center Court around 10:30 a.m. with only minutes left before the anticipated follow-on plane attack. Six men and Kathryn Greenwell divided into two groups and walked to different areas of the Center Court, increasing the odds that some of them would survive another air attack. An eerie silence fell over the court as Carter, Murphy, Smith, Greenwell, Robert Candido, David Brown, and Anthony Freeman waited for the plane; firefighters and others had remained there as well. After receiving the all clear notification maintenance crews resumed their work to save the building.[38]

Word of the supposed inbound aircraft was late in reaching the Heating and Refrigeration Plant, so that operators continued to monitor systems, waiting for the water pressure to rise before restarting the cooling plant. Once it rose sufficiently everyone had to be ready to activate all plant components in precise sequence. Nothing could go wrong, especially in the condenser system that pulled water from the Potomac River and put it through several filtering screens. Everyone knew the chilled water was indispensable to keeping the Pentagon functioning as a command center. Once the pressure reached a normal level Kuney gave the go-ahead to start the sequence to bring the plant back on line. The 10-minute process ending about 10:30 a.m. permitted the cooling of the major computer and telephone systems. None of the critical components had to shut down.[39]

Still responding to the warning of a second attack, police arrived at the plant and ordered everyone into the nearby parking lot except Maguire, who volunteered to stay and monitor the stabilized systems. Kuney soon returned to the plant, put some coins in a vending machine for a couple of sodas, and, handing a drink to Maguire, asked about the terrorists, "Do you think they'll come back?" "Nah," replied Maguire. Shortly after the presumed threat ended police allowed everyone to return to the plant to tackle restoring chilled water to the Navy Annex building.[40]

The Pentagon's electrical system also suffered critical damage. After the plane crashed, mangled live wires threatened to electrocute survivors, firefighters, and rescue workers. Arcing from short-circuited lines could rekindle fires, spark explosions of jet fuel vapors, and damage components of the electrical system throughout the entire building.[41]

Electrician Matthew Morris, just inside Corridor 6 off A-E Drive when the crash occurred, stood about a hundred yards from the destroyed area. Running along the drive toward the impact site, he saw people climbing over the chain link fence across the drive near Corridor 4. After helping to unlock the gate in the fence he was appalled to see people emerging through the heavy smoke from the C-4 electrical vault, which carried 13,800 volts of electricity. The vault's doors to the drive and its inner doors had all been blown open, and part of its ceiling caved in. Peering into the deep vault, Morris saw water on the floor and heard the transformers humming even though they were twisted off their bases. He quickly went inside as more people were coming out, saw digital displays still operating, and pulled disconnect switches to cut all voltage.[42]

From the A-E Drive Morris hurried through the building to the E Ring and outside to check on the temporary emergency power generator for Wedge 1, mounted on a trailer. He found it burning. The airplane had grazed it, igniting its hundreds of gallons of fuel. Fortunately his coworker, John Robinson, had not been performing his weekly maintenance on the generator at the time of the crash. After the explosion Robinson had run to A-E Drive, saw the injured emerging from the C Ring, and found and drove a small utility vehicle to transport them to the DiLorenzo Clinic or the North Parking area for evacuation. The police ordered Morris away from the building for his own safety and would not let him reenter from the west side. He kept in touch with the BOCC and Steven Carter by radio.[43]

Shortly after impact Morris's supervisor, William Thomas, ran to a vault in the basement and began to identify and pull levers to cut the flow of electricity to the crash site. For the next few hours he and electricians coordinated with fire officials through the BOCC to cut power to firefighting areas. An old wiring maze that carried electricity from other parts of the building complicated their search for sources of power to some live wires arcing and sending out flashes of sparks. Computer servers still working from emergency battery-operated "uninterruptible power supply" components also caused concern. When part of the NMCC lost power, workers set up generators.[44]

Voltage disconnections also caused the BOCC to lose some of its power. Then about 11:10 a.m. an electrician pulled a switch for Wedge 1 that cut remaining power to the BOCC causing it to lose computers and telephones. Earlier it had lost its backup electrical power when the plane hit the wedge's temporary emergency generator. After Greenwell left the center and headed up a flight of stairs to the smaller, less capable alternate BOCC, she spent her time between that site, the Building Management Office at 2A258, and the Center Court, mostly responding to phone calls and passing messages.[45]

The air in the building worried managers, workers who remained in their offices, and first responders, fearful that carbon monoxide, cyanide, asbestos, lead from paint, and other toxins might be circulating. The building's industrial hygienist, Matthew Skowronski, quickly set up equipment to check levels of common gases. The Arlington County Fire Department tested for carbon monoxide in the NMCC. The Safety and Occupational Health Branch of WHS called on contractors to remove water-soaked plaster and asbestos that fell from ceilings onto furniture and floors. Within 24 hours, in addition to contractors, Army environmental specialists were testing air throughout the building. PENREN contractors continued to conduct routine air sampling, the results serving as cross-checks to other tests. Filters, coils, and grills were repeatedly changed or cleaned to improve air quality. The Labor Department's Occupational Safety and Health Administration assisted with matters involving asbestos and structural damage. The Environmental Protection Agency collected air, water, and debris samples and monitored conditions for first responders, Pentagon occupants, and residents in the surrounding community.[46]

Immediately after the plane hit, WHS Director Doc Cooke, responsible for overall management of the building, hurried to the entrance closest to Rumsfeld's office to check the emergency security arrangements and evacuation procedures. During the day and into the evening, he did not leave the building, providing the secretary with information on casualties and the building's condition and security. In turn he received reports from DPS Chief John Jester, Director of Real Estate and Facilities (RE&F) Paul Haselbush, and the latter's deputy, Ralph Newton.[47]

Haselbush and Newton had responsibility for the building's maintenance and security. In accordance with their continuity of operations procedures, they moved to their alternate command post in a satellite office on Army Navy Drive, beyond South Parking. The continuity plan remained fresh in their minds because a month earlier a fire in the Pentagon had produced smoke that caused a partial building evacuation, prompting Haselbush to direct his staff to update the directorate's emergency plans.[48]

Federal Facilities Division Chief Irby and Building Manager Bryant kept Haselbush and Newton, who closely monitored the activity of the maintenance crews and police officers, informed about the activity of the BOCC; Jester relayed security information. They received calls also from division chiefs accounting for employees and contractors and tried to determine the number of people in the damaged wedges at the time of the attack, all the while keeping Cooke and other officials abreast of the situation.[49]

About mid-afternoon Cooke informed Newton that Rumsfeld wanted the Pentagon open for business the next day. All morning that had been the gritty intent of the maintenance crews, who knew the Pentagon symbolized the nation's defense. Carter spoke for them when asked if the building evacuation would be 100 percent. "Not on our watch," he replied.[50]

While the crash site smoldered and the roof continued to burn, Haselbush and Newton took measures to prepare the building and its occupants for as normal a day as possible on 12 September. They and their staff tried to determine how much was habitable and if utilities could sustain the return of the workforce; checked on the building's air quality; discussed ways to inform employees about conditions at the Pentagon; and provided assistance in preparing information for Rumsfeld. Problems of transportation and parking required that Haselbush's staff also keep in touch with incident command officials and police authorities to learn which roads would remain closed around the Pentagon; coordinate with the Washington Metropolitan Area Transit Authority on the resumption of train and bus service to the Pentagon; reroute DoD shuttle buses; and find additional parking spaces since South Parking was taken over by numerous emergency vehicles. They also consulted with Jester to identify new security requirements for the building.[51]

Fire Chief Plaugher did not welcome Rumsfeld's directive to bring back the workforce on 12 September—the roof still burned and the air at the impact site was contaminated. Worried that fire gases might travel throughout the building, fire officials directed the placement of barriers to prevent anyone from approaching the impact site and surrounding areas without authorization and protective gear. FBI representatives, too, were concerned because the area was a crime scene. Yellow crime scene tape and guards declared sections of the building between Corridors 2 and 7 off limits. Wooden wall barriers were built later to further restrict access to the impact site.[52]

Nancy Judd, head of the RE&F contracting office, spent much of the day on 11 September along the Potomac River bank, along with other civilians and military, helping care for infants and youngsters from the evacuated Pentagon Child Development Center, located adjacent to North Parking. Most parents had rushed from the building to the center and then to the river bank to retrieve their children. Many others frantically made their way through massive traffic jams to get to the center. In the late afternoon Judd arrived at the RE&F alternate command site.[53]

On learning of the expected return of workers to the Pentagon the next day, Judd, after consultation with Haselbush, immediately let a service contract to clean soot and smoke from habitable areas and arranged for a recovery management firm specializing in cleanups after disasters to send a 50-person work crew on the morning of the 12th. For the next few weeks they cleaned the building 24 hours a day, washing floors, walls, ceilings, windows, doors, vents, and light fixtures.[54]

By evening on the 11th the firefighters and maintenance crews had thus far preserved the Pentagon. The roof still burned, but ruinous damage was confined to the crash area; utilities functioned in most of the building. The widespread smoke did not prevent holding two significant conferences during the evening.

Confident and reassuring, Rumsfeld held a brief press conference in the Pentagon at 6:42 p.m., especially to demonstrate to the American people and the world that despite the damaging attack the Pentagon still operated. Most of the attending press people had been working outdoors several hundred yards from the building, on South Joyce Street near the Navy Exchange gas station, the closest they were permitted to the crash site. The staff of Assistant Secretary of Defense for Public Affairs Victoria Clarke helped the press haul their equipment to the Pentagon and pass through tight security checks.[55]

Sen. Carl Levin, chairman of the Senate Armed Services Committee, and Sen. John Warner, the committee's ranking minority member, had asked to come to the Pentagon to show bipartisan support. Appreciating their concern, Rumsfeld welcomed them. After visiting the crash site the senators participated in the press conference, joined by JCS Chairman General Shelton just arrived from Europe and Secretary of the Army White, back from the alternate command location. Near the end of his remarks Rumsfeld pointedly declared that the briefing was taking place in the Pentagon and that "the Pentagon's functioning. It will be in business tomorrow." He spoke of casualties but said it was too early to have firm figures because roster checks were still under way. In response to a question he stated that the FBI had secured the site.[56]

After the conference the secretary went to the White House to listen to the president, returned from Omaha, speak to the nation at 8:30 p.m. Earlier in the evening on his helicopter ride from Andrews Air Force Base to the White House, the president had flown over the Pentagon to see for himself the extent of the destruction. After the speech Bush met with Rumsfeld and other top advisers.[57]

At the Pentagon immediately after Rumsfeld's press conference, Cooke and MDW Commander General Jackson met with representatives from security, firefighting, and search and rescue organizations; building maintenance; PENREN; and the military services to discuss responsibilities. The FBI announced that later that night it would establish a Joint Operations Center (JOC) at the nearby Fort Myer Community Center, where staffs of federal and local agencies would answer questions and provide updated information.[58]

Open for Business on 12 September

Some of the thousands of military personnel, civil servants, and contractors who returned to the Pentagon on 12 September, determined to keep the building in operation, arrived well before sunrise to avoid traffic jams and find parking. At some points in the E Ring embers had flared up during the night, and fire persistently consumed the dry wood under areas of the slate roof. Anthony Conques recalled, "I came in the next morning around 5:00, and the worst part for me was looking out over the courtyard at the bandages, bags, and debris, and in the dark the building was still on fire. . . . In the dark it was eerie—the orange flames and smoke, the shining lights from the firefighting efforts—it was surreal and upsetting." Most poignant for workers was knowing that the building entombed colleagues and friends.[59]

As the chief of the RE&F Office of Space Policy and Acquisition, Conques had to find office space in the National Capital Region for displaced workers. With the help of the General Services Administration (GSA) he found quarters in three buildings in Crystal City in Arlington, two subway stops from the Pentagon. The RE&F staff and GSA acquired desks, chairs, computers, and telephones and arranged for cabling and electrical power for 3,000 people, down from the original estimate of 5,000 displaced by fire, smoke, and water; many people found space with colleagues either within the Pentagon or elsewhere in the area. Through Cooke, Conques coordinated with the military department administrative assistants: J. B. Hudson (Army), John LaRaia (Navy), and William Davidson (Air Force). Douglas Benton of the GSA cut through red tape for them. Within five days all displaced employees were at alternate work stations.[60]

Two stubborn problems on 12 September could have forced Rumsfeld from the building after all. Had the roof fire continued to spread it would have destroyed an antenna cluster located atop the building; destruction of the antennas would have seriously degraded the NMCC's communications capability, forcing a relocation of the center and DoD leaders. Firefighters battling the blaze beneath slate roof areas through the 12th succeeded in keeping the flames from the communication gear. Likewise, water pouring from fire hoses into the building threatened to short-circuit the Pentagon's main telephone switching room. Quick action by building maintenance workers using pumps and sandbags saved the critical equipment.*[61]

For many days after the attack managers and employees faced scores of urgent, unusual problems, exhibiting impressive skill and in some instances courage under hazardous conditions. On the 12th, electrician Robert McCloud led a team to assess the condition of the building's high-voltage electrical distribution system. Using a flashlight in smoky, wet electrical vaults he began the process of restoring power to parts of the building. Later, in full firefighting gear the team entered the collapsed impact area where they sought the source of a live connection and disconnected a battery still trying to power a computer server backup system. Kuney, with a team of employees and contractors on the lawn immediately in front of the crash site, used a generator, air compressor, and pump to remove thousands of gallons of water from a utility vault damaged by the attacking aircraft. They hastened to pump the water out so it would not touch steam pipes in the vault.[62]

The RE&F contracting office quickly arranged for contractors to tear off damaged roof slate and cover the openings with tarpaulins and wood to protect the floors beneath in the event of rain. No matter how waterproof they made the roof, however, heat from warm days that followed affected wet, dark, sealed areas of otherwise undamaged sections of the building and unleashed a wild growth of mold that would require removal of walls and ceilings and extensive environmental testing in the ensuing weeks.[63]

Maintenance crews worked around the clock for weeks after 11 September. Robert Cox, chief of the technical staff of the Federal Facilities Division, spoke for many of the civil servants and contractors: "Everyone I know and talk to who was involved in this intensive effort unanimously felt privileged to be a part of it. There were so many people … who like me got many phone calls from

* After 11 September the Pentagon renovation eliminated these vulnerabilities.

family and friends worried about [our] safety. This was overwhelming. . . . There was an amazing feeling of satisfaction that went with the whole effort."[64] Closing valves, pulling switches, testing the air, pumping water, setting up generators, and hundreds of other jobs helped to reestablish the physical environment in the Pentagon that the department needed to carry out its responsibilities. Office workers responded with as much toughness and resilience as the building itself, returning to their jobs the next day while fires still burned and rescue and recovery efforts continued.

That terrorists, rather than accidental or natural occurrences, caused the Pentagon's damage, made it crucially important to maintain continuity of operations. DoD had to act immediately to safeguard the nation against other possible strikes and prepare for military action against those who facilitated and perpetrated the attacks. The department's resourcefulness in carrying on effectively under extreme conditions reflected the steadfast dedication of its leaders and rank and file—military and civilian.

Chapter VII

Securing the Pentagon

Security provided by the police, FBI, and military was indispensable to the efforts to save and protect the Pentagon's people and to limit damage to the building on 11 September and the days that followed. For the Pentagon police—the Defense Protective Service—and more than 30 other law enforcement agencies and military units that came to its assistance the attack created immediate, immense security requirements. Together they faced a myriad of problems far beyond the capacity of DPS to handle alone: overseeing evacuation of the building, rescuing survivors, guarding the building and grounds, collecting evidence, safeguarding the building's secrets, protecting against possible additional terrorist strikes, controlling traffic in a wide area, and keeping intruders and the curious away from the site. All this required the services of more than two thousand federal, state, local, and military police, and other military units, some of whom remained on the job for months, even years. With the security provided by the police and the military, the firefighters could concentrate on their formidable tasks, as could search and rescue units, medical teams, engineers, cleanup and construction crews, and even chaplains and the family assistance center. Involvement of so many different agencies could have created jurisdictional and chain of command problems, but the incident command system and the compelling sense of responsibility and urgency experienced by all responders made effective cooperation possible.

Defense Protective Service

The DPS, led by Chief John Jester, had responsibility for security and law enforcement on the Pentagon Reservation. Approximately 250 armed officers, trained at the Federal Law Enforcement Training Center in Georgia, patrolled the building and grounds, guarded entrances, screened deliveries, responded to bomb threats, formed an Emergency Response Team commonly known as a special weapons and tactics (SWAT) team, and staffed the Protective Services Unit that guarded the secretary of defense, other high-ranking DoD officials, and visiting dignitaries. The DPS also supervised contract security guards at 45 DoD leased facilities around the National Capital Region. Additionally, some 50 unarmed DPS members operated the locksmith and building pass offices and had responsibility for installing and maintaining alarms and intrusion detection devices, securing classified material, and promoting industrial and information security.[1]

The Pentagon required extensive security arrangements around the clock to protect not only the people in the building, but also command and control operations, communication equipment, and a vast number of classified documents. To safeguard foreign official visitors, DPS worked with the United States Secret Service, the Department of State, and the Central Intelligence Agency. Whenever the Pentagon became the target of protest demonstrations DPS coordinated with civilian and military agencies in the region. Managing the flow of 100,000 tourists who visited the building each year also required coordination with other agencies.[2]

During the 1980s and 1990s DPS studied the lessons learned from truck bombings against Americans abroad and at home. Despite the steep costs, Jester and others strongly advocated incorporating as part of the Pentagon renovation such changes as blast-proof windows, a remote facility for truck deliveries, a blast wall between South Parking and the building, moving the Metro bus terminal further from the structure, and rerouting the exit path from the Metro train station—all measures eventually carried out.[3]

The 1995 sarin nerve gas attack in a Tokyo subway prompted DPS to initiate planning to counter a terrorist chemical or biological attack on the Pentagon. For Exercise Cloudy Office in 1998 DPS employed a scenario in which sarin was released after terrorists breached security, reached the office of the secretary of defense, and took hostages. The exercise, participated in by 500 people from local, state, and federal agencies, "killed" 26 people and "contaminated" 100 at the Pentagon. By 2001, however, DPS had made little progress in acquiring chemical and biological detection equipment, a key component of its counterterrorism planning.[4]

Because the Pentagon lay in the flight path of Reagan National Airport, the 16th busiest in the country, DPS also considered the possibility of the crash of an airplane into the building, an event it thought more likely to be accidental than deliberate. In 2000 DPS held a tabletop exercise with a scenario of a single-engine aircraft hitting the roof and bursting into flames.[5]

During these exercises DPS regarded the Arlington County Fire Department as the first responder since it normally served the Pentagon for fire and medical incidents. Arlington officials introduced DPS to the incident command system.* On the other hand, although the Arlington police were the law enforcement and security arm for the firefighting incident commander, they did not have jurisdiction on the Pentagon Reservation. Chief Edward Flynn of the Arlington County Police Department and Jester, however, knew each other well as members of the police chiefs committee of the Metropolitan Washington Council of Governments. Membership in the committee afforded Jester opportunities to get to know his counterparts throughout the region.[6]

On 11 September Jester, at his desk in room 4A275, received a telephone call from Glenn Flood, a public affairs specialist in the Office of the Secretary of Defense, alerting him to the first strike in New York City. Turning on his television set he saw United Flight 175 plunge into the second tower. When Lieutenant Michael Nesbitt, who ran the day-to-day operations in the DPS Communications Center on the 1st Floor, telephoned the chief asking if he knew of the New York plane crashes, Jester directed him to send a message to the building's Real Estate and Facilities Directorate reassuring all that the Pentagon remained secure—its Terrorist Threat Condition stayed at "Normal," meaning no present

* See Chapter IV.

threat of terrorist activity. Terrorist Threat Condition, renamed Terrorist Force Protection Condition in June 2001—a term not yet widely used in September 2001—ranged from Normal to four higher levels, Alpha through Delta.[7]

No one in DPS received warning of a hijacked aircraft on its way to the Washington area. Reacting to the news from New York City, Army Deputy Administrative Assistant Sandra Riley telephoned Jester and asked, "What do we have in place to protect from an airplane?" He replied, "Nothing." The Pentagon did not have an antiaircraft system on the roof of the building or on the grounds. Even if DPS had received word of an inbound plane, it had no plan to counter a suicide air attack. Had a warning been issued in time, DPS's only effective response would have been evacuation and dispersal of the building's occupants.[8]

A surface attack was a different matter. After reviewing contingency plans and procedures for tightening security with DPS Major James Phillips, Jester proceeded to the offices of Doc Cooke, head of the Washington Headquarters Services, and Paul Haselbush, Jester's immediate supervisor and director of Real Estate and Facilities. He informed them of DPS procedures to beef up patrols outside the building and impose stricter security checks at entry points. Before returning to his office Jester met with Deputy Chief John Pugrud and discussed the tighter security arrangements. He directed Pugrud to notify the DPS Communications Center to raise the Force Protection Condition to Alpha, meaning that a general threat of possible terrorist activity existed which required enhanced security.[9]

Pugrud had the phone in his hand dialing the center when Flight 77 hit. He heard the crash more than felt it. When the phone call was answered, he could hear the center's alarms activating and radio calls taking place. The dispatcher yelled, "We've been hit! We've been hit! Wedge one. Wedge one." DPS Officer Mark Bright, who was standing outside the building, saw the plane fly low over the Navy Annex and slam into the building. He radioed in his report, sped in his police cruiser to the crash site, and called in a description of the scene. Other officers also radioed the center.[10]

In his office about 600 feet from the crash site Jester thought the shaking and loud noise was caused by a heavy load of furniture on a pallet rolling over an uneven expansion joint. He heard someone yell, "We've been hit!" His first thought was "No, not here. It can't happen here." He looked out the window, saw smoke, ran down the stairs to the Communications Center, and shouted, "Get a camera up there!" Some of the center's eight monitor screens mounted on a wall remained blank because the crash had destroyed the camera nearest the impact site and cut connectivity to others.[11]

One monitor came on automatically, showing debris and doors blown off their hinges in Corridor 5. Officer Jesse DeVaughn brought up an image from a camera at the Navy Annex that had zoomed in on the roiling red flames and smoke. Nesbitt thought he was looking at the nearby gas station on South Joyce Street, so when he called to notify the Arlington County Fire Department of reports that a plane had hit the Pentagon, he also reported a fire at the gas station. Nesbitt then refocused the Annex camera to clearly show a normal gas station scene and the blaze at the Pentagon.[12]

In the meantime Jester told Nesbitt to use the public address system to order everyone to evacuate but not to use Corridors 3 and 4. The chief ran to the Center Court, then over to A-E Drive where he saw black smoke and raging flames. With others he tried to enter the building, but the intense heat forced them back. He heard shouts about windows ready to blow. Jester ran back to the Communications Center and told Nesbitt, "Mike, you've got to get Fire or somebody in here because people are trapped. They're burning alive." Jester ran out to A-E Drive again, heard people shouting for fire extinguishers, and directed DPS officers to find some, but he feared the equipment could do little against the horrible flames he had just seen and felt. The officers found extinguishers in the Remote Delivery Facility and brought them to A-E Drive. Moving on to the Center Court for a while, Jester tried to gather information and coordinate DPS activity, then headed for the impact site on the west side of the building, arriving after the E Ring floors had collapsed at 10:15 a.m.[13]

Although smoke began to filter into the Communications Center, DPS personnel remained at their posts, communicating with the ACFD and agencies with medical evacuation helicopters and responding to and monitoring radio calls, while utilizing 11 phone lines. Knowing that a move to the untested, off-site backup center further from the building could disrupt DPS communications for nearly an hour and might even result in a long-term disconnect, they were determined to remain in place and function as the DPS communication hub despite the thickening smoke and warnings about another hijacked airliner on its way to the area.[14]

Immediately after the crash, DPS officers rushed to the devastated area to rescue people. Officers Fred Hodges and Marc Baker left their police cruiser near the crash site and ran to help terrified people fleeing the inferno. "It seemed like an eternity before the fire trucks arrived, but it was only five minutes," Hodges recalled. Officer David Webster pedaled his bike from the Pentagon Metro bus area to the impact site where he helped people exit from Corridors 5 and 6. He met Master Police Officer George Clodfelter who with Officer Jose Rojas pulled victims from the burning building near the Heliport. One of these had hair and clothes on fire. Officer Arthur Rosati plunged into the smoke in a hallway to grab and guide a lieutenant colonel to safety. On meeting Clodfelter, who had blood all over his shirt, he heard him say, "This is insane."[15]

From the Remote Delivery Facility Officer James Murphy and K-9 Officer Isaac Ho'opi'i ran to the building, entering it through the double doors at the Heliport entrance. They attempted to move deeper into the 1st Floor but smoke and heat drove them back. Murphy then ran to a window and pulled people out. Ho'opi'i reentered the structure at a different point and carried people to safety. The heavy smoke caused some victims to lose their bearings, but the calming instructions from Ho'opi'i guided them to safety. In one pitch-dark room thick with smoke, William Sinclair, with severely burned hands and arms, heard Ho'opi'i say over and over, "If you can hear me, head toward my voice," which he did. Sinclair called Ho'opi'i his "guardian angel." Officers Bruce Centner and W. T. Carpenter joined other rescuers in the A-E Drive, leading injured survivors to safety and operating fire extinguishers to help others exit the building.[16]

DPS Major James Koerber, Investigator Robins Mapp, and two Virginia State troopers entered the building from the Heliport side, braving the smoke and heat to help dazed and injured people escape from the destruction. Koerber had rushed to the scene from the Navy Annex with Officers Michael Benedict and John Kinnard. Despite the threat of a building collapse, Mapp, Koerber, and the troopers removed debris, called out to survivors, and searched halls and rooms. On the 4th Floor above the aircraft entry hole, when smoke and heat disoriented one of the troopers, Officers Donald Behe and Abraham Diaz took him out of the Pentagon to paramedics who sent him to the hospital. Increasingly dangerous conditions also forced the others to leave the building shortly before the floors collapsed.[17]

Duty required many DPS personnel to remain at their posts within the building and at main entrances during and after the evacuation. Officers William McNeil, Richard Brown, and James Griggs, among those protecting the National Military Command Center and other JCS offices, could respond only with makeshift, barely effective means when the smoke reached them. McNeil used wet paper towels on his mouth and nose to filter out the smoke. Offered a dust mask, Brown readily donned it for the meager protection it offered. Griggs relied on wet tissues to breathe through and to soothe his irritated eyes.[18]

Although often at risk, no DPS officers were killed or seriously injured on 11 September. Unfortunately, Allen Boyle, a DPS contract worker installing alarms in Wedge 1, had apparently taken a break on the west side by Corridor 4, was close to the impact point, and perished.[19]

DPS and the Pentagon Building Management Office had responsibility for the orderly evacuation of the approximately 20,000 military and civilian personnel, contractors, vendors, and visitors in the building. They conducted periodic fire drills and provided floor plans, exit routes, and guidance about evacuations. Each organization had to select its own assembly area and publicize its exit paths. In the unrenovated wedges frequent false alarms accidentally triggered by maintenance work had often led to occupants not leaving until they received confirmation of a fire or other incident. On 16 August 2001 Cooke reported to DoD senior managers that a few days earlier while a fire burned in the cafeteria area some people ignored alarms and DPS evacuation directions. He stressed the importance of emergency response training for DoD personnel and urged managers to consult a circular recently issued by building management explaining supervisory responsibilities in the event of a fire or other dangerous situations. For the new, recently occupied Wedge 1, an evaluation after 11 September found that "many survivors said that they were not aware of evacuation plans for the areas of the building in which they worked and that there had been no drills during the period of time they occupied their new space."[20]

Since a local fire was not thought to warrant the evacuation of the entire building, the fire alarm systems in the renovated Wedge 1 and the unrenovated Wedges 2-5 were not designed to sound throughout the entire structure. The explosion and fires destroyed or damaged some alarms; others automatically activated. Alarms in corridors on the opposite side of the building from the crash site did not automatically activate; occupants and DPS officers set them off manually. DPS personnel and building maintenance workers also entered alarm control rooms near the building apexes and activated alarms for an entire wedge. A pre-recorded voice evacuation message and an alarm sounded in the new and old wedges, but in the old wedges the message was often unintelligible. In addition, DPS's patched together "Big Voice" public address system, allowing an officer to issue specific exit instructions during an evacuation, did not amplify well or reach all parts of the building; in some parts it was difficult or impossible to understand.[21]

Jester wanted the entire building evacuated except for critical command sites. Knowing that some people could not hear or understand the alarms or might ignore them if they were unaware of the plane crash, Pugrud instructed the staff of the Security Services Branch to join armed officers to pound on doors and enter offices from the 5th Floor to the Basement, ordering everyone to leave. Locked emergency doors at the Mall and River Entrances required people to find other routes. Deputy Secretary Wolfowitz directed a guard to open the emergency door near the River Entrance that became an exit route. Officers unlocked the Mall emergency door as well.[22]

By and large the massive evacuation directed by DPS was orderly, but emotions ran high. Some people in South Parking were dazed and crying. On the River side, D.C. Harbor Patrol Officer Jeffrey Blevins observed: "Everybody was running out. The first group that we were dealing with were the ones that were just kind of in shock. They didn't know what was going on; they just knew there was an explosion." Army Colonel Bruce Bachus heard people "yelling and screaming" as they ran past him. John Irby, head of the Federal Facilities Division, observed, "Out in the corridor you could see the terror on people's faces as they left. There was no question that it was not a drill." People with disabilities received help if they needed it; most got out with little difficulty.[23]

DPS could not help the many Pentagon evacuees who carried wireless telephones but could not send their calls through the communication networks. Local television reporter David Statter referred to the situation as "cellular gridlock." Navy Lieutenant (jg) James McDonner noted that about 15 to 20 people using his phone tried unsuccessfully to make connections. Sometimes if a call got through, the caller would ask others in the crowd if they wanted to send a message to a relative via a third party. Army Major Carl Jaley reached his sister in Seattle and gave her a list of names and numbers to phone on behalf of others. Army Colonel Mark Volk's wife received a call from a stranger telling her that her husband was fine and that the caller could not talk at length because she had to continue contacting people on a list. Telephones connected to wires functioned much more reliably than cell phones; people formed long queues at pay phones such as those in the Pentagon City shopping mall to await their turn to call family, friends, and supervisors.[24]

Jester moved through the crowd to meet Incident Commander Schwartz at South Parking and walked with him to South Hayes Street under the I-395 overpass where Schwartz set up his command post to elude the second hijacked airliner reportedly headed toward the Pentagon. A man in motion the rest of the day, Jester went back and forth between the I-395 location and the crash site when he was not in the Pentagon at the DPS Communications Center or providing status briefings for Rumsfeld, Cooke, and others. Major Koerber, who eventually arrived at the I-395 command post, during Jester's absence functioned as the DPS liaison with the incident commander. Pugrud stayed in the Center Court as the police liaison with Fire Battalion Chief Dale Smith. Jester had ordered the recall of all off-duty officers. Many rushed to the Pentagon without a recall message, but massive traffic jams delayed their arrival. Once there, heavy smoke in the armory made it difficult to retrieve service weapons. After the attack DPS raised the Force Protection Condition to Delta, the highest level; officers took maximum security measures.[25]

FBI and the Crime Scene

In the vanguard of federal government responders racing to support the rescue, firefighting, and security operations at the Pentagon, FBI Special Agent Christopher Combs had taken action in accordance with the Federal Response Plan first issued in 1992. Shortly after the attack, the Federal Emergency Management Agency activated the plan. Designed to bring together 28 federal departments and agencies and the American Red Cross to aid state and local governments in coping with presidentially declared disasters and emergencies, the plan identified lead federal agencies to perform 12 emergency support functions such as conducting search and rescue operations, handling and disposing of hazardous materials, and providing health and medical services. In 1995 President Bill Clinton issued Presidential Decision Directive (PDD) 39, "United States Policy on Counterterrorism," and in 1997 an annex based on PDD 39 was added to the Federal Response Plan expanding the plan's scope to include acts of terrorism.[26]

As the lead federal agency responsible for dealing with terrorism within the United States, the Department of Justice had delegated operational responsibility to the FBI. Responsible for "crisis management," primarily law enforcement functions, the FBI was charged to anticipate, thwart, respond to, and resolve terrorist incidents. FEMA, as lead agency for "consequence management," was charged with coordinating federal efforts to protect public health and safety, restore government services, and provide emergency relief. In January 2001 the FBI and FEMA issued the "United States Government Interagency Domestic Terrorism Concept of Operations Plan," affirming FEMA's lead role in consequence management and the FBI's in crisis management.*[27]

On his arrival about 9:50 a.m. Combs reported to Schwartz, and asked how the FBI could support him. Schwartz told Combs, who was well-known to him, that he wanted intelligence about the attack. The agent had secure radio contact with the FBI's Washington Field Office at Judiciary Square in Washington, which had direct lines to the Strategic Information Operations Center at FBI headquarters on Pennsylvania Avenue. He passed to Schwartz reports from the Field Office and warned him shortly before 10:15 a.m. that the fourth hijacked airliner was on a direct flight path to Washington. When the airliner threat vanished after the 20-minute countdown, Combs received and relayed the all clear report from the Field Office.[28]

FBI agents arriving at the Pentagon reported to Combs, who initially exercised FBI command and control on scene. Later in the afternoon Assistant Special Agent in Charge Robert Blecksmith took over on-scene command, and on 13 September Special Agent in Charge Arthur Eberhart assumed the responsibility.[29]

* The FBI defined a terrorist incident as "a violent act or an act dangerous to human life, in violation of the criminal laws of the United States, or of any state, to intimidate or coerce a government, the civilian population, or any segment thereof, in furtherance of political and social objectives."

To establish for the record the cause of the explosion and fire the FBI conducted interviews with eyewitnesses and learned that a commercial airliner had hit the building, dispelling early suspicions and reports that a truck bomb or small commuter plane had caused the damage. Seeking to collect lasting visual evidence, an FBI agent asked for assistance from two combat photographers, Marine Corporal Jason Ingersoll and Navy Petty Officer Kevin Rimrodt, who took photographs of the damaged building, the debris field, the path of the plane, and also the crowds of people who gathered to watch, among whom it was thought there might be terrorists. When another hijacked airliner was thought to be on its way, the agent asked Ingersoll and Rimrodt to stand where they could photograph the incoming aircraft if it smashed into the building. The photographers watched as everyone fled, leaving them behind at an exposed site to wait for the next catastrophic strike. The all clear signal brought them special relief. Other photographers boarded helicopters to take aerial shots of the Pentagon.[30]

As the fire raged, FBI agents identified grid zones and formed a line of Arlington police officers, military personnel, and others to walk shoulder to shoulder on the west side lawn to search for remnants from the airliner. Keeping clear of rescue and firefighting efforts, agents then identified, photographed, removed, and bagged pieces of the airplane and personal effects. Although much of the plane disintegrated within the Pentagon, the searchers found many scraps and a few personal items widely scattered on the grass and Heliport. Plane remnants varied from half-dollar size to a few feet long. Anxious to hunt for investigative leads, the FBI scoured the debris field as soon as possible to prevent souvenir seekers from helping themselves or fire trucks from running over, crushing, and destroying evidence. That morning and afternoon and the next day they conducted line sweeps, systematically searching through the debris, finding the larger plane pieces to the north of the impact point.[31]

Seeking assured security for the Pentagon area, Combs met briefly with Jester in South Parking and again at the Incident Command Post under the I-395 overpass. Both worried that terrorists would again hit the Pentagon and agreed that members of the DPS SWAT team should protect the command post. To control entrance to the area, Arlington County officers augmented the FBI and DPS by guarding the perimeter of the reservation along Route 27, now closed to all but emergency vehicles. Arlington Battalion Chief Randy Gray on the west side of the edifice remembered, "When I got my assignment I looked up and there were guys with guns all around. I felt that they had my back. It was important to know that our back was covered so I could concentrate on my job." Fire Chief Plaugher directed the Arlington County Emergency Operations Center to obtain 2,000 feet of chain link fence for access control, and a contractor began installation that day.[32]

Not overly concerned that the terrorists might have carried chemicals or biological agents on board Flight 77 since a plane crash was an ineffective delivery mode for toxic substances, Combs and Schwartz nonetheless wanted additional air testing at the site to detect chemical, biological, and radiological weapons of mass destruction.* The county's Emergency Operations Center asked FEMA to arrange for the Department of Health and Human Services to deploy the National Medical Response Team (NMRT) to conduct tests for poisons possibly released by the hijackers. Based in and managed by Arlington County, the NMRT's 36 members lived and worked in the region; team members arrived at the site within hours. After tests proved negative, the team focused on setting up and operating a decontamination tent to wash down workers in their protective clothing as they left the Pentagon after shoring up columns, clearing paths through rubble, and locating and removing human remains.[33]

Inside the building, late that night and around the clock afterward, Special Agents John Adams and Thomas O'Connor led teams recording locations of human remains and numbering, tagging, and photographing them. Aircraft parts were placed in a pile on the lawn and then in a steel container or a tent for examination and disposal by National Transportation Safety Board (NTSB) officials. When loads of debris were trucked to North Parking for more detailed sifting, the FBI took custody of recovered items deemed to be evidence. DPS provided initial safekeeping for classified documents and disks.[34]

The aircraft's flight data and cockpit voice recorders, the so-called "black boxes," were found 14 September about 4:00 a.m. in the Pentagon near the hole in the inner C Ring wall. The FBI transferred custody of the canisters to the NTSB for analysis. Both recorders had been installed in the rear of the aircraft beneath the tail. The badly damaged voice recorder yielded no information, but the flight recorder provided data about altitude, speed, and headings.[35]

* See also Chapter VI for a discussion of air quality.

For command operations, the FBI stationed its mobile command post near the Heliport. At 6:00 a.m. on 12 September, it established a Joint Operations Center at the Fort Myer Community Center, in accordance with federal plans requiring that after a terrorist incident the FBI set up a JOC to include federal, state, and local officials with crisis management and consequence management responsibilities. Such quick action was possible because months earlier the agency had surveyed regional sites and selected Fort Myer as a JOC location to coordinate the law enforcement response to expected disruptive and violent protests during World Bank and International Monetary Fund meetings scheduled for Washington later in September. Twenty-six government organizations sent representatives to the JOC, commanded by Special Agent in Charge Timothy Bereznay.[36]

To assist the FBI with its evidence search, DPS and contractors gave agents videos from two cameras positioned north of the crash site. The recently installed digital cameras were still undergoing testing as part of a security system enabling a guard in a protective booth to identify drivers in cars heading toward the parking lot for the Pentagon Mall Entrance and to raise turnstile arms permitting entry. The cameras captured images of the west facade bursting into a huge fireball as Flight 77 crashed. An image a second before the explosion showed an indistinct view of the plane at nearly ground level heading toward the building.[37]

The FBI investigation involved far more than the Pentagon. On the morning of the crash agents raced to Dulles Airport in Virginia, where American Airlines Flight 77 had originated, to collect evidence and interview ticket agents, security personnel, baggage and food handlers, and others. At its peak the global investigation involved 7,000 agents, making it the largest and most complex investigation in the bureau's history. The FBI named its overall investigation of the 11 September attacks PENTTBOM, an acronym for "Pentagon, Twin Towers bombing."[38]

Federal, State, and Local Police and the Old Guard

Within minutes of the attack, federal, state, and local civilian police officers reached the Pentagon. Among the first to respond were helicopters from the U.S. Park Police Aviation Unit near the Anacostia River in Washington. When an alarm sounded and the emergency circuit "crash" phone rang in the unit office,

Sergeant Ron Galey answered the call from the Reagan National Airport air traffic controller, who reported that the tower had just lost track of a Boeing 757 aircraft in the vicinity of the Pentagon. Galey, Sergeant Kenneth Burchell, and their crews quickly took off in two medical evacuation helicopters, arriving at the Pentagon within minutes. As Burchell landed on the Route 27 cloverleaf he could see people on fire running from the building. He loaded two burn victims and flew them to the Washington Hospital Center. The center's MedStar helicopter landed to transport another victim. Galey remained airborne when the tower at Reagan National gave him air traffic control responsibility because the thick billowing smoke from the explosion blocked the tower's view and overwhelmed its ventilation system. He soon passed control responsibility to a District of Columbia Metropolitan Police Department helicopter equipped with communication systems. Landing to transport more victims and finding none on the west side of the building, he remained on the ground until the rumored threat of another airliner attack passed. Galey then went airborne over the Pentagon to send live images of the scene to Secret Service, FBI, Metropolitan Police, and Park Police operations centers. Park Police helicopters also carried incident command team members aloft to examine the extent of the conflagration and structural damage. Afterward, they flew security-related missions throughout the region.[39]

The first on-scene commander for the Arlington County Police Department, Lieutenant Robert Medairos, arranged with DPS that his officers would secure the perimeter of the Pentagon Reservation, freeing DPS to focus on the building and grounds. Lieutenant Brian Berke and Sergeant James Daly moved quickly to keep all but emergency traffic off the feeder roads to Route 27 immediately west of the crash site. Police officers closed the route to regular traffic and prevented first responders from parking vehicles haphazardly and blocking emergency lanes.[40]

In the absence of Chief Flynn and two deputy chiefs, attending out-of-town conferences, responsibility for command of the Arlington police on the scene fell to Captain Rebecca Hackney, a district commander. Arriving at the Pentagon before the E Ring collapse she moved with her mobile command post further away from the crash site to Route 27. When the threat of a second air attack loomed, she relocated the post under a highway overpass near Route 27 with a line of sight to the fire. Hackney, who had received training in the incident

Above: An FBI-directed line sweep in front of the Pentagon Heliport to find evidence of the terrorist attack.
Below: Remnant of the fuselage from Flight 77.

Secretary Rumsfeld at his Pentagon press conference the evening of 11 September, with (left to right) Secretary of the Army Thomas White, Chairman of the Joint Chiefs of Staff General Hugh Shelton, Sen. John Warner (R-Va.), and Sen. Carl Levin (D-Mich.).

"Mayor of the Pentagon" David O. (Doc) Cooke, Director of Administration and Management.

Above: Personnel emerge from the A-E Drive access road leading into Center Court.

Below: Soldiers from the Military District of Washington arrive at the Pentagon Reservation.

Dogs and handlers in search and rescue operations.

John Jester (left), chief of the Defense Protective Service.

Decontamination.

Preparing to transport body bags.

Heliport air tower controllers' burnt cars.

Damaged interior offices sheared open by the collapse of the E Ring.

Above: Clock in Room 3E452, located near the "hinge" of the collapsed floors. The 9/11 Commission determined that the plane hit the building at 9:37 a.m.
Below: An inside view.

Lieutenant General John Van Alstyne directed the assistance program for families of victims.

Joyce Rumsfeld, the wife of the defense secretary, visits Sheila Moody, 13 September 2001.

Above: Days after the attack, the lawn west of the Pentagon filled with vehicles, equipment, and tents for command and control, search and recovery, shoring, demolition, and security.
Below: "Camp Unity" in South Parking provided a respite from search and recovery operations.

Piece of the aircraft that struck the Pentagon.

Flight data recorder found in the building near the hole in the inner C Ring wall leading to A-E Drive.

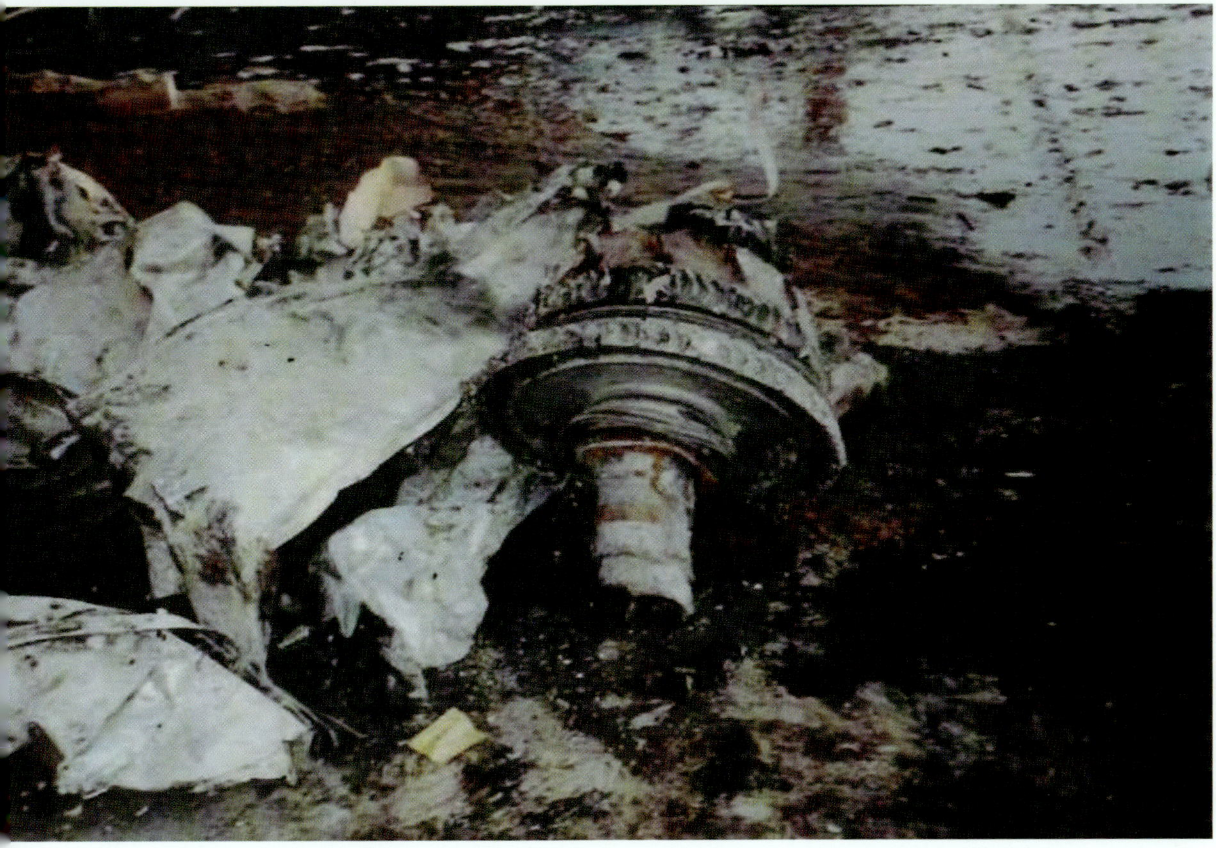

Above: One of the larger pieces of debris from Flight 77.
Below: FBI representatives Arthur Eberhart and Van A. Harp (left) hand over management of the crash site to Major General James Jackson, Commander, U.S. Army Military District of Washington, 26 September 2001 .

Above: Demolition in preparation for reconstruction.
Below: The inner E Ring wall still stands days after the collapse.

Above: Debris sifting operations in North Parking.
Below: Reconstructing the damaged area.

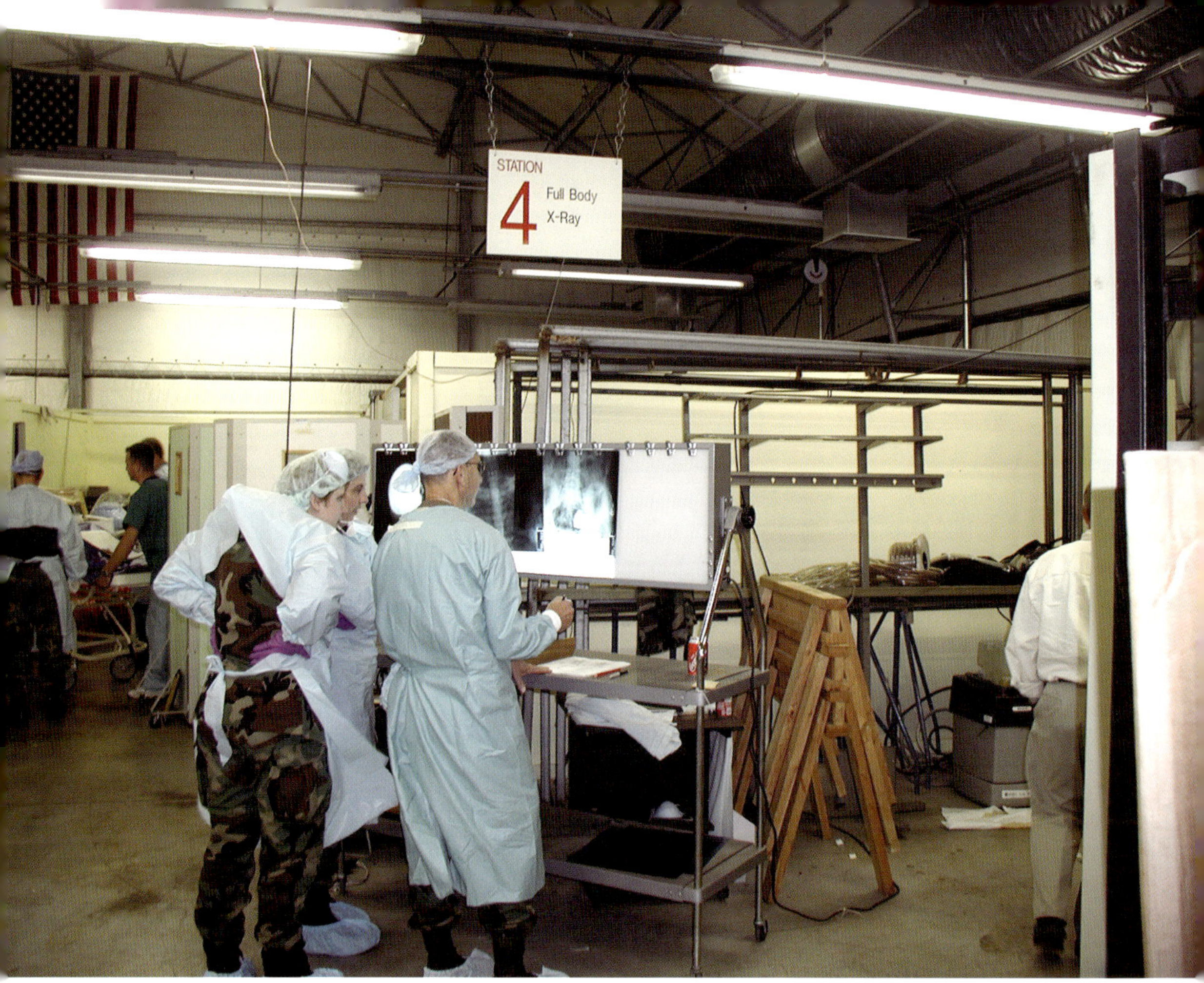

Above: Using radiology to help identify victims at the Dover Port Mortuary.

Right: Identifying victims at the Dover Port Mortuary.

Impromptu memorial near the Navy Annex.

Soldiers from Company B, 3rd U.S. Infantry Regiment, "The Old Guard."

Pentagon workers attend October 2001 memorial service for victims of the 9/11 attack.

command system, immediately directed officers to assume prescribed responsibilities: directing vehicle traffic and pedestrians, planning logistics, setting up a staging area, requesting mutual aid as needed, and protecting the firefighters.[41]

With thousands of Pentagon occupants crossing nearby streets en masse, police cars and fire trucks racing to the scene, helicopters landing and lifting off, and automobile traffic stopping as occupants gawked at the burning building, roads around the Pentagon had to be closed to non-emergency traffic. Arlington County and Virginia State police, experienced in blocking entry ramps and detouring traffic along routes near the building for two annual races—the Marine marathon and the Army 10-mile run—quickly closed key intersections and points. Sergeant Richard Keevill, one of the first Virginia state troopers on the scene to coordinate road closings, had years of experience working with DPS and Arlington police. Arlington County deputy sheriffs, detectives, and park rangers assisted in partially shutting down four major routes and more than a half-dozen streets.[42]

Virginia troopers closed the northbound lanes of I-395 nine miles south of the Pentagon at the intersection of I-95 and I-495 (Washington Beltway), blocking all entry ramps. Park Police closed Arlington Memorial Bridge and the George Washington Memorial Parkway; D.C. Metropolitan police closed the 14th Street Bridge. Sixteen Fairfax County motorcycle officers augmented the patrols of the Arlington motorcycle police, keeping pedestrians off roads and away from emergency access lanes, redirecting sightseers heading toward the Pentagon, and searching for aircraft debris on I-395. Also helping with road closings and pedestrian traffic were officers from the Treasury Department's U.S. Mint Police and a lone officer from the Justice Department's U.S. Border Patrol, Assistant Chief Patrol Agent Jeffrey Parsons from Del Rio, Texas, in town on business. Parsons felt the explosion and saw the smoke from his hotel near South Parking. He changed into his uniform with sidearm, donned his "Smokey the Bear" hat, and positioned himself at a key intersection on Army Navy Drive, keeping it clear for emergency vehicles. He stayed at the post all day.[43]

In the District of Columbia the White House and Capitol were hurriedly evacuated, the federal and D.C. governments dismissed workers, and companies closed their doors. Thousands of people poured out, clogging transportation routes; gridlock gripped the region, and some people abandoned their cars. Viewing abandoned vehicles near the Pentagon as possible bombs, police dispatched K-9 dog explosive detection teams to investigate. The D.C. Harbor Patrol and the U.S. Coast Guard checked for explosive devices under the 14th Street Bridge and kept boats from docking under Potomac River bridges. About 10:30 a.m. a report in official channels, repeated through the rumor mill, mistakenly stated that a car bomb had exploded at the State Department. Reports about truck bombs at the Capitol, fires on the Mall, and a "suspicious" rental truck near the Pentagon, possibly loaded with explosives, added to the confusion. Sergeant Keith Bohn of the Park Police recalled, "There were a lot of things coming up. All of a sudden, everything was just unbelievable—to check bridges for abandoned cars which were believed to be packed with explosives. So, we were running from one report of things to another report. Actually, in the city nothing else, in essence, happened that day, but ... lots of fear was running rampant."[44]

Arlington Deputy Police Chief Stephen Holl drove hurriedly from Richmond, Virginia, arrived at the Arlington Police command post under the overpass about noon, and took over from Hackney. A few hours later Flynn returned from New Jersey and assumed command. In one of his first actions, Holl ordered the implementation of a decision to stage police resources at Arlington Fire Station 5, about a mile from the Pentagon. Police officers from the county and neighboring jurisdictions were to report there to receive instructions and assignments before moving on to the Pentagon.[45]

A signatory to both the Northern Virginia Law Enforcement Mutual Aid Agreement and the Northern Virginia Sheriffs Mutual Aid Agreement, Arlington County invoked prescribed actions on 11 September. In response, a host of local Virginia jurisdictions sent police officers and/or sheriffs to Station 5 over the duration of the emergency: City of Alexandria, Fairfax County, City of Fairfax, City of Falls Church, Loudoun County, City of Manassas, Prince William County, Fauquier County, and George Mason University. From Maryland help came from the City of Greenbelt, Montgomery County, Prince George's County, and the City of Rockville. Officials from these localities had experience working together through the Metropolitan Washington Council of Governments.[46]

Help came also from a number of specialized law enforcement organizations. Agents from the Alexandria office of Virginia's Alcohol Beverage and Control Board arrived at the River Entrance side of the Pentagon not long after the plane struck and assisted the injured, drove people to hospitals, and helped to evacuate the Child Development Center, as did National Park rangers. Personnel from the Treasury Department's Bureau of Alcohol, Tobacco, and Firearms arrived at the Pentagon about 11:00 a.m. and immediately assisted the Arlington police with site security. The Justice Department's Immigration and Naturalization Service sent officers who helped guard the perimeter from 6:00 p.m. until 6:00 a.m. for the next few nights. Holl welcomed this support: "It was nice to have 20 extra federal agents in their raid jackets with their guns walking around because we don't know who was out there surveying us and how we responded and where our weaknesses might be. So it was great to be able to plug them at different posts and confuse people, if nothing else."[47]

Under a mutual aid agreement with the District of Columbia, Flynn asked Metropolitan Police Chief Charles Ramsey for help with crowd and traffic control; Ramsey sent about 50 officers on 12 September. On the 11th the Metropolitan police had their hands full in the District supporting Secret Service agents and Capitol and Park Police guarding the White House, the vice president's residence, the Capitol, and monuments. They also responded when the Union Station train depot was evacuated because of a truck bomb scare, put extra patrols at the city's critical infrastructure facilities, and tried to manage the traffic chaos in the city's business and government sections. That morning Ramsey received a report that six planes from Europe were flying under radar coverage and heading toward the District of Columbia. Fortunately a Federal Aviation Agency representative assigned to the police command center determined the information to be incorrect.[48]

While Arlington police provided security for the rescue and firefighting operations at the Pentagon, they maintained patrols in neighborhoods and responded to calls from frightened citizens and business owners concerned about suspicious people and packages. Captain Hackney recalled, "The officers were going from call to call to call to call." Within a fortnight Arlington County shifted more Pentagon perimeter patrols to officers from neighboring jurisdictions, freeing Arlington police for regular patrol duties and securing the county's high-value facilities.[49]

The organized military role in support of firefighting, rescue, and police operations expanded in size and scope after arrival at the Pentagon from Fort

McNair in Washington of General Jackson, not long after noon. As commander of the Army's Military District of Washington, Jackson had responsibility for security, ceremonial, and training duties in the National Capital Region but not at the Pentagon. Aware of the huge and urgent demands of the emergency, Director of the Army Staff Lieutenant General John Pickler told Jackson to provide military support for operations at the crash site. Later in the day, Jackson met with Army Secretary Thomas White who told him that Rumsfeld wanted the Army to take the lead among the military services in supporting the emergency response at the Pentagon. This lead role followed established policy assigning to the Army executive agent responsibilities for DoD assistance to local civilian authorities during disasters and emergencies nationwide.[50]

On arrival Jackson met with Chief Plaugher, whom he had met previously, and informed him of the deployment of the MDW engineer company from Fort Belvoir for search and rescue operations.* The general also met later with Schwartz. He joined Schwartz's unified command team that included representatives from the FBI, DPS, FEMA, and Arlington police. That evening he ordered his mobile command vehicle positioned close by the incident commander's; after a few days he moved immediately adjacent to Schwartz's command post.[51]

Soon after arriving at the scene Jackson relieved about a hundred volunteer Pentagon military of all ranks who continued to stand by at the crash site waiting to carry stretchers, replacing them with 3rd U.S. Infantry (Old Guard) soldiers stationed at Fort Myer. The general recalled: "My first thought was to get some kind of cohesive unit in here, specifically the Old Guard down there, then start to release these volunteers to get them out of the way. . . . Not that they weren't doing exactly what they were supposed to do, it's just the sooner I could get guys in class A and Bs [uniforms] out of here and have troops in fatigues who could be doing things for us, the better off we were. I wanted NCOs in charge of small units, and officers in charge of bigger units."[52]

Old Guard soldiers spent the next few weeks participating in search and rescue/recovery operations as their primary mission,† but they also performed security duties. In the evening of the 11th, dressed in battle dress uniforms but

* See Chapter IV.
† See Chapter V.

without weapons, some went to Arlington Cemetery to assist Park Police in clearing people from an area affording a good vantage point for observing the burning building. The soldiers also joined in searching for airplane parts, as did Naval Criminal Investigative Service agents who conducted line sweeps of the cemetery the next morning and found evidentiary items.[53]

The first night, platoons of soldiers donned dust masks and joined DPS officers in putting up FBI crime scene tape at Pentagon hallway entrances on all floors from Corridors 2 to 7 and then stood sentry duty. The next day some people returning to work, seeing that hallways between Corridors 6 and 7 were not damaged, asked to be allowed to retrieve personal items and professional data, but the guards, as ordered, allowed no one in without special authorization. Private Keith Dooley recalled, "If any general or anybody wanted to go up to their offices, we didn't let them just for the fact that there's a bunch of doors that were still open with Top Secret . . . in there, and they didn't want anybody going in there until everything was checked out." In other areas guards prevented people from entering offices possibly contaminated with asbestos, lead paint, and unhealthy air.[54]

An exception had to be made for the staff of the OSD Graphics Office in 2E271. They received permission to return to their space in the off-limits area to produce much-needed charts showing the extent of damage on each of the Pentagon's floors from fire, water, and smoke as maintenance crews provided the information. The graphics specialists worked around the clock preparing materials for emergency operations and press briefings. The FBI examined rooms in the building and authorized their release as soon as possible. After a few weeks, however, people still could not return to some cleared but damp, dark, and warm offices because of the thick mold that posed a health hazard. Eventually plywood walls were constructed to keep unauthorized people away from hallways closest to the impact site, the "hot zone."[55]

The Old Guard also pulled guard duty at the North Parking area. The FBI, assisted by officers from a large number of federal, state, and local agencies, used the location to sift through tons of material from the impact site in search of human remains, personal effects, airplane remnants, documents, and other items. Around the mound of debris, the sifting lane, and the evidentiary piles were tents and a newly installed security wire fence. Illumination from generator-powered floodlights allowed the search to continue around the clock.[56]

Above the sifting area, Route 27 and its exit ramp to Route 110 North adjoined the lot. Despite the closed roads curious spectators walked to the site to watch the work and sometimes took photos, even though signs warned against doing so. Unarmed soldiers stood guard for "presence" and to augment armed personnel from the DPS, FBI, U.S. Marshal Service, and local police who kept people moving and confiscated camera film.[57]

Tightened Security and Military Police

In the days following the attack DPS contended with the many problems brought on by the expanded security requirements. Captain Randall Harper functioned as the DPS on-site commander, with Lieutenant William Stout as assistant commander. DPS worked from a command post consisting in succession of a vehicle, a small truck, tents, and a borrowed mobile van. Stout attended Schwartz's unified command meetings as well as FBI briefings. Leaves and training for DPS personnel were cancelled; for the next four months all worked 12-hour shifts instead of the usual 8 hours. Radio communication among DPS guards outside the building worked well as long as batteries lasted; recharging equipment received constant use and newly purchased batteries kept the radios functioning. Unfortunately the different radio frequencies employed prevented DPS from talking with officers from local police departments. Communication greatly improved after the Secret Service and Verizon Communications set up cellular telephone towers on the Pentagon grounds and distributed cell phones to security personnel and others.[58]

Force Protection Condition Delta required the highest security at the Pentagon, but the thousands of people who responded without clearance to the emergency enormously complicated the situation on 12 September. With the workforce returning in large numbers police searched cars and required drivers and passengers to identify themselves. South Parking still held many automobiles left from the day before; emergency support vehicles rapidly filled the empty space. Police routed cars to partially cordoned-off North Parking. Automobile security checks caused long traffic backups extending to some of the reopened highways and bridges near the Pentagon; lines stretched for miles into the District of Columbia and Virginia. Metro trains and buses did not stop at the Pentagon the morning of the 12th, but fortunately the Pentagon City station lay within easy walking distance. Within days workers were allowed to park at the Pentagon City mall and at Reagan National Airport, which remained closed to air traffic for 23 days, easing North Parking congestion.[59]

For better security DoD shuttle buses were rerouted from South Parking to Boundary Channel Drive, further from the building. The Joint Operations Center gave emergency cargo priority clearance for access. Arlington police and state troopers provided escorts for deliveries to search and recovery operations. DPS directed trucks to an area where a K-9 explosive detection unit could check cargo. For inspections and responses to bomb threats, DPS received K-9 assistance from the Army, federal, and other police agencies. They found no explosive cargo or bombs.[60]

To protect the Incident Command Post and watch for suspicious activity, Arlington County SWAT and anti-sniper teams, DPS teams, and others took up positions atop the tall Drug Enforcement Administration building across from the Pentagon City mall and on the roofs of the Navy Annex and Pentagon. Arlington officers also assisted DPS in guarding hotels in nearby Crystal City where DoD had arranged billeting for families of victims and for search and rescue units. The day after the attack some people who had not heard from family members gathered on the Navy Annex hill overlooking the Pentagon and just beyond the police off-limits boundary, where they had a clear view of the building as they awaited word about their missing relatives. Soon the site became a memorial to the victims with family, friends, colleagues, neighbors, and strangers leaving photos, notes, flags, and other items of remembrance. On Saturday, 15 September, Coneleous Alexander, a Navy Annex building manager, and a contractor installed a memorial board on the hill; it soon filled with photographs of those who died at the Pentagon. Police guarded the site, visitors, and memorabilia.[61]

More police arrived on 12 September between 7:00 and 9:00 a.m., when two companies of the 115th Military Police Battalion of the Maryland National Guard, commanded by Lieutenant Colonel Bernard Liswell, reached the Pentagon to assist with security; joined by a headquarters company that evening the battalion remained until 30 September. The soldiers guarded the temporary morgue, hallways, and classified storage areas. They also secured the perimeter of the crash site and the sifting operations in North Parking, denying access to reporters, photographers, and onlookers. When the president and later the prime minister of Japan visited the site the battalion provided additional security. Over three weeks, the military police detained only a few people at the crash site, one of them an Army general officer not authorized to be at the scene.[62]

Providing security became a growing concern as the lawn between the west facade and Route 27 became increasingly congested with command post vehicles, vans, trucks, trailers, cranes, front-end loaders, other heavy equipment, tents, generators, and power and telephone lines. The fence Plaugher had ordered ran along Route 27, forming the outer perimeter of the crash site. DPS established and guarded five entry points through the fence.[63]

In South Parking there sprang up "Camp Unity," an accumulation of tents and facilities for the food and aid assistance from the Red Cross and Salvation Army; chaplains and counselors; supplies and food services donated by commercial establishments; a small post exchange; ice and hand-washing stations; light towers, telephones, and latrines. NCIS Special Agent Michelle Jackson, who worked on the sifting operation, observed: "Food was never a problem. You never had to leave the scene. You could eat, drink, change your clothes, brush your teeth—all right there." Army Private First Class Michael Chandler from the Old Guard was pleasantly surprised that he did not have to eat field rations day after day. Army Specialist William Corcoran, who also labored on recovery operations, later commented that the support elements were "heaven sent, I mean really. They made it a lot more bearable."[64]

Some who came to the Pentagon were pretenders or freelancers. The absence of an effective identification system to control the large number of people that passed through the outer perimeter fence to support firefighting and recovery operations worried incident command, DPS, and FBI officials. The day after the attack DPS arrested three people in firefighting gear who were not firefighters. "When you have a major event, certain people are like moths around a light bulb," noted Jester. "They come to the scene as thrill seekers."[65]

On the 12th the FBI and DPS quickly removed from the west side of the building anyone who was not fighting the fire or doing search and rescue work. As people returned they were screened and given color-coded plastic wrist bands provided by DPS and the Arlington police; the supply of 2,000 bands was soon exhausted.[66]

The following day DPS used its photo identification computer system to make badges, but the large number processed caused the unit to burn out. Finally DPS and the FBI procured from the Secret Service five mobile stations that mass-produced photo badges. Members of the Army Band from Fort Myer operated the equipment and compiled lists of badge recipients who had displayed agency identification and a driver's license. Eventually everyone connected with firefighting, search and rescue, criminal investigation, security, and building operations had a badge. Some 4,000 people, an excessive number, received badges that allowed access to all sites including the dangerous and sensitive impact zone within the building.[67]

Authorities reviewed badge lists, asked fire, military, and security organizations for priorities, and compiled a new short list of people who received red badges allowing access to the devastated areas of the Pentagon, now referred to as the "red zone." A fence close to the building further restricted access. At first DPS and military police and then U.S. marshals guarded the inner perimeter and checked for badges. Security was ironclad. The day Plaugher escorted Vice President Cheney to the site, they tried to enter the red zone even though the vice president did not have a badge. The guard said, "I'm sorry, Mr. Vice President," and denied him entry. Plaugher eased the refusal by telling Cheney that he probably did not want to enter the building because he would then have to be decontaminated. The vice president replied, "Absolutely right. I don't need a field shower."[68]

Granting access to destroyed and damaged offices required taking precautions. Representatives from the two largest offices demolished in the attack, the Army's Office of the Deputy Chief of Staff for Personnel and the Navy Command Center, urgently requested permission to retrieve documents, disks, and hardware from the damaged areas. The Army's servers and routers on the 2nd Floor were far enough from the impact site to survive, but they were threatened by water and smoke damage. Fire officials examined the area for structural integrity, after which the FBI checked and allowed access to the server room. Starting on 13 September and working all the next day technicians, accompanied by DPS officers and military police, removed the heavy equipment from racks and transported it to the nearby Hoffman Building in Alexandria, Virginia, where the Personnel Office had been reconstituted. On 13 September NCIS Special Agent Dennis Becker led a team into the Navy Command Center. During the next week the team brought out highly classified documents and disks and equipment, making sure that remaining safes were secure for later retrieval.[69]

A steady stream of requests for access to rooms in off-limits areas of the Pentagon flowed to the incident commander; people urgently wanted to retrieve personal belongings and professional items. MDW officials at the Joint Operations Center evaluated and prioritized requests from organizations and people of all ranks. Firefighters, engineers, and FBI agents inspected the sites before they authorized entry. Workers in protective clothing were led to the offices by escorts concerned with safety and security. Later, the FBI cleared rooms and turned them over to Pentagon renovation personnel who permitted employees from affected offices to enter and claim belongings.[70]

The enormous task of securing and disposing of many thousands of documents from destroyed and damaged offices fell to DPS and the FBI.[71] Unclassified documents included information readily available to the public, personnel data protected by the Privacy Act, or information marked "For Official Use Only." Classified documents included those marked Confidential, Secret, Top Secret, and higher levels, in paper format, on disks, and in computers, stored in safes or kept on desks and in file cabinets within highly secure rooms.

When the aircraft's impact blew holes through the C Ring wall between Corridors 4 and 5, it also blew many documents into A-E Drive. DPS officers retrieved and guarded them. During the search for human remains and evidence, stacks of charred and wet papers were carried through the holes and placed on the drive for DPS to remove. Initially, the FBI set up an evidence recovery point near the Heliport where documents mixed with other debris were taken. Classified documents raked up during the sifting operation in North Parking were brought in wheelbarrows to massive document piles; there teams of agents from the military criminal investigative agencies and intelligence organizations clad in Tyvek protective clothing examined them for disposition.[72]

Within weeks, as PENREN contractors began demolition at the crash site, hundreds of burned, crushed, and mangled file cabinets and safes weighing from 350 to 1,200 lbs., many stuffed with classified material, were brought to the fenced, lighted yard of the DPS incinerator. Many could not be identified because affixed tin plates and cards had melted or burned. Ruined combination locks and damaged suspension systems prevented drawers from opening, as did damage to containers that had fallen between floors. More often than not the DPS locksmiths—Marion "Snake" Cochran, Michael Dooley, and John Bukowski—could cut through locking bolts, but they could not easily open drawers. One morning, after working for hours at the backbreaking task, Dooley asked to borrow the Arlington County Fire Department's "jaws of life" hydraulic equipment used for prying open cars at devastating accidents. The apparatus operated so efficiently that DPS ordered its own machine, receiving it the next day. As the locksmiths opened about 300 safes, DPS had security and records managers of affected offices provide teams of people to review the contents—sometimes undamaged, sometimes still smoking and charred—for ownership and disposition.[73]

On 20 September the continuing need for police help was alleviated when active-duty military police arrived at Fort Myer from Fort Bragg, North Carolina, to work with DPS on access control and physical security. The convoy of Humvees consisted of troops from the 503rd Military Police Battalion (Airborne), commanded by Lieutenant Colonel Wade Dennis. The 293rd MP Company from Fort Stewart, Georgia, joined them the next day.[74]

The MPs and DPS officers joined with Secret Service and Virginia State and Arlington County police to provide security for the memorial service on 11 October at the Pentagon parade ground, attended by thousands of building occupants, families of victims, Secretary Rumsfeld, and President Bush. Because Route 110 passed close enough to the Pentagon for terrorists to detonate a truck full of explosives next to the building, in December the MPs and Virginia State troopers worked in tandem to close it to all truck traffic until a bypass could be constructed. Also in December the MPs began training with Metro Transit police on bus evacuation techniques in the event that the large bus terminal at the Pentagon became the site of an incident. Additional MP companies—the 988th from Fort Benning, Georgia, and the 978th from Fort Bliss, Texas—arrived before the end of the year. Military police remained at the Pentagon for approximately two years after 11 September until the DPS, beginning in May 2002, could grow sufficiently in size and expertise to transform itself into the Pentagon Force Protection Agency.[75]

The high state of emergency wound down before the end of September. Within 10 days after the plane hit the building, firefighters and search and rescue teams had extinguished all fires and hot spots and had concluded rescue and recovery operations. At 7:00 a.m. on 21 September, Schwartz passed incident command to FBI Special Agent Eberhart. The FBI remained in control of the Pentagon crime scene until 7:00 a.m. on 26 September when Eberhart passed command to General Jackson. Old Guard soldiers removed a flag from one of the shored columns and folded and presented it to FBI officials during a small change-of-command ceremony. A few days later Jackson turned control of the site back to the director of the Washington Headquarters Services.[76]

On the larger scene, in the skies above the Pentagon, Air Force F-16 fighters guarded the nation's capital as they had since 11 September, when at 9:30 a.m., only seven minutes before the Pentagon was hit, the first three armed Air National Guard fighters had taken off from Langley Air Force Base, Virginia, and via a circuitous route over the ocean headed for the Baltimore area to intercept Flight 11, mistakenly thought to be flying south toward Washington. Redirected to head for Washington because of an FAA report of another unidentified aircraft (Flight 77) six miles southwest of the city, the fighters flew at a maximum subsonic speed of 660 m.p.h., but were too late to intercept the airliner. After the fighters arrived over the capital two of them established a combat air patrol over the Pentagon by 10:10 a.m. at an altitude of about 20,000 feet. Warned that hijacked United Flight 93 was off course in the Cleveland area and presumed to be heading toward Washington, the two fighters set up a 20-mile racetrack pattern patrol over the area. The third Langley fighter, after investigating and identifying two aircraft near the Potomac as a military helicopter and a police helicopter, flew at low altitude around Washington, following instructions from the Secret Service to protect the White House.[77]

The low-flying Langley jet frightened many Pentagon evacuees who had been warned that another hijacked aircraft was on its way to the area. They heard the fighter before they saw it and mistook it for the dreaded second airliner. In the Center Court assisting firefighters, Lieutenant Commander Dale Rielage went "face first in the grass" as the roaring jet neared the building and overflew it. Some people in the crowd walking from North Parking toward the Memorial Bridge ducked into the woods towards the river to hide from the fighter. Recognition of the plane as "friendly" brought relief and reassurance; some people cheered.[78]

Meanwhile in the president's absence on the 11th, Vice President Cheney directed actions from the White House. The threat of further possible attack on the nation's capital from the missing hijacked United Flight 93 and possibly still other aircraft as yet unknown, created the tragic dilemma of whether or not to authorize fighters to shoot them down. In a telephone conversation some time before 10:20 a.m. the president authorized Cheney to order the shootdown of hijacked planes, which he did by sending word to the National Military Command Center in the Pentagon which communicated the order to NORAD. At 10:39 the vice president informed Secretary Rumsfeld of the shootdown order.[79]

Within the hour Air National Guard fighters from Andrews Air Force Base, Maryland, augmented the initial patrols by the Air Force fighters from Langley. Thereafter during the day Air National Guard fighter aircraft came from air bases at Richmond, Virginia, and Atlantic City, New Jersey; at times as many as 12 fighters flew patrol over the capital area. Navy and Marine Corps aircraft also contributed to the improvised air defense on 11 September, as did Air Force tanker planes and E-3 Airborne Warning and Aircraft Control Systems (AWACS). Combat air patrols over the Washington area became a fixture until the spring of 2002. Thereafter, intermittent patrols were flown by fighters kept on alert.[80]

The extraordinary scale of Pentagon security after the attack was the product of immediate and ongoing cooperation among the federal, state, and local security agencies augmenting DPS and the military. The 9/11 Commission in its report highlighted the effectiveness of the collaboration:

> While no emergency response is flawless, the response to the 9/11 terrorist attack on the Pentagon was mainly a success for three reasons: first, the strong professional relationships and trust established among emergency responders; second, the adoption of the Incident Command System; and third, the pursuit of a regional approach to response. Many fire and police agencies that responded had extensive prior experience working together on regional events and training exercises.

Jester strongly agreed: "We knew each other, and we had worked together. So the cooperation just happened. There [was] no 'Who are you, what is your jurisdiction, why are you here?'"[81]

DPS and the FBI, stretched thin, welcomed the reinforcements required to secure the Pentagon Reservation. Understanding the historic nature of the emergency, most police officers wanted to be a part of the action, guarding against another attack and protecting those in their charge. The many responders who closed roads, guarded doorways and sites, investigated bomb threats, and patrolled on foot and in vehicles performed indispensable security functions, working long days with a heightened sense of duty. The massive security presence enabled the recovery effort to proceed apace and assured the Pentagon workforce that they could safely return to their desks and the job of protecting the nation.

Chapter VIII

Caring for the Dead and the Living

Within the first few hours of the attack injured people were treated by medics at the Pentagon and at clinics and hospitals elsewhere. Of the 189 fatalities, only one, Antoinette Sherman, a civilian employee of the Army, died in hospital. The remains of the others who perished at the Pentagon were transported to the Dover Port Mortuary for final identification. There, a small army of military and civilian experts, using traditional forensic procedures and advanced technologies, identified the remains of all but five of the victims.

The fragmented condition of many of the human remains greatly complicated the forensic investigation, requiring two months of intensive effort that prolonged the anguish of the families of the missing. The Defense Department immediately initiated measures to help the families through this painful period. Opened early on the morning of the 12th and operating for one month, the Pentagon Family Assistance Center (PFAC) served as the central source of information and coordination for the families. Casualty assistance officers were assigned to each family, and civilian and military authorities drew up policies regarding burial, compensation, legal, and other matters. DoD staffs, other government agencies, and numerous relief organizations and volunteers aided the families in making their arrangements.[1]

Identifying the Dead

As they removed bodies from the building, rescuers were at first uncertain about where to establish a temporary morgue. On the afternoon of the attack many body bags were laid out in the Center Court in anticipation of it becoming the field morgue. It had the advantage of relative privacy since entry to the building was closely controlled. But by the time soldiers of the Old Guard began bringing out bodies on the 12th, the FBI had set up a protected and controlled temporary morgue in North Parking; refrigeration units stood by at the Remote Delivery Facility loading dock. The Army had dispatched its sole active mortuary affairs unit, the 54th Quartermaster Company, from Fort Lee, Virginia, and activated a reserve unit, the 311th, based in Puerto Rico, that arrived on the 15th.[2]

The location and nature of the emergency, overlapping layers of jurisdiction, and statutory regulations that governed military operations added a legal dimension to identifying and laying to rest the remains of the dead, both military and civilian. Normally, the Commonwealth of Virginia exercised authority over crimes committed within its borders. But the unusual circumstance of an attack on U.S. soil by foreign terrorists and the resultant national emergency caused the Departments of Justice and Defense to assume jurisdiction. Navy Captain Glenn Wagner, director of the Armed Forces Institute of Pathology (AFIP), described that decision:

> So jurisdiction became a very important aspect since it clearly was an act of terrorism and the FBI was running the operation. The FBI and the US Attorney General really wanted to keep this on the federal side and were relieved to get confirmation that the Pentagon was [an] exclusive[ly] federal jurisdiction and that there wouldn't have to be any more state involvement than was absolutely necessary in the search and recovery. At that particular point the AFIP in the mobilization of our resources and the mobilization of DoD resources became a priority.[3]

The FBI, in consultation with the Office of the Assistant Secretary of Defense for Health Affairs, directed AFIP to carry out forensic identification at the Dover Port Mortuary at Dover Air Force Base, Delaware, the Defense Department's only active port mortuary. Virginia's chief medical examiner requested and received a letter from the U.S. attorney general relieving the state of forensic and mortuary responsibilities. Death certificates would be issued at Dover on behalf of the Commonwealth of Virginia.[4]

Until forensic activity shifted away from the Pentagon to Dover, AFIP senior staff coordinated on-site with the FBI, Arlington County Fire Department, and state law enforcement officials, as well as their own chain of command, headed by the commander of the Military District of Washington. All parties worked together to recover remains while preserving crime scene evidence. After being photographed and labeled in a controlled area, twice daily beginning on the 13th, in the continuous custody of the FBI the remains were transported under Virginia State Police and Fairfax County motorcycle officer escort from the Pentagon to Davison Army Airfield at Fort Belvoir, some 15 miles south of the Pentagon. From there Army CH-47 Chinook helicopters transported them 100 miles northeast to the Dover Port Mortuary. To ensure proper legal custody and continuous evidentiary control, FBI agents accompanied the remains until they were released to the medical examiner in Dover. As the bodies arrived at the base a brief plane-side prayer service was held and a Dover AFB honor guard removed the remains from the planes.[5]

Since 1955 the Dover Port Mortuary had been the primary receiving point for America's military personnel and civilian employees and their families who died on overseas assignments. Although a new state-of-the-art facility lay in its future, in September 2001 the Mortuary building was a typical military prefab structure—nondescript, metal-sided, with a concrete floor, fenced off from the rest of the base. Its interior, resembling a warehouse with high ceilings and minimal furnishings, contained administrative offices, a storage room, spaces for receiving and holding remains, medical examination and autopsy rooms, a mortuary clothing and supplies area, and a casket room.[6]

The permanent Air Force staff consisted of one mortuary affairs officer, two mortuary specialists, one noncommissioned officer in charge, and three administrative personnel, supported by the 512th Memorial Affairs Squadron and the 436th Services Squadron.[7] AFIP, the triservice organization supervising the greatly augmented operation at the Mortuary, had its origin, explained Captain Wagner, in the "Army Medical Museum established in the Civil War by the Army Surgeon General's directive to study combat injuries and infectious diseases. Its first forensic case was the autopsy or medical postmortem of Abraham

Lincoln followed by that of John Wilkes Booth." The Institute expanded in size and mission over the years; by 2001 it occupied nine buildings on the grounds of Walter Reed Army Medical Center in Washington.[8]

For its Dover assignment AFIP assembled some 50 specialists and more than 400 personnel from across the country to conduct, according to Wagner, "one of the most comprehensive forensic investigations in U.S. history."[9] The experts, scientists, and technicians included military personnel under the direction of the Armed Forces Medical Examiner (AFME), a component of AFIP; regional and reserve medical examiners; forensic anthropologists from the Smithsonian Institution, the FBI, and the Army's Central Identification Laboratory in Hawaii; autopsy assistants from AFIP and the National Naval Medical Center in Bethesda, Maryland; experts from AFME's Armed Forces DNA Identification Laboratory; dental investigators headed by the director of AFIP's Department of Oral and Maxillofacial Pathology; and other staff support, including photographers.[10] Wagner, the site commander, reported his day-to-day activities through the Air Force and its Air Mobility Command, and on a "case-by-case basis" to the Army Surgeon General's office and the deputy assistant secretary of defense for military personnel policy. In addition, casualty representatives served as liaison between the military services and the Dover activity.[11]

To perform its singular role in military medicine AFIP possessed the expertise required for complex forensic investigations. But the old Mortuary building had not been designed for a task of the magnitude now under way. The hugely expanded staff of investigators and their sophisticated equipment created crowded conditions. The dental area alone had to accommodate banks of computers, x-ray machines, digital sensors, and other specialized equipment. Oral pathologist Navy Captain Douglas Arendt, AFIP's chief of forensic odontology, recalled that they used space carved from "the shell of an old whole body radiography area that was full of trash when we got there. . . . We found a corner and so we just moved out the trash."[12] Inadequate air conditioning and lighting as well as pest control problems contributed to the unpleasant conditions. Administrative complications owing to the large number of agencies involved caused further slowdowns. The AFIP After-Action Report noted, for example, that it was unclear at first who would acquire the records of the Flight 77 casualties;[13]

while the FBI ultimately assumed that responsibility, it took weeks to gather the records.

The immense burden of family and national grief weighed heavily on all those engaged at Dover, motivating them to issue frequent and as accurate information as possible. Their work attracted intense public, media, and official attention. Emotional newscasts ran day and night. AFIP's Public Affairs Office was swamped by inquiries.[14] Congressional offices pressed for updates. Senior Army and Navy leaders called about subordinates or old friends among the soldiers and sailors killed in the attack; some flag and general officers visited repeatedly. Captain Wagner observed that "the intensity of this investigation, the personalness of this investigation, resulted in significant flag interest at every level, in all service[s] … because everybody wanted to have the information before the next guy."[15]

Remains of the 183 victims and the 5 hijackers sent to Dover bore the identification tags attached during the recovery effort. On arrival they were scanned for the presence of unexploded ordnance or other metallic elements and photographed. Where possible, FBI agents took fingerprints that could be matched against a database containing the prints of DoD uniformed personnel and civilian employees. Whole-body radiographs documented injuries, the age of victims, and the presence of teeth and jewelry.[16]

Wallets, purses, credit cards, badges, military "dog tags," or other identifying materials accompanied some bodies. These and any other personal effects kept with the remains throughout the identification process were removed, photographed, and accounted for; two individuals were always present to witness the handling of such items. Once it was determined that these items had no further use as evidence, they were forwarded to casualty assistance officers who returned them to next of kin.[17]

When characteristics of a body could be described, examiners recorded victims' height, weight, and skin and hair coloring. Compiled and compared with reference information including blood type, this data helped to identify many people. Autopsies also aided identification, disclosing scars, birthmarks, or other identifying features as well as the presence of specific prescription drugs in the body. Such information could be checked against medical records of likely casualties, although this approach was inexact. Where possible, autopsies were performed to help determine the cause of death, needed for the issuance of death certificates. Moreover, next of kin often wanted to know how a person had died. The mortuary staff compiled reports on the cause of death when that information became conclusive; eventually autopsy reports were made available to the families.[18]

The tremendous energy generated by the impact of the airliner as it slammed into the building fragmented many bodies, making it impossible to identify them by visual means or by doing an autopsy. In these instances forensic anthropologists and state-of-the-art techniques and equipment were brought to bear. Eight anthropologists worked alongside the radiologists and pathologists. Investigators matched the DNA profiles of 50 military fatalities with the samples kept on file at the Armed Forces Repository of Specimen Samples for the Identification of Remains. In other instances, they compared specimens with the DNA supplied by family members.[19]

DNA evidence, regarded by the public and the courts as the "gold standard" for identification, was not, however, always available because in many instances it too had been destroyed. For example, the most precise form, nuclear DNA, whose testing reveals unique characteristics, degrades quickly and is vulnerable to fire. The second type, mitochondrial DNA, more resistant to high temperatures, can require a month or more of laboratory time to process, and since only the mother's mitochondrial DNA carries on to subsequent generations, its use for proof of identity often requires additional genealogical research.[20]

Particularly where there existed no soft tissue evidence or other markers for recognition, forensic dentistry proved a powerful tool. Air Force Colonel Charles Pemble headed the group of odontologists, other dentists, and technicians from the 436th Dental Flight at Dover and the 81st Dental Squadron from Keesler Air Force Base, Mississippi. Pemble pointed out that dental examinations often furnish definitive data since teeth, which are calcified structures, are the hardest substances in the human body and generally much less susceptible than soft tissue to destruction by blunt force trauma or fire. Moreover, the arrangement of teeth is unique to each person. The forensic team employed traditional methods as well as a computer software program known as WIN ID that permitted postmortem dental radiology to be compared with antemortem dental records. Through the use of such advanced digital and other technologies, the oral pathologists completed their work in just one month. Odontologist Arendt estimated that 65 identifications resulted solely from the dental investigation.[21]

Findings confirmed that most victims had died swiftly; comparatively few died from slower-acting burns or asphyxiation attributable to the fire itself. The greatest number died from blunt force injuries. The remainder died from other causes or from effects that could not be determined. "Given the level of char and fragmentation," Captain Wagner thought that the "real challenge" in identification and determining the cause of death had not been the "DoD folks" but the contractors and the airplane passengers and crew for whom it was more difficult to reconstitute medical and dental records. Only five victims—two from the Army, two from the Navy, and one aboard the aircraft—could not be identified from remains. Although analysis indicated the hijackers' remains, their individual identities could not be determined since there was no reference dental or DNA information. The FBI took custody of them.[22]

By mid-November the identification process was complete. Medical evidence and other relevant materials were turned over to the military services whose task throughout had been to prepare the remains for burial and communicate with the families of the dead. The Army and Navy assigned liaison personnel to assist with these arrangements, the Defense Intelligence Agency coped with its civilian dead, and the FBI with the people on board the airplane, including the hijackers. To the Army's Office of the Deputy Chief of Staff for Personnel fell the sad duty of fielding a liaison team to deal with the various matters required for final disposition. Lieutenant Colonel Harold Campbell of the Mortuary Affairs and Casualty Support Division explained that the job was "finding health and dental records; working family reference samples for DNA if necessary; awards and decorations for uniforms; posthumous promotions; the information that the Medical Examiner would need to do the State of Virginia death certificate." The team also forwarded information about the identification of remains and about personal effects and shipping arrangements and, finally, dressed the Army dead for cremation or burial.[23]

Headed by Thomas Ellis, civilian chief of DCSPER's Mortuary Affairs Branch, the team included Sergeant First Class Thomas Jones of the Disposition Branch and Staff Sergeant Robert Bryson of the Repatriation and Family Affairs Branch. Jones had left a month or so earlier for an assignment in Japan but requested to return for this duty. Campbell considered him "uniquely qualified" in that he was "one of the few NCOs that [had] ever worked an incident.... He knew what was going on and having him back was helpful." Reservist Major Richard Chaloupka, a licensed funeral director and embalmer in the Alaska State Medical Examiner's Office, was recalled for duty at Dover. He and Sergeant First Class Albert Brown, who had been present at the crash scene, relieved Ellis and Bryson at the Mortuary.[24]

The Navy also sent a three-member liaison team, but unlike the Army team the Navy men had no previous training in mortuary affairs. The senior officer in charge, Naval Reserve Captain Stephen O'Brien, had previously dealt only with the death of a subordinate. Master Chief Petty Officer Gale Bond, stationed with the Bureau of Naval Personnel (BUPERS) in Millington, Tennessee, was in Washington at the time of the attack, where he learned he was the only BUPERS "representative on the East Coast of the United States right now . . . within driving distance" of Dover, and he had a rental car. On his way out of town, Bond picked up the third member, Hospitalman First Class Prince Brown, who was to provide administrative support.[25] Although they lacked training for their temporary assignment and had never met nor worked together, the three men performed their duty with commitment and sensitivity.

The military services had to clarify and resolve several internal jurisdictional matters. Although all the services were represented and cooperated, as DoD's executive agent in mortuary affairs the Army took the lead in the operation. Even so it had to determine whether its personnel office, DCSPER, or its logistics office, DCSLOG, should take charge. Ultimately the Central Joint Mortuary Affairs Office decided that both offices would provide staff support to the MDW commander.[26] Because of the Army's years of practical experience dealing with mortuary matters, it had highly detailed procedures and regulations in place, as Colonel Campbell explained:

> As a matter of culture, if you look at Navy regulations and Air Force regulations and Army regulations and pamphlets, the Army is usually more anal in its description of what you can and can't do, how to do, what to do; and the other Services are kind of like: You have a flat tire? Fix it. We say: You have a flat tire. Open your trunk. Get out your jack. Get out your spare. Check your spare. Jack up the car. And because

> the Army's publications have been more detailed, that's why they were more helpful.[27]

With a murkier chain of command for mortuary affairs, at first the senior Navy officer, Captain O'Brien, wondered, "Who do we work for. . . . What is my authority to make decisions?" He continued to chafe over the lack of joint coordination, the failure to establish "a military command post set up ... to bring structure to the effort, to focus the issues, to update the entire group on the status of the remains, on the status of records, personal effects."[28] The Navy's internal casualty notification process also proved cumbersome and time-consuming—"ludicrous" as far as Bond was concerned.[29]

Moreover, the Navy personnel office demanded constant updates from its liaison staff. According to Bond, "they wanted voice reports five times a day and a written report about four times a day." But in his workspace he had neither internet connectivity nor print capability. "I've got a telephone that sometimes works, sometimes doesn't." Citing the pressure on their time and psyches, the team members finally persuaded BUPERS to accept a daily situation report. The team also had to coordinate the flow of information among nearly 200 different individuals assigned to approximately 38 agencies and offices. They compiled a checklist of 37 items, including the deceased's personal effects, full personal data, and whether the individual's remains should be viewed. They took great care, aware that any mistake, even the misspelling of a middle name on a death certificate, could cause problems.[30]

When the identification and notification procedures ended, the service liaison teams faced their most painful task—dressing or draping the remains of the military dead in full regalia, regardless of their condition, before they were released for burial or cremation. The Mortuary maintained complete sets of military dress uniforms, ribbons, decorations, badges, and other emblems of rank and accomplishment. Posters on the walls displayed proper wear. MDW provided the Army uniforms. Bond arranged for the purchase of new Navy uniforms. The uniforms reflected promotions to which the decedents were posthumously entitled. End-of-tour commendations and Purple Heart medals were affixed. Once the remains were ready for release the liaison officers received and briefed the escorts on their duties, then signed over the remains to them. Civilian remains were not dressed for burial at the Mortuary but were respectfully covered, and like those of the military placed in caskets and returned to their families or designated funeral homes.[31]

Organizing for Family Assistance

While the dead remained in military hands during the forensic investigation, Pentagon officials undertook to see to the needs of the living—the families of the victims. Such care had long been a solemn and committed obligation of the military establishment; regulations and procedures provided for assistance to the bereaved. However, the character of the Pentagon disaster made it unique in Department of Defense experience—its immediacy, the location and scale, and the varied nature of the victims: military and civilians, male and female adults, children, and foreign nationals on board the plane. Moreover, the military dead were multiservice—Army and Navy. These circumstances pointed clearly to the need for a joint response orchestrated by the Office of the Secretary of Defense and involving resources of all the military services as well as elements of the civilian sector. A centralized organization at one location would facilitate coordination of the large number of agencies providing support.

David Chu, DoD undersecretary for personnel and readiness, exercised overall responsibility for personnel policy. Under his charge came the Office of Family Policy headed by Meg Falk, which monitored matters relating to the education, medical care, and employment of American dependents at military bases around the world, and aided dependents after the death of a service member overseas. As Falk and her staff evacuated their 1B700 office after the attack, hurrying out by way of the Center Court to North Parking and then driving to an Air Force office in nearby Crystal City, she began to ponder what needed to be done in the emergency. Realizing that the likelihood of a large number of casualties would require setting up a family assistance center, she sought and received authorization from Chu to do "whatever it takes."[32]

The most immediate requirement was to find a location for the center that offered adequate space and parking. After considering and discarding several possibilities, Falk, with strong support from members of the local community and the help of Arlington's assistant county manager, John Mausert-Mooney, secured use of the Crystal City Sheraton Hotel, little more than a mile from the

Pentagon. Although he could not be certain of reimbursement from the government, hotel manager Perry Ahmed quickly agreed to the arrangement.[33]

To take charge of what became known as the Pentagon Family Assistance Center (PFAC), Chu turned to his deputy assistant secretary for military personnel policy, Lieutenant General John Van Alstyne, an infantry officer and a Vietnam combat veteran, a reticent man of whom Falk spoke as the "heart and soul of that Center." Chu called him a "hero." Van Alstyne had been in the Pentagon only a month when he was confronted with the "nightmarish scene" on 11 September and accepted the sensitive task. A year later, in one of the few remarks he made about his experience, he recalled that he pulled up a desk and chair in the hotel lobby and "that became my command center for family assistance. I lived there for a full month." Center staff members later expressed a grateful consensus that Van Alstyne ran it with the efficiency of a well-managed military operation but with notable modesty and compassion.[34]

Pentagon Family Assistance Center

As word of the attack spread on the morning of the 11th, distraught family and friends rushed to the Pentagon hoping for news of the injured, missing, or dead. That day and throughout the night chaplains at the site stayed with the fearful bystanders near the temporary morgue and escorted a group of about 30 to the Sheraton in the morning. At 7:00 a.m. on 12 September, less than 22 hours after Flight 77's deadly attack, they found the Pentagon Family Assistance Center up and running with a hastily assembled staff of about 50 volunteers from the Army, Navy, Air Force, Marine Corps, Office of the Secretary of Defense, and the private sector.[35]

While making arrangements for the center location, Falk also gave thought to staffing it. Seeking experienced help, she telephoned the Navy Fleet and Family Support Center at Hampton Roads, Virginia, to confer with a team that had counseled the families of sailors killed in the terrorist attack on the destroyer USS *Cole* in Aden, Yemen, the year before. By 4:00 p.m. six team members were cleared to go; they arrived that night and were present for PFAC's opening the next morning.[36]

By then the military departments and other agencies had also inaugurated family assistance services. The Army Community Service headquarters staff, alerted almost immediately after the attack, began to receive calls as early as 10:00 a.m. on an existing toll-free phone number.[37] American Airlines set up an inquiry office at Dulles Airport; the Department of Justice Office for Victims of Crime went into action. In order that all might speak with one voice, Chu directed that the separate services stand down; PFAC became the combined headquarters for DoD components and other federal agencies, the airlines, and relief organizations.[38]

PFAC's professional staff increased rapidly. Organized into management, administration, and operations sections, the center had as its mission to provide information concerning recovery and identification of deceased victims, inform families about benefits and funeral and memorial services, and assist their "return to normalcy."[39]

For his deputy Van Alstyne requested a reserve general officer; Brigadier General James Spivey, the Army assistant chief of chaplains for mobilization and reserve affairs, took on the assignment. After arriving on 14 September, Spivey, who had served in combat areas, assumed responsibility for 24-hour daily operations, briefed and counseled families, and, after the closure of PFAC, headed the successor Pentagon Family Assistance Resource and Referral Office. Falk monitored and coordinated day-to-day activities and policy matters and advised on casualty and mortuary affairs. An Army attorney who had worked for Van Alstyne at the Pentagon, Lieutenant Colonel Thomas Emswiler, oversaw the legal research and services available from a considerable number of attorneys and paralegals. Members of the team from the Navy Fleet and Family Support Center consulted on organizational and other matters. Van Alstyne assigned Air Force Major Jay Dougherty to handle billing issues and logistics with the hotel.[40] Navy Commander Yvette BrownWahler, also from Van Alstyne's Pentagon office, spent much of her time conferring with the Army and Navy casualty offices and the Defense Intelligence Agency about the status of the missing. Reflecting on the working relationship of the management team, BrownWahler asserted that "we ended up becoming basically one brain. You know we created this cocoon and I could tell somebody to do something because the General wanted it done, or I thought it should be done or whatever else and it just, it got done. You didn't have to check up."[41]

The military services brought to the operation well-formulated family support programs and staffs with years of hands-on experience. OSD, on the other hand, normally concerned with policy, had no practical experience in providing family support. Established ad hoc as a joint organization but without command authority, PFAC had to rely on voluntary cooperation in obtaining resources from the military services and other federal agencies. It did not, for example, task the services to assign any specific number of people to PFAC. Some critical service components remained apart from the center—one such, the Navy Casualty Assistance Calls Office at the Washington Navy Yard, did not place an operational cell at the hotel for several weeks. But Navy Lieutenant Commander Elizabeth Stair, who took charge of volunteer staffing and military manning, informed personnel working at the assistance center that "this is a team effort, and if somebody needs your help, you help them." She turned to Navy master chiefs who typically maintained close ties with one another; through those networks many PFAC requests were processed successfully.[42] PFAC became the duty station for staff from Army Community Service who provided information to the Army leadership, assuring them, according to co-director Delores Johnson, that the Army families were "getting the kind of service they need and they deserve." Then "we settled in to do business as a joint element and it flowed very smoothly."[43]

The OSD public affairs office handled the internal release of information about the victims. On 13 September it released an estimate of the people unaccounted for. The next day it provided the names of the Army, Navy, and Defense Agencies' military and civilians unaccounted for. The FBI had responsibility for information about the passengers on Flight 77. Each agency informed the families which organizations would serve them over the longer term.[44]

The center remained open 24 hours daily. Staff and volunteers typically worked one of three eight-hour shifts; many put in much longer hours.[45] Van Alstyne received a financial commitment from Chu for federal payment to the Sheraton for lodging where needed and for feeding the staff and volunteers and the victims' relatives. For the next month the hotel served meals on a 24-hour basis at no charge to the families or the workers.[46]

A half-dozen employees from Falk's Office of Family Policy became the central administrative unit that tracked, among other matters, staffing levels.

Having learned from the *Cole* experience and other disasters, they took steps to organize media coverage by arranging to have public affairs officers stationed at the assistance center. They provided space for the media on the first floor and at prearranged times gave them tours of the center, but journalists and broadcasters were not permitted to enter the meeting rooms during briefings. Chu emphasized the importance of having a senior officer in charge with the authority to say to the media and others, "No, this is not a circus, this is not a voyeuristic event."[47] Noncommissioned officers greeted family members at the lobby door; families and appropriate visitors could come and go at the Sheraton with anonymity if they chose.[48]

By 3:00 p.m. on its first day of operation, 12 September, PFAC had established a call center with a toll-free telephone number to keep communication open for families outside the Washington area. The telephone bank remained essential even after commercial air transportation resumed on 13 September.[49] As information became available and could be released, next of kin could learn who had been confirmed dead and who was still considered missing. They could proffer a claim for survivor benefits and speak with a therapist or social worker for psychological support. The call center also served the staff in tracking down information on the missing and next of kin.[50]

Consolidation of resources and the presence of victims' families at PFAC aided in the identification of remains at the Dover Mortuary. The Armed Forces DNA Identification Laboratory under the direction of deputy director James Canik organized the collection of blood samples at the assistance center. Technicians explained the process and purpose and then took samples from family members to match with victims whose DNA data were not on file at the laboratory.[51]

Since World War II the services had regularly assigned a commissioned or senior noncommissioned officer to assist the family of any military member killed in the line of duty. Titled Casualty Assistance Officers in the Army and Casualty Assistance Calls Officers in the Navy, they normally had a rank equivalent to or greater than the deceased service member.[52] With the 11 September attack the services broke with their practice of furnishing casualty officers only to the families of military personnel and assigned such officers to the families of civilian victims as well. Finding casualty officers was reported to be a "relatively easy task" since the intense emotional impact of the attack elicited an eager willingness to help.[53] The Defense Intelligence Agency provided representatives for families of its dead employees. American Airlines and the FBI, in consultation with the National Transportation Safety Board's Family Affairs Office, did likewise for the passengers and crew of Flight 77.[54] When remains at Dover were positively identified, casualty officers informed next of kin that the victim's official status had changed from missing to dead. They signed for and then handed over to the family the deceased's personal belongings and passed along relevant information regarding survivor benefits and burial options.

Coordination lapses between the involved agencies, attributable in part to the improvised joint nature of the operation, created some difficulties for casualty officers. Initially they received instructions simultaneously from their parent services and from PFAC, and they had to deal with dissimilar procedures for civilians and military.[55] A few of the victims fell under more than one category. For example, Bryan Jack, an airplane passenger, was a Pentagon employee, and the captain of Flight 77, Charles Burlingame III, was a retired Navy reservist. Colonel Campbell, principal coordinator for the Army's casualty process, noted that the casualty officers "had a great deal of difficulty figuring out what they were supposed to do and what the benefits were and what was really happening because they would get advice and assistance and guidance from multiple offices from multiple agencies. So there was never any one single voice."[56] In a questionnaire filled out after completing the assignment, one casualty officer wrote, "The victim was a passenger on American Flight 77. Coordination of information gathering between the Navy and American Airlines was sorely lacking." Another stated: "More coordination between agencies. Too much redundancy and confusion of benefits."[57] Undersecretary Chu later acknowledged that "over the years there has been a sort of archaeological accretion of legislation" that left uncertainties about the rights of the dead and their families. After 11 September DoD twice sought and received additional legislative authority from Congress to remove the uncertainties.[58] The assistance center attempted to clarify these issues by providing additional training and briefings.

Besides the challenge of mastering the regulations, the casualty officers could not be expected to handle alone the intense emotional reactions to the traumatic information they conveyed. Here other PFAC staff members helped families cope not only with their losses but also with practical concerns. Colonel William Huleatt's group of mental health professionals included active duty military personnel, government civilian therapists, Red Cross and community mental health volunteers, and a six-person team from the Department of Veterans Affairs National Center for Post-Traumatic Stress Disorder in Palo Alto, California. Their expertise ranged from child psychiatry to marriage counseling. PFAC reported that on average 20 military and civilian counselors were available 24 hours a day.[59]

Relatives and friends could turn also to chaplains for pastoral care. When invited, chaplains consulted on decisions regarding burials, especially the uncertainty about whether to leave the deceased on forensic hold, as described by Campbell: "We had twenty some families who received additional portions [of remains] after they had done their initial interment. Which meant they then had to either disinter the original casket and put the subsequent portions . . . in an acceptable container and bury it on top of the original casket or treat it as cremation or hold it to be put in with the group remains, when all the unidentifiable portions [were] interred as a group burial."[60] One of the chaplains made "approximately 18 visits to family members facing these decisions, some of whom were angry, some accepting, but all in pain."[61]

Not only were spiritual and psychological needs of the families attended to, but a medical aid station staffed with doctors, nurses, and technicians remained open around the clock. Additionally, military and civilian benefits officers and other specialists were available in the days after the attack. Representatives of the military TRICARE medical program worked with military families on medical benefits and claims processing. Civilian personnel officers established standard procedures for determining benefits and entitlements in coordination with relevant federal agencies such as the Office of Personnel Management. To afford adults an opportunity to use these services, the center provided free child care on the third floor of the Sheraton at what was called Kids' Place.[62]

A large contingent of attorneys contributed legal expertise. Headed by Colonel Emswiler, the core group of Judge Advocate General reservists was augmented by the Army's 10th Legal Support Organization based in Richmond, Virginia, and a number of Coast Guard lawyers. Another 110 private attorneys and paralegals from Virginia, Maryland, and the District of Columbia offered pro bono advice. Legal assistance covered probate, domestic relations, estate planning, power of attorney, and the ramifications of pension, retirement, and social security benefits. Lawyers helped families gain access to victims' bank accounts and other financial assets, dealt with the Internal Revenue Service, and responded to child custody questions. Seemingly simple matters such as retrieving family vehicles from Pentagon parking lots could require legal intervention because victims whose remains had not yet been identified were officially still "missing" and their property could not be disposed of.[63]

A host of public and private organizations augmented the work of the center. OSD authorized the Army Emergency Relief Society, Navy and Marine Corps Relief Society, Air Force Aid Society, the Federal Employee Education & Assistance Fund, and the United Services Organization (USO) to accept donated funds for victims and their families. Other relief agencies and charitable organizations such as the American Red Cross and Salvation Army delivered services. State and federal entities stepped in, including the Virginia Criminal Injuries Compensation Fund, Veterans Benefits Administration, Social Security Administration, and the Federal Emergency Management Agency. Navy Federal Credit Union and Pentagon Federal Credit Union representatives stood by to discuss financial and insurance matters.[64]

Assistance came also from ad hoc groups and unexpected sources. The DCSPER Family Volunteer Group collected and relayed information, consulted about finances, and helped with chores for the many affected families of that organization.[65] On 12 September Therapy Dogs Incorporated volunteered its own "expertise." The group's four-legged members, trained to respond positively to the embrace of strangers and play easily with children, visited senior citizens and others in need of companionship. Falk laughingly remembered that the "kids would pull their tails and pull their ears and these dogs wouldn't even blink."[66] Not only did they become favorites of the children, but also of adults waiting in the lobby or meeting upstairs in the conference and counseling rooms.[67]

From the beginning Van Alstyne deemed it a paramount obligation to keep the families informed. He established a daily routine, giving briefings in the hotel's large conference ballroom at 10:00 a.m. and 4:00 p.m.[68] After announcing the number of remains recovered and identified he invited questions from the audience. Experts, including the superintendent of Arlington National Cemetery, a representative from the Dover Port Mortuary, and a member of the OSD casualty assistance office, were invited to speak. When search and rescue activities at the Pentagon shifted to search and recovery, 35 workers and officials from Arlington, Fairfax, and Montgomery Counties, the Old Guard, and Army engineers briefed the families. Before and after the assembly Van Alstyne and other senior personnel often met privately with family members; they also arranged for formal counseling.[69]

At the twice-daily gatherings Van Alstyne spoke as the definitive voice of the government in reporting the status of the casualties. He conducted the emotionally charged meetings calmly, with straightforwardness, patience, and sometimes humor. Spivey described him as "very candid, very, very gentle, and very understanding and compassionate, but at the same time very straightforward."[70] The general explained that he was not a public affairs officer. Rather, he described himself as "an infantry officer of thirty-five years, and I've learned how to deal in the facts, and that's what I'm going to do. Now you may not like the facts. You ask me a question, I will answer. If you ask me a question and I don't have the answer, I'm not going to tell you [that I do]. I'm not going to try to hoodwink you." Spivey could see that Van Alstyne "built a bond of trust with those people. They identified with him. They trusted him."[71] Falk agreed completely, affirming that "all the families want is accurate information and he was so respectful of those families." She believed that his "commanding presence, his authoritative persona," his remarks delivered in his slow deliberate Texas drawl, caused the families to "revere" him.[72]

The sessions could be distressingly painful. Sometimes, because of the condition of the remains, the general and his staff urged that a coffin not be opened for viewing—"do not put that image in your mind for the rest of your life," counseled BrownWahler. When somebody broke down while asking a question, Van Alstyne often stepped away from the podium to console the bereaved until he or she regained composure and could continue.[73] Reports that the status of a casualty had been officially changed from missing to dead provoked a variety of responses, sometimes deep and overwhelming grief, sometimes relief at resolution. Robert Jaworski, director of the resource services office, part of the Army office that suffered the largest number of fatalities, recalled the comfort it seemed to give to one victim's daughters when told their mother's remains had been identified.[74]

PFAC staff and even the chaplains, who had more experience with tragedy, were greatly moved by the sorrow they witnessed. Lieutenant Colonel William Lee, a chaplain with the Maryland National Guard, recalled how at the recovery site at the Pentagon "a stillness fell over the recovery workers as a child's pajamas were pulled from the debris." A Barbie doll followed, then a child's foot. But it wasn't until Lee went to PFAC that it became horribly personalized. When he learned about the child whose remains he had seen, probably, he thought, those of eight-year-old Zoe Falkenberg, "my heart nearly stopped, and hot tears welled in my eyes." Apparently she loved to dance and "had perfect ballerina feet."[75]

Besides waiting to receive the remains, many families were anxious for any personal effects found with the bodies or recovered elsewhere. As searchers sifted the debris in the Pentagon and North Parking, they collected items that belonged to the victims and survivors of the crash—nameplates, photographs, uniforms and other clothing, award certificates, coffee mugs, day planners, credit cards, wallets, purses, and much more. Personal items were sent to the Joint Personal Property Depot set up at Fort Myer and manned by some 110 of the Army Reserve's mobilized 311th Quartermaster Company, commanded by Lieutenant Colonel Cortez Puryear. The soldiers at the depot, explained the Army's Thomas Kuhn, "clean everything. They catalogue everything. They record where it was found in the building. It's very, very detailed. And it's all boxed up, photographs were taken of all of it."[76] At its peak, running a 24-hour operation, the unit produced copies of a register, mostly photographs, of about 310 pages. It was shown to survivors and to families of the missing and dead; keepsakes that were recognized and claimed were handed over. The depot officially closed on 20 September although some items were returned afterward.[77]

Among its many sad but beneficial activities PFAC coordinated the somber visits of the victims' relatives and friends to the crash site. Mental health experts insisted that going to the Pentagon, even as crews sifted through the wreckage, would expedite the healing for next of kin struggling to come to terms with death under terrifying circumstances, with no bodies yet to see or touch or bury. When one family member asked why the news media could get closer to the building than they, Van Alstyne secured permission for a formal visit, even though the site was still cordoned off and Route 27 closed to traffic. The first occasion came the weekend of 15-16 September after the attack, when chartered buses transported family members, accompanied by military chaplains and counselors. The superintendent of Arlington National Cemetery brought the relatives small American flags to take with them.[78]

MDW commander General Jackson greeted the group on arrival for the first visit. A member of the Arlington County Fire Department played the mournful notes of a bagpipe, and Arlington County police officers rendered honors. From an observation platform decorated with flags and flowers and screened to prevent media intrusion, the viewers could see the burned and badly damaged western side of the building and the feverish work under way to shore up the structure and recover remains. Although the fire had essentially been extinguished, even as the group watched, a small remnant of the building caved in. Members of the Army's Old Guard stood by to provide information when requested about the airliner, the damage on each floor, the progress of the recovery, and other details. Falk was "amazed at the number of family members who wanted to know every detail. . . . No matter how hard it is you've got to give it to them. You don't dance around the truth. You give it to them straight, unequivocal and that's what these Old Guard members did." In fact, one soldier felt that talking to family members boosted his own resolve as he continued to comb through the debris: "It didn't make me happy, but it sure made me feel good about what I was doing and made me want to perform my best." Families could stay as long as they wished, and as the day lengthened and became colder, the Red Cross passed out blankets. Return trips took place over the next several weeks, usually on Saturday and Sunday nights, including one led by General Spivey for the families and friends of American Airlines employees killed on Flight 77. A table in the small viewing area became a memorial of sorts, filled with flowers, pictures, and mementos.[79]

PFAC staff relied on the counselors to advise about other activities or decisions that might be either therapeutic or disturbing for the families. One recommendation was to discourage co-workers of the dead or missing from coming to the Sheraton. To see someone from a nearby office who had survived the attack when a family member had not, or to be given harrowing accounts about the day, perhaps a story related to one of the deceased, might be traumatic.[80] Those who wished to see friends or colleagues of the victims were encouraged to do so privately, not at the Sheraton. When requested, chaplains arranged meetings between family members and those who worked in the same offices as the deceased. In those instances Chaplain Donna Weddle found that "they provided great support for each other."[81]

The assistance center strove to protect the privacy and sensitivities of the families but did not try to cloister them. Public recognition of the enormity of their loss helped in some small way to sustain those whose lives were so shockingly affected. A number of media and political figures, celebrities, and other well-known or distinguished persons were welcomed at the center. Senior government civilian and military leaders made themselves available even as they planned the nation's response to the terrorist act. Secretary of Defense Rumsfeld met with the families, as did Secretary of the Army Thomas White, Secretary of the Navy Gordon England, the Joint Chiefs of Staff and other flag officers, the sergeant major of the Army, and cabinet members. Among the visitors appreciated for her unassuming presence was Linda Carter, a Washington-area resident and star of the 1970s television series "Wonder Woman," who dropped by regularly to sit quietly with families. Sen. Jean Carnahan of Missouri made a particularly strong impression. She volunteered to answer phones at the center and when asked to speak, gave a moving and heartfelt talk about how she coped after the sudden loss of her own husband and son who had been killed in a plane crash just 11 months earlier.[82]

Besides discussing with families deeply personal and often private matters, center members sought to keep them informed about broader aspects of the recovery effort at the Pentagon and reactions to the event in the outside world. To maintain consistency in the information delivered and to avoid giving credence to rumors Van Alstyne occasionally restricted the kind of news released. In one instance, a congressman talked about retribution in a manner that greatly upset several of the listening family members; thereafter the general interviewed beforehand all would-be speakers.[83]

The human desire to alleviate pain, ease the specter of death, and comfort the bereaved is a powerful social force. A generous outpouring of gifts and expressions of sympathy for the victims' families arrived in the form of flags, quilts, toys, stuffed animals, books, and numerous other items. At first these donations filled one table, then four tables, and they continued to pour in by the thousands even after the center closed its doors in October.[84] These tokens of concern and respect added to the cherished remembrances of the relatives. Soon after the center opened, they asked to display photographs of the missing and dead. The hotel staff set up tables on which white napkins folded into the shape of stars were laid on a blue tablecloth, with red and white cloths for the stripes. The tables, with a large American flag on the wall behind, were soon covered with photographs and mementos and usually surrounded by flowers sent by citizens.[85]

The large conference hotel was transformed in that month. The ballroom with its wrenching personal display came to represent not only raw individual grief but also communal mourning, a shared commemoration of the lives lost. Falk called it "sacred ground" that she and Van Alstyne encouraged staff members to visit every day "to remind us of why we were there."[86] It was evident that the center staff and volunteers carried out their duties as gatekeepers at some emotional cost to themselves. Van Alstyne admitted to Falk that heading the Family Assistance Center ranked only behind his combat tours in South Vietnam as the most stressful experience of his life. He added, his self-effacing humor coming to the fore, that "if this ever happens again, just make sure that whoever they select for this job is mean, ornery and expendable."[87]

Continuity and Commemoration

The initial trickle of 30 people who arrived at the Sheraton on 12 September grew to a flood. Friends and family including children of the victims from the Pentagon and Flight 77 joined the waiting. Hundreds of volunteers and a like number of relatives could be found in the building at any one time. The center received 2,545 people in its first week and counted over 2,500 volunteers during its month-long tenure, providing services to an average of 466 people each day and directly assisting 170 families of victims.[88]

The Pentagon Family Assistance Center ceased operation at the Sheraton on 12 October, but family assistance did not end. To extend services through the end of the month the Pentagon Family Assistance Resource and Referral Office (PFARRO), Phase II or "aftercare" as some termed it, was set up. For continuity of leadership, General Spivey became the officer in charge and Brown-Wahler his deputy. Although OSD funded it and retained control, the office staff came mostly from the Army and Navy: senior noncommissioned officers, casualty affairs liaison officers, information and referral representatives, phone center operators, plus an Army attorney, a mental health counselor, and a family support coordinator. The Red Cross also sent representatives.[89]

Located in Crystal City in the Polk Building, a leased facility with restricted access, PFARRO chiefly provided referral services. Although it offered walk-in assistance and maintained a hotline, the office did not attempt to be the round-the-clock center and safe haven of its predecessor. Services did not go beyond pastoral, mental health, and legal matters. The reduced mission and staffing meant that daily briefings, 24/7 operations, on-site housing and transportation, food service, and child care were no longer available. The office distributed a resource and referral guide to family members; it informed those who lived outside the National Capital Region about available support from government agencies and military installations in their area. In addition, an Internet website supplied updated information.[90] Although PFARRO significantly scaled back family services, it continued to support the casualty officers' ongoing responsibilities in dealing with such difficult matters as "forensic hold," when remains of the dead had not been returned to next of kin by the time PFAC closed.[91]

On Sunday, 16 September, the Dover Mortuary reported the first four preliminary victim identifications; the final identification came on 11 November. On the 15th the Armed Forces Medical Examiner stated that no remains could be found to substantiate the identity of five people killed—two Army, two Navy, and one young child from the airliner. The Army recommended formal, simultaneous notification of all family members that the process was complete. Falk, as director of the Office of Family Policy, informed OSD and service officials, the FBI, and representatives of the families including the five for whom remains could not be identified. Casualty assistance officers met with the families, all of whom agreed to release information to the public at the same time, on Friday, 16 November 2001, at 5:00 p.m. Eastern Standard Time.[92]

Caring for its own is a bedrock military obligation—"fulfilling that Army promise," as one official phrased it, maintaining the "reciprocal commitment" from "cradle to grave" between the department and service members and their families, said another.[93] In the last chapter of this response to exceptional circumstance, surprise, and violent death on 11 September, the Pentagon implemented long-established traditions through carefully detailed programs supervised by well-trained military and civilian professionals, supported by an impressive logistical capability, to bury its dead and offer comfort to the bereaved.

Sustaining the injured survivors, standing by the families whose lives were forever changed on that day, and memorializing the men and women who were killed remained a quiet but ongoing responsibility of the Department of Defense. When PFARRO closed on 1 November 2001, OSD's Office of Family Policy, the military services, and American Airlines reclaimed the mission of seeing to the welfare of the people who suffered such grievous loss on the morning of 11 September. The first Pentagon memorial service took place a month after the catastrophe on 11 October, followed by another on the one-year anniversary. Plans for a permanent memorial overlooking the scene of destruction began even as the destroyed part of the Pentagon was being rebuilt and reoccupied.

The honors and tribute paid to the fallen expressed both the nation's grief and its resolve.

Afterword

The 11 September 2001 terrorist attacks on New York and Washington confronted the United States with a new and covert form of aggression of global dimension difficult to defend against and capable of inflicting great harm and damage. Although they could not prevent the attacks, the military forces responded in the hours and days afterward with a greatly heightened level of alertness and protection and prepared for offensive action against the terrorists in Afghanistan. The Defense Department ordered the deployment of land, sea, and air forces in accordance with prescribed alert procedures. The vital role of the Pentagon in directing the deployment and response of U.S. military forces worldwide was never more manifest even as key portions of the building lay in ruins.

While saving lives and preserving the building were the immediate imperatives on 11 September, keeping the Pentagon up and running was essential to command and control of U.S. forces. The National Command Authority (NCA)—the president and the secretary of defense—relied on the established procedures and the communications capabilities of the command centers in the Pentagon to exercise effective command and control. While alternate facilities existed, they were inferior to the Pentagon in their capacity to meet maximum command and control requirements. The success on 11 September and following days in sustaining continued operation of the Pentagon helped reassure President Bush and Secretary Rumsfeld that they would be able to exercise expeditious direction of U.S. forces to cope with the emergency.

Maintenance of the building's operational capability owed much to the building management staff, which performed the arduous and often dangerous task of ensuring the continued provision of vital services—power, water, and air conditioning—without which the building could not function. Although their labors succeeded in meeting the NCA's immediate needs, it also became obvious that the Pentagon Renovation Program would have to incorporate important additional changes to satisfy new requirements, some of them deriving directly from the attack experience. These requirements included modernizing, hardening, and strengthening utilities, modernizing and renovating command centers, and building new security and fire safety features into the building's design.[1]

The most pressing and overriding need was to rid the building of the widespread damage done by fire, smoke, water, and mold that had compelled the evacuation of thousands of employees to temporary quarters elsewhere for weeks and months. Nevertheless, large numbers of employees reported for work on 12 September. By 24 September work areas that had not sustained structural damage—Corridors 6 1/2 to 2 1/2 clockwise, or about 66 percent of the building—had been reoccupied. In the following months most of the sections of the building that had been evacuated were reoccupied, including parts of Wedges 1 and 2.[2]

On 11 October 2001, one month after the attack, by which time the Pentagon and surrounding area had been largely cleared of the mountains of debris, a service of remembrance was held at the site. The large American flag that had been draped over the top of the building on 12 September was lowered after 29 days and folded with full military honors. Bush and Rumsfeld addressed an audience of many thousands of Pentagon workers and families of the deceased gathered to honor the victims of the assault. Rumsfeld spoke feelingly of the dead and thanked "those who came to assist that day and afterwards." The president promised that "the wound to this building will not be forgotten, but it will be repaired. Brick by brick, we will quickly rebuild the Pentagon."[3]

Responsibility for rebuilding fell to the Pentagon Renovation Program Office, whose staff throughout 11 September and in the days and weeks that followed had been instrumental in limiting damage to the stricken building and supporting in so many ways the recovery effort—from supplying building diagrams to the firefighters to shoring up critical areas and providing essential materials and equipment. PENREN had been engaged for almost a decade in planning and overseeing the renovation of the building. It followed naturally that it should undertake demolition and reconstruction of the structurally damaged area—all five floors of Rings E, D, and C between Corridors 4 and 5, in all some 400,000 square feet.

Delayed because of the 11 October memorial ceremony, demolition did not start until 18 October. Working two 12-hour shifts seven days a week, strongly motivated crews completed the job on 19 November, almost four weeks ahead of the "aggressive eight week schedule" and months ahead of what would have been the normal schedule.[4] Reconstruction of the huge damaged area of the Pentagon also made remarkable progress in the 10 months following completion of demolition. Some 3,000 dedicated construction workers labored two 10-hour shifts six days a week, completing restoration of Wedge 1 Ring E between Corridors 4 and 5 by 11 September 2002, one year after the attack, permitting occupants to move into offices in the ring. In thanking and praising the workers, Deputy Secretary Wolfowitz declared that "like the mythical Phoenix bird, the building, too, has risen from its ashes to be reborn." Indeed, from the beginning the reconstruction effort had been named the Phoenix Project. Completion of work on the remaining portion of the damaged area permitted full occupancy of Wedge 1 by February 2003. Thereafter, with increased appropriations of money by Congress, renovation of the building proceeded at a much accelerated pace that permitted advancing the scheduled date of completion to 2010 instead of 2014, as had been the plan prior to 11 September.[5]

Of the more than a hundred Pentagon inhabitants and responders requiring hospital treatment, a number who suffered serious injuries and lasting effects remained the object of continuing anxious attention from the government and the public. The president, secretary of defense, and other officials, including the highest-ranking officers of the military services, visited military and civilian victims in hospitals. Their expressions of concern and appreciation reflected the emotion of a caring public.[6]

The strong sentiment for lasting commemoration of the victims of the 11 September attack led to planning for two memorials—one inside the building and one outside. In May 2002 an American Heroes Memorial opened on the 3rd Floor apex area of Corridors 9 and 10 to display temporarily the many items of tribute and remembrance that had poured into the Pentagon from the American public. These included letters, poems, cards, paintings, quilts, candles, mobiles, and statues that had previously been exhibited in the halls of the building.

A permanent memorial and adjacent chapel opened later in 2002 in the 1st Floor E Ring at the point of Flight 77's impact. In the center of the memorial room is a book with a page and picture for each of the 184 victims. On either side is an etched list with all of the names. In the chapel, the most prominent feature is a pentagon-shaped art glass window, five feet from point to point, including individual pieces of glass for each of the 184 victims. The window was dedicated on 11 September 2002 and the chapel on 12 November 2002.[7]

The permanent outdoor memorial, authorized but not funded by Congress, was planned for an almost two-acre site near the Heliport. A DoD advisory group, including family members of some of the victims, approved a location 165 feet west of the Pentagon in April 2002 and conducted a design competition. The winning design, announced in March 2003, called for 184 cantilevered benches placed along the path taken by Flight 77, each with an illuminated reflecting pool. Planned also were some 80 paperbark maple trees to provide shade. To pay for the construction, under the direction of the Pentagon Renovation Program Office, a fundraising group led by families of the victims launched a campaign in April 2004 to obtain the necessary funds. On 15 June 2006 a groundbreaking ceremony at the site signaled the beginning of construction of the memorial.[8]

Buried in Arlington Cemetery are 64 of those killed in the attack on the Pentagon. Also buried there is a casket containing the unidentified remains of victims presumed to be those of five people who could not be individually identified: Dana Falkenberg, Colonel Ronald Golinski, USA (Ret.), U.S. Navy Electronics Technician 1st Class Ronald Hemenway, James Lynch, and Rhonda Rasmussen. The casket also contains the remains of some others that families desired to be included. Over the shared grave is a five-sided granite memorial on which the names of all 184 dead are inscribed in raised silver letters.[9]

In another traditional expression of homage, the Defense Department awarded medals and decorations to the dead, to the injured, to the rescuers, and to other responders who performed over and above the call of duty. On behalf of their deceased, military families received the Purple Heart. Civilian families received the Medal for the Defense of Freedom, a new award created by the secretary of defense in October 2001 as the civilian equivalent of the Purple Heart. These medals were awarded also to the injured military and civilians. The Army, Navy, Air Force, Marine Corps, and Defense Intelligence Agency awarded these and other medals and certificates of distinction to more than 200 of their employees. Another new award, the Medal for Valor, created in September 2001 to recognize acts of heroism or sacrifice by civilians, was presented to 17 Defense Protective Service officers and 22 Real Estate and Facilities Directorate employees.[10]

Appendices

Appendix A

List of 9/11 Pentagon Fatalities*

Name	Military/Civilian	Affiliation
Ambrose, Paul W.	Civilian	Flight 77
Amundson, Craig S.	SPC	Army
Barnes, Melissa R.	YN3	Navy
Beilke, Max J.	Civilian	Army
Betru, Yeneneh	Civilian	Flight 77
Bishundat, Kris R.	IT2	Navy
Blagburn, Carrie R.	Civilian	Army
Boone, Canfield D.	LTC	Army
Booth, Mary Jane	Civilian	Flight 77
Bowen, Donna M.	Contractor	Army
Boyle, Allen P.	Contractor	OSD
Brown, Bernard C., II	Civilian	Flight 77
Burford, Christopher L.	ET3	Navy
Burlingame, Charles F., III	Civilian	Flight 77
Caballero, Daniel M.	ET3	Navy
Calderon-Olmedo, Jose O.	SFC	Army
Calley, Suzanne M.	Civilian	Flight 77
Carter, Angelene C.	Civilian	Army
Carver, Sharon A.	Civilian	Army
Caswell, William E.	Civilian	Flight 77
Chada, John J.	Civilian	Army
Chapa, Rosa Maria	Civilian	DIA
Charlebois, David M.	Civilian	Flight 77
Clark, Sara M.	Civilian	Flight 77
Cooper, Julian T.	Contractor	Navy

* Excluding the five plane hijackers. Military ranks are as of time of death.

Name	Military/Civilian	Affiliation
Cottom, Asia S.	Civilian	Flight 77
Cranford, Eric A.	LCDR	Navy
Davis, Ada M.	Civilian	Army
Debeuneure, James D.	Civilian	Flight 77
DeConto, Gerald F.	CAPT	Navy
Dickens, Rodney	Civilian	Flight 77
Dickerson, Jerry D.	LTC	Army
Dillard, Eddie A.	Civilian	Flight 77
Doctor, Johnnie, Jr.	IT1	Navy
Dolan, Robert E., Jr.	CDR	Navy
Donovan, William H.	CDR	Navy
Droz, Charles A., III	Civilian	Flight 77
Dunn, Patrick W.	CDR	Navy
Earhart, Edward T.	AG1	Navy
Edwards, Barbara G.	Civilian	Flight 77
Elseth, Robert R.	LCDR	Navy
Falkenberg, Charles S.	Civilian	Flight 77
Falkenberg, Dana	Civilian	Flight 77
Whittington (Falkenberg), Leslie A.	Civilian	Flight 77
Falkenberg, Zoe	Civilian	Flight 77
Fallon, Jamie L.	SK3	Navy
Ferguson, James J.	Civilian	Flight 77
Fields, Amelia V.	Civilian	Army
Fisher, Gerald P.	Contractor	Army
Flagg, Darlene E.	Civilian	Flight 77
Flagg, Wilson F.	Civilian	Flight 77
Flocco, Matthew M.	AG2	Navy
Foster, Sandra N.	Civilian	DIA
Gabriel, Richard P.	Civilian	Flight 77
Getzfred, Lawrence D.	CAPT	Navy
Ghee, Cortez	Civilian	Army
Gibson, Brenda C.	Civilian	Army
Golinski, Ronald F.	Civilian	Army
Gray, Ian J.	Civilian	Flight 77
Hale-McKinzy, Diane	Civilian	Army
Hall, Stanley R.	Civilian	Flight 77
Halmon, Carolyn B.	Civilian	Army
Heidenberger, Michele M.	Civilian	Flight 77
Hein, Sheila M.S.	Civilian	Army
Hemenway, Ronald J.	ET1	Navy

Name	Military/Civilian	Affiliation
Hogan, Wallace C., Jr.	MAJ	Army
Holley, Jimmie I.	Civilian	Army
Houtz, Angela M.	Civilian	Navy
Howell, Brady K.	Civilian	Navy
Hurt, Peggie M.	Civilian	Army
Hyland, Stephen N., Jr.	LTC	Army
Hymel, Robert J.	Civilian	DIA
Ivory, Lacey B.	SGM	Army
Jack, Bryan C.	Civilian	Flight 77
Jacoby, Steven D.	Civilian	Flight 77
Johnson, Dennis M.	LTC	Army
Jones, Judith L.	Civilian	Navy
Judge, Ann C.	Civilian	Flight 77
Kegler, Brenda	Civilian	Army
Keller, Chandler R.	Civilian	Flight 77
Kennedy, Yvonne E.	Civilian	Flight 77
Khan, Norma C.	Civilian	Flight 77
Kincaid, Karen A.	Civilian	Flight 77
Lamana, Michael S.	LT	Navy
Laychak, David W.	Civilian	Army
Lee, Dong Chul	Civilian	Flight 77
Lewis, Jennifer	Civilian	Flight 77
Lewis, Kenneth E.	Civilian	Flight 77
Lightbourn-Allen, Samantha L.	Civilian	Army
Long, Stephen V.	MAJ	Army
Lynch, James T., Jr.	Civilian	Navy
Lynch, Terence M.	Contractor	Army
Lyons, Nehamon, IV	OS2	Navy
Marshall, Shelley A.	Civilian	DIA
Martin, Teresa M.	Civilian	Army
Mason-Acker, Ada L.	Civilian	Army
Mattson, Dean E.	LTC	Army
Maude, Timothy J.	LTG	Army
Maxwell, Robert J.	Civilian	Army
May, Renée A.	Civilian	Flight 77
McKenzie, Molly L.	Civilian	Army
Menchaca, Dora M.	Civilian	Flight 77
Mickley, Patricia E.	Civilian	DIA
Milam, Ronald D.	MAJ	Army
Moran, Gerard P., Jr.	Contractor	Navy

Name	Military/Civilian	Affiliation
Morris, Odessa V.	Civilian	Army
Moss, Brian A.	ET2	Navy
Moy, Teddington H.	Civilian	Army
Murphy, Patrick J.	LCDR	Navy
Newton, Christopher C.	Civilian	Flight 77
Nguyen, Khang Ngoc	Contractor	Navy
Noeth, Michael A.	DM2	Navy
Olson, Barbara K.	Civilian	Flight 77
Ornedo, Ruben S.	Civilian	Flight 77
Padro, Diana B.	Civilian	Army
Pak, Chin Sun (Wells)	SPC	Army
Panik, Jonas M.	LT	Navy
Patterson, Clifford L., Jr.	MAJ	Army
Penninger, Robert	Civilian	Flight 77
Ploger, Robert R., III	Civilian	Flight 77
Ploger, Zandra F.	Civilian	Flight 77
Pontell, Darin H.	LTJG	Navy
Powell, Scott	Contractor	Army
Punches, Jack D.	Civilian	Navy
Pycior, Joseph J., Jr.	AW1	Navy
Raines, Lisa J.	Civilian	Flight 77
Ramsaur, Deborah A.	Civilian	Army
Rasmussen, Rhonda S.	Civilian	Army
Ratchford, Marsha D.	IT1	Navy
Reszke, Martha M.	Civilian	Army
Reuben, Todd H.	Civilian	Flight 77
Richard, Cecelia E.	Civilian	Army
Rowenhorst, Edward V.	Civilian	Army
Rowlett, Judy	Civilian	Army
Russell, Robert E.	Civilian	Army
Ruth, William R.	CW4	Army
Sabin, Charles E., Sr.	Civilian	DIA
Salamone, Marjorie C.	Civilian	Army
Sammartino, John P.	Civilian	Flight 77
Scales, David M.	LTC	Army
Schlegel, Robert A.	CDR	Navy
Scott, Janice M.	Civilian	Army
Selves, Michael L.	Civilian	Army
Serva, Marian H.	Civilian	Army
Shanower, Dan F.	CDR	Navy

Name	Military/Civilian	Affiliation
Sherman, Antoinette M.	Civilian	Army
Simmons, Diane M.	Civilian	Flight 77
Simmons, Donald D.	Civilian	Army
Simmons, George W.	Civilian	Flight 77
Sincock, Cheryle D.	Civilian	Army
Smallwood, Gregg H.	ITC	Navy
Smith, Gary F.	Civilian	Army
Sopper, Mari-Rae	Civilian	Flight 77
Speisman, Robert	Civilian	Flight 77
Statz, Patricia J.	Civilian	Army
Stephens, Edna L.	Civilian	Army
Steuerle, Norma L.	Civilian	Flight 77
Strickland, Larry L.	SGM	Army
Taylor, Hilda E.	Civilian	Flight 77
Taylor, Kip P.	MAJ	Army
Taylor, Leonard E.	Civilian	Flight 77
Taylor, Sandra C.	Civilian	Army
Teague, Sandra D.	Civilian	Flight 77
Teepe, Karl W.	Civilian	DIA
Thurman, Tamara C.	SGT	Army
Tolbert, Otis V.	LCDR	Navy
Troy, Willie Q.	Civilian	Army
Vauk, Ronald J.	LCDR	Navy
Wagner, Karen J.	LTC	Army
Waller, Meta L. (Fuller)	Civilian	Army
White, Maudlyn A.	SSG	Army
White, Sandra L.	Civilian	Army
Willcher, Ernest M.	Contractor	Army
Williams, David L.	LCDR	Navy
Williams, Dwayne	MAJ	Army
Woods, Marvin R.	Civilian	Navy
Yamnicky, John D., Sr.	Civilian	Flight 77
Yancey, Vicki	Civilian	Flight 77
Yang, Shuyin	Civilian	Flight 77
Yokum, Kevin W.	IT2	Navy
Young, Donald M.	ITC	Navy
Young, Edmond G., Jr.	Contractor	Army
Young, Lisa L.	Civilian	Army
Zheng, Yuguang	Civilian	Flight 77

APPENDIX B

National Transportation Safety Board Reports*

* Excerpts from original.

NATIONAL TRANSPORTATION SAFETY BOARD

Office of Research and Engineering
Washington, D.C. 20594

February 19, 2002

Flight Path Study - American Airlines Flight 77

A. SUBJECT AIRCRAFT

Location:	Arlington, VA
Date:	September 11, 2001
Time:	09:38 AM Eastern Daylight Time
Flight:	American Airlines Flight 77
Aircraft:	Boeing 757-200, registration: N644AA
NTSB#:	DCA01MA064

B. GROUP

N/A

C. SUMMARY

This document provides a brief description of the flight path of the aircraft based on information obtained from various sources of recorded radar of the subject aircraft both before and after the hijacking events. Information from the Flight Data Recorder (FDR) recovered on scene is also used to develop the description. Flight paths are overlaid onto maps of the area, and time histories of altitude data are presented

American Airlines Flight 77 – Flight Profile

The following description of American Airlines Flight 77 is based on data from the flight data recorder (FDR) recovered from the crash site, as well as radar data obtained from the Federal Aviation Administration's Air Route Traffic Control Centers, approach control at Washington Dulles Airport, and the U.S. Air Force 84th Radar Evaluation Squadron.

Figure 1 shows the flight path of the aircraft from take off at Washington Dulles airport to the crash site at the Pentagon. Figure 2 shows the aircraft's altitude profile for the 1 hour and 17 minute duration of the flight, and figure 3 shows the flight path during the final maneuver before impact.

American Airlines Flight 77 departed Washington Dulles at 8:20 AM (point A in Figures 1 and 2) and reached its assigned cruising altitude of 35,000 feet at about 8:46 AM (B). The final routine radio transmission from the flight was received at 8:51 AM. The flight appeared normal until a deviation from the assigned course occurred at approximately 8:55(C), when the aircraft started a turn to the south. One minute later, radar stations stopped receiving transponder returns from AA77. At 8:56, FAA's Indianapolis Center Air traffic control facility attempted to contact the flight several times, with no response. By 9:00 (D) the airplane was heading to the east, and shortly thereafter began to descend from 35,000 feet. The autopilot remained engaged during the turn, and during the initial descent from 35,000 feet.

At approximately 9:07 AM, the airplane leveled off at 25,000 feet and made a slight course change to the east-northeast (E). One minute later, the autopilot was disconnected for approximately 3 minutes. During these three minutes, heading remained steady, yet variations in altitude as low as 22,000 feet are noted. When the autopilot was re-engaged, the airplane leveled again at 25,250 feet, and then began to descend again at 9:22 AM. At approximately 9:29 AM, when the aircraft was approximately 35 miles west of the Pentagon, the autopilot was disconnected (F) as the aircraft leveled near 7000 feet. Slight course changes were initiated, during which variations in altitude between 6800 and 8000 feet were noted.

At 9:34 AM, the aircraft was positioned about 3.5 miles west-southwest of the Pentagon, and started a right 330-degree descending turn to the right. At the end of the turn, the aircraft was at about 2000 feet altitude and 4 miles southwest of the Pentagon. Over the next 30 seconds, power was increased to near maximum and the nose was pitched down in response to control column movements. The airplane accelerated to approximately 460 knots (530 miles per hour) at impact with the Pentagon. The time of impact was 9:37:45 AM.

Jim Ritter
Chief, Vehicle Performance Division
NTSB

8:19:20	LCW	American seventy seven your departure frequency will be one two five point zero five runway three zero cleared for take off. [IAD 1211-1226 LCW]
8:19:27	AAL-77	twenty five point five cleared for take off runway ah three zero American seventy seven. [IAD 1211-1226 LCW]
8:20:26	LCW	American seventy seven turn left heading two seven zero contact departure. [IAD 1211-1226 LCW]
8:20:31	AAL-77	two seventy heading departure American seventy seven thanks sir good day. [IAD 1211-1226 LCW]
8:20:43	ND	American seventy seven Dulles departure radar contact climb and maintain five thousand. [IAD 1215-1230 ND]
8:20:47	AAL-77	five thousand American seventy seven. [IAD 1215-1230 ND]
8:22:05	ND	American seventy seven climb and maintain one one thousand eleven thousand. [IAD 1215-1230 ND]
8:22:08	AAL-77	up to one one thousand American seventy seven. [IAD 1215-1230 ND]
8:23:23	ND	American seventy seven cleared direct LINDEN contact Dulles one one eight point six seven. [IAD 1215-1230 ND]
8:23:28	AAL-77	direct LINDEN eighteen sixty seven American ah seventy seven **. [IAD 1215-1230 ND]
8:23:43	AAL-77	* American ah seventy seven with you passing nine decimal one for eleven one one thousand. [IAD 1215-1230 NH]
8:23:47	NH	American seven seven Dulles approach climb maintain one seven thousand. [IAD 1215-1230 NH]
8:23:50	AAL-77	one seven thousand American seventy seven. [IAD 1215-1230 NH]
8:25:33	NH	American seventy seven contact Washington center one two zero point six five good flight. [IAD 1215-1230 NH]
8:25:37	AAL-77	twenty six five American seventy seven thank you maam good day. [IAD 1215-1230 NH]
8:25:49	AAL-77	ah center American seventy seven with you passing one three decimal zero for one seven thousand. [ZDC 1220-1236 05R]
8:25:57	05R	American seventy seven Washington center roger climb and maintain flight level two seven zero. [ZDC 1220-1236 05R]
8:26:00	AAL-77	two seven zero American seventy seven. [ZDC 1220-1236 05R]
8:30:38	05R	American seventy seven contact Washington center one three three point two seven. [ZDC 1220-1236 05R]
8:30:42	AAL-77	ah thirty three twenty seven American seventy seven thanks sir good day. [ZDC 1220-1236 05R]
8:31:05	AAL-77	* American seventy seven passing two five decimal one for two seven oh. [ZDC 1223-1246 03R]
8:31:23	03R	American seventy seven ah climb, climb maintain flight level two niner zero sir. [ZDC 1226-1246 03R]
8:31:30	AAL-77	two nine zero American seventy seven. [ZDC 1226-1246 03R]
8:34:16	03R	American seventy seven turn twenty degrees right vector for your climb. [ZDC 1226-1246 03R]
8:34:19	AAL-77	turn twenty right American seventy seven. [ZDC 1226-1246 03R]
8:37:31	03R	American seventy seven recleared direct Charleston climb maintain cor -- correction recleared direct Henderson sir climb maintain flight level three niner zero. [ZDC 1226-1246 03R]
8:37:39	AAL-77	direct HENDERSON out of two nine for three nine oh requesting three five zero for a final American seventy seven. [ZDC 1226-1246 03R]
8:37:55	AAL-77	center American ah seventy seven you copy request for three five zero as a final? [ZDC 1226-1246 03R]
8:37:59	03R	American seventy seven ah roger maintain flight level three five zero I'll show that as your flinal. [ZDC 1226-1246 03R]
8:38:03	AAL-77	ah three five zero for a final American seventy seven thank you sir. [ZDC 1226-1246 03R]

8:39:30	03R	American seventy seven amend your altitude maintain flight level three three zero for traffic. [ZDC 1226-1246 03R]
8:39:36	AAL-77	American seven seven stop at three three zero. [ZDC 1226-1246 03R]
8:40:03	03R	American seventy seven contact Indy center one two zero point two seven. [ZDC 1226-1246 03R]
8:40:06	AAL-77	twenty twenty seven American seventy seven thanks sir good day. [ZDC 1226-1246 03R]
8:40:13	AAL-77	center American seventy seven with you level three three zero. [ZDC 1234-1409 HNN-R]
8:40:15	HNN-R	American seventy seven Indy center roger squawk, three seven four three. [ZDC 1234-1409 HNN-R]
8:40:19	AAL-77	three seven four three American seventy seven. [ZDC 1234-1409 HNN-R]
8:43:51	HNN-R	American seventy seven climb and maintain flight level three five zero. [ZDC 1234-1409 HNN-R]
8:43:55	AAL-77	thirty three, three five oh American seventy seven. [ZDC 1234-1409 HNN-R]
8:47:16	HNN-R	American seventy seven turn ten degrees to the right vectors for traffic. [ZDC 1234-1409 HNN-R]
8:47:20	AAL-77	ten right American seven seven. [ZDC 1234-1409 HNN-R]
8:50:47	HNN-R	American seventy seven cleared direct ah FALMOUTH. [ZDC 1234-1409 HNN-R]
8:50:51	AAL-77	ah direct FALMOUTH American seventy seven thanks. [ZDC 1234-1409 HNN-R]
8:56:32	HNN-R	American seventy seven Indy. [ZDC 1234-1409 HNN-R]
8:56:46	HNN-R	American seventy seven Indy. [ZDC 1234-1409 HNN-R]
8:56:53	HNN-R	American seventy seven American Indy. [ZDC 1234-1409 HNN-R]
8:57:12	HNN-R	American seventy seven American Indy radio check how do you read? [ZDC 1234-1409 HNN-R]
8:57:27	HNN-R	American ah seventy seven American radio check how do you read? [ZDC 1234-1409 HNN-R]
8:58:16	HNN-R	American seventy seven Indy radio check how do you read? [ZDC 1234-1409 HNN-R]
8:58:20	DAC-RA	American seventy seven center. [ZDC 1249-1317 DAC-RA]
8:58:41	HNN-R	American ah seventy seven ah Indy center how do you read? [ZDC 1234-1409 HNN-R]
8:58:51	HNN-R	American seventy seven Indy radio check how do you read? [ZDC 1234-1409 HNN-R]
8:59:32	DAC-RA	American seventy seven center. [ZDC 1249-1317 DAC-RA]
9:00:25	HNN-R	American seventy seven Indy. [ZDC 1234-1409 HNN-R]
9:00:56	DAC-RA	Indy center calling American seventy seven American seventy seven. [ZDC 1249-1317 DAC-RA]
9:00:56	DAC-R	Indy center calling American seventy seven American seventy seven. [ZDC 1249-1317 DAC-R]
9:03:06	HNN-R	American seventy seven Indy. [ZDC 1234-1409 HNN-R]
9:15:15	AAL-683	[called AAL-77 on guard at center request]. [ZDC 1249-1317 DAC-RA]

NATIONAL TRANSPORTATION SAFETY BOARD

Office of Research and Engineering
Washington, D.C. 20594

February 13, 2002

Study of Autopilot, Navigation Equipment, and Fuel Consumption Activity Based on United Airlines Flight 93 and American Airlines Flight 77 Digital Flight Data Recorder Information

by John O'Callaghan and Daniel Bower, Ph.D.

A. SUBJECT AIRCRAFT

Location:	Arlington, VA
Date:	September 11, 2001
Time:	09:38 AM Eastern Daylight Time
Flight:	American Airlines Flight 77
Aircraft:	Boeing 757-200, registration: N644AA
NTSB#:	DCA01MA064

Location:	Shanksville, PA
Date:	September 11, 2001
Time:	10:03 AM Eastern Daylight Time
Flight:	United Airlines Flight 93
Aircraft:	Boeing 757-200, registration: N591UA
NTSB#:	DCA01MA065

B. GROUP

American Flight 77: Daniel Bower, Ph.D.
Senior Aerospace Engineer
NTSB, RE-60
490 L'Enfant Plaza E, SW
Washington, DC 20594

United Flight 93: John O'Callaghan
National Resource Specialist - Aircraft Performance
NTSB, RE-60

C. SUMMARY

This document describes information obtained from the Digital Flight Data Recorders (DFDRs) of the subject aircraft concerning the use of the airplane autoflight and navigation systems both before and after the hijacking events, and presents fuel on board calculations based on the DFDR fuel flow data.

D. AUTOFLIGHT SYSTEMS DESCRIPTION AND ACTIVITY

Numerous parameters on the DFDRs record the status of various autopilot modes and navigation equipment settings. Analysis of these parameters provides some indication of the way the autopilot and navigation equipment was used by those operating the aircraft, both before and after the hijackings.

The Boeing 757 autopilot can control both the vertical movement of the airplane (climbs, level flight, and descents), as well as its horizontal movement (direction of flight). In addition, the autothrottle automatically controls the engine thrust required for different maneuvers. Taken together, the autopilot and autothrottle comprise the "autoflight" system. The manner in which the autoflight system maneuvers the airplane is governed by different autopilot and autothrottle "modes." In some modes, the autoflight system obtains all the information it needs to fly the airplane from the Flight Management Computer (FMC), which has been pre-programmed (or re-programmed in flight) by the flight crew to fly the desired route at the desired altitudes and speeds. In other modes, the autoflight system obtains required information from the Mode Control Panel (MCP), a set of controls on the instrument panel with which the crew specifies desired headings, altitudes, speeds, and climb or descent rates. In general, more crew interaction is required when the autoflight system is operated from the MCP than from the FMC, because with the MCP each change in flight condition must be initiated by a crew input on the MCP, whereas changes in flight condition can be pre-programmed into the FMC and so will occur automatically in modes that use the FMC for input.

The Flight Director is an instrument that provides pitch and roll guidance to the pilot when flying manually, by displaying "command bars" on the Attitude Direction Indicator (ADI), which is an electronic version of an artificial horizon. The pitch and roll commands issued by the Flight Director, if followed by the flying pilot, will result in a flight path identical to the flight path that would be flown by the autopilot itself. This flight path is a function of the autopilot mode, and the programming of the FMC or values set in the MCP. The autoflight system calculates the pitch and roll maneuvers that will result in the desired flight path; with the autopilot on, the autopilot executes these pitch and roll maneuvers itself. With just the Flight Director on, the system only provides control input guidance to the pilot, and the pilot must make the control inputs, or the airplane will not follow the desired flight path. The Flight Director and autopilot can both be on at the same time, or each can be on independently.

AAL 77 Autoflight Activity

Figure 1 shows a time history of the various autopilot and autothrottle modes engaged on Flight 77, from takeoff from Dulles airport to the end of the DFDR data at impact with the Pentagon. Also shown in the Figure are the values of speeds, altitudes, headings, and Mach that the airplane flew. The values set in the MCP by the pilots (both the American Airlines pilots and the hijack pilots) had a recording error when recorded on the DFDR, and could not be determined.

For most of the flight, until after the hijackers turned the airplane back towards Washington, both the Captain's and First Officer's Flight Directors were on. During the takeoff, the autopilot was off, and the Flight Director was issuing roll commands based on inputs made in the MCP, and pitch commands based on inputs coming alternatively from the FMC (when in VNAV mode) or from the MCP (when in Altitude Hold or Flight Change modes). Once the flight was cleared to its 35,000 ft. cruising altitude, the autopilot was engaged in LNAV and VNAV modes, which use inputs from the FMC to guide the airplane along the desired horizontal and vertical flight path. During the ascent, and while at the cruise altitude, the right (First Officer's) autopilot was engaged, and heading select mode was used to maneuver the airplane horizontally.

The autothrottle was engaged throughout the initial part of the flight. During the climb the autothrottle mode varied between climb thrust mode, airspeed hold mode, flight level change mode, and Mach mode. Upon reaching the cruise altitudes, first at 33,000 feet, then 35,000 feet, the autothrottle switched to a Mach number hold cruise mode, applying thrust to achieve a Mach number of 0.83.

A few minutes after the hijackers took control of the cockpit (at approximately 08:52), the horizontal mode was changed to a heading select and the airplane began a 180-degree turn back towards Washington. After the new heading was selected, and up until the last nine minutes of the flight, the autopilot operated in modes that receive inputs from the MCP (i.e., target values of altitude, speed, and heading set directly by the operators of the aircraft) rather than from the FMC. The autopilot was off for the last eight minutes of the flight. For the remainder of the flight, the horizontal mode remained in heading select and the vertical mode was operated in altitude hold, altitude, or flight level change mode. Similarly, the autothrottle remained in either airspeed mode or mach mode, except during times of flight level changes.

At about 09:08, after a flight level change was initiated from 25,000 feet, the First Officer's flight director, the autopilot, and the autothrottle all disengaged. This disengagement was concurrent with a right (First Officer's) autopilot warning. The autopilot remained off for approximately two minutes, and then re-engaged on the left side (Captain's side). The autopilot disengaged again, concurrent with an autopilot warning on the left side. After about a half a minute of disengagement, the left autopilot was re-engaged and the autothrottle was re-engaged soon after. Over the next ten minutes, the autothrottle was engaged and disengaged several times, while the aircraft remained at 25,000 feet, until remaining engaged in the flight level change mode during descent from 25,000 feet.

At approximately 9:29, while at an altitude of 7000 feet and approximately 30 nautical miles from Washington Reagan National Airport, the autopilot and autothrottle were disengaged. These remained off during the 360-degree, descending turn to impact with the Pentagon.

UAL 93 Autoflight Activity

Figure 2 shows a time history of the various autopilot and autothrottle modes engaged on Flight 93, from takeoff from Newark to the end of the DFDR data at impact. Also shown in the Figure are the values of speeds, altitudes, headings, and climb/descent rates set in the MCP, along with the values of those parameters that the airplane actually flew.

For most of the flight, until shortly after the hijackers took control of the cockpit (at approximately 09:30), both the Captain's and First Officer's Flight Directors were on. During the takeoff, the autopilot was off, and the Flight Director was issuing roll commands based on inputs made in the MCP, and pitch commands based on inputs coming alternatively from the FMC (when in VNAV mode) or from the MCP (when in Altitude Hold or Flight Change modes). Once the flight was cleared to its 35,000 ft. cruising altitude, the autopilot was engaged in LNAV and VNAV modes, which use inputs from the FMC to guide the airplane along the desired horizontal and vertical flight path.

The autothrottle was engaged throughout the flight. During the climb the autothrottle mode varied between climb thrust mode, airspeed hold mode, and flight level change mode. Upon reaching the 35,000 cruise altitude, the autothrottle switched to a Mach number hold cruise mode, applying thrust to achieve a Mach number of 0.82.

At about 09:33, the autoflight modes started to change. Both the Captain and First Officer's flight directors were turned off, and at about 09:34 the autopilot was turned off briefly. After the autopilot was reengaged (less than a minute later), up until the last three minutes of the flight it operated in modes that receive inputs from the MCP (i.e., target values of altitude, speed, heading, and descent rate set directly by the operators of the aircraft) rather than from the FMC. The autopilot was off for the last three minutes of the flight.

The autothrottle switched from a Mach hold mode to an airspeed hold mode at about 9:33:30, and remained in this mode for the remainder of the flight, except for brief periods where the airspeed was either below or above pre-set limits and the autothrottle adjusted thrust in an attempt to correct the situation (these are the MIN SPD and SPD LIMIT modes).

From 09:33 to the time the autopilot was turned off (about 10:00), the airplane was maneuvered horizontally via the heading select and heading hold modes, with the desired heading set on the MCP. The bottom graph in Figure 2 shows the magnetic heading selected in the MCP was 120 degrees, and also shows the airplane turning towards that heading. From the airplane's position at this point, a magnetic heading of 120 degrees would put the airplane on course for Washington, D.C.. At 09:57, the heading selected in the MCP is changed to 90 degrees. About half a minute later, the autopilot switches from heading hold to heading select modes, and the airplane turns to the 90 degree heading selected in the MCP.

From 09:33 to the time the autopilot was turned off, the airplane was maneuvered vertically using the vertical speed and altitude hold modes. In the vertical speed mode, the desired rate of climb or descent is set in the MCP. In altitude hold mode, the airplane maintains the altitude at which the altitude hold mode button on the MCP is pressed. As shown in Figure 2, initially the vertical speed selected was about +1,500 ft/min, and the airplane climbed accordingly. Interestingly, at the same time, the altitude selected in the MCP was 9,600 feet (lower than the current airplane altitude). At about 09:38 the autopilot entered altitude hold mode at 40,700 feet. A couple of minutes later, the autopilot re-entered vertical speed mode, with a descent rate of -4,200 feet/minute selected in the MCP, and the airplane started to descend. At about 09:47, this descent rate in the MCP was adjusted to about -1,300 feet/minute. At around the same time, the altitude set in the MCP was adjusted to about 5,000 feet. This suggests that the intent of the operators may have been to descend to 5,000 feet.

At about 10:00, the autopilot was turned off, and remained off for the remaining three minutes of the flight.

D. NAVIGATION SYSTEMS DESCRIPTION AND ACTIVITY

The Boeing 757 keeps track of its own position using the Inertial Navigation System (INS), which uses acceleration sensors to calculate the motion of the airplane over the ground. The INS position calculation is periodically updated and corrected using data from ground based radio navigation stations, called "very high frequency omnirange stations" (VORs). By tuning a receiver to the signals broadcast from a VOR, the bearing from the airplane to the VOR can be determined. Tuning in two or more stations and knowing the positions of each, a fix of the airplane position can be obtained.

The 757 has two VOR receivers. The crew can manually tune each of these receivers to a desired station (provided the station is in range), and view the airplane's bearing relative to the station on a special display mode on the Electronic Horizontal Situation Indicator (EHSI). This mode is most often used when the crew wants to fly either towards or away from the selected VOR station, along a specific bearing or "radial" to or from the station. In other modes, the airplane will automatically tune in VOR stations along the airplane's route in order to obtain position fixes. The system generally selects stations whose bearings from the airplane differ by about 90 degrees; this configuration results in the most accurate position fixes.

AAL 77 Navigation System Activity

Figure 3 shows the VOR stations tuned to by the two VOR receivers on American Flight 77. The EFIS mode determines the type of display shown on the EHSI. During the initial part of the flight, the EFIS is in “MAP” mode. In this mode, the EHSI displays an airplane symbol pointed towards the top of the display, with the magnetic heading and track shown in a partial compass rose at the top of the display. Various points of interest - VOR stations, fixes, airports, and so on - can be displayed in their correct position relative to the airplane. The planned and projected route of flight can also be displayed in the MAP mode. The range of the MAP mode can be adjusted from 5 miles to 160 nautical miles, depending on the detail or scale of map required. At about 09:08:20, the display switched to VOR mode; in this mode, the EHSI displays the airplane's angular deviation or position relative to a specified radial from the selected VOR.

The points during the flight at which the VOR receivers were tuned to new frequencies are shown on the map in Figure 2 as yellow diamonds. The points shown occur after the hijackers took control of the cockpit. Lines from the airplane flight path to the stations indicate the VOR stations tuned by the left and right VOR receivers. The point on the flight path from which the lines originate are the points at which the station was first tuned, i.e., the points at which the VOR station frequency selected by each receiver changed.

Note that while the EFIS was initially in MAP mode, the left and right VOR receivers were tuned to stations whose bearings from the airplane differed by about 90 degrees, at the time at which the VOR station pairs were changed. This illustrates the method the system uses for obtaining VOR position fixes to update the INS.

During the turn back to the east, the frequency of the right VOR receiver was set to 111.0 MHz, corresponding to the VOR station located at Washington Reagan National Airport (DCA). At the time the DCA frequency was selected, the station was too far away for its signals to be received by the receiver. The right VOR receiver remained tuned to the DCA VOR for the remainder of the flight, except for a 1-minute period at 9:15. The left VOR receiver was tuned to various frequencies, but was tuned to 113.5 (AML in Herndon, VA near Dulles Airport) at approximately 9:08. At approximately 9:18, the left distance measuring equipment (DME) began receiving information from the AML VOR. After receiving the DME signal, the airplane remained on a constant heading towards the Washington area. At 9:32, both VOR receivers were tuned to the DCA VOR.

UAL 93 Navigation System Activity

Figure 4 shows the VOR stations tuned to by the two VOR receivers on United Flight 93. At the bottom of the Figure, the EFIS mode is shown. For most of the fight, the EFIS is in “MAP” mode.

As in Figure 3, the points during the flight at which the EFIS mode switched to MAP mode and then to VOR mode are shown on the map in Figure 4 as yellow diamonds. The VOR stations tuned by the left and right VOR receivers are indicated by lines from the airplane flight path to the stations. The point on the flight path from which the lines originate are the points at which the station was first tuned.

As with Flight 77, while the EFIS was in MAP mode, the left and right VOR receivers were tuned to stations whose bearings from the airplane differed by about 90 degrees, at the time at which the VOR station pairs were changed. Again, this illustrates the method the system uses for obtaining VOR position fixes to update the INS.

Shortly after the EFIS was switched to VOR mode, the frequency of the left VOR receiver was set to 111.0 MHz, corresponding to the VOR station located at Washington Reagan National Airport (DCA). At the time the DCA frequency was selected, the station was too far away for its signals to be received by the receiver. If DCA VOR had been in range, the display on the EHSI could have been used to show the airplane's position relative to an inbound radial to DCA, and thus help navigate the airplane towards DCA. The selection of the DCA VOR frequency in the airplane's left VOR receiver suggests that the operators of the airplane had an interest in DCA, and may have wanted to use that VOR station to help navigate the airplane towards Washington.

The magnetic heading of 120 degrees selected in the autopilot MCP was the correct heading for flying to Washington. However, even though the EFIS was in the MAP mode at the time, it was in the 80 nautical mile range setting, and so would not have shown DCA on the display; consequently, it is unlikely that the hijackers used the map display on the EHSI to deduce the correct heading for Washington. It follows that the hijackers had some other means of obtaining this heading.

A surprising element in the navigation of flight 93 is the rapid descent from cruise altitudes while still approximately 260 nautical miles from the (presumed) target. If the hijacker's destination was Washington, they started their descent very prematurely. Figure 5 compares the descent profiles of all four airplanes hijacked on September 11. Note that by the time AAL 11, UAL 175, and AAL 77 descended below 5,000 feet, they were all within 10 NM of their targets. UAL 93, on the other hand, descended to 5,000 feet while still 135 NM from Washington.

E. FUEL CONSUMPTION AND FUEL REMAINING CALCULATIONS

AAL 77 Fuel Consumption

Figure 6 shows AAL flight 77's fuel flow to each engine as recorded by the DFDR, and the sum of these, equal to the total fuel flow. By integrating the total fuel flow with time, the amount of fuel consumed throughout the flight can be calculated. Subtracting the fuel consumed from the initial fuel load then gives the amount of fuel remaining, as shown in the bottom plot of Figure 6.

Based on ACARS transmissions to the airplane, the fuel load on the airplane when on the ramp was 48983 lbs. This results in about 36,200 lb. of fuel remaining upon impact with the Pentagon (the end of the DFDR data).

UAL 93 Fuel Consumption

Figure 7 shows fuel flow and fuel remaining for UAL Flight 93, calculated in the same way as just described for AAL Flight 77.

Based on ACARS transmissions to the airplane, the fuel load on takeoff was 48,700 lb. This results in about 37,500 lb. of fuel remaining upon impact (the end of the DFDR data). If instead of descending to about 5,000 feet over Pennsylvania, Flight 93 had continued cruising at 35,000 feet to Washington, it would have arrived over Washington with about 35,500 lb. of fuel on board.

____

John O'Callaghan

____

Daniel Bower, Ph.D.

List of Abbreviations

ACFD	Arlington County Fire Department
ACPD	Arlington County Police Department
AFIP	Armed Forces Institute of Pathology
AFME	Armed Forces Medical Examiner
AOC	Army Operations Center
BOCC	Building Operations Command Center
BUPERS	Bureau of Naval Personnel
DIA	Defense Intelligence Agency
DoD	Department of Defense
DPS	Defense Protective Service
ECC	Emergency Communications Center
EMS	Emergency Medical Services
EOC	Emergency Operations Center
FAA	Federal Aviation Administration
FBI	Federal Bureau of Investigation
FEMA	Federal Emergency Management Agency
GSA	General Services Administration
ICS	Incident Command System
IMCEN	Information Management Support Center
IRT	Initial Reconnaissance Team

IST	Incident Support Team
JOC	Joint Operations Center
JTTF	Joint Terrorism Task Force
MDW	Military District of Washington
MWAA	Metropolitan Washington Airports Authority
NCC	Navy Command Center
NCIS	Naval Criminal Investigative Service
NCRS	National Capital Response Squad
NEADS	Northeast Air Defense Sector
NMCC	National Military Command Center
NMRT	National Medical Response Team (Department of Health and Human Services)
NORAD	North American Aerospace Defense Command
NTSB	National Transportation Safety Board
ODCSPER	U.S. Army Office of the Deputy Chief of Staff for Personnel
OSD	Office of the Secretary of Defense
PAC	Pentagon Athletic Center
PENREN	Pentagon Renovation Program Office
PFAC	Pentagon Family Assistance Center
PFARRO	Pentagon Family Assistance Resources and Referral Office
QDR	Quadrennial Defense Review
RDF	Remote Delivery Facility
RE&F	Real Estate and Facilities
RSW	U.S. Army Resource Services—Washington
SCIF	Sensitive Compartmented Information Facility
SWAT	Special Weapons and Tactics
US&R	Urban Search and Rescue
WHS	Washington Headquarters Services

Notes

Certain conventions—abbreviations and short forms of titles—have been used to save space. For fuller identification of sources, including complete information about interviews and published works, readers may consult the bibliography.

I. TARGET: THE PENTAGON

1. Except where otherwise indicated the following description of the Pentagon is drawn from Goldberg, *The Pentagon: The First Fifty Years*. Supplementary information is derived from e-mail Dr. Georgine Glatz (Chief Engineer, Pentagon Renovation and Construction Program Office) to Alfred Goldberg, 10 Oct 06.
2. Office of the Secretary of Defense, *A Status Report to the Congress on the Renovation of the Pentagon*, 1 Mar 91, 4-7 (these annual reports will hereafter be referred to as OSD, *Status Report*, with the date); ibid, 1 Mar 95, 6-12; ibid, 1 Mar 02, 13.
3. *Defense Authorization Act for FY 1991* (PL 101-510) Sec 2804, 5 Nov 90; *DoD Appropriation Act, FY 1995* (PL 103-335), Sec. 8149, 30 Sep 94; *Engineering News-Record*, 4 Sep 00, 58.
4. OSD, *Status Report*, 1 Mar 02, 3, 6, 25, 56-57, 80; ibid, 1 Mar 00, 51, 85; ibid, 1 Mar 01, 14, 90-91; e-mail Neal A. Shelly to Alfred Goldberg, 4 Aug 05.
5. "Building Performance Evaluation, The 9-11 Terrorist Attack—Pentagon" (hereafter "PENREN Report"), 6:3-4; OSD, *Status Report*, 1 Mar 00, 4, 51, 84; ibid, 1 Mar 02, 19; interv Evey, 22 Oct 01, 14.
6. OSD, *Status Report*, 1 Mar 02, 4, 28, 45; ibid, 1 Mar 00, 73.
7. *9/11 Commission Report*, 60-61, 68-70, 71, 190.
8. Ibid, 223-31, 252-53; indictment, *United States of America v. Zacarias Moussaoui* (E. D. Va., Dec 01), 8-9, http://www.usdoj.gov/ag/moussaouiindictment.htm.
9. *9-11 Commission Report*, 1-8, 32.
10. Ibid, 17, 20-22, 285.

11. Ibid, 10-14, 32-33.
12. Ibid, 4, 278, 285.
13. Ibid, 33; Prepared Statement of Monte R. Belger to the National Commission on Terrorist Attacks upon the United States, 9-11 Commission Hearings, 17 Jun 04, 2, http://www.911commission.gov/hearings/hearing12/belger_statement.pdf.
14. *9-11 Commission Report*, 2-3, 8-9, 33, 225; 9-11 Commission, "The Four Flights," staff statement no. 4, 5, http://www.9-11commission.gov/staff_statements/index.htm#statements. A passenger on the plane, Barbara Olson, wife of U.S. Solicitor General Theodore Olson, called her husband and told him of being herded to the rear of the plane; see Tim O'Brien, "Wife of Solicitor General Alerted Him of Hijacking from Plane," 12 Sep 01, http://archives.cnn.com/2001/US/09/11/pentagon.olson/index.html.
15. *9/11 Commission Report*, 33-34, 27-28.
16. Ibid, 37, 39; Center for Cooperative Research, "Context of 8:30 a.m., Rookie in Command of the NMCC," 9/11 timeline at http://www.cooperativeresearch.org/context.jsp?item=a830rookienmcc; "Statement of Captain Charles J. Leidig, Jr., before the National Commission on Terrorist Attacks upon the United States, 9-11 Commission Hearings," 17 Jun 04, http://www.9-11commission.gov/hearings/hearing12/leidig_statement.pdf; "PENREN Report," 2:1 (msg); Rossow, *Uncommon Strength*, 12.
17. ACPD Incident Reports (Witness Section) filed by Barry Foust and Richard Cox, 11 Sep 01, Dep-Chief Holl ACPD; telcon Foust and Nancy Berlage, 3 Aug 06; telcon Cox and Nancy Berlage, 28 Jul 06.
18. Interv Rabogliatti, 5 Nov 01, 1; interv Chiarelli, 5 Feb 02, 15.
19. American Society of Civil Engineers, *The Pentagon Building Performance Report* (hereafter *ASCE Report*), 12-14, 18.
20. Gross, "9/11 and Operation Noble Eagle," 7-8.
21. *ASCE Report*, 20.
22. Ibid, 12.
23. Ibid, 20, 40; "PENREN Report," 2:8.
24. *ASCE Report*, 28, 34, 37; "PENREN Report," 2:2.
25. "PENREN Report," 2:9, 6:15-16; interv Pugrud, 1 Nov 01, 3; interv Perez, 10 Oct 01, 9; interv K. Cox, 2 Aug 02, 6; *ASCE Report*, 40; interv Powell, 29 Oct 01, 9; DoD, "Flight Data and Cockpit Voice Recorders Found," news release 425-01, 14 Sep 01, http://www.defenselink.mil; FBI Evidence Response Team, Penttbom, First Floor-West Graphic w/atchd list of dead, 26 Nov 01, AttOfc EDVa.
26. *ASCE Report*, 58; "PENREN Report," 6:4, 9-12; e-mail Dr. Georgine Glatz to Alfred Goldberg, 27; Paul Jackson, ed, *Jane's All the World's Aircraft, 2000-2001*, 622, 627; *ASCE Report*, 50.

II. THE DEADLY STRIKE

1. OSD, *Status Report*, 1 Mar 02, 4.
2. "Arlington County After-Action Report," B-15.
3. September 11, 2001, Bios on Victims, OSD Hist. There is no attribution of compiler or date.
4. Pers acct Collier, 13 Sep 01.
5. "PENREN Report," 1:2, 3.
6. Interv Boger, 14 Nov 01, 10-15.
7. Interv Jaworski, 11 Dec 01, 2, 7, 10-13, 19.
8. Interv Moody, 13 Sep 01, 2-7.
9. Donna St. George, "Pentagon Survivor Wounds are Slow to Heal," *Washington Post*, 11 Sep 03, 1; Greg Zoroya, "The Cruzes, Injured at the Pentagon, Juan Cruz Santiago," *USA Today*, 11 Sep 02, D4.
10. Donna St. George, "Hope Breathes Beneath Wounds," *Washington Post*, 2 Dec 01, 1; Donna St. George, "Alive, But Not As She Was," *Washington Post*, 10 Sep 02, 1.
11. See Appendix A; interv Hudson, 25 Feb 02, 9-11.

12. Interv Gallop, 31 Oct 01, 7-17.
13. "Navy Command Center Pull Together," unpaginated manuscript (see sections, "The Survivors" and "Schematic"), Nav Hist. The dimensions of the Command Center are computed from the Schematic.
14. Interv McKeown, 25 Oct 01, 2-7.
15. Interv Shaeffer, 21 Jun 02, 3-9, 15-17, 22, 24, 29, 36.
16. Interv Lhuillier, 13 Dec 01, 2-3, 5-6, 9-17; interv Capets, 2 Nov 01, 17.
17. Interv Lhuillier, 10-14; interv Cole, 6 Dec 01, 8-9; interv Capets, 10-14, 17; interv Humbert, 4 Jan 02, 7-9.
18. Interv Gully, 6 Dec 01, 3-5; interv Polasek, 6 Dec 01, 5-6; interv Cole, 7-8.
19. See Appendix A.
20. Agency Space Allocation Diagram, Floor One, Pre-9-11-01, PENREN Office; interv Gonzales, 13 Feb 02, 2, 6-9, 13.
21. Interv Cordero, 4 Mar 02, 3-6, 8-9, 11; interv Gonzales, 18-19, 26, 28; Lewis A. Prombain (DIA),"Recognition of Heroic Acts," w/atchmt, nd, OSD Hist.
22. Interv Morrison, in "PENREN Report," 2:21-22.
23. Ibid, 2:23-24.
24. Rossow, *Uncommon Strength*, iv-v, viii-ix, xii; "PENREN Report," 6:14-15.
25. "PENREN Report," 6:6-8, 17.
26. Interv Parham, 4 Dec 01, 4-14.
27. Interv Zappalla, 9 Oct 01, 2-6.
28. Interv Olaes, 13 Sep 01, 3-6; interv Petrovich, 21 Sep 01, 5-9; Rossow, *Uncommon Strength*, 34-36, 38-39.
29. Interv Grant, 26 Feb 02, 32-40; interv Maxfield, 16 Nov 01, 4-8, 13-14; interv Rose, 23 Jan 02, 9-16; Rossow, *Uncommon Strength*, 38, 43-44.
30. "PENREN Report," 6:15.
31. Rossow, *Uncommon Strength*, 39-40; pers acct McNair, 29 Oct 01, 1.
32. Interv Wills, 12 Jul 02, 3-4; interv Stevens, 13 Dec 01, 3-4; interv Grunewald, 2 Nov 01, 3.
33. Interv Grunewald, 4-13, 20-21; interv Carden, 29 Oct 01, 3-14.
34. Rossow, *Uncommon Strength*, 41, 49.
35. Interv Wills, 4-8; interv Stevens, 6-8; pers acct McNair, 1-2.
36. Interv Petrovich, 21 Sep 01, 8-12; interv Petrovich, 1 Nov 01, 23-26; interv Stevens, 12; interv Wills, 16-17.
37. Interv Beans, 6 Nov 01, 1-2, 5-6, 8-18, 21, 27.
38. Rossow, *Uncommon Strength* (Appendix A has pictures of 29 victims; Appendix B lists names of injured).
39. Interv Birdwell, 7 Mar 02, 5, 7, 9-11, 13-15, 24; interv Knoblauch, 28 Nov 01, 9-10; pers acct R. Wallace, nd, 1; interv Menig, 14 Feb 02, 7-9.
40. Interv Wood, 1 Mar 02, 11-15; interv Eikenberry, 6 Feb 02, 5-6.
41. Interv Wood, 16-21; interv Eikenberry, 7-10.
42. Interv Kensinger, 2 Aug 02, 26; FBI Evidence Response Team, Penttbom, First Floor-West Graphic w/atchd list of dead, 26 Nov 01, AttOfc EDVa; September 11, 2001, Bios on Victims, OSD Hist.
43. Interv P. Murphy, 19 Sep 01, 4-10.
44. Interv Zitterkopf, 27 Nov 01, 4-7.
45. Interv Livingstone, 19 Feb 02, 2-6; interv Kern, 24 Jan 02, 3-6.
46. Interv Livingstone, 5-6; interv Kern, 7-10; interv Crane Group #1, 25 Feb 02, 8-10.
47. Interv Livingstone, 6-8; interv Kern, 8; interv Wirick, 27 Jun 02, 3-4; interv Crane Group #2, 25 Feb 02, 17-18.
48. Interv Kern, 8-9; interv Livingstone, 7-8; interv Wirick, 4-6, 25; interv Crane Group #2, 14, 16, 17-18; "PENREN Report," 6:12.
49. Interv Braswell, 30 Oct 01, 2-7; interv Kern, 9-14; interv Livingstone, 8-14; interv Crane Group #1, 29; interv Crane Group #2, 21-24.

50. "Arlington County After-Action Report," A-13; interv Combs, 11 July 05, 11.

III. THE RESCUERS

1. Interv White, 19 Apr 02, 14-15; interv Gray, Gibbs, and Smith, 3 Feb 06, 3-4; interv T. Hodge, 30 Oct 01, 8; interv Jackson, 7 Jan 02, 12. Chief Smith was known by both names, Jerome and Dale.
2. Interv Schwartz, 17 Apr 02, 41-44.
3. Interv Perrin, 1 Nov 01, 6-7, 9-14; interv S. Kelly, 1 Nov 01, 5-7; interv Oliver, 31 Oct 01, 8, 10-22, 32.
4. Interv Schuetz, 13 Sep 01, 5-8, 10-14; interv Vera, 20 Sep 01, 4-5, 7-18, 21; interv P. K. Carlton, 4 Dec 01, 11.
5. Interv Schuetz, 8; interv Lirette, 30 Nov 01, 13.
6. Interv Tarantino, 25 Sep 01 (corrected transcript), 1, 3-5.
7. Interv Thomas, 23 Jan 02, 5-6; interv Lirette, 7-10; interv Tarantino, 4-5; interv Powell, 29 Oct 01, 2, 4, 6, 10; interv P. K. Carlton, 21-22.
8. Interv Powell, 5-9; interv K. Cox, 5-8; interv P. K. Carlton, 13.
9. Interv Tarantino, 5.
10. Interv Henson, 23 Jan 02, 5-9; interv C. Lewis, 25 Apr 02, 4-7.
11. Interv Thomas, 9-10; interv Tarantino, 5; interv Powell, 11-12.
12. Interv Tarantino, 6-7; interv Thomas, 11-12; interv Henson, 10; interv P. K. Carlton, 12-13.
13. Interv Henson, 11; interv Tarantino, 6-7; interv Thomas, 12-13; interv Powell, 12-13; interv P. K. Carlton, 11-13.
14. Interv Knoblauch, 28 Nov 01, 6-9; pers acct R. Wallace, 1; interv McKinnon, nd, 3-7; interv Davies, 12 Dec 01, 4; interv Richon, 27 Nov 01, 5.
15. Interv McKinnon, 8-9; interv Knoblauch, 9-10; interv Birdwell, 7 Mar 02, 14-15. For an account of Birdwell's ordeal, see Chapter II.
16. Interv McKinnon, 11, 15; interv Knoblauch, 10; interv Baxter, 30 Nov 01, 5-8; interv Birdwell, 18-19; interv Wassel, 9 Apr 03, 17.
17. Interv Ogletree, 29 Jan 02, 4-6; interv Birdwell, 20, 22, 42.
18. Interv Davies, 5-6; interv Knoblauch, 10-11; pers acct R. Wallace, 1; interv McKinnon, 12-15.
19. Interv Thurman, 20 Sep 01, 2, 5-6, 8-12, 13-16, 23; interv Knoblauch, 11; interv Davies, 6-7; pers acct R. Wallace, 1.
20. Interv Davies, 7-8; interv Knoblauch, 11-12; interv McKinnon, 14-19, 21; interv Balisle, 28 Jun 02, 7-8.
21. Interv Perez, 10 Oct 01, cover sheet, 6-7.
22. Interv Balisle, 5-7.
23. "Arlington County After-Action Report," A-22-23; interv Toti, 10 Oct 01, 1-2, 14, 17, 19-21; interv Combs, 9.
24. Interv Rumsfeld, 23 Dec 02, 5-7; interv Wassel, 19-20; Video Rcd, WUSA 9, 9:41 a.m. to 10:55 a.m.
25. Interv Leibner, 23 Jan 02, passim.
26. Interv Combs, 11-12; "Arlington County After-Action Report," A-30, C-46; ACPD "Incident History Detail," 11 Sep 01, entries 10:41:31 and 10:42:55, DepChief Holl ACPD.

IV. FIGHTING THE FIRE

1. Lilly and Walz, "Tower Terror," *Pentagram*, 16 Nov 01, 1; "Washington's Heroes," *Newsweek* web exclusive, 29 Sep 01, http://www.msnbc.msn.com/id/3069699/; interv A. Wallace, 30 Oct 01, 36-38; interv Skipper, 30 Oct 01, 3; interv Boger, 5; interv Garofola, 20 Sep 01, 31; interv Valenzo, 30 Oct 01, 6-7; interv Pollygus, 8 Nov 01, 2, 10, 13-14; interv Kidd, 14 Nov 01, 2, 4-5; interv Suvari, 9 Apr 02, 21-22; interv P. Murphy, 11; telcon Maj Damien Marsh (co-pilot of Marine One on 9-11) and Nancy Berlage, 7 Jul 06; telcon Maj Brian Foley (pilot of second Marine helicopter accompanying POTUS)

and Nancy Berlage, 6 Jul 06; telcon Charles Campbell (Chief FMMCFD) and Nancy Berlage, 13 Apr 06; e-mail Sgt Bobby M. Thomas (PFPA) to Diane Putney, 20 Apr 06. The president had taken off from the Pentagon Heliport on 10 September on his way to Florida. The South Lawn of the White House was unavailable for helicopter usage due to a special event; see Patrick Gavin, "The Day Before," *Washington Post*, 5 Sep 04.

2. Interv A. Wallace, 6-7, 36-38, 43 (quote, 7); interv Skipper, 3; interv Valenzo, 7; facsimile A. Wallace to Kelly, 17 Sep 03, w/atchmt, ACFD.
3. Interv A. Wallace 7-10; interv Skipper, 3-4; interv Schwartz, 112, described the initial fireball as burning fuel; interv Kidd, 6-8; Lilly and Walz, "Tower Terror," 2; interv Boger, 12-14.
4. "Arlington County After-Action Report," A-4; interv Skipper, 5; interv Gilroy, 30 Oct 01, 10; interv A. Wallace, 8-12, 14.
5. Interv Skipper, 6, 8; interv A. Wallace, 20; William Toti, "Six Thousand Antoinettes," nd, Nav Hist; interv Toti, 10 Oct 01, 14-16 (quotes, 16); Toti "One Year Later Frozen in Time," 37.
6. Interv A. Wallace, 12-19, 40; interv Leibner, 10-11; interv Skipper, 5; Ward, "Attack on the Pentagon," 24; interv Afforder, 30 Oct 01, 14-15; interv Hamlet, 26 Feb 02, 16; interv Reardon, 20 Oct 01, 10; interv Bruno, 15 Apr 02, 12-14; interv Cruz-Cortez, 21 Feb 02, 13-15.
7. Interv Afforder, 3; interv Valenzo, 7; Ward, "Attack on the Pentagon," 33.
8. Ward, "Attack on the Pentagon," 25; on ECC general operations, telcon Capt Michelle Nuneville (Arlington ECC) and Nancy Berlage, 9 Dec 05; "Arlington County After-Action Report," 9, 44, A-4, 34-35, 44, C-26; ACPD Incident Reports filed by Barry Foust, Richard Cox, and Ralph D. Rice, Jr., 11 Sep 01, DepChief Holl ACPD; telcon Richard Cox and Nancy Berlage, 28 Jul 06; telcon Barry Foust and Nancy Berlage, 3 Aug 06; e-mail John Lisle (Media Relations, ACPD) to Nancy Berlage, 4 Aug 06, w/atchmt digital recording, "Excerpt Released to Public of Arlington ECC Police Response Tape, 11 Sep 01," Arlington ECC.
9. A hospitality room fire was reported at 1001 Wilson Boulevard in the Rosslyn neighborhood. Arlington ECC Fire Dispatch Recording, 11 Sep 01, Arlington ECC; "Arlington County After-Action Report," A-4-5, 7, 9, 34; Ward, "Attack on the Pentagon," 25; interv Burroughs, 5 Dec 01, abstract, 2; interv, Schwartz, 14-15.
10. Ward, "Attack on the Pentagon," 33; "Arlington County After-Action Report," A-44; interv Owens, 20 Mar 02, 23, 27 (quote, 23).
11. Interv Valenzo, 10-12; interv Gilroy, 14; "Arlington County After-Action Report," A-6-7; interv Schwartz, 16, 19-20; interv White, 7; Ward, "Attack on the Pentagon," 25; interv Gray, Gibbs, and Smith, 2; e-mail Derek Spector (Truck 105 ACFD) to Nancy Berlage, 18 Aug 06; telcon Capt Steve McCoy (Eng 101 ACFD) and Nancy Berlage, 17 Aug 06.
12. Brewster, "Belvoir Firefighter among First Responders at Pentagon," 1; interv Valenzo, 3, 9-10 (quote, 9); interv Afforder, 5; interv Gilroy, 9-11; interv Surette, 30 Oct 01, 3-4; interv Ladd, 30 Oct 01, 11, 12.
13. Interv Reardon, 8-9 (quote); Lilly and Walz, "Local Heroes: FMMC Fire Department Reflects on Attacks," 4.
14. Interv Ladd, 12-13; interv Surette, 7-8; interv T. Hodge, 6 (quote); interv Valenzo, 13; interv Reardon, 9; e-mail Michael Thayer (FMMCFD) to Nancy Berlage, 1 May 06, w/atchmt, "Chart of Ft. Myer Firefighters Names and Assignments on 11 Sept 01"; interv Valenzo, 10-11. Many individuals described the day's scenes as resembling a movie: see for example interv Howes, 3 Dec 01, 9, 23; interv Thumann and Zegowitz, 20 Dec 01, 16; interv Tinsley, 20 Dec 01, digital recording.
15. Interv Ladd, 12-15; interv Valenzo, 11-12; interv Reardon, 9-13; interv Wallace, 31; interv T. Hodge, 4-6; interv Surette, 8-9.
16. Interv Valenzo, 21; interv Gilroy, 10-18, 21 (quote, 16); Brewster, "Belvoir Firefighter among First Responders at Pentagon," 2.
17. Interv Defina, 3 Dec 01, 4-5; interv Durrer, 3 Dec 01, 4-5.
18. Interv Defina, 3-6; interv Howes, 4; interv Durrer, 6-12, 26 (quotes, 6, 7, 26); e-mails Capt Michael Defina to Nancy Berlage, 14, 24 Aug 06.

19. Interv Henry, 5 Dec 01, digital recording; interv Durrer, 11-12.
20. Interv Defina, 4, 6-9; interv Durrer, 27; Ward, "Attack on the Pentagon," 24; "Arlington County After-Action Report," A-6; MWAA Fire Response radio transmissions, 11 Sep 01, MWAA.
21. Interv A. Thompson, 12 Dec 01, abstract, 2; interv Thumann and Zegowitz, 12-13; interv Martin, 12 Dec 01, 2-6, 9 (quote, 6); MWAA Fire Response radio transmissions, 11 Sep 01.
22. Interv Schwartz, 9-15 (quotes, 9, 13, 14).
23. The agreement was The Greater Metropolitan Washington Area Fire/Rescue Services Mutual Aid Operations Plan (2001). See telcon Calvin Smith (Metropolitan Washington COGs) and Nancy Berlage, 12 Apr 06; interv Plaugher, 22 Apr 02, 83-85; interv Schwartz, 35-36; interv Gray, Gibbs, and Smith, 33; interv Owens, 9.
24. Interv Schwartz, 16; "Arlington County After-Action Report," A-20; interv Eberhart, 15 Jan 02, 7-8; interv Combs, 9-10; interv Jester, 31 Jan 06, 2-4. For explanation of the ICS see course materials at the National Wildfire Coordinating Group website, http://nwcg.gov/online.html; http://www.training.fema.gov/EMIWeb/IS/ICS Resource/index.htm; and Kane, "The Incident Command System and the Concept of Unified Command at a Terrorist Incident." On the Department of Defense's relationship with the incident command system in 2001 compared with the present, see Joint Chiefs of Staff, *Joint Pub 3-08: Interagency Coordination During Joint Operations*, vol 1, 9 Oct 96: 2:7-10, and Joint Chiefs of Staff, *Joint Pub 3-08: Interagency, Intergovernmental Organization, and Nongovernmental Organization Coordination During Joint Operations*, vol 1, 17 Mar 06, iii, 2:7-11. Presidential Decision Directive 39, as modified by subsequent provisions, specifies national policy regarding terrorism and assigns specific missions to designated federal departments and agencies; see unclassified synopsis at Department of Justice, http://www.ojp.usdoj.gov/odp/docs/pdd39.htm.
25. Interv Schwartz, 24, 31; interv Combs, 5; "Arlington County After-Action Report," A-23-24.
26. "Arlington County After-Action Report," A-6, 21, 23, 25-26; interv Schwartz, 16, 32-35, 53-54; interv Gray, Gibbs, and Smith, 32.
27. Interv Gray, Gibbs, and Smith, 15-16, 26, 28.
28. Interv Combs, 1, 6-7; interv Schwartz, 25-26, 39; U.S. General Accounting Office, *Combating Terrorism*, 3.
29. "Final Report: The Role of the Volunteer Fire Service in the September 11, 2001 Terrorist Attacks"; interv Smoot, 5 Dec 01, tape recording; interv Cayer, 29 Nov 01, tape recording.
30. Interv Plaugher, 4, 10, 13-14, 35-36 (quote, 36); "Arlington County After-Action Report," A-21; interv Kelley, 19 Apr 02, 8.
31. Interv Plaugher, 14-16; interv Burchell, 20 Nov 01, 12; interv Bohn, 19 Nov 01, 8.
32. Different groups experienced problems of varying degree, depending on location, department, and type of radio. In the A&E Division, Chief Smith found that the D.C. units lacked functional radios, while Chief Gray and Captain Gibbs had little difficulty communicating with Arlington firefighters. Several officers believed the greatest problem was not faulty or incompatible equipment, but that too many people tried to use the same radio channels simultaneously: interv G. M. Thompson, 30 Oct 01, 10; interv Gray, Gibbs, and Smith, 4, 7, 15; interv Gilroy, 17; interv Ladd, 15-16.
33. Interv T. Hodge, 10 (quote); interv Defina, 22; interv Valenzo, 19-20 (quote); on chaos, interv Gilroy, 26; interv Gray, Gibbs, and Smith, 7-8; interv G. M. Thompson, 10.
34. Interv Defina, 13-14, 22; interv Ramsey, 30 Nov 01, 22; Eversburg, "The Pentagon Attack on 9-11," 7.
35. Interv Ladd, 17; interv Defina, 14; Gilroy recalls that before the collapse, some of his units were able to enter via Corridor 4 and go toward the blast site (see interv Gilroy, 20-21); interv Gray, Gibbs, and Smith, 6; interv Valenzo, 13-14.
36. Interv T. Hodge, 8; interv Ladd, 19; interv Reardon, 15.
37. Interv Hood, 5 Dec 01, digital recording; interv M. Murphy, 5 Dec 01, abstract, 2.
38. Interv Howes, 14-16; interv M. Murphy, abstract, 2; interv Thumann and Zegowitz, 23.
39. Interv Schwartz, 44; on staggering, interv Defina, 13; interv Gray, Gibbs, and Smith, 5; interv Howes, 12-14; interv Reardon, 18.

40. Interv Kuney and Maguire, 26 Oct 01, 16; interv Ladd, 14; "PENREN Report," 2:13-14; interv Howes, 12; interv Reardon, 11, 14; interv Bryant, 31 Oct 01, 10; interv Carter, 19 Nov 01, 11; interv Conques, 25 Oct 01, 4; interv Morris, 05 Dec 01, 4, 12; interv Viner and Kelly, 25 Oct 01, 8; interv Durrer, 13, 18; interv Henry, digital recording; interv Defina, 12.
41. Interv Reardon, 14; interv Defina, 6, 12; interv Durrer, 12-13; interv Howes, 5-6, 9-12; interv Valenzo, 15.
42. Interv Valenzo, 14, 21; interv Gray, Gibbs, and Smith, 19; interv Gilroy, 15-16 (quote, 15); interv A. Wallace, 23, 25-26, 30; interv G. M. Thompson, 10-11.
43. Interv Gray, Gibbs, and Smith, 2-4, 7-8, 11-12, 24; interv Gilroy, 24.
44. Interv Combs, 10-11; interv T. Hodge, 8-9 (quote); interv A. Wallace, 23-24; interv Gray, Gibbs, and Smith, 27; interv Schwartz, 45; Arlington ECC Fire Dispatch Recording, 11 Sep 01.
45. *ASCE Report*, 10, 28, 35, 39, 58; Titus, "Shoring," 10, Fig 9; "PENREN Report," 2:7; e-mail Dr. Georgine Glatz to Alfred Goldberg, 30 Dec 05.
46. Interv Valenzo, 14; interv Gilroy, 20-21; interv Afforder, 10; interv Reardon, 16; interv Gray, Gibbs, and Smith, 6-7; on pancaking, interv Durrer, 16 (quote) and interv Martin, 25-26; interv Henry, digital recording ("knife" quote); interv DiPaula, 29 Oct 01, 11, 5-6, 26-28; interv Bohn, 18.
47. Interv Combs, 11-14; interv Schwartz, 27-28; "Arlington County After-Action Report," A-13, 47; map indicating mobile command post locations, facsimile Jacquelyn Brown (ACFD) to Nancy Berlage, 31 Aug 06, OSD Hist.
48. Interv Combs, 11-14; on the communications challenge see, "Arlington County After-Action Report," A-30, 36, C-46; interv Gray, Gibbs, and Smith, 4, 16; interv Hazelwood, 28 Jan 02, 10; interv McCormick, 25 Oct 01, 4; interv Irby, 19 Nov 01, 5; interv Woodson, 8 Nov 01, 6; interv Nelson, 9 Nov 01, 4.
49. Interv Howes, 14; "Arlington County After-Action Report," A-13; interv Hood, digital recording; interv Jester in Murphy, *September 11, An Oral History*, 246; interv McKinnnon, 28 Nov 01, 21.
50. Interv Perez, 17; eyewitness acct Glasbrenner, "What About the Children," DAC's Response to Tasker 01-05616, sub ROU-Request for Information Concerning the Sep 11, 2001 Attack on the Pentagon, OpNE CMH.
51. Interv Gray, Gibbs, and Smith, 11-13; "Arlington County After-Action Report," A-11, 66; interv Carter, 7-8; interv Greenwell, 9 Nov 01, 13-14; interv Hilliard, 6 Nov 01, 6-8; interv D. Murphy, 28 Nov 01, 3-4; interv Brady, 5 Nov 01, 4; interv Candido, 12 Dec 01, 4-5; interv Smith, 29 Oct 01, 3.
52. Pers acct Collier, 13 Sep 01; interv Lescault, 27 Nov 01, 11-12.
53. Some recall being prevented from reentering the building as a general policy, not only due to a threatened inbound plane. Interv Balisle, 6-8; interv Morehead, 30 Oct 01, 24-26; interv Schwartz, 42-43; interv Robinson, 5 Dec 01, 3; interv Hood, digital recording; interv Perez, 7, 12, 14-15; interv Parks, 27 Sep 01, 3-4, 7; interv Brady, 6-7; "Command Performance: County Firefighters Take Charge of the 9-11 Pentagon Emergency," 12-15; Captain Gibbs and Chief Smith recalled that the military personnel did not resist the instructions they gave (interv Gray, Gibbs, and Smith, 8).
54. Interv Schwartz, 28-29; interv Combs, 13-14. The 10:40 a.m. time derives from APCD, "Incident History Detail," entries 10:41:31 and 10:41:55, DepChief Holl ACPD.
55. On blurring of time perception, see for example interv Howes, digital recording. On confusion over the timing of collapse and inbound aircraft, see Schwartz, 27-28, 45-46; interv Paull, 26 Feb 02, 9-10; and interv Hackney, 28 May 02, 11-12. On multiple evacuation warnings in the morning, see Fort Myer Fire Department Log, 11 Sep 01, Doc 109, OpNE CMH; e-mail David Statter (WUSA9) to Diane Putney, 9 Feb 07, w/atchmt pers acct Statter; memrcd John White (ACFD), sub Pentagon Incident 9/11/01, nd, ACFD; interv Durrer, 14-16; interv Howes, 14-16; interv Hood, digital recording; interv Huntley, 8 Feb 02, 25-28, 34; interv Henry, digital recording; interv Waring, 1 Nov 01, 23-27, 6, 11-12. See interv Penn, 17 Apr 02, 37-38, on National air tower reports. Some may have mistaken as threats helicopters that were in Washington airspace around the time of the collapse (*9-11 Commission Report*, 41-43, 465, n224; interv Bohn, 9-13; interv Burchell, 6-11) or the military jets that flew over D.C. in the morning (interv Martin, 5-9). On bomb scare, see interv Gray, Gibbs, and Smith, 12.

56. Interv Penn, 38 ("get go" quote); interv Durrer, 14-16 (quote, 15); interv Howes, 14-17 (quote, 17); interv Hood, digital recording; interv M. Murphy, abstract, 2; "Arlington County After-Action Report," A-16, 30; Henry, digital recording.
57. Interv White, 10-11. White had previously used this strategy effectively when he and other personnel were evacuated from the scene of the bombed Murrah Federal Building in Oklahoma City in 1995. Interv Howes, 14; interv A. Wallace, 32-33.
58. Interv McKethan, 28 Dec 01, digital recording; interv Tinsley, 20 Dec 01, digital recording; interv Thumann and Zegowitz, 16-25 (quote, 25); interv Gray, Gibbs, and Smith, 20.
59. Interv Durrer, 18; interv Hood, digital recording; interv Schwartz, 109; interv Howes, 16-17; interv McKethan, digital recording; interv Condrell, 30 Oct 01, 13; Rosenbaum, Hunt, and Pitts, "Review of 9/11 Pentagon Scenario from the Fire Fighters', Fire Marshal's and Fire Protection Engineer's Perspectives," 18, 30-31.
60. Interv Gray, Gibbs, and Smith, 22; interv McKethan, and interv Tinsley, both digital recordings; interv M. Murphy, abstract, 2; interv Howes, 18.
61. Interv Henry, digital recording; interv Gray, Gibbs, and Smith, 19.
62. Interv Martin, 11-12.
63. Interv Gray, Gibbs, and Smith, 22-23; interv Martin, 13.
64. Interv Gray, Gibbs, and Smith, 21-22; interv Schwartz, 101; interv Perez, 8; on the water pressure problem see interv Kuney and Maguire, 12-17.
65. Interv Martin, 12-13; interv Gray, Gibbs, and Smith, 22-23.
66. "PENREN Report," 3:6; interv Morris, 3-5, 7, 14; interv Schwartz, 102 (quote); Titus, "Shoring," 8; *ASCE Report*, 52.
67. Interv Schwartz, 102 (quote); interv Defina, 15; interv Howes, 17-18; interv Gray, Gibbs, and Smith, 28-29.
68. Interv Thumann and Zegowitz, 34-36.
69. Interv Defina, 15-17; interv Howes, 19-22; interv McKethan, digital recording; interv Beavers, 6 Dec 01, digital recording.
70. Interv Gilroy, 19, 21; interv Defina, 23; interv Thumann and Zegowitz, 34, 41; interv M. Murphy, abstract, 2; interv McKethan, digital recording.
71. Interv Navas, 28 Nov 01, 18-19; interv Hazelwood, 11-12.
72. Interv Fitzharris, 12 Dec 01, 4-5; interv Condrell, 23-24; interv Gray, Gibbs, and Smith, 8-9, 22; interv Kuney and Maguire, 20; interv Martin, 14, 21-22; interv Burroughs, abstract, 2.
73. "Arlington County After-Action Report," A-30.
74. Interv Fitzharris, 4.
75. For original roofing details, see "The Pentagon," booklet signed Sept 42, box 1305, Subj Files, OSD Hist; materials from Chief Engineer's Office, PENREN, including Roof Plans and Misc. Details Section D, Drawing no. 7185, circa 1942, roofing artifacts, photos, and drawings, now in OSD Hist; interv Martin, 26-28; interv Schwartz, 103; interv McCormick, 25 Oct 01, 11-12; "PENREN Report," 8:6.
76. Interv Condrell, 18; interv Drumming, 18 Dec 01, 12-13; mtg, former Pentagon Fire Marshal Diane Pitts and OSD Historical staff, 24 Feb 06, OSD Hist Office.
77. Interv Howes, 23-24.
78. Interv McKethan, digital recording; interv Drumming, 15-16; "Arlington County After-Action Report," A-16; interv Valenzo, 28; interv Drumming, 9-12 (quotes); interv Tinsley, digital recording.
79. Interv Owens, 36; interv Schwartz, 103-06; interv Newton, 19 Nov 01, 18; interv Bryant, 20-21; interv Carter, 26.
80. Interv Schwartz, 104; interv Owens, 36 (quote); interv Bethke, Campbell, and Brown, 24 Jan 02, 31.
81. Interv Schwartz, 105; interv Nelson, 9 Nov 01, 8-9; interv Cochran, 3 Dec 01, 5; interv Gray, Gibbs, and Smith, 4, 25-26; interv Schwartz, 105; interv Martin, 26-28; interv Kelley, 11-13; interv Irby, 14.
82. Interv Thumann and Zegowitz, 64; interv Schwartz, 106-07; interv Howes, 23-24; interv Martin, 26-28 (quote), interv Howes, 24; "Arlington County After-Action Report," A-16; interv McCormick, 25 Oct 01, 11-12; interv Luczak, 7 Nov 01, 8; interv Drumming, 13.

83. Interv Kelley, 13; atchmt, "End of Tour Duty Report of 115th MP Bn MNG," 5, e-mail Joseph Balkoski (Command Hist, MDNG) to Diane Putney, 24 Jan 07.
84. Interv Schwartz, 107-08; interv Kelley, 14-15; Arlington County, Va. press release, 12 Sep 01, issued at 6:08:54 p.m.; interv Judd, 29 Oct 01, 16-17; Real Estate & Facilities, "Initial Damage Assessment—Roof," generated 13 Sep 01, 0800, Pentagon Damage Assessment, OSD Graphics.
85. Interv Schwartz, 98-99, 113-14.
86. Ibid, 48-51.
87. Interv Douglas, 17 Oct 01, 17; interv Barta, 19 Oct 01, 10-12; interv Godbehere, 18 Oct 01, 19.
88. Shirer, "MDW Engineer Company," 1.
89. Interv Barta, 5, 16, 19-24, 26, 28.
90. Ibid, 30-31; interv Brown, 14-15.
91. Interv Godbehere, 23-26 (quote, 26), 30.
92. Ibid, 25; interv Brown, 15-16.
93. Interv Balvanz, 17 Oct 01, 19-20; interv Erdelyi, 19 Oct 01, 20-28.
94. Interv Schwartz, 48-50; interv White, 27-28.
95. Titus, "Shoring," 2.
96. Ibid, 3.
97. Interv Schwartz, 49-50; interv Mathias, 12 Dec 01, 13, 16-17, 19, 21-26; Titus, "Shoring," 1, 7.
98. Titus, "Shoring," 7-8, 25; interv Kelley, 60.
99. "PENREN Report," 6:5, 9.
100. Titus, "Shoring," 19-20.
101. Interv Starette, 23-24; interv Barta, 35-37.
102. Titus, "Shoring," 25.
103. Interv Kilsheimer, 29 Oct 01, 1-3, 7-9, 10, 19; interv Viner and Kelly, 11, 18; interv Sullivan, 18 Oct 01, 13; interv Fitzharris, 7-8, 12, 21, 23, 40; PBS Online News Hour, "The Pentagon: One Year Later," 6 Sep 02, http://www.pbs.org/newshour/bb/terrorism/july-dec02/pentagon_9-06.html.
104. Interv Penn, 9-10; interv White, 24-26; "Arlington County After-Action Report," A-53-59, D-2, 8.
105. Interv Penn, 2-3, 9-12, 34; "Arlington County After-Action Report," D-2-4; interv Plaugher, 18-20; interv Flynn, 20 May 02, 5, 7.
106. Interv Penn, 12, 14.
107. Ibid, 12-15; interv Schwartz, 49-50; "Arlington County After-Action Report," D-4.
108. Interv Schwartz, 53-54; interv White, 22-27; interv Kelley, 56-57; interv Penn, 27, 41.
109. Interv Penn, 16-17, 36; interv White, 24-26; Dennis Ryan, "Hamburgers, Chicken, Steak, Boots, Prayer, More at Camp Unity," *MDW News Service*, 21 Sep 01, http://www.mdw.army.mil/news/Hamburgers-chicken-steak-boots-prayer.html#NavSkip.
110. Interv Gray, Gibbs, and Smith, 29; interv Schwartz, 55-56; interv Plaugher, 70-73.
111. Interv Penn, 13-14 (quote), 36-37; Hannah Mack Lapp, "A Visit at Camp Unity: First Person Reflections," Nov 01, http://www.emu.edu/ctp/footpaths/vol3no3/page6.html.
112. Interv Schwartz, 58-68 (quote, 63); "Command Performance," 17-20; interv Combs, 21-22; interv Jester, 16-17.
113. Interv Schwartz, 91; interv Kelley, 13, 16-21; atchmt, "End of Tour Duty Report of 115th MP Bn MNG," 5, e-mail Joseph Balkoski to Diane Putney, 24 Jan 07.
114. Interv Schwartz, 62-68, 91; interv Kelley, 13, 16-19; interv White, 31-35.
115. Interv Plaugher, 35-41.
116. Ibid, 39, 45, 61-70 (quote, 39); see for example, "America Counts Its Dead," 12 Sept 01, http://www.newscientist.com/article.ns?id=dn1279; "Command Performance," 22-23.
117. Interv Kelley, 44-45.
118. Interv Mix, 13 Dec 01, 14; interv Mayer, 29 Nov 01, 14-15; interv Hurley, 25 Sep 01, 14; interv Corcoran, 24 Sep 01, 15; interv Borrego, 2 Oct 01, 7-8; interv Kelley, 32-33; Brinsfield "The Attack on the Pentagon: The Ministry of Army Chaplains," 43; Samantha L. Quigley, "Firefighters Visit Walter Reed, Bethesda, Pentagon," 25 Mar 05, news archive, http://www.defenselink.com; "Chronology: The

Day After," 12 Sep 01, http://archives.cnn.com/2001/US/09/12/wednesday.chronology; Jim Garamone, "Bush Visits Pentagon, Meets Rescuers," 12 Sep 01, AFPS News Articles, news archive, http://www.defenselink.com.

V. TREATING THE INJURED, SEARCHING FOR REMAINS

1. Interv Lutgen, 7 Dec 01, 5.
2. "Arlington County After-Action Report," A-44-45; interv Roser, 10 Oct 01, 5-6.
3. Interv Geiling, 17 Dec 01, 3-5.
4. Jamieson, "The U.S. Air Force and 11 September 2001," 37; "Arlington County After-Action Report," B-17.
5. Interv Geiling, 7.
6. Interv Felicio, nd, in Marble and Milhiser, *Soldiers to the Rescue*, 15-16; interv L. Brown, 29 Nov 01, 2-6; interv Brown in Marble and Milhiser, *Soldiers to the Rescue*, 7; interv Glidewell, 10 Oct 01, 8; "Arlington County After-Action Report," B-4.
7. Interv Glidewell, 9-14.
8. Interv Baxter, 5-7; interv Lirette, 30 Nov 01, 5.
9. Interv Baxter, 8-11(quote, 10), 14, 16; interv Lirette, 8-9.
10. Jamieson, "The U.S. Air Force and 11 September 2001," 38-40, 44.
11. Condon-Rall, *Disaster on Green Ramp*, 3, 6, 27, 115-16.
12. Interv Horoho, 27 Sep 01, 2, 9-12.
13. Ibid, 27.
14. "Arlington County After-Action Report," B-5; interv Roser, 3, 7-10.
15. Interv Vafier, 8 Jan 02, 1-2, 5-6, 10,
16. Interv Sepulveda, 6 Dec 01, 2-6, 11, 14-15; interv Horoho, 39.
17. Interv White, 9.
18. Interv Brown in Marble and Milhiser, *Soldiers to the Rescue*, 8.
19. Interv Durm, 12 Oct 01, 15; Jamieson, "The U.S. Air Force and 11 September 2001," 44; interv E. Murphy, 25 June 02, 8; interv L. Brown, 8-12.
20. Interv Horoho, 27 Sep 01, 16-17, 24-27; interv White, 10-14; interv Vafier,11; interv Brown, interv Pernell in Marble and Milhiser, *Soldiers to the Rescue*, 9, 111.
21. Interv White, 15.
22. Ibid, 19.
23. Interv Brown in Marble and Milhiser, *Soldiers to the Rescue*, 9.
24. Interv Bucci in ibid, 62.
25. Interv Lirette, 9-10.
26. Marble and Milhiser, *Soldiers to the Rescue*, 143.
27. Interv Vafier, 12.
28. Interv Burchell, 8-9; "Arlington County After-Action Report," B-6.
29. Marble and Milhiser, *Soldiers to the Rescue*, 141.
30. "Arlington County After-Action Report," B-7; interv Nesbitt, 7 Nov 01, 3-4.
31. Interv Penn, 20.
32. Interv Shaeffer, 17.
33. Interv Lutgen, 6; "Arlington County After-Action Report," B-13; interv Mayer, 6-7; interv Yantis, 8 Feb 02, 64.
34. Interv L. Brown, 14; interv Hanfling, 7 Dec 01, 18; "Arlington County After-Action Report," B-12, Fig B-3.
35. Interv J. McGuire, 7 Dec 01, 5.
36. "Arlington County After-Action Report," B-3, 5.
37. Interv Mayer, 1, 3.
38. Jamieson, "The U.S. Air Force and 11 September 2001," 45-50.

39. Interv Mayer, 9.
40. "Arlington County After-Action Report," B-12, 14, Fig B-3.
41. Rossow, *Uncommon Strength*, 86-87.
42. Brinsfield, "The Attack on the Pentagon: The Ministry of Army Chaplains," 13-32.
43. Ibid, 45-51, 103; interv Horoho, 30-31.
44. Interv Schwartz, 48-49; interv Penn, 24-26.
45. Interv Ingersoll, 28 Feb 02, 16, 22; interv Farrrington, 18 Dec 01, 23, 25.
46. Interv Penn, 32.
47. Interv Ingersoll and Rimrodt, 12 Jun 02, 41-42; interv Eberhart, 13. Eberhart estimated that the crime scene covered about 30,000 square feet on each of the five floors.
48. Casualty map, FBI Evidence Response Team, 26 Nov 01, AttOfc EDVa.
49. Interv Gouen, 25 Sep 01, 10; interv Boatwright, 2 Oct 01, 4-6.
50. Interv Craft, 2 Oct 01, 5.
51. Interv Frauman, 25 Sep 01, 14.
52. Interv Farrar, 25 Sep 01, 11; interv Hanfling, 25-26 (quote, 26).
53. Interv Stanton, 14 Mar 06, 9, 20; interv Ingersoll, 19-20; interv Rimrodt, 15 Feb 02, 13-14, 16; interv Ingersoll and Rimrodt, 43-44.
54. Interv Stokes, 25 Sep 01, 6.
55. "Arlington County After-Action Report," C-57; interv Penn, 32-33; interv Ingersoll, 16, 20; interv Rimrodt, 16.
56. Interv Rimrodt, 17, 18.
57. Interv Frauman, 15.
58. Interv Ingersoll and Rimrodt, 48-49.
59. Interv Eberhart, 22.
60. Interv Yantis, 37.
61. Interv Stokes, 7; interv Cunningham, 2 Oct 01, 23.
62. Interv Boatwright, 7-8; interv Corcoran, 10-12; interv Craft, 6-7; interv D. Davis, 2 Oct 01, 18, 20; interv Kovacic, 23 Oct 01, 6; interv Stokes, 8-9.
63. "Arlington County After-Action Report," C-54; interv Stokes, 12; interv Litchfield, 2 Oct 01, 11-12.
64. Interv Penn, 34.
65. Interv Gallivan, 2 Oct 01, 18.
66. Interv Myers, 25 Sep 01, 10.
67. Interv D. Davis, 15, 19.
68. Interv Farrar, 9, 20.
69. Interv O'Neill, 2 Oct 01, 13.
70. Interv Watson, 25 Sep 01, 10-11.
71. Interv Farrar, 19.
72. Interv Farrington, 30.
73. Interv Litchfield, 10.
74. Interv Malmquist, 2 Oct 01, 14.
75. Interv Wolfe, 3 Oct 01, 8; interv Boatwright, 16.
76. Interv Frauman, 17.
77. Interv Wolfe, 12.
78. Interv Munoz, 2 Oct 01, 12.
79. Interv Reynolds, 25 Sept 01, 9-10.
80. Interv Farrar, 35.
81. Interv Malmquist, 7, 16-17.
82. Interv Wolfe, 17.
83. "Arlington County After-Action Report," C-55.
84. Interv Eberhart, 22-23.

85. Interv Roemer, 11 Feb 02, 10-11; interv Lugaila, 19 Nov 01, 14-15, 20-21. Lugaila stated that 30 dogs were employed.
86. Interv Lugaila, 22, 24, 26, 35; interv Roemer, 13-15.
87. Interv Eberhart, 24; interv Lugaila, 43; interv Roemer, 12; interv Rimrodt, 23.
88. Interv Roemer, 15-16.
89. Interv Lugaila, 48.
90. "Arlington County After-Action Report," C-56; interv Rimrodt, 22.
91. Interv Eberhart, 12, 23, 32-33.

VI. UP AND RUNNING

1. *9/11 Commission Report*, 38-39, 325; *Public Papers: Bush 2001*, 2:1098-99; Bill Adair and Stephen Hegarty, "The Drama in Sarasota," *St. Petersburg Times*, 8 Sep 02, http://www.sptimes.com/2002/09/08/911/The_drama_in_Sarasota.shtml.
2. *9/11 Commission Report*, 325-26, 554, n 1. The notion of a threat to Air Force One stemmed from a misunderstood communication.
3. Interv Rumsfeld, 5-6.
4. Ibid, 5; interv Giambastiani, 18 Jul 02, 8 (quote); "Secretary Rumsfeld Interview with Parade Magazine," 12 Oct 01, 1, transcripts archive, 18 Nov 01, http://www.defenselink.mil; interv Davis and Oldach, 20 Jul 06, 2, 5-8; interv Wassel, 13-14. Davis and Oldach were members of the Protective Service Unit of the Defense Protective Service.
5. Interv Rumsfeld, 6 (quote); interv Clarke, 2 Jul 02, 8; interv Davis and Oldach, 2-3, 10-11, 12; "Rumsfeld Interview with Parade," 1; interv Wassel, 15-17.
6. Interv Davis and Oldach, 11, 12-13; *9/11 Commission Report*, 38, 43-44; interv Rumsfeld, 5; Donald Rumsfeld, "Testimony Prepared for Delivery to the National Commission on Terrorist Attacks Upon the United States," 23 Mar 04, 11, speeches archive, http://www.defenselink.mil; interv Giambastiani, 1 Aug 02, 1-3; interv Wolfowitz, 19 Apr 02, 3, 7; interv Clarke, 8; interv Wassel, 20-21. Wassel set up the call from Air Force One and heard the secretary's answers to such questions as "Are you okay?" and "Is the Pentagon still intact?" This seems to be the telephone call mentioned in *9/11 Commission Report*, 43, for which "no one can recall the content of this conversation." Wassel was not interviewed by the commission. Based on his account, it seems that Rumsfeld had not previously talked with the president, so Rumsfeld's attempt to call Air Force One from his Pentagon office was not successful. The president told the commission that "he could not reach key officials, including Secretary Rumsfeld, for a period of time." See *9/11 Commission Report*, 40, 43, 465, n 232 (quote, 40). For some of the NMCC's activity on 11 September, see *9/11 Commission Report*, 17-18, 35-38, 42-44.
7. *9/11 Commission Report*, 37-38, 40, 43-44; interv Rumsfeld, 7-8; Rumsfeld, "Testimony to the National Commission," 11; interv Giambastiani, 1 Aug 02, 2-7; interv Wolfowitz, 3-5; interv Cambone, 8 Jul 02, 3-4; interv Clarke, 8-10, 12; interv Di Rita, 27 Jun 02, 5; "Secretary Rumsfeld Interview with the *Washington Post*," 9 Jan 02, 4, 5, transcripts archive, http://www.defenselink.mil.
8. Interv Wolfowitz, 5-6; interv Giambastiani, 1 Aug 02, 3-4. Lawrence Di Rita, special assistant to Rumsfeld, stated that the White House directed that federal departments activate alternate command sites as a precaution (interv Di Rita, 5). The *9/11 Commission Report*, 38, states that Deputy National Security Advisor Stephen Hadley passed on the order.
9. Interv Plaugher, 31-34 (quote, 32); interv White, 16-17; interv Giambastiani, 1 Aug 02, 4-6; interv Rumsfeld, 7; interv Wolfowitz, 5; interv Cambone, 4; interv Clarke, 11.
10. Interv Wolfowitz, 6-7; interv Di Rita, 8; interv Giambastiani, 1 Aug 02, 5-9. Giambastiani stated, "At 12:18 there were fifty aircraft in the air" (5). These were probably associated with law enforcement or emergency operations; see Ned Preston (FAA Historian), "Chronology of the Attacks of September 11, 2001," Office of Public Affairs, Federal Aviation Administration, Doc 24, OpNE CMH. In the months after 11 September, computer and communication systems at the alternate site were signifi-

cantly upgraded and improved under authority newly transferred from the Army to the Office of the Secretary of Defense.

11. For discussion of the plane hitting the Navy Command Center see Chapter II. After 11 September a unified command center was eventually established that co-located service watch cells with the NMCC and Executive Support Center.
12. Interv Tracey and Sweeney, 28 Sep 01, 4; interv Totushek, 5 Feb 02, 6; Shupe, "Operation Noble Eagle," 4.
13. Interv Tracey and Sweeney, 4-5; interv Rabogliatti, 6.
14. Interv Tracey and Sweeney, 5; interv Masso, 11 Dec 01, 17; interv Godfrey, 7 Nov 01, 5-6; interv Rabogliatti, 5-7; interv Alexander, 5 Nov 01, 2, 6.
15. Interv McAtee, 25 Sep 01, 3-7.
16. Ibid, 5; interv Sweeney, 13 Mar 02, 7-8; interv Rabogliatti, 8; Shupe, "Operation Noble Eagle," 8.
17. Atchmt, summary of interv BrigGen George Flynn, Jones's military secretary, by Fred Allison (Historian, USMC) [Apr 06], e-mail Allison to Diane Putney, 21 Apr 06; interv P. Murphy, 11; Jones, *Boys of '67*, 363-65.
18. Interv Chiarelli, 6-7, 10-11; Rossow, *Uncommon Strength*, 64-65.
19. Interv Chiarelli, 3-4, 7-8; Rossow, *Uncommon Strength*, 64-65.
20. Interv Chiarelli, 14 (quote); Rossow, *Uncommon Strength*, 65-66. For information about warnings of hijacked aircraft approaching Washington before the Pentagon was struck, see *9/11 Commission Report*, 25-27, 37, 39.
21. Interv Chiarelli, 18-25; Rossow, *Uncommon Strength*, 68. At the alternate site Wolfowitz received Rumsfeld's approval for White to return immediately to the Pentagon, where White believed he belonged. See interv Wolfowitz, 5.
22. Rossow, *Uncommon Strength*, 68-69; interv Spindler, 27 Nov 01, 10-11; interv Bachus, 6 Mar 02, 10-11, 23-25; e-mail Alvin Nieder to Diane Putney, 13 Mar 06.
23. Interv Spindler, 8-9, 15; interv Boggess, 8 Dec 01, 5-7. Accountability was extra difficult for the Army because the crash destroyed personnel records in the DCSPER offices. See interv M. Lewis, 12 Dec 01, 7-10; Rossow, *Uncommon Strength*, 20-22, 83-85. In the early evening on 11 September, Lewis and Lt. Col. William Kelly had the difficult task of calling families to inquire if any of the missing had telephoned or arrived home, and too often the heart-wrenching reply was "no."
24. Perry Jamieson notes, "11 Sep 01 CSAF Staff Meeting and Attack on Pentagon," 12 Sep 01, 1, AF Hist Studies; Jamieson, "The U.S. Air Force and 11 September 2001," 3.
25. "USAF After-Action Report," 2-3, 9.
26. "USAF After-Action Report," 2-3; Jamieson, "The U.S. Air Force and 11 September 2001," 45-46. On 10 May 2002 a DoD Inspector General report addressed the deployment to McGuire AFB: DoD, OIG, *Health Care: DoD Medical Support to the Federal Response Plan*.
27. Interv Greenwell, 1-3, 10; interv Carter, 4; interv Bryant, 9; interv Candido, 12 Dec 01, 2. For broadcast news transcripts describing the activity of the building maintenance crews on 11 September, see CBS Evening News, "How the Pentagon Was Saved on 9/11," 9 Sep 02, and "The Unsung Pentagon Heroes," 10 Sep 02, (locate by title) http://www.cbsnews.com. For the videos see "September 11/Pentagon Heroes," CBS Evening News, 9, 10 Sep 02, http://openweb.tvnewsvanderbilt.edu/.
28. Interv Greenwell, 3; interv Carter, 1-3; interv Irby, 3-4.
29. Interv Carter, 3-6, 10; interv Greenwell, 3-5 (quotes, 3). Over the years the Incident Command Post was usually located in the Center Court. See "PENREN Report," 3:4.
30. Interv Carter, 4-6, 15; interv Greenwell, 8-9; interv Bryant, 3-4; interv Pugrud, 4; interv Smith, 3; interv McCormick, 3-4, 19-20. For efforts by Juan Rodriguez, Kevin Hawkins, Anthony Freeman, Thomas Hayden, and Yong Kim to reenter the building from A-E Drive to rescue people see memo John F. Irby for AsstDir for Labor Mgt, 16 Oct 01, OSD Hist. See also the account of Daniel Murphy entering the building from A-E Drive in a second memo Irby for AsstDir for Labor Mgt, 16 Oct 01, OSD Hist. Later McCormick and Smith, members of the Pentagon Emergency Action Team, donned

their firefighting gear and went to steam rooms and other parts of the building to assess damage. See interv Carter, 23-24; interv McCormick, 5-7.

31. Interv Greenwell, 6-7.
32. Ibid, 7; e-mail Kathryn Greenwell to Diane Putney, 4 Jan 06; interv Carter, 11, 14-15, 19; interv D. Murphy, 10; interv Bryant, 11-12; interv R. Cox, 15 Nov 01, 4.
33. "Arlington County After-Action Report," A-10; interv Gray, Gibbs, and Smith, 19; interv Carter, 25; interv White, 16-17; interv Greenwell, 9; interv Candido, 2, 11; interv Haselbush, 19 Oct 01, 14.
34. Interv Carter, 13-14; interv Irby, 7-8; interv Morris, 11; interv R. Cox, 4.
35. Interv Carter, 7, 9-10, 20-21; interv Kuney and Maguire, 1, 3, 5, 7, 12-16; e-mail Brian Maguire to Diane Putney, 21 Feb 06; interv Irby, 2-3, 6-7; interv Bryant, 7-8, 11.
36. Interv Kuney and Maguire, 13-15. A chilled water backup system existed but it was not yet operational, and the broken pipes would also affect its performance.
37. Interv Carter, 7, 9; "Arlington County After-Action Report," A-13; interv Smith, 5, 8; interv D. Murphy, 3-4, 12-13.
38. Interv Carter, 7-9; interv Greenwell, 12-14; interv Gray, Gibbs, and Smith, 11. The medical personnel evacuated patients from the Center Court. See interv L. Brown, 17-18.
39. Interv Kuney and Maguire, 7-8, 15-16, 35.
40. Ibid, 22 (quotes); e-mail Brian Maguire to Diane Putney, 4 Nov 05. The restoration of the chilled water to the Annex required Kuney and James Graves later in the afternoon to enter the utility vault near the Heliport in front of the crash site. The aircraft had ripped open the vault door, and debris hung dangerously from above as the two men waded through two feet of water to examine the condition of water and steam pipes. See interv Kuney and Maguire, 17-20, 25-27, and memo Irby for Asst-Dir for Labor Mgt, 15 Oct 01, OSD Hist. A team from Washington Gas and Light had arrived at the Pentagon around 10:50 a.m., and after coordinating with the incident commander and FBI entered the vault near the Heliport and closed valves on the Pentagon's natural gas line. See interv Cook, 17 Apr 02, 10-11, 14.
41. Interv Irby, 2; interv Morris, 14; interv Bryant, 16-17.
42. Interv Morris, 2-5, 8, 16; interv Carter, 5, 12-13; interv D. Murphy, 9-10. Morris brought a ladder from the vault to A-E Drive for use by the survivors at the 2nd Floor window near Corridor 4. See Chapter II.
43. Interv Morris, 8-9, 11-12; interv Robinson, 1-3, 13-14; interv Smith, 13-14.
44. Interv Morris, 5, 7-8; interv D. Murphy, 5; interv Bryant, 8-10; interv Carter, 12-13, 17; interv Breeden, 5 Dec 01, 4; interv Smith, 4; "PENREN Report," 10:6.
45. Interv Greenwell, 8-9, 11; interv Carter, 11-12; interv Candido, 3.
46. Interv Plaugher, 33; interv Clarke, 16; interv Newton, 19-20; interv Haselbush, 21; interv Irby, 14-15; interv D. Murphy, 5-6; interv R. Cox, 7-10, 13-14; interv Hilliard, 6 Nov 01, 8, 11; interv Breeden, 5; interv Luczak, 11; interv Bryant, 19, 23; interv Penn, 28; memo Ralph E. Newton for AdmAsst to SecA et al, [24 Sep 01], OSD Hist; "Arlington County After-Action Report," A-68; OSHA, "September 11, 2001: Attack on America," news release USDL 01-307, 14 Sep 01, http://www.yale.edu/lawweb/avalon/sept_11/osha_001.htm. For a "synopsis of analyses completed by various environmental, health, and safety experts," see "Environmental Health Response to the September 11, 2001 Attack on the Pentagon."
47. Interv Cooke, 18 Oct 01, 4-8; interv Haselbush, 2, 10, 13; interv Newton, 5-6, 8.
48. Interv Haselbush, 6-7, 12-13; interv Newton, 2, 4-5; interv Conques, 3; interv Candido, 6; interv White, 53; Bradley Graham, "At the Pentagon: Response Hampered by Confusion, Lack of Preparedness," *Washington Post*, 16 Sep 01.
49. Interv Haselbush, 1, 13; interv Newton, 4-7, 10, 17, 20; interv Irby, 4-6; interv Carter, 16.
50. Interv Newton, 7-8; interv Rumsfeld, 10; interv Di Rita, 8; interv Wassel, 25; interv Irby, 10-11; interv Carter, 9-10, 19-20, 29 (quote, 19); interv R. Cox, 15.
51. Interv Newton, 6-11, 16, 18-19. The OSD Graphics and Presentation Division set up a "post incident" Internet site to communicate with employees. See interv Nelson, 10, 12.

52. Interv Plaugher, 34; interv Pugrud, 7-8; interv Haselbush, 17; interv Pickens, 23 Oct 01, 11; interv Irby, 11, 13.
53. Interv Judd, 7-10. The Child Development Center was eventually moved from the Pentagon Reservation.
54. Interv Judd, 13-16; interv Haselbush, 17-18; interv R. Cox, 10; interv Luczak, 11-12.
55. Interv Clarke, 15; interv Giambastiani, 1 Aug 02, 8; "DoD News Briefing on Pentagon Attack," 11 Sep 01, transcripts archive, http://www.defenselink.mil.
56. Interv Rumsfeld, 10; "DoD News Briefing on Pentagon Attack," 1-3 (quote, 2). The Office of Personnel Management issued a news release stating that on 12 September federal agencies in the D.C. area would be open under an unscheduled leave policy allowing employees to take leave without prior approval. See OPM, "Federal Government Status," news release, 11 Sep 01, http://www.opm.gov/news/federal-government-status,438.aspx.
57. *Public Papers: Bush 2001*, 2:1099-1100; *9/11 Commission Report*, 330, 326; interv Cambone, 5.
58. Interv Newton, 11-12, 14-16; interv Irby, 11-13, 16-17; interv Haselbush, 7; interv White, 32.
59. Interv Clarke, 20; interv Irby, 13; interv Conques, 5 (quote).
60. Interv Conques, 6-9, 11, 18; interv Haselbush, 20; e-mail David Butler (WHS Defense Facilities Directorate) to Alfred Goldberg, 20 Sep 06.
61. Interv Irby, 14; "Arlington County After-Action Report," A-16; interv Fitzharris, 35; interv White, 43.
62. Memo Kent A. Womack for AsstDir for Labor Mgt, 25 Oct 01, memo Edgar W. Fruit for AsstDir for Labor Mgt, 18 Oct 01, OSD Hist; interv Robinson, 5-8; interv D. Murphy, 7; interv Carter, 17; interv Kuney and Maguire, 21.
63. Interv Luczak, 8-9; interv Judd, 26; interv Haselbush, 16; interv Irby, 15; interv Newton, 20.
64. Interv R. Cox, 15-16 (quote); interv Carter, 31; interv Newton, 26; interv Irby, 20. Individuals from OSD/WHS who were awarded the Medal for Valor for rescuing people and keeping the Pentagon in operation were John Brady, Timothy Breeden, Robert Candido, Steven Carter, Donald Ellis, Anthony Freeman, Michael Gargano, Kenneth Goodnight, James Graves, Kathryn Greenwell, Kevin Hawkins, Thomas Hayden, Leroy Hilliard, Yong Kim, Donald Kuney, Brian Maguire, Robert McCloud, Charles McCormick, Daniel Murphy, John Robinson, Juan Rodriguez, and Dennis Smith. See "Personnel Hilites," *WHS Newsletter*, 3.

VII. SECURING THE PENTAGON

1. Interv Jester, 19 Oct 01, 21; "Defense Protective Service After-Action Report: The Pentagon on 9-11" (hereafter "DPS After-Action Report"), [19]; "Arlington County After-Action Report," C-31, 38; Kennedy, "Renovation of Pentagon Includes Tighter Security." The Pentagon Reservation, approximately 280 acres, includes the Pentagon, Navy Annex, Heating and Refrigeration Plant, other facilities, and parking lots. See 10 USC §2674. The DPS numbers are authorized strength; not all positions were filled on 11 September.
2. "DPS After-Action Report," [32]; "Pentagon Tours," http://www.dtic.mil/ref/html/Welcome/tours.html.
3. Interv Jester, 19 Oct 01, 12; interv Irby, 18-19; interv Nesbitt, 19 Jun 06, 15-16. Deputy Secretary of Defense John Hamre had also strongly advocated better security for the Pentagon (see interv Haselbush, 19 Oct 01, 3). The Metro renovations were accomplished after 11 September 2001.
4. Interv Jester, 19 Oct 01, 20; ibid, 31 Jan 06, 2; Alicia Borlik, "DoD Drill Tests Response to Terrorist Attack," 9 Jun 98, AFPS News Articles, news archive, http://www.defenselink.mil; "Pentagon Undergoes Mock Terrorist Attack," 30 May 98, http://www.cnn.com/US/9805/30/terror.pentagon/; interv Pugrud, 1 Nov 01, 8.
5. Defense Protective Service special ed newsletter "911" (hereafter DPS newsletter "911"), nd, 3; interv Jester, 19 Oct 01, 1-2; ibid, 31 Jan 06, 6-8; "Arlington County After-Action Report," 2. See Chapter V for discussion of the Pentagon's medical clinics staging a tabletop exercise in May 2001 under the scenario of a twin-engine aircraft hitting the building.

6. Interv Jester, 19 Oct 01, 5-6, 14; ibid, 31 Jan 06, 3, 5; interv Nesbitt, 7 Nov 01, 1; interv Plaugher, 22 Apr 02, 6.
7. Interv Jester, 19 Oct 01, 2-3; interv Nesbitt, 7 Nov 01, 2; ibid, 19 Jun 06, 1-2. DoD Instruction 2000.16, 14 Jun 01, changed the terminology. For definitions see http://www.brussels.army.mil/force_protection_condition.htm and http://www.ala.usmc.mil/fpcon.asp. For recollections of people receiving word of the "Normal" condition see interv Carter, 19 Nov 01, 3; interv Luczak, 7 Nov 01, 2; interv Woodson, 4; "PENREN Report," 4:1.
8. Interv Jester, 19 Oct 01, 1; interv Nesbitt, 7 Nov 01, 4-5; interv Riley, 24 Jan 02, 4 (quote).
9. Interv Phillips, 9 Nov 01, 2; interv Jester, 19 Oct 01, 2-3; interv Pugrud, 1; FPCON definitions athttp://www.brussels.army.mil/force_protection_condition.htm.
10. Interv Pugrud, 2; DPS newsletter "911," 12 (quote); *Henderson Hall News*, 28 Sep 01, http://www.dcmilitary.com/dcmilitary_archives/stories/092801/10797-1.shtml.
11. Interv Jester, 19 Oct 01, 3-4 (quotes); interv Nesbitt, 19 Jun 06, 2-3. Some of the cameras at the Pentagon were inoperable because of construction work. See interv Austin and Pennington, 9 Nov 06, 11, 20.
12. Interv Nesbitt, 19 Jun 06, 2-3; ibid, 7 Nov 01, 3; DPS newsletter "911," 4; e-mail Capt Michael Nesbitt to Diane Putney, 9 Aug 06.
13. Interv Jester, 19 Oct 01, 4; interv Nesbitt, 7 Nov 01, 3-4 (quote); interv Jester, 31 Jan 06, 13-14.
14. Interv Nesbitt, 7 Nov 01, 3-5, 8; interv Jester, 31 Jan 06, 17-18; "Arlington County After-Action Report," C-35-36.
15. *Henderson Hall News*, 28 Sep 01, 2-6 (quotes, 6, 4); memos John N. Jester, Paul K. Haselbush for AsstDir for Labor Mgt, both 22 Oct 01, sub Hodges, Baker, Webster, Clodfelter, Rojas, and Rosati citations, OSD Hist. See also Jose Rojas, Jr., transcript of jury trial, 11 Apr 06, vol 17A, *United States v. Zacarias Moussaoui*. For a list of DPS recipients of the Medal for Valor, see, "Personnel Hilites," *WHS Newsletter*, 3.
16. Memos John N. Jester, Paul K. Haselbush for AsstDir for Labor Mgt, 22 Oct 01, 7 and 13 Feb 02, 28 Mar 02, sub Ho'opi'i, Murphy, Centner, and Carpenter citations, OSD Hist; DPS newsletter "911," 13; *Henderson Hall News*, 28 Sep 01; CNN news, "Voice of an Angel," 1 (quote), http://www.cnn.com/SPECIALS/2002/america.remembers/stories/heroes/hoopii.html. Sinclair and Ho'opi'i reunited on national television; Ho'opi'i became widely recognized. See Glen Finland, "The Guardians," *Washington Post*, 11 Sep 05.
17. Memos John N. Jester, Paul K. Haselbush for AsstDir for Labor Mgt, 22 Oct 01, 14 Feb 02, sub Koerber, Behe, Diaz, and Mapp citations, OSD Hist. For rescue accounts by two Virginia state troopers see memos Trooper Myrlin Wimbish for 1st Sgt Richard S. Keevill, 23 Nov 01, Trooper Michael S. Middleton for Keevill, nd, Virginia State Police. For an account of rescue assistance from personnel from the Arlington County Sheriff's Office, see interv Young, 23 May 02.
18. DPS newsletter "911," 3-5.
19. Interv Jester, 19 Oct 01, 5; interv Nesbitt, 7 Nov 01, 8-9; Jonathan Pitts, "A Caring Man, A Cruel Irony," http://cf.newsday.com/911/victimsearch.cfm?id=986; "Radian Receives Pentagon Phoenix Award," http://www.radianinc.com/press_releases/01.15.03.htm.
20. Interv Pugrud, 4; interv Newton, 2; interv Nesbitt, 19 Jun 06, 12-13; interv Bryant, 26; "Arlington County After-Action Report," C-33; memo D. O. Cooke for service secretaries, 16 Aug 01, OSD Hist; "PENREN Report," 9:2, 3:7, 5:4 (quote).
21. Interv Irby, 8-9; interv Candido, 4; "PENREN Report," 9:1, 4; interv Carter, 4; interv Jester, 31 Jan 06, 10-11; interv Nesbitt, 19 Jun 06, 9-11; ibid, 7 Nov 01, 3; interv Newton, 23-24; "Arlington County After-Action Report," C-35; memo Arthur H. Hildebrandt (AssocGenCoun, Mgt) for Office of Program Appraisal, 1 Oct 01, 1, in "DON Consolidated Lessons Learned"; "DPS After-Action Report," [33].
22. Interv Jester, 31 Jan 06, 10-11; interv Pugrud, 2; memo Hildebrandt for Office of Program Appraisal, 1 Oct 01, 1 in "DON Consolidated Lessons Learned"; memo RAdm S. G. Smith (Office of Program Appraisal) for UnderSecN, 9 Oct 01, 5, in ibid; interv Sweeney, 4-5; atchmt, pers acct Stauber, e-mail

Maj Francis Burns to Stephen Lofgren, 11 Oct 01, OpNE CMH; Bob Whitmer, "Per Rumsfeld's Orders: The Briefing Will Go On," 3, http://www.defendamerica.mil/articles/Dec2002/a122602a.html. For the Mall doors being open see interv Yantis, 18; interv Eggerton, 28 Nov 01, 8; pers acct Stone, 10 Oct 01, 2-3.

23. Interv Newton, 4; interv McCormick, 18-19; interv Blevins, 13 Dec 01, 2; interv Bachus, 6; interv Irby, 8 (quote); "PENREN Report," 5:4.
24. Video Recording, WUSA 9, 9:41 a.m. to 10:55 a.m. (quote); interv McDonner, 13 Dec 01, 7; interv Dossel, 28 Sep 01, 9-10; interv Yantis, 35; interv Bass, 11 Oct 01, 12; interv Volk, 1 May 02, 19.
25. Interv Jester, 31 Jan 06, 15, 17, 19; ibid, 19 Oct 01, 4, 6, 8; "Arlington County After-Action Report," C-33, 35; interv Nesbitt, 7 Nov 01, 5; interv Harper, 14 Jul 06, 12; interv Pugrud, 4, 5.
26. "FEMA Fully Activated in Response to Apparent Terrorist Events," 11 Sep 01, http://www.fema.gov/news/newsrelease.fema?id=5696; Federal Response Plan, Apr 99, foreword and table of contents; sanitized PDD 39, 21 Jun 95, http://www.fas.org/irp/offdocs/pdd39.htm; FEMA Federal Response Plan Notice of Change, 7 Feb 97, FEMA 229, chg 11, http://www.fas.org/irp/offdocs/pdd39_frp.htm. The federal response preceded the presidential declaration of disaster—allowable by law. The president issued an emergency declaration for Arlington County on 13 September and declared the Pentagon and the surrounding region a disaster area on 21 September. The Federal Response Plan was later revised and renamed the National Response Plan.
27. "Terrorism 2000/2001," 7 (definition quote); DoJ synopsis PDD 39, 1, http://www.ojp.usdoj.gov/odp/docs/pdd39.htm; "CONPLAN: United States Government Interagency Domestic Terrorism Concept of Operations Plan," Jan 01, http://www.fbi.gov/publications/conplan/conplan.pdf. In 1998 Clinton signed PDD 62 which codified and clarified activities of U.S. agencies in combating terrorism and established the Office of the National Coordinator for Security, Infrastructure Protection and Counter-Terrorism. See abstract of PDD 62 from Office for State and Local Domestic Preparedness Support, http://permanent.access.gpo.gov/lps9890/lps9890/www.ojp.usdoj.gov/osldps/lib_pdd62.htm.
28. Interv Combs, 3-12; interv Schwartz, 25-26; "Arlington County After-Action Report," A-20, 45, 47.
29. Interv Combs, 7-8, 24-25; "Arlington County After-Action Report," A-22; interv Eberhart, 15 Jan 02, 6-7. FBI members from both the National Capital Response Squad (NCRS) and the Joint Terrorism Task Force (JTTF) arrived at the Pentagon within the hour. See "DPS After-Action Report," [21]. Combs was a member of the NCRS, consisting of evidence, SWAT, and weapons of mass destruction/hazardous material teams. The JTTFs, first established in 1980, brought together federal, state, and local law enforcement agencies.
30. Interv Combs, 6, 25; interv Plaugher, 28-29; interv Rimrodt, 6-8; interv Ingersoll and Rimrodt, 12 Jun 02, 21-23, 27, 30-31, 36-37; interv Ingersoll, 9-10. A third person, identified as Sergeant Marshall Paull, also took photographs. Joining the rescue effort, MSgt Morris gave his camera to Ingersoll. See interv Ingersoll and Rimrodt, 22, 30.
31. Interv Combs, 7-8, 16; interv Holl, 28 May 02, 34; interv Panther, 28 May 02, 12-13; interv Hanfling, 16; interv Rimrodt, 9-11; interv Ingersoll, 10-11, 15; interv Ingersoll and Rimrodt, 24-25, 31-32, 34.
32. Interv Combs, 9, 16-17, 20; "DPS After-Action Report," [16]; interv Jester, 31 Jan 06, 6, 23; interv Gray, Gibbs, and Smith, 21 (quote); interv Plaugher, 30, 43. Arlington County paid for the fence purchase and subsequently received partial reimbursement from FEMA. See interv Penn, 27.
33. Interv Combs, 25-26; interv Gray, Gibbs, and Smith, 17-18; interv Schwartz, 51-53; interv Penn, 24-26; "Arlington County After-Action Report," A-68; National Disaster Medical System, Office of Emergency Preparedness, Dept of Health and Human Services, "Terrorist Attacks" situation report #40, 18 Oct 01, 1600hrs EST, 2, http://www.911da.org/crr/documents/2928.pdf.
34. Interv Eberhart, 12, 22-23; interv Combs, 23; interv Jester, 19 Oct 01, 11; interv Rimrodt, 16-26; interv Perryman, 2 Oct 01, 9; interv Boatwright, 6; interv Ingersoll, 16-21; "Arlington County After-Action Report," C-35, 39, 54.
35. Interv Hanfling, 33; "Remarks of Carol Carmody, Vice-Chairman, National Transportation Safety Board . . . ," 27 Feb 02, 1, http://www.ntsb.gov/speeches/carmody/cc020227.htm; CNN transcript

aired 14 Sep 01, 06:33, http://transcripts.cnn.com/TRANSCRIPTS/0109/14/se.47.html; DoD, "Flight Data and Cockpit Voice Recorders Found"; "War on Terror: Speed Likely Factor . . . ," 23 Feb 02, 2, http://www.cbsnews.com/stories/2002/02/25/attack/main501989.shtml; H.R. 3336, "Safe Aviation . . . ," 19 Jul 05, 3, 109 Cong, 1 sess, http://thomas.loc.gov/cgi-bin/query/z?c109:H.R.3336. IH:; illustration, "Pentagon First Floor-West," FBI Evidence Response Team, AttOfc EDVa; e-mails Michael Lombardi (Boeing historian) to Diane Putney, 14 Jun 06; NTSB, Vehicle Recorders Division, "Specialist's Factual Report of Investigation Digital Flight Data Recorder," no. DCA01MA064, 31 Jan 02, http://www.ntsb.gov/info/AAL77_fdr.pdf.

36. "Arlington County After-Action Report," C-49, 51, 52; interv Combs, 17; interv White, 32, 34.
37. Interv Jester, 31 Jan 06, 13; e-mail John Pugrud to Diane Putney, 11 Oct 06; interv Austin and Pennington, 3-8. In March 2002 a few still images from one of the videos were supposedly "leaked" to the press which widely publicized them. See http://www.msnbc.msn.com/id/12818225/print/1/displaymode/1098/. On 16 May 2006 DoD released the two videos to the Judicial Watch organization, which had submitted a Freedom of Information Act request for them in December 2004. DoD also placed the videos on its Internet website. See "Videos of American Flight 77 Striking the Pentagon on September 11, 2001," OSD/JS FOIA Requester Service Center Reading Room, http://www.dod.mil/pubs/foi/reading_room/. The videos are also exhibits for *United States v. Zacarias Moussaoui*. (See prosecution trial exhibits, P200022, http://www.vaed.uscourts.gov/notablecases/moussaoui/exhibits/.) The date and time on the P200022 still images indicate when the still pictures were made from the video. See interv Austin and Pennington, 8, 13-15.
38. Interv Eberhart, 5; timeline of FBI history, entry 11 Sep 01, http://www.fbi.gov/libref/historic/history/historicdates.htm; Michael E. Rolince (ActAsstDir, FBI) testimony before S Judiciary Cte, 24 Jun 03, 3, http://www.fbi.gov/congress/congress03/rolince062403.htm.
39. Interv Galey, 20 Nov 01, 3-10; interv Burchell, 5-14; Bill Line, "National Capital Region Contributions to September 11th Help Efforts," National Park Service, http://www.nps.gov/remembrance/dcarea/dc_press.html. All departures from the airport had been cancelled by the FAA directive issued at 9:26 a.m., and at 9:45 a.m. the FAA ordered all civil aircraft to land at the nearest airport, diminishing the traffic into Reagan National. See FAA Historian's "Chronology," Doc 24, OpNE CMH.
40. "Arlington County After-Action Report," C-7; interv Hackney, 29; interv Holl, 15.
41. "Arlington County After-Action Report," C-6, 13-14, 16; interv Hackney, 4-5, 10-15, 18-19, 21-22.
42. Interv Flynn, 25, 32; "DPS After-Action Report," [3, 15]; interv Hackney, 6-8; interv Jester, 19 Oct 01, 15; "Arlington County After-Action Report," A-6, C-8-9, 20, D-13; interv Gavin, 28 May 02, 8-9.
43. "Arlington County After-Action Report," C-25; interv Holl, 32; ACPD "Incident History Detail," 11 Sep 01 entries 10:03:11, 10:09:39, 16:35:11, DepChief Holl ACPD; interv Alt, 28 May 02, 7; interv R. Carlton, 15 Apr 02, 8-13; interv Parsons, 13 Dec 01, 1, 32-37, 40-41. The motorcycle unit of the Prince George's County Police Department also assisted on 11 September by escorting medical personnel in the morning and trucks carrying lighting equipment in the evening from Andrews AFB to the Pentagon. See interv Weishaar, 23 Jan 02, tape recording.
44. "Arlington County After-Action Report," D-13; interv Holl, 14; interv Ramsey, 22; interv Blevins, 13 Dec 01, 6; MDW Provost Marshal timeline, 11 Sep [01], SAIC, http://www.911digitalarchive.org/crr/documents/2698.pdf; interv Eberhart, 9; interv Suvari, 21, 30; interv Pollygus, 33; interv Bohn, 8-9 (quote).
45. Interv Holl, 7, 9; interv Flynn, 8, 16; interv Hackney, 20; "Arlington County After-Action Report," C-6-7, 13.
46. "Arlington County After-Action Report," C-16, 21; interv Gavin, 21; "DPS After-Action Report," [16].
47. "2002 Annual Report," VA Dept ABC, 14; ACPD "Incident History Detail," 11 Sep 01 entry 11:04:32, DepChief Holl ACPD; Covert, "Search and Recovery," 20, 21; interv Holl, 17-18 (quote, 18).
48. Interv Ramsey, 4-10, 21-23.
49. Interv Hackney, 16-17, 35 (quote); interv Flynn, 39; "Arlington County After-Action Report," C-24.

50. Summary of interv Col Egon Hawrylak, 1 Apr 02, [2], National Guard Bureau, "Comprehensive Reference Resource for September 11, 2001," September 11 Digital Archive, http://www.911da.org/crr/documents/5118.pdf; interv Jackson, 7 Jan 02, 25, 27, 36.
51. Interv Jackson 18-22, 31-34, 40, 49-51; summary of interv Hawrylak, [2-3].
52. Interv Jackson, 12-13 (quote); summary of interv Hawrylak, [2].
53. Summary of interv Hawrylak, [2]; interv Cunningham, 7; interv Telgren, 2 Oct 01, 5, 6; Shupe, "Operation Noble Eagle," 7.
54. Interv Telgren, 5-6; interv Farrar, 14; interv Pugrud, 8; interv Haselbush, 17; interv K. Dooley, 2 Oct 01, 6 (quote); interv Norton, 25 Sep 01, 7; "Arlington County After-Action Report," C-40.
55. Interv Brassell and Harris, 1 Nov 01, 4; interv Smith, 11; "Arlington County After-Action Report," C-40; interv Hurley, 11 (quote).
56. Interv Malmquist, 17-18; interv Corcoran, 8; interv Litchfield, 12; "Arlington County After-Action Report," C-55.
57. Interv Malmquist, 18-20; interv Corcoran, 8-9; interv Boatwright, 10-11; interv Stout, 23 Jun 06, 16-17, 19.
58. Interv Stout, 2-4; interv Harper, 6-7, 14; "DPS After-Action Report," [9, 11, 26]; interv Jester, 31 Jan 06, 17-19; ibid, 19 Oct 01, 11; interv Nesbitt, 7 Nov 01, 6. On 11 September Major Koerber was the on-site commander followed by Captain Stanley until Chief Jester asked Stanley to focus on security for the leased facilities; Harper and Stout manned the day shift.
59. Interv Jester, 19 Oct 01, 13-14; ibid, 31 Jan 06, 22; interv Stout, 2; interv Nelson, 9 Nov 01, 10, 17-18; MWAA Public Affairs Office, news release, 20 Jun 06.
60. Interv Nelson, 11-12; interv Holl, 34-35; interv Stout, 4, 14; "DPS After-Action Report," [16].
61. Interv Alt, 15-16, 22; "Arlington County After-Action Report," C-16, 21; Sandra Jontz and Patrick Dickson, "Pentagon Employees Try to Resume Jobs Amid Disaster," *Stars and Stripes*, 13 Sep 01, 4, http://ww2.pstripes.osd.mil/01/sep01/ed091301m.html; interv Alexander, 10-11. There were other temporary memorials near the Pentagon, and on 30 Nov 01 WHS arranged for a moving company to package and move the items to storage. See DoD, "DoD to Preserve Mementos from Pentagon 'Memorial,'" news release 606-01, 29 Nov 01, releases archive, http://www.defenselink.mil.
62. Interv Jester, 19 Oct 01, 18; atchmt, "End of Tour Duty Report of 115th MP Bn MNG," e-mail Joseph Balkoski to Diane Putney, 24 Jan 07.
63. "Arlington County After-Action Report," C-40-41; interv Stout, 4, 10-11.
64. "Arlington County After-Action Report," A-54, 56; interv Jackson, 44-46; Shupe, "Operation Noble Eagle," 11 (Jackson quote); interv Chandler, 25 Sep 01, 9; interv Corcoran, 12 (quote); interv Stout, 11.
65. Interv Jester, 19 Oct 01, 10.
66. ACPD command post notes, 13 Sep 01, entries 0823, 1150, DepChief Holl ACPD; interv Stout, 6-8; interv Combs, 20-21; "Arlington County After-Action Report," C-23; e-mails Lt Jason Bower (PFPA) to Diane Putney, 31 Oct, 1 Nov 06.
67. Interv Jester, 19 Oct 01, 11; "DPS After-Action Report," [16-17]; interv Combs, 21; "Arlington County After-Action Report," C-40. For the 4,000 estimate, see the reference to 3,700 while the issuance process was still under way in ACPD command post notes, 15 Sep 01, entry 0930 briefing, DepChief Holl ACPD.
68. Interv Combs, 21-22; "Arlington County After-Action Report," C-58-59; "DPS After-Action Report," [17]; "Pentagon Site Access Badge Requirements . . . ," nd, DepChief Holl ACPD; interv Stout, 7-10; interv Plaugher, 45 (quote).
69. Rossow, *Uncommon Strength*, 105-06; Shupe, "Operation Noble Eagle," 9-10; interv Kelley, 25.
70. Interv Kelley, 25-26; interv White, 36-38; "Arlington County After-Action Report," A-68; interv Smith, 11; interv Nesbitt, 7 Nov 01, 10; interv Fitzharris, 22. Sgts Christian Hale and Randall Peterson handled the escort service for DPS. See interv Stout, 20; interv Nesbitt, 7 Nov 01, 10.

71. Interv Jester, 19 Oct 01, 11; "Arlington County After-Action Report," C-35. Michael Copeland led the DPS effort to recover and safeguard classified documents. See interv Stout, 20; interv Nesbitt, 19 Jun 06, 28.
72. Interv Pugrud, 5; Covert, "Search and Recovery," 20-21; Shupe, "Operation Noble Eagle," 10-11, 19; "Arlington County After-Action Report," C-57.
73. Interv Cochran, 6-13; interv M. Dooley, 5 Dec 01, 8-19.
74. Interv Dennis and Byrd, 26 Nov 01, 8-9, 18-21; interv Nesbitt, 7 Nov 01, 10; interv Mascelli, 9 Jan 02, 18-22; "DPS After-Action Report," [18]; DPS newsletter "911," 8. The HQ/HQ Detachment and the 118th Military Police Company (Airborne) of the 503rd Military Police Battalion (Airborne) arrived at the Pentagon on 20 September 2001.
75. DPS newsletter "911," 9; interv Friedl, 28 Oct 03, 18-19; DoD, "DoD Establishes Pentagon Force Protection Agency," news release 241-02, 9 May 02, releases archive, http://www.defenselink.mil. The 7th Chemical Company from Fort Polk, Louisiana, arrived at the Pentagon in October 2001. See interv Dennis and Byrd, 8, 21.
76. Arlington County, "Arlington Transfers Pentagon Site to FBI," news release, 21 Sep 01, DepChief Holl ACPD; Rossow, *Uncommon Strength*, 96; interv Eberhart, 12, 32-33. Eberhart provided the 26 September date contradicting the "Arlington County After-Action Report," C-49; the MDW still had to turn the command back to OSD's Washington Headquarters Service. See interv Haselbush, 24; interv Jackson, 23-24; interv Fitzharris, 23.
77. Two of the F-16s were armed with missiles and a loaded 20-mm. internal gun while the third F-16 carried no missiles because it was a spare aircraft. Gross, "9-11 and Operation Noble Eagle," 9-11; *9/11 Commission Report*, 26-34.
78. Interv Rielage, 29 Mar 02, 24-25 (quote, 25); e-mail Kathleen Heincer (Pentagon librarian) to Diane Putney, 29 Nov 06; interv Young, 23 May 02, 30; interv Bohn, 9-10; interv Holl, 11; interv Slifer, 8 Oct 01, 11-12; interv Martin, 8-9; interv White, 18-19; interv Thumann and Zegowitz, 18-20; interv Perez, 14-15; interv Heggood, 6 Feb 02, 11-12; interv McKinnon, 21-22.
79. For when and to whom the shootdown order was communicated in the chain of command see *9/11 Commission Report*, 40-45.
80. Ibid, 44; Gross, "9-11 and Operation Noble Eagle," 11-15, 17, 29, 45. See also Scott, "F-16 Pilots Considered Ramming Flight 93," 71-73.
81. *9/11 Commission Report*, 314; interv Jester, 19 Oct 01, 14 (quote); ibid, 31 Jan 06, 2-3, 6.

VIII. CARING FOR THE DEAD AND THE LIVING

1. "Response to the Terrorist Attack on the Pentagon: Pentagon Family Assistance Center (PFAC) After Action Report" (hereafter "PFAC After Action Report"), 63, C-4.4. The source of casualty officers for the DIA personnel is not recorded; interv Bethke, Campbell, and Brown, 24 Jan 02, 94-95.
2. "Arlington County After-Action Report," A-47, C-55; interv Durm, 21-22; interv Bethke, Campbell, and Brown, 24 Jan 02, 25; Rossow, *Uncommon Strength*, 93-94.
3. Interv Wagner, 1 Mar 02, 27.
4. Ibid, 8-9; "Arlington County After-Action Report," A-47, C-51.
5. "Arlington County After-Action Report," C-55; Rossow, *Uncommon Strength*, 95; Ruggeri, "The Dover Air Force Base Port Mortuary," 72; interv R. Carlton, 15 Apr 02, 36-37.
6. Write-up of tour given to Naval Historical Center Pentagon Team, 14-15 Nov 01, Nav Hist.
7. Ruggeri, "The Dover Air Force Base Port Mortuary," 70; Peterson, "Psychological Intervention with-Mortuary Workers after the September 11 Attack," 84.
8. Interv Wagner, 2-3, 35.
9. Peterson, "Psychological Intervention," 84; Wagner and Kelly, "*Operation Noble Eagle*: Forensic and Psychological Aspects," 81.

10. "After-Action Report, Operation Noble Eagle" (hereafter "AFIP After-Action Report"), Encl 1, Encl 2-1; Hammonds and Kelly, "*Operation Noble Eagle*: DNA Laboratory Plays Key Role," 4; Peterson, "Psychological Intervention," 84.
11. Interv Wagner, 33; Rossow, *Uncommon Strength*, 94-95; "AFIP After-Action Report," 2; Wagner and Kelly, "*Operation Noble Eagle*: Forensic and Psychological Aspects," 81; Kelly, "*Operation Noble Eagle*: AFIP Responds to September 11th Pentagon Terrorist Attacks," 1; Kelly, "*Operation Noble Eagle*: Forensic Anthropologist Provides Expertise Following September 11 Attack," 6.
12. Interv Arendt, 1 Mar 02, 16.
13. "AFIP After-Action Report," 5, 9.
14. Ibid, 10.
15. Interv Wagner, 31-32.
16. Wagner and Kelly, "*Operation Noble Eagle*: Forensic and Psychological Aspects," 81; Pemble, "Forensic Dentistry and Forensic Dental Identification," 12; Kelly, "*Operation Noble Eagle*: Radiologic Pathology Provides Dover Support," 10.
17. In the Army, personnel of the Casualty and Memorial Affairs Operations Center coordinated with the families of deceased for the delivery of remains and return of personal effects; see Rossow, *Uncommon Strength*, 91.
18. Interv Wagner, 22, 24; interv O'Brien, 2 July 02, 36.
19. Interv Wagner, 14; Hammonds and Kelly, "*Operation Noble Eagle*: DNA Laboratory," 4-5.
20. Interv Wagner, 19, 40.
21. Pemble, "Forensic Dentistry," 14-15, 18; Kelly, "Noble Eagle," 7; interv Arendt, 5-7, 9.
22. "AFIP After-Action Report," 3, Encl 1; FBI list, ME Cause, 13 Dec 01, AttOfc EDVa; interv Wagner, 10; interv Bethke, Campbell, and Brown, 105; memcon Charles Pemble (DepDir AFIP) w/Rebecca Welch, 19 May 06.
23. Interv Bethke, Campbell, and Brown, 79, 87, 89, 106.
24. Ibid, 39, 87; interv Chaloupka, 8 Feb 02, 4.
25. Interv Bond, 14 Nov 01, 2, 3; "After-Action Report NLO," 2.
26. Interv Bethke, Campbell, and Brown, 6-7, 20, 35-36, 41, 45, 82.
27. Ibid, 81.
28. Interv O'Brien, 15 Nov 01, 9, 24.
29. Interv Bond, 12.
30. Ibid, 8-9, 12, 15; "After-Action Report NLO," 4, Appendix B, C.
31. Write-up of tour 14-15 Nov 2001, Nav Hist; interv Bethke, Campbell, and Brown, 89; interv O'Brien, 15 Nov 01, 11-13, 15; interv Bond, 28; interv Chaloupka, 11-14; memcon Pemble and Welch, 19 May 06.
32. Interv Falk, 8 July 02, 7, 12; interv Chu, 1 Feb 02, 4.
33. "Arlington County After-Action Report," D-9; interv Falk, 9-11.
34. Interv Falk, 16, 28; interv Chu, 5; "Aggies and Local Residents Pause to Commemorate Sept. 11, 2001," *Aggie Daily*, Texas A&M University, 11 Sep 02, http://tamu.edu/univrel/aggiedaily/news/stories/02/091102-12.html.
35. "PFAC After Action Report," 4.
36. Ibid, 3; interv Falk, 7, 12.
37. "After-Action Report: The ACS's Response to the Attack on the Pentagon" (hereafter "ACS After-Action Report"), 3; interv Johnson and Gifford, 14 Mar 02, 7-8.
38. Interv Johnson and Gifford, 35.
39. Brinsfield, "Attack on the Pentagon: The Ministry of Army Chaplains," 124-25.
40. Ibid, 119; "PFAC After Action Report," 10, A-3.1; interv Falk, 15, 18; Lessons Learned from the USS *Cole* Crisis (internal notes, nd) were made available to the staff (see Doc 45, OpNE CMH).
41. Interv BrownWahler, 30 Jan 02, 6, 34.
42. Interv Stair, 9 Oct 01, 2, 4, 7, 10, 13-14, 18.
43. Interv Johnson and Gifford, 36, 38; "ACS After-Action Report," 17.

44. News releases, 13 and 14 Sep 01, releases archive, http://www.defenselink.mil.
45. "PFAC After Action Report," 9.
46. Ibid, 16, 20.
47. Interv Chu, 5.
48. Brinsfield, "Attack on the Pentagon: The Ministry of Army Chaplains," 120; "PFAC After Action Report," 12, 19; interv Falk, 13, 24.
49. *9/11 Commission Report*, 327.
50. Rossow, *Uncommon Strength*, 115-16; "PFAC After Action Report," 4, 24, 25-26.
51. Hammonds, "*Operation Noble Eagle*: Helping Pentagon Families Who Lost Loved Ones, AFIP Personnel Staff Special Assistance Center," 12.
52. John Molino (DASD Military Community and Family Policy), "Briefing on Casualty Notification," transcript archive, 26 Mar 03, http://www.defenselink.mil.
53. Interv J. Hodge, 15 Nov 01, 5.
54. Rossow, *Uncommon Strength*, 116. As a result of the Federal Aviation Disaster Family Assistance Act of 1996, the National Transportation Safety Board, American Red Cross, and major air carriers developed an arrangement to care for families affected by aviation disasters; see "Remarks of Carol Carmody Vice-Chairman, National Transportation Safety Board . . ."; Huleatt, "Pentagon Family Assistance Center Inter-Agency Mental Health Collaboration and Response," 68 (Huleatt indicates that the Marine Corps provided CAOs to Defense contractors, 69); interv Kuhn, 8 Feb 02, 21-22.
55. Interv Hodge, 9.
56. Interv Bethke, Campbell, and Brown, 99.
57. "PFAC After Action Report," 28, C-4.12, 4.14.
58. Interv Chu, 9.
59. "PFAC After Action Report," 30-31; interv BrownWahler, 11.
60. Interv Bethke, Campbell, and Brown, 91.
61. Brinsfield, "Attack on the Pentagon: The Ministry of Army Chaplains," 81-82.
62. "PFAC After Action Report," 26, 28-29, 35, 37.
63. Ibid, 10-11, 35-36.
64. Ibid, 38-45, B-2.8; Brinsfield, "Attack on the Pentagon: The Ministry of Army Chaplains," 121-22.
65. Rossow, *Uncommon Strength*, 116-19.
66. Interv Falk, 19.
67. "PFAC After Action Report," 44-45; Rudi Williams, "'Therapy Dogs' Help Relieve Stress for Families, Staff, Volunteers," news archive, 11 Oct 01, http://www.defenselink.mil.
68. About two weeks after the briefings began, on reaching a consensus with the families Van Alstyne cut back the briefings to one per day. See interv Falk, 33-34.
69. Brinsfield, "Attack on the Pentagon: The Ministry of Army Chaplains," 58; "PFAC After Action Report," 12-14.
70. "PFAC After Action Report," 125.
71. Ibid, 126.
72. Interv Falk, 16.
73. Ibid, 17.
74. Interv Jaworski, 39.
75. Brinsfield, "Attack on the Pentagon: The Ministry of Army Chaplains," 136.
76. Interv Kuhn, 19.
77. Interv Puryear, 24 Sep 02, 3-6, 9.
78. Interv Falk, 26-27.
79. "PFAC After Action Report," 21, 46-77; Brinsfield, "Attack on the Pentagon: The Ministry of Army Chaplains," 59; interv Falk, 26, 27; interv Perryman, 15; interv BrownWahler, 7-8.
80. Interv Falk, 35; the wounded were considered a medical responsibility and also excluded, which, according to interv BrownWahler, 13, left them "out of the loop."
81. Brinsfield, "Attack on the Pentagon: The Ministry of Army Chaplains," 58.

82. Interv Falk, 29.
83. Ibid, 17; interv BrownWahler, 13.
84. Some staff expressed concern that the donations became excessive and commercialized and were inefficiently screened for security, distribution, and other purposes.
85. Interv BrownWahler, 16.
86. Interv Falk, 25.
87. Ibid, 32.
88. "PFAC After Action Report," 18; interv Stair, 20, notes that a list of the volunteers required about 40 pages of Excel spreadsheets.
89. Memo DASD (Molino) for DASs Army, Air Force, PDAS Navy, "On-Going Support for Families of Victims of the Pentagon Attack," 5 Oct 01, Doc 30, and PRRO briefing, 10 Oct 01, Doc 49, both in OpNE CMH.
90. SOP for PRRO, 1 Oct 01, Doc 48, and PRRO info briefing, 10 Oct 01, Doc 52, both in OpNE CMH; "ACS After-Action Report," briefing 14 Mar 02, 19ff.; interv Johnson and Gifford, 51, 57-58.
91. A briefing stated that 66 percent of the "missing persons" had been positively identified as of 7 October 2001; see PFARRO info brief, 7 Oct 01, 2, Doc 55, OpNE CMH.
92. Rossow, *Uncommon Strength*, 97-98; interv Bethke, Campbell, and Brown, 106, 108; interv Brown-Wahler, 17.
93. Interv Kuhn, 29; interv Falk, 2, 3.

AFTERWORD

1. OSD, *Status Report*, 1 Mar 99, 57-59.
2. Memo Ralph Newton (DepDir Real Estate and Facilities) for AdminAsst to SecA et al, 24 Sep 01, OSD Hist.
3. *Public Statements: Rumsfeld 2001*, 3:2162; *Public Papers: Bush 2001*, 2:1217.
4. OSD, *Status Report*, 1 Mar 02, ii, 17-19.
5. Ibid, 1 Mar 03, 6, 17-19; ibid, 1 Mar 02, ii; ibid, 1 Mar 04, 4; Gerry Gilmore, "Pentagon Phoenix Project Workers Are Heroes, Wolfowitz Says," 11 Sep 02, AFPS News Articles, news archive, http://www.defenselink.mil.
6. WHS Building Circular, PBM-01-1, 7 May 02, OSD Hist.
7. Kathleen T. Rhem, "Military Clergymen Dedicate Pentagon Memorial Chapel," 12 Nov 02, AFPS News Articles, news archive, http://www.defenselink.mil; Tara Bahrampour, "Pentagon Pulls Veil From Hallowed Spot," *Washington Post*, 11 Sep 05, 1.
8. OSD, *Status Report*, 1 Mar 04, 19-21; ibid, 1 Mar 05, 19; Timothy Dwyer, "9-11 Memorial to Reflect Pangs of Loss, Recollections of Joy," *Washington Post*, 16 Jun 06, B1.
9. Steve Vogel, "Lost, and Sometimes, Never Found," *Washington Post*, 13 Sep 02, B1; Frank S. Murray, "Pentagon Celebrates Rebuilding; Honors Dead," *Washington Times*, 12 Sep 02, 1.
10. DoD, "Defense of Freedom Medal Unveiled," news release 463-01, 27 Sep 01, and DoD, "Department of the Navy Honors Pentagon Heroes," news release 642-01, 17 Dec 01, both at releases archive, http://www.defenselink.mil; Lisa Burgess, "FBI Turns Pentagon Crash Site Over to Army for Rebuilding, Renovation Phase," *Stars and Stripes*, 28 Sep 01, 1-2; Linda D. Kozaryn, "Pentagon Honors First Responders for Valor," 6 Mar 02, AFPS News Articles, news archive, http://www.defenselink.mil.

Selected Bibliography

Most of the information for this book was derived from the hundreds of oral history interviews with participants in the events of 9/11 and the days that followed. The interviews were conducted by the historical offices of the military services and OSD; they are in the possession of the originating offices as indicated in the list below. Also of prime importance were a number of published and unpublished reports that merit special acknowledgement. The published reports include *The Pentagon Building Performance Report; The 9/11 Commission Report: Final Report of the National Commission on Terrorist Attacks upon the United States;* and *Uncommon Strength: The Story of the U.S. Army Office of the Deputy Chief of Staff for Personnel during the Attack on the Pentagon, 11 September 2001.* Two unpublished reports were especially helpful: "Building Performance Evaluation, The 9-11 Terrorist Attack—Pentagon" and the "Arlington County After-Action Report on the Response to the September 11 Terrorist Attack on the Pentagon."

INTERVIEWS

Air Force Historical Support Office, Washington, D.C.

Beavers, Craig. Interviewed by George Watson, 6 December 2001.

Carlton, Paul K. Interviewed by Perry Jamieson and James S. Nanney, 4 December 2001.

Cayer, Richard. Interviewed by George Watson, 29 November 2001.
Smoot, Jacob. Interviewed by George Watson, 5 December 2001.
Weishaar, Daniel. Interviewed by George Watson, 23 January 2002.

Historical Office, Office of the Secretary of Defense, Arlington, Va.
Alexander, Coneleous. Interviewed by Richard Hunt, 5 November 2001.
Austin, Brian and Steve Pennington. Interviewed by Diane Putney, 9 November 2006.
Brady, John. Interviewed by Richard Hunt, 5 November 2001.
Brassell, Kathleen and John Harris. Interviewed by Stuart Rochester and Roger Trask, 1 November 2001.
Breeden, Timothy M. Interviewed by Richard Hunt, 5 December 2001.
Bryant, Michael. Interviewed by Diane Putney, 31 October 2001.
Cambone, Stephen A. Interviewed by Alfred Goldberg and Rebecca Cameron, 8 July 2002.
Candido, Robert H. Interviewed by Richard Hunt, 12 December 2001.
Carter, Steven. Interviewed by Diane Putney, 19 November 2001.
Chu, David. Interviewed by Alfred Goldberg and Rebecca Cameron, 1 February 2002.
Clarke, Victoria. Interviewed by Alfred Goldberg and Rebecca Cameron, 2 July 2002.
Cochran, Marion, Jr. (Snake). Interviewed by Diane Putney, 3 December 2001.
Combs, Christopher. Interviewed by Alfred Goldberg, Diane Putney, and Rebecca Welch, 11 July 2005.
Condrell, Stacie. Interviewed by Ronald Landa and Rebecca Cameron, 30 October 2001.
Conques, Anthony. Interviewed by Diane Putney, 25 October 2001.
Cooke, David O. (Doc). Interviewed by Alfred Goldberg and Diane Putney, 18 October 2001.
Cox, Robert. Interviewed by Richard Hunt, 15 November 2001.
Davis, Aubrey and Gilbert Oldach. Interviewed by Diane Putney, 20 July 2006.
Di Rita, Lawrence. Interviewed by Alfred Goldberg and Stuart Rochester, 27 June 2002.
Dooley, Michael. Interviewed by Diane Putney, 5 December 2001.
Evey, Lee. Interviewed by Alfred Goldberg and Diane Putney, 22 October 2001.
Fitzharris, Rich. Interviewed by Alfred Goldberg, Roger Trask, and Rebecca Cameron, 12 December 2001.
Friedl, Joseph. Interviewed by Alfred Goldberg and Rebecca Welch, 28 October 2003.
Giambastiani, Edmund P., Jr. Interviewed by Alfred Goldberg and Rebecca Cameron, 18 July 2002 and 1 August 2002.
Gibbs, Chuck. See Gray, Gibbs, and Smith.
Godfrey, Steven L. Interviewed by Richard Hunt, 7 November 2001.
Gray, Frances A. Interviewed by Diane Putney, 8 November 2001.
Gray, Randy, Chuck Gibbs, and Jerome Dale Smith. Interviewed by Rebecca Welch and Nancy Berlage, 3 February 2006.
Greenwell, Kathryn. Interviewed by Diane Putney, 9 November 2001.
Harper, Randall. Interviewed by Diane Putney, 14 July 2006.
Haselbush, Paul K. Interviewed by Alfred Goldberg, Stuart Rochester, and Diane Putney, 19 October 2001.

Hilliard, Leroy. Interviewed by Richard Hunt, 6 November 2001.

Irby, John F. Interviewed by Diane Putney, 19 November 2001.

Jester, John. Interviewed by Alfred Goldberg, Diane Putney, and Stuart Rochester, 19 October 2001.

_______. Interviewed by Diane Putney, 31 January 2006.

Judd, Nancy. Interviewed by Diane Putney, 29 October 2001.

Kelly, Jack. See Viner and Kelly.

Kilsheimer, Allyn. Interviewed by Ronald Landa and Rebecca Cameron, 29 October 2001.

Kuney, Donald and Brian Maguire. Interviewed by Diane Putney, 26 October 2001.

Luczak, Linda. Interviewed by Diane Putney, 7 November 2001.

Maguire, Brian. See Kuney and Maguire.

McCormick, Charles. Interviewed by Diane Putney, 25 October 2001.

Morris, Matthew. Interviewed by Diane Putney, 5 December 2001.

Murphy, Daniel J. Interviewed by Diane Putney, 28 November 2001.

Nelson, Rick. Interviewed by Diane Putney, 9 November 2001.

Nesbitt, Michael. Interviewed by Stuart Rochester and Roger Trask, 7 November 2001.

_______. Interviewed by Diane Putney, 19 June 2006.

Newton, Ralph. Interviewed by Diane Putney, 19 November 2001.

Oldach, Gilbert. See Davis and Oldach.

Pennington, Steve. See Austin and Pennington.

Phillips, James. Interviewed by Stuart Rochester and Richard Hunt, 9 November 2001.

Pickens, Edwin. Interviewed by Alfred Goldberg and Rebecca Cameron, 23 October 2001.

Pugrud, John. Interviewed by Stuart Rochester and Roger Trask, 1 November 2001.

Rabogliatti, R. E. Interviewed by Richard Hunt, 5 November 2001.

Robinson, John. Interviewed by Diane Putney, 5 December 2001.

Rumsfeld, Donald H. Interviewed by Alfred Goldberg and Rebecca Cameron, 23 December 2002.

Smith, Dennis. Interviewed by Diane Putney, 29 October 2001.

Smith, Jerome Dale. See Gray, Gibbs, and Smith.

Stanton, Tom. Interviewed by Alfred Goldberg, Diane Putney, Nancy Berlage, and Rebecca Welch, 14 March 2006.

Stout, William. Interviewed by Diane Putney, 23 June 2006.

Sullivan, Michael. Interviewed by Alfred Goldberg and Diane Putney, 18 October 2001.

Viner, William and Jack Kelly. Interviewed by Ronald Landa and Rebecca Cameron, 25 October 2001.

Wassel, Joseph M. Interviewed by Alfred Goldberg and Rebecca Cameron, 9 April 2003.

Wolfowitz, Paul. Interviewed by Alfred Goldberg and Rebecca Cameron, 19 April 2002.

Woodson, Alvina. Interviewed by Diane Putney, 8 November 2001.

Marine Corps History Division, Quantico, Va.

Blevins, Jeffrey. Interviewed by Fred Allison, 13 December 2001.

Bohn, Keith. Interviewed by Gary Solis, 19 November 2001.

Burroughs, Charles. Interviewed by Fred Allison, 5 December 2001.

Defina, Michael T. Interviewed by Fred Allison, 3 December 2001.
Drumming, Charles J. Interviewed by Fred Allison, 18 December 2001.
Durrer, John T. Interviewed by Fred Allison, 3 December 2001.
Farrington, Michael K. Interviewed by Fred Allison, 18 December 2001.
Garofola, Timothy J. Interviewed by Fred Allison, 20 September 2001.
Henry, Cary. Interviewed by Fred Allison, 5 December 2001.
Hood, Walter J. Interviewed by Fred Allison, 5 December 2001.
Howes, Charles Thomas. Interviewed by Fred Allison, 3 December 2001.
Lugaila, James. Interviewed by Fred Allison, 19 November 2001.
Martin, James B. Interviewed by Fred Allison, 12 December 2001.
McKethan, Gary. Interviewed by Fred Allison, 20 December 2001.
Mix, Ronald. Interviewed by Fred Allison, 13 December 2001.
Murphy, Michael K. Interviewed by Fred Allison, 5 December 2001.
Murphy, Peter M. Interviewed by Gary Solis, 19 September 2001.
Ramsey, Charles H. Interviewed by Fred Allison, 30 November 2001.
Schuetz, Dustin P. Interviewed by Fred Allison, 13 September 2001.
Thompson, Adrian H. Interviewed by Fred Allison, 12 December 2001.
Thumann, John and Richard Zegowitz. Interviewed by Fred Allison, 20 December 2001.
Tinsley, David. Interviewed by Fred Allison, 20 December 2001.
Vafier, James. Interviewed by Gary Solis, 8 January 2002.
Vera, Michael. Interviewed by Fred Allison, 20 September 2001.
Zegowitz, Richard. See Thumann and Zegowitz.

Naval Historical Center, Washington, D.C.

Arendt, Douglas. Interviewed by Gary Hall, Carol O'Hagan, and Kathleen Wright, 1 March 2002.
Balisle, Phillip. Interviewed by Gary Hall and Michael McDaniel, 28 June 2002.
Bond, Gale Wallace. Interviewed by Gary Hall, Michael McDaniel, Carol O'Hagan, Karen Loftus, Kathleen Wright, and Jeff Luthi, 14 November 2001.
Braswell, Donald. Interviewed by Michael McDaniel, 30 October 2001.
BrownWahler, Yvette. Interviewed by Gary Hall, Carol O'Hagan, Karen Loftus, and Kathleen Wright, 30 January 2002.
Burchell, Kenneth S. Interviewed by Gary Hall, Michael McDaniel, Carol O'Hagan, Karen Loftus, and Kathleen Wright, 20 November 2001.
Capets, Charles. Interviewed by Michael McDaniel, 2 November 2001.
Cole, Sarah. Interviewed by Michael McDaniel and Richard Fahy, 6 December 2001.
Cordero, Kathy. Interviewed by Carol O'Hagan, Robert Sawyer, and Kathleen Wright, 4 March 2002.
Crane Group #1. Interviewed by Gary Hall, Michael McDaniel, and Kathleen Wright, 25 February 2002.
Crane Group #2. Interviewed by Gary Hall, Michael McDaniel, and Kathleen Wright, 25 February 2002.

Dossel, Carl W. Interviewed by Robert Schneller and Michael McDaniel, 28 September 2001.

Eberhart, Arthur R. Interviewed by Robert J. Cressman and Timothy L. Francis, 15 January 2002.

Falk, Mary Margaret (Meg). Interviewed by Randy Papadopoulos, Julie Kowalski, and Richard Tate, 8 July 2002.

Galey, Ronald. Interviewed by Gary Hall, Michael McDaniel, Carol O'Hagan, Karen Loftus, and Kathleen Wright, 20 November 2001.

Gonzales, Paul. Interviewed by Carol O'Hagan, Karen Loftus, and Robert Sawyer, 13 February 2002.

Gully, Steven. Interviewed by Michael McDaniel and Richard Fahy, 6 December 2001.

Hanfling, Daniel. Interviewed by Lara Bornstein, 7 December 2001.

Hazelwood, Kevin. Interviewed by Carol O'Hagan and Kathleen Wright, 28 January 2002.

Henson, Jarrell. Interviewed by Michael McDaniel and Gary Hall, 23 January 2002.

Humbert, Megan. Interviewed by Gary Hall, Michael McDaniel, and Karen Loftus, 4 January 2002.

Ingersoll, Jason. Interviewed by Carol O'Hagan, Robert Sawyer, and Kathleen Wright, 28 February 2002.

_______ and Kevin Rimrodt. Interviewed by Randy Papadopoulos and Kathleen Wright, 12 June 2002.

Kern, Dennis. Interviewed by Gary Hall and Michael McDaniel, 24 January 2002.

Lescault, Randall. Interviewed by Michael McDaniel and Karen Loftus, 27 November 2001.

Lewis, Charles. Interviewed by Gary Hall and Michael McDaniel, 25 April 2002.

Lhuillier, Jason. Interviewed by Michael McDaniel and Carol O'Hagan, 13 December 2001.

Livingstone, Susan. Interviewed by Gary Hall, Michael McDaniel, and Randy Papadopoulos, 19 February 2002.

Lutgen, Deborah. Interviewed by Andre Sobocinski, 7 December 2001.

Masso, Edward. Interviewed by Michael McDaniel and Gary Hall, 11 December 2001.

Mathias, Melven. Interviewed by Gary Weir, 12 December 2001.

Mayer, Thomas. Interviewed by Lara Bornstein, 29 November 2001.

McAtee, Thomas. Interviewed by Randy Papadopoulos and Thomas Blake, 25 September 2001.

McDonner, James. Interviewed by Gary Hall and Michael McDaniel, 13 December 2001.

McGuire, Jean. Interviewed by Andre Sobocinski, 7 December 2001.

McKeown, Nancy. Interviewed by Karen Loftus and Carol O'Hagan, 25 October 2001.

Navas, George. Interviewed by Gary Hall and Michael McDaniel, 28 November 2001.

O'Brien, Stephen. Interviewed by Gary Hall, Michael McDaniel, Carol O'Hagan, Karen Loftus, Kathleen Wright, and Jeffrey Luthi, 15 November 2001.

_______. Interviewed by Randy Papadopoulos and Julie Kowalski, 2 July 2002.

Ogletree, Natalie. Interviewed by Carol O'Hagan and Karen Loftus, 29 January 2002.

Parks, William Paul. Interviewed by Thomas Blake, Michael McDaniel, Ray Pietrzak, and Randy Papadopoulos, 27 September 2001.

Parsons, Jeffrey Mark. Interviewed by John Darrell Sherwood, 13 December 2001.

Paull, Marshall. Interviewed by Carol O'Hagan and Kathleen Wright, 26 February 2002.

Perez, Samuel. Interviewed by Gary Hall, Carol O'Hagan, and Randy Papadopoulos, 10 October 2001.

Polasek, Jesse. Interviewed by Michael McDaniel and Richard Fahy, 6 December 2001.

Powell, Craig. Interviewed by Michael McDaniel, 29 October 2001.

Rielage, Dale C. Interviewed by Michael McDaniel, 29 March 2002.

Rimrodt, Kevin. Interviewed by Robert Sawyer and Kathleen Wright, 15 February 2002.

_______. See Ingersoll and Rimrodt.

Roemer, Eileen. Interviewed by Gary Hall, Carol O'Hagan, Karen Loftus, Robert Sawyer, and Kathleen Wright, 11 February 2002.

Sepulveda, Noel. Interviewed by Lara Bornstein, 6 December 2001.

Shaeffer, Kevin. Interviewed by Randy Papadopoulos, Gary Hall, Michael McDaniel, Karen Loftus, and Julie Kowalski, 21 June 2002.

Starrett, Mike. Interviewed by Gary Weir, 4 December 2001.

Sweeney, Mary Jo. Interviewed by Gary Hall and Michael McDaniel, 13 March 2002.

_______. See Tracey and Sweeney.

Tarantino, David. Interviewed by Michael McDaniel and Gary Weir, 25 September 2001.

Thomas, David. Interviewed by Michael McDaniel and Gary Hall, 23 January 2002.

Toti, William. Interviewed by Michael McDaniel, 10 October 2001.

Totushek, John. Interviewed by Gary Hall, Michael McDaniel, and Carol O'Hagan, 5 February 2002.

Tracey, Patricia and Mary Jo Sweeney. Interviewed by Gary Weir, Ray Pietrezak, and Michael McDaniel, 28 September 2001.

Wagner, Glenn. Interviewed by Gary Hall, Carol O'Hagan, and Kathleen Wright, 1 March 2002.

Wirick, Gail Elizabeth. Interviewed by Gary Hall and Michael McDaniel, 27 June 2002.

Zitterkopf, Joan. Interviewed by Michael McDaniel and Karen Loftus, 27 November 2001.

Office of Medical History, Office of the Surgeon General, U.S. Army, Falls Church, Va.

Baxter, John. Interviewed by Debora Cox, 30 November 2001.

Durm, William. Interviewed by Debora Cox, 12 October 2001.

Geiling, James. Interviewed by Debora Cox, 17 December 2001.

Glidewell, Jennifer. Interviewed by Debora Cox, 10 October 2001.

Horoho, Patty. Interviewed by Debora Cox, 27 September 2001.

Lirette, Paul. Interviewed by Debora Cox, 30 November 2001.

Murphy, Eileen. Interviewed by Debora Cox, 25 June 2002.

Roser, John F. Interviewed by Debora Cox, 19 October 2001.

U. S. Army Center of Military History, Washington, D.C.

Afforder, Jeff. Interviewed by Donna Majors, 30 October 2001.

Alt, Richard. Interviewed by George Dover, 28 May 2002.
Bachus, Bruce. Interviewed by Robert Rossow and Austin Shellenberger, 6 March 2002.
Balvanz, Joseph. Interviewed by Robert Smith, 17 October 2001.
Barta, Aaron. Interviewed by Robert Smith, 19 October 2001.
Bass, Samuel. Interviewed by Robert Rossow, 11 October 2001.
Beans, Michael. Interviewed by Frank Shirer, 6 November 2001.
Bethke, Paul A., Harold W. Campbell, and Albert J. Brown. Interviewed by Robert Rossow and Frank Shirer, 24 January 2002.
Birdwell, Brian. Interviewed by Frank Shirer and George Dover, 7 March 2002.
Boatwright, Doyle. Interviewed by Frank Shirer, 2 October 2001.
Boger, Sean. Interviewed by Kelly Strand, 14 November 2001.
Boggess, Corrina. Interviewed by Robert Rossow, 8 December 2001.
Borrego, Travis B. Interviewed by Kim Holien, 2 October 2001.
Brown, Albert J. See Bethke, Campbell, and Brown.
Brown, Fred W. Interviewed by George Dover, 17 October 2001.
Brown, Lorie. Interviewed by Robert Rossow, 29 November 2001.
Bruno, Eduardo. Interviewed by Austin Shellenberger, 15 April 2002.
Byrd, Robert. See Dennis and Byrd.
Campbell, Harold. See Bethke, Campbell, and Brown.
Carden, Martha. Interviewed by Stephen Lofgren, 29 October 2001.
Carlton, Richard. Interviewed by Kelly Strand, 15 April 2002.
Chaloupka, Richard. Interviewed by Frank Shirer, 8 February 2002.
Chandler, Michael. Interviewed by Kim Holien, 25 September 2001.
Chiarelli, Peter. Interviewed by Frank Shirer, 5 February 2002.
Cook, Richard J. Interviewed by Robert Smith and Austin Shellenberger, 17 April 2002.
Corcoran, William. Interviewed by Frank Shirer, 24 September 2001.
Cox, Kenny R. Interviewed by Frank Shirer, 2 August 2002.
Craft, James D. Interviewed by Frank Shirer, 2 October 2001.
Cruz-Cortez, Roxane. Interviewed by Mark Mantini, 21 February 2002.
Cunningham, Steven. Interviewed by Stephen Lofgren, 2 October 2001.
Davies, John. Interviewed by Robert Rossow, 12 December 2001.
Davis, David. Interviewed by Stephen Lofgren, 2 October 2001.
Dennis, Wade F. and Robert Byrd. Interviewed by George Dover, 26 November 2001.
DiPaula, Michael. Interviewed by Dennis Lapic, 29 October 2001.
Dooley, Keith. Interviewed by Eric Villard, 2 October 2001.
Douglas, Robert F. Interviewed by George Dover, 17 October 2001.
Eggerton, Albert S. Interviewed by Robert Rossow, 28 November 2001.
Eikenberry, Karl. Interviewed by Frank Shirer and Stephen Lofgren, 6 February 2002.
Erdelyi, Timothy. Interviewed by Dennis Lapic, 19 October 2001.
Farrar, Robert. Interviewed by Eric Villard, 25 September 2001.
Flynn, Edward. Interviewed by Stephen Lofgren and Randy Papadopoulos, 20 May 2002.
Frauman, Joshua B. Interviewed by Eric Villard, 25 September 2001.
Gallivan, Dakota. Interviewed by Frank Shirer, 2 October 2001.

Gallop, April. Interviewed by Dennis Lapic, 31 October 2001.
Gavin, Mary. Interviewed by Steve Walker and Randy Papadopoulos, 28 May 2002.
Gifford, Holly. See Johnson and Gifford.
Gilroy, Dennis. Interviewed by George Dover, 30 October 2001.
Godbehere, Eric K. Interviewed by Robert Smith, 18 October 2001.
Gouen, Matthew R. Interviewed by Eric Villard, 25 September 2001.
Grant, Regina. Interviewed by Austin Shellenberger and Robert Rossow, 26 February 2002.
Grunewald, Robert. Interviewed by Robert Rossow, 2 November 2001.
Hackney, Rebecca. Interviewed by Donna Majors and George Dover, 28 May 2002.
Hamlet, Kirk. Interviewed by Mark Mantini, 26 February 2002.
Heggood, Paul D. Interviewed by Frank Shirer, 6 February 2002.
Hodge, John. Interviewed by Frank Shirer, 15 November 2001.
Hodge, Thomas. Interviewed by Donna Majors, 30 October 2001.
Holl, Stephen. Interviewed by Stephen Lofgren and Randy Papadopoulos, 28 May 2002.
Hudson, Joel B. Interviewed by Frank Shirer and Stephen Lofgren, 25 February 2002.
Huntley, Henry. Interviewed by George Dover, 8 February 2002.
Hurley, Randolph. Interviewed by Frank Shirer, 25 September 2001.
Jackson, James T. Interviewed by Robert Smith and Frank Shirer, 7 January 2002.
Jaworski, Robert L. Interviewed by George Dover and Frank Shirer, 11 December 2001.
Johnson, Delores F. and Holly Gifford. Interviewed by Austin Shellenberger, 14 March 2002.
Kelley, Shawn Stephan. Interviewed by Frank Shirer and Dennis Lapic, 19 April 2002.
Kelly, Sean M. Interviewed by Austin Shellenberger, 1 November 2001.
Kensinger, Philip. Interviewed by Stephen Lofgren, 2 August 2002.
Kidd, Jacqueline. Interviewed by Kelly Strand, 14 November 2001.
Knoblauch, Karl. Interviewed by Robert Rossow, 28 November 2001.
Kovacic, Jason Paul. Interviewed by Eric Villard, 23 October 2001.
Kuhn, Thomas N. Interviewed by Frank Shirer and Robert Rossow, 8 February 2002.
Ladd, F. Brian. Interviewed by George Dover, 30 October 2001.
Leibner, Lincoln. Interviewed by Stephen Lofgren, 23 January 2002.
Lewis, Mark L. Interviewed by Robert Rossow, 12 December 2001.
Litchfield, Glenn Robert. Interviewed by Frank Shirer, 2 October 2001.
Malmquist, Matthew. Interviewed by Frank Shirer, 2 October 2001.
Mascelli, Alex. Interviewed by Dennis Lapic, 9 January 2002.
Maxfield, Betty. Interviewed by Dennis Lapic, 16 November 2001.
McKinnon, William T. Interviewed by Robert Rossow, 28 November 2001.
Menig, Janet C. Interviewed by Frank Shirer, 14 February 2002.
Moody, Sheila. Interviewed by Frank Shirer, 13 September 2001.
Morehead, Edwin. Interviewed by Stephen Lofgren, 30 October 2001.
Munoz, Gilbert. Interviewed by Stephen Lofgren, 2 October 2001.
Myers, John. Interviewed by Eric Villard, 25 September 2001.
Norton, Benjamin. Interviewed by Frank Shirer, 25 September 2001.

Olaes, Dalisay. Interviewed by Leo Hirrel and Frank Shirer, 13 September 2001.
Oliver, Darrell. Interviewed by Dennis Lapic, 31 October 2001.
O'Neill, Mark. Interviewed by Eric Villard, 2 October 2001.
Owens, Thomas W. Interviewed by George Dover, 20 March 2002.
Panther, Thomas. Interviewed by George Dover, 28 May 2002.
Parham, Ann. Interviewed by Robert Rossow, 4 December 2001.
Penn, Mark L. Interviewed by Frank Shirer and Kelly Strand, 17 April 2002.
Perrin, Mark. Interviewed by Dennis Lapic, 1 November 2001.
Perryman, David A. Interviewed by Frank Shirer, 2 October 2001.
Petrovich, Michael. Interviewed by Frank Shirer, 21 September 2001.
_______. Interviewed by Robert Rossow, 1 November 2001.
Plaugher, Edward P. Interviewed by Stephen Lofgren, Dennis Lapic, Randy Papadopoulos, and Kathleen Wright, 22 April 2002.
Pollygus, Anthony. Interviewed by Dennis Lapic, 8 November 2001.
Puryear, Cortez. Interviewed by Robert Rossow, 24 September 2002.
Reardon, Roger. Interviewed by Donna Majors, 20 October 2001.
Reynolds, Joel K. Interviewed by Frank Shirer, 25 September 2001.
Richon, George. Interviewed by Robert Rossow, 27 November 2001.
Riley, Sandra R. Interviewed by Frank Shirer, 24 January 2002.
Rose, Tony. Interviewed by Dennis Lapic and Robert Rossow, 23 January 2002.
Schwartz, James H. Interviewed by Stephen Lofgren, Dennis Lapic, Randy Papadopoulos, and Kathleen Wright, 17 April 2002.
Skipper, Mark. Interviewed by Donna Majors, 30 October 2001.
Slifer, Isabelle. Interviewed by Robert Rossow, 8 October 2001.
Spindler, Mark. Interviewed by Robert Rossow, 27 November 2001.
Stair, Elizabeth A. Interviewed by Stephen Lofgren, 9 October 2001.
Stevens, Lois. Interviewed by Robert Rossow, 13 December 2001.
Stokes, Steven. Interviewed by Stephen Lofgren and Robert Rossow, 25 September 2001.
Surette, Bruce. Interviewed by Donna Majors, 30 October 2001.
Suvari, Sulev. Interviewed by Robert Smith, 9 April 2002.
Telgren, Jason. Interviewed by Leo Hirrel and Kim Holien, 2 October 2001.
Thompson, G. M. Interviewed by Frank Shirer, 30 October 2001.
Thurman, John Lewis. Interviewed by Frank Shirer, 20 September 2001.
Valenzo, Vance. Interviewed by Austin Shellenberger, 30 October 2001.
Volk, Mark. Interviewed by Stephen Lofgren, 1 May 2002.
Wallace, Alan. Interviewed by Austin Shellenberger, 30 October 2001.
Waring, Robert. Interviewed by Austin Shellenberger, 1 November 2001.
Watson, Ryan. Interviewed by Stephen Lofgren, 25 September 2001.
White, John J. Interviewed by Stephen Lofgren, 19 April 2002.
Wills, Marilyn. Interviewed by Stephen Lofgren and Frank Shirer, 12 July 2002.
Wolfe, Rob. Interviewed by Stephen Lofgren, 3 October 2001.

Wood, John. Interviewed by Stephen Lofgren, 1 March 2002.
Yantis, Timothy Ryan. Interviewed by Frank Shirer, Stephen Lofgren, and Randy Papadopoulos, 8 February 2002.
Young, Charles. Interviewed by Donna Majors, 23 May 2002.
Zappalla, Stephen. Interviewed by Robert Rossow, 9 October 2001.

PERSONAL ACCOUNTS

U.S. Army Center of Military History, Washington, D.C.
Collier, Craig, 13 September 2001.
McNair, Philip, 29 October 2001.
Stauber, Ricky S., 11 October 2001.
Stone, Jeanette, 10 October 2001.
Wallace, Roy, n.d.
Virginia State Police, Area 45 Office, Arlington, Va.
Middleton, Michael S., n.d.
Wimbish, Myrlin, 23 November 2001.

AUDIO AND VIDEO RECORDINGS

Arlington County (Va.) Emergency Communications Center, Fire Dispatch Audio Recording,11 September 2001.
__________. Police Response Audio Recording, 11 September 2001.
Department of Defense, "Videos of American Flight 77 Striking the Pentagon on September 11, 2001," OSD/JS FOIA Requester Service Center Reading Room, http://www.dod.mil/pubs/foi/reading_room/.
Metropolitan Washington Airports Authority, Fire Response Radio Transmissions, Audio Recording, 11 September 2001.
WJLA 7 News, Washington, D.C., Video Recording, 11 September 2001.
WUSA 9 News, Washington, D.C., Video Recording, 11 September 2001.

REPORTS

Published

American Society of Civil Engineers. *The Pentagon Building Performance Report.* Reston, Va.: ASCE, January 2003. [cited as *ASCE Report*]
Department of Defense, Office of the Inspector General. *Health Care: DoD Medical Support to the Federal Response Plan.* Report No. D-2002-087. 10 May 2002, http://www.dodig.mil/audit/reports/fy02/02.087.pdf.
The 9/11 Commission Report: Final Report of the National Commission on Terrorist Attacks upon the United States. New York: W. W. Norton & Company, 2004.

Office of the Secretary of Defense. *A Status Report to the Congress on the Renovation of the Pentagon*. 1 March 1991; 1 March 1995; 1 March 1999; 1 March 2000; 1 March 2001; 1 March 2002; 1 March 2003; 1 March 2004; 1 March 2005.

Rossow, Robert. *Uncommon Strength: The Story of the U.S. Army Office of the Deputy Chief of Staff for Personnel during the Attack on the Pentagon, 11 September 2001*. Washington, D.C.: Department of the Army, Office of the Deputy Chief of Staff, G1. n.d.

U.S. General Accounting Office. *Combating Terrorism: Issues to be Resolved to Improve Counterterrorism Operations*. GAO/NSAID 99-135. 13 May 1999.

U.S. Joint Chiefs of Staff. *Joint Pub 3-08: Interagency Coordination During Joint Operations*. Vol I. 9 October 1996.

__________. *Joint Pub 3-08: Interagency, Intergovernmental Organization, and Nongovernmental Organization Coordination During Joint Operations*. Vol I. 17 March 2006.

Unpublished

"After-Action Report NLO." Navy Liaison Office, Dover Air Force Base. 23 January 2002.

"After-Action Report, Operation Noble Eagle." Armed Forces Institute of Pathology. 30 January 2002. [cited as "AFIP After-Action Report"]

"After-Action Report: The ACS's Response to the Attack on the Pentagon." U.S. Army Community and Family Support Center. n.d. [cited as "ACS After-Action Report"]

"Arlington County After-Action Report on the Response to the September 11 Terrorist Attack on the Pentagon." July 2002. http://www.arlingtonva.us/Departments/Fire/edu/about/FireEduAboutAfterReport.aspx.

"Building Performance Evaluation, The 9-11 Terrorist Attack—Pentagon." Building Performance Evaluation Task Force, Pentagon Renovation and Construction Program Office. 1 June 2002. [cited as "PENREN Report"]

"Defense Protective Service After-Action Report: The Pentagon on 9-11." Pentagon Force Protection Agency. n.d. [cited as "DPS After-Action Report"]

"DON Consolidated Lessons Learned for 11 September 2001 and Aftermath." Binder. Department of the Navy, Office of Program Appraisal. 9 October 2001.

"End of Tour Report of 115th MP Battalion, Maryland National Guard, 11-30 Sep 01." Historical Report No. 115MP/1. JFHQ Command Historian, 5th Regiment Armory, Baltimore, Md. n.d.

"Environmental Health Response to the September 11, 2001 Attack on the Pentagon." Deployment Health Support Directorate and Deputy Assistant Secretary of Defense (Force Health Protection and Readiness). 15 January 2004. http://www.deploymentlink.osd.mil/pentagon_911/index.htm.

"Final Report: The Role of the Volunteer Fire Service in the September 11, 2001 Terrorist Attacks." TriData Corporation for National Volunteer Fire Council. 1 August 2002. http://www.nvfc.org/pdf/rolevolfiresvc911.pdf.

"Response to the Terrorist Attack on the Pentagon: Pentagon Family Assistance Center (PFAC) After Action Report." Office of Undersecretary of Defense (Personnel and Readiness). March 2003. [cited as "PFAC After Action Report"]

"Terrorism 2000/2001." U.S. Department of Justice, Federal Bureau of Investigation. FBI Publication No. 308. n.d. http://www.fbi.gov/publications/terror/terror 2000_2001.htm

"2002 Annual Report." Virginia Department of Alcohol Beverage Control. n.d.

"USAF After-Action Report for Initial Headquarters Air Force (HAF) Response to OPERATION NOBLE EAGLE." Air Force Historical Studies Office. 17 October 2001.

DOCUMENT COLLECTIONS

Arlington County (Va.) Police Department. Collection of documents, including incident reports, command post notes, and "incident history detail," assembled for use of historians, courtesy of ACPD Deputy Chief Stephen Holl. [cited as DepChief Holl ACPD]

Arlington County (Va.) Public Library, Local History Collection. RG 133, Records Related to the September 11, 2001, Terrorist Attacks on the Pentagon, 2001-2002.

Historical Office, Office of the Secretary of Defense, Arlington, Va. Subject files and collection relating to 9/11. [cited as OSD Hist]

Naval Historical Center, Washington, D.C. 9/11 Pentagon Incident collection. [cited as Nav Hist]

U.S. Army Center of Military History, Washington, D.C. Operation Noble Eagle MHD Task Force collection. [cited as OpNE CMH]

U.S. Attorney's Office for Eastern District of Virginia. Materials related to *United States v. Zacarias Moussaoui*. [cited as AttOfc EDVa]

BOOKS

Condon-Rall, Mary Ellen. *Disaster on Green Ramp: The Army's Response*. Washington, D.C.: U. S. Army Center of Military History, 1996.

Goldberg, Alfred. *The Pentagon: The First Fifty Years*. Washington, D.C.: OSD Historical Office, 1992.

Jackson, Paul, ed. *Jane's All the World's Aircraft, 2000-2001*. Coulsden and Alexandria: Jane's, 2000.

Jones, Charles. *Boys of '67: From Vietnam to Iraq, the Extraordinary Story of a Few Good Men*. Mechanicsburg, Pa.: Stackpole Books, 2006.

Marble, Sanders and Ellen Milhiser. *Soldiers to the Rescue: The Medical Response to the Pentagon Attack*. Washington, D.C.: Office of the Surgeon General, 2004.

Murphy, Dean E. *September 11, An Oral History*. New York: Doubleday, 2002.

Public Papers of the Presidents of the United States: George W. Bush, 2001. Vol II. Washington, D.C.: Office of the Federal Register, National Archives and Records Administration, 2003.

Public Statements of Secretary of Defense Donald H. Rumsfeld, 2001. Vol III. Historical Office, Office of the Secretary of Defense. n.d.

ARTICLES

Brewster, Casondra. "Belvoir Firefighter among First Responders at Pentagon." *Military District of Washington News*, 4 October 2001.

Brinsfield, John. W. "The Attack on the Pentagon: The Ministry of Army Chaplains—In Their Own Words." In *Courageous in Spirit, Compassionate in Service: The Gunhus Years*. U.S. Army Chief of Chaplains, History Office, July 2003.

Covert, Craig. "Search and Recovery." *NCIS Bulletin*, Summer 2002.

Eversburg, Rudy. "The Pentagon Attack on 9-11: Arlington County (VA) Fire Department Response." *Fire Engineering*, November 2002.

Gross, Charles J. "9/11 and Operation Noble Eagle." In *History of the Air National Guard, 2001-2004*. National Guard Bureau Historical Services Division. n.d.

Hammonds, Michele. "*Operation Noble Eagle*: Helping Pentagon Families Who Lost Loved Ones, AFIP Personnel Staff Special Assistance Center." *AFIP Letter* 159, no. 5, October 2001.

__________ and Christopher C. Kelly. "*Operation Noble Eagle*: DNA Laboratory Plays Key Role in Pentagon, Somerset County Victim Identifications." *AFIP Letter* 159, no. 5, October 2001.

Huleatt, William J. "Pentagon Family Assistance Center Inter-Agency Mental Health Collaboration and Response." *Military Medicine*, September 2002.

Kelly, Christopher C. "*Operation Noble Eagle*: AFIP Responds to September 11th Pentagon Terrorist Attacks." *AFIP Letter* 159, no. 5, October 2001.

__________. "*Operation Noble Eagle*: Forensic Anthropologist Provides Expertise Following September 11 Attack." *AFIP Letter* 159, no. 5, October 2001.

__________. "*Operation Noble Eagle*: Radiologic Pathology Provides Dover Support." *AFIP Letter* 159, no. 5, October 2001.

Kennedy, Harold. "Renovation of Pentagon Includes Tighter Security." *National Defense Magazine*, 2003. www.nationaldefensemagazine.org/issues/2003/Dec/Renovation.htm.

Lilly, Jennifer and Chris Walz. "Local Heroes: FMMC Fire Department Reflects on Attacks." *Pentagram*, 2 November 2001.

__________. "Tower Terror." *Pentagram*, 16 November 2001.

"Personnel Hilites." *WHS Newsletter*, Spring 2002.

Peterson, Alan L., et al. "Psychological Intervention with Mortuary Workers after the September 11 Attack: The Dover Behavioral Health Consultant Model." *Military Medicine*, September 2002.

Ruggeri, Eric D. "The Dover Air Force Base Port Mortuary." *American Funeral Director*, September 2001.

Scott, William B. "F-16 Pilots Considered Ramming Flight 93." *Aviation Week & Space Technology*, 9 September 2002.

Shupe, Barbara. "Operation Noble Eagle D.C.'s Largest Crime Scene: NCIS Responds." *NCIS Bulletin*, Summer 2002.

Toti, William. "One Year Later Frozen in Time." *U.S. Naval Institute Proceedings*, September 2002.

Wagner, Glenn N. and Christopher C. Kelly. "*Operation Noble Eagle*: Forensic and Psychological Aspects of the Armed Forces Institute of Pathology's Response to the September 11 Pentagon Attack." *Military Medicine*, September 2002.

Ward, Michael J. "Attack on the Pentagon: The Initial Fire and EMS Response." *Journal of Emergency Medical Services*, April 2002.

UNPUBLISHED PAPERS AND MANUSCRIPTS

"Command Performance: County Firefighters Take Charge of the 9-11 Pentagon Emergency." Paper by Pamela Varley for Arnold Howitt for Executive Session on Domestic Preparedness at John F. Kennedy School of Government, Harvard University, 2003.

Jamieson, Perry D. "The U.S. Air Force and 11 September 2001." Air Force Historical Studies Office. n.d.

Kane, John. "The Incident Command System and the Concept of Unified Command at a Terrorist Incident." Paper presented to the Community Response to the Threat of Terrorism symposium, November 2001. http:/www.riskinstitute.org/PERI.PTR/Terrorism_LIB_1309.htm.

Pemble, Charles W., III. "Forensic Dentistry and Forensic Dental Identification." Keesler Air Force Base teaching manuscript. Updated 2001.

Rosenbaum, Eric, Sean P. Hunt, and Diane Pitts for Hughes Associates, Inc. Fire Science and Engineering. "Review of 9/11 Pentagon Scenario from the Fire Fighters', Fire Marshal's and Fire Protection Engineer's Perspectives." Slide show printout. n.d.

Shirer, Frank. "MDW Engineer Company." U.S. Army Center of Military History. n.d.

Titus, Leo J., Jr. "A Review of the Temporary Shoring Used to Stabilize the Pentagon after the Terrorist Attacks of September 11th, 2001." Paper submitted to the Department of Civil Engineering, University of Maryland, May 2002.

Acknowledgements

It is impossible to acknowledge all those who lent advice, assistance, and support to this endeavor. Those who made particularly noteworthy contributions, in addition to those mentioned already in the Preface, include the following:

The leaders of the JCS and military service historical offices participated in oversight and support of the project throughout, reviewing drafts, furnishing information, and offering encouragement. They are: Brigadier General David Armstrong (USA Ret), Director, Joint Staff Historical Office; Jeffrey Clarke, Chief Historian, U.S. Army Center of Military History; William Dudley, Director, Naval Historical Center; Rear Admiral Paul Tobin (USN Ret), Director, Naval Historical Center; Richard Anderegg, Director, Air Force History; and Charles Melson, Senior Historian, Marine Corps Historical Center.

At all stages of the project, particularly relating to the physical aspects of the Pentagon building, Georgine Glatz, Chief Engineer of the Pentagon Renovation Program Office, provided constant guidance and invaluable advice including close reading and review of drafts of the manuscript.

Stephen Lofgren of the U.S. Army Center of Military History directed the extensive Army 9/11 oral history program and provided an insightful critique of the original draft.

Catherine Zickafoose, Brenda White, and the staff of the OSD Graphics Office lent expert assistance with charts, photographs, and graphic elements. Shannon Giles skillfully prepared the text and layout of the book.

Paul Dorsette of DoD's Document Automation and Production Service and Michael Barnes and Cheryl Hall of the U.S. Government Printing Office provided critical help on procurement issues; GPO's Jeffrey Turner, Lottie Mitchell, Maureen Whelan, and Jennifer Wilson offered generous advice and assistance on publication planning.

Elaine Everly of the OSD Historical Office performed the indispensable and onerous task of checking citations for the documentation for the book, participated in the editing, and assisted with preparation of the appendices.

Ruth Sharma of the OSD Historical Office typed, checked, and tracked numerous drafts of the manuscript with her usual skill and reliability.

Interviewees and interviewers who contributed to the project are listed in the bibliography.

Among others who deserve mention, their names listed in alphabetical order, are: Regina Akers, Deane Allen, Fred Allison, Joseph Balkoski, Jeffrey Barlow, Pamela Bennett, Mattia Bernardoni, Robert Boyd, William Brazis, Jacqui Brown, Jaya Chaterjee, Anthony Conques, Graham Cosmas, Robert Cressman, Sandy Doyle, Mark Evans, John Fox, Timothy Francis, Gerard Francisco, James Garamone, John Glennon, John Greenwood, Charles Gross, Caitlin Hitt, Stephen Holl, William Hopper, Amy Hunt, Richard Hunt, Perry Jamieson, Erno Kolodny-Nagy, Julie Kowalski, Ronald Landa, Mark Langerman, Kathleen Lloyd, Ted Lopatkiewicz, Philip Lundeberg, Megan Maples, Jackie McGuire, David Novak, Diane Pitts, Sarah Roberts, Max Rosenberg, Aberdeen Sabo, Robert Schneller, John Sherwood, Thomas Stanton, David Statter, Richard Stewart, Robert Stone, Carolyn Thorne, Roger Trask, Aurelie Trur-Nicli, George Watson, Gary Weir, Mark Wertheimer, Kathleen White, Patricia Wilson, and Jason Witteman.

Index

Note: For ranks of military personnel, see corresponding text.

About the Authors

ALFRED GOLDBERG received his Ph.D. in history from The Johns Hopkins University. After service with the Army Air Forces in World War II, he was a historian with the U.S. Air Force Historical Division and a senior staff member of the Rand Corporation. Since 1973 he has been the Historian of the Office of the Secretary of Defense. He is co-author of *The Army Air Forces in World War II* (7 volumes) and author of *The Pentagon: The First Fifty Years*. He is the general editor of the *History of the Office of the Secretary of Defense* series.

SARANDIS (RANDY) PAPADOPOULOS received a Ph.D. in history from the George Washington University. He has been a Lecturer in History at George Washington and the University of Maryland, College Park, and is currently a historian in the Contemporary History Branch of the U.S. Naval Historical Center. Papadopoulos is a Trustee of the U.S. Commission on Military History and the author of numerous papers and reports.

DIANE T. PUTNEY earned her Ph.D. in history from Marquette University. As a historian with the U.S. Air Force, she served as Pentagon Team Chief for the Air Force History Support Office. Presently she is a historian with the Historical Office, Office of the Secretary of Defense. She is the author of *Airpower Advantage: Planning the Gulf War Air Campaign, 1989-1991* and editor of *ULTRA and the Army Air Forces in World War II*.

NANCY K. BERLAGE received her Ph.D. from The Johns Hopkins University. She currently works in the Historical Office, Office of the Secretary of Defense, where she is an editor and consultant on the DoD Acquisition History Project. Previously, she was assistant editor for *The Papers of Dwight David Eisenhower* and a senior historian for History Associates Inc. She has published in academic journals and books and taught at Johns Hopkins and Towson universities.

REBECCA HANCOCK WELCH obtained her Ph.D. from the George Washington University. She has been a historian with the Smithsonian Institution, the Office of Air Force History, where she authored *Training to Fly: Military Flight Training, 1907-1945*, and the Historical Office, Office of the Secretary of Defense, where she headed the oral history program.